SOCIOLOGICAL CONCEPTS AND TERMINOLOGY

SOCIOLOGICAL CONCEPTS AND TERMINOLOGY

Identification, Categorisation and Classification Schemes

Lalit P. Pathak

ANMOL PUBLICATIONS PVT. LTD.
NEW DELHI-110 002 (INDIA)

ANMOL PUBLICATIONS PVT. LTD.
4374/4B, Ansari Road, Daryaganj
New Delhi-110 002

Sociological Concepts and Terminology

First Edition 1998
ISBN 81-7488-981-7

PRINTED IN INDIA

Published by J.L. Kumar for Anmol Publications Pvt. Ltd., New Delhi-110 002 and Printed at Mehra Offset Press, Delhi.

Dedicated

To the memory of my father
Late Mr. Chooramani Pathak whose
last present to me before his death
in 1952, were a few ink tablets.

Contents

Preface

Identification of main fields or areas of a discipline in the form of main concepts used in it, is an essential step in designing an information retrieval tool. Most of the existing general classification schemes were designed by one or two individuals, mostly by their individual experience and expertise. Full comprehension of all the subjects in the universe of documentary knowledge and mapping these subjects and their individual concepts according to their discipline-specific significance is not possible for one or a few individuals. Even depending on one or a few specialists in a field, does not provide a balanced picture of the main concepts of a discipline according to their relative significance. Under the circumstances, the only other alternative is to take the views of a maximum number of practicing professionals in the field, and consolidate their views for identifying the most significant concepts in that discipline.

With this objective, this research study was undertaken to identify some of the main concepts, and the terms used for them by sociologists, and to examine how far, bibliographic information retrieval tools, used in libraries and information centers, have been able to provide them in their schedules. For this, identification of the main concepts of sociology, that are dealt, discussed, taught and written about, by sociologists, was necessary, and after giving due consideration to various alternative sources, terms used in the chapter headings of the sociology textbooks were adjudged to be the best source. It was also felt necessary that the sample should be a satisfactory representative of the universe of sociology textbooks, and the period coverage also should span as maximum as possible. Hence, 100 introductory textbooks of sociology covering the period 1939 to 1990 have been considered, for the present study.

Concepts and the terms representing them, have been identified out of 87 books, that were found relevant, out of 100 books initially selected. All the concepts, dealt in the form of terms used in the chapter headings, by at least 3 authors, have been identified and treated as the main concepts of sociology. The number of authors using a chapter heading for a concept and the total proportion of these books used for a concept, has been quantified and treated as the relative significance given to that concept, by all the authors. The concepts identified in this way, have been arranged under 10 broad categories and each main concept placed in relation to other concepts, on the basis of its definition, explanation, and usage in some subject-dictionaries. Broader, narrower, and related terms used for a concept, by all the textbook authors, in the form of division of a book into sections and chapters has also been considered for relative placement. Finally, some bibliographic information retrieval tools have been evaluated for the provision in them, for these main concepts. The study implies that the concepts, based on the opinion of a large number of practicing professionals are certainly significant, and can be treated as the main concepts, from the subject-specific point of view, as such, these need to be provided in all types of information retrieval tools pertaining to sociology. The method also deserves to be applied for identifying the main concepts of other social sciences also.

Lalit P. Pathak

1
Introduction

Statement of the Problem

Information storage and retrieval tools are required to represent the concepts of a discipline or field of knowledge to the best extent possible, in their terminology. As such, identification of the concepts used in a discipline is a prerequisite for designing any bibliographic information storage and retrieval tools (BIRTs). Some theory based classification schemes and other retrieval tools provide guidelines about the methodology for selection of isolates representing the concepts relating to the specific disciplines, but clear methodology is not available to identify the main concepts and the terms representing them, that need to be included invariably as headings in the information retrieval tools. One of the major criteria for evaluating the information retrieval tools is, to see how far they have been able to take into consideration main concepts of a discipline how the main concepts have been categorized and how the categories themselves and the concepts within categories have been arranged.

Schedule for sociology was examined in some of the classification schemes and it was observed that some of the main concepts used in sociology are either not included at all or provided subordinate placing. The arrangement is also not based on the proper categorization of concepts as displayed in the literature of the subject. Such a situation results in the scattering of the literature on related concepts, non-retrieval of all the related documents being searched by users and a lack of correspondence between the terms used in the literature of the subject by sociologists and their representation in the information retrieval tools.

The present study aims to identify the concepts used in sociology, and out of these concepts, categorize some main concepts, that represent major areas of literature in the field. The identified concepts will be arranged in a helpful and filiatory sequence, on the basis of the definition, explanation, and usage of each concept in the literature. Finally, the study will try to evaluate some of the bibliographic information retrieval tools, with regard to the provision in them for the main identified concepts.

There have been several approaches to decide about the concepts that need to be accommodated in the terminology of an information retrieval tool. Hulme (1911) suggested the criterion of 'literary warrant' or 'bibliographic warrant '. [1] Bliss emphasized on 'educational and scientific consensus' as the basis of selection of terms.[2] Lancaster and Ranganathan want 'user warrant' also taken into consideration. Hulme's 'literary warrant' meant that the terms used in a schedule of class headings should be based on accurate survey and measurement of the classes of literature. Mills says 'insofar as the making of a library classification should always begin with the literature, and use as its raw material, the concepts manifested in that literature, then it may be said to be based on literary warrant, although not in the sense that Hulme used the term.'[3] Later on Mills says 'In conclusion, we may say that, the characteristics used in library classification are usually to be found clearly expressed in the literature, and that the theoretical problem involved in deciding their 'naturalness' or 'artificiality' is largely irrelevant '.[4]

Objectives and Hypotheses

A preliminary observation of some of the bibliographic information retrieval tools gave an indication that the tools, available currently, do not represent the concepts used in the literature, adequately. It was also presumed that, some methodology could be evolved to identify the main concepts of a discipline, that are generally used in the literature of that subject. The concepts identified in this way can be compared with the provision for them in the information retrieval tools.

Thus, the study has been undertaken with the following main objectives:

1. To develop a methodology for identifying the main concepts pertaining to a discipline in social sciences, so as to use the terms representing these concepts in the information retrieval tools;
2. To identify the concepts used and the form of terms used in sociology with the help of this methodology;
3. To arrange these main concepts in a filiatory and helpful sequence on the basis of their definition, explanation and usage in the literature of sociology;
4. To find out the relative significance of each concept, and in this way categorize the concepts into some significance groups, thus enabling to find out the most significant concepts of sociology ; and
5. To evaluate some information retrieval tools with regard to the provision in them for the main concepts of sociology and the categorization and arrangement adopted.

Hypotheses

1. Significant concepts of a discipline can be identified with the help of the terms used for chapter headings in the textbooks;
2. Terminology used in the information retrieval tools does not represent all the main sociological concepts ; and
3. Concepts used in a field of study can be ranked according to their relative significance for use as headings in the information retrieval tools.

Interrelationship between Concepts and Terms

Concepts are described as units of thought. These are mental images formed by generalization. A concept is defined as an aspect of thought, it is a kind of unit, in terms of which one thinks. Marion J. Levy Jr., while writing on some methodological problems says "A concept, as that term is used here, is a means of inter-subjective communication. For these purposes, concepts are represented by signs, mostly words. These words, in order to fulfill such purposes, must have inter-subjective meanings . . . . A concept may be defined as simply a name for the members of a given class, the class may be of any sort. The definition or referent of a concept involves the logical analysis of the class to which the concept is applied "[5] Chinoy describes the nature of concepts and writes "A concept is a general term that refers to all members of a particular class of objects, events, persons, relationships, processes, ideas."

Writing on science and concepts, Chinoy says " The first step toward the understanding of sociology, as of any scientific discipline, is the mastery of its basic concepts . . . . The concepts of sociology, then, provide the intellectual instruments with which the sociologist works. They define the phenomena to be studied, and they differentiate sociology from other social science, each of which has its own body of concepts. The focus attention upon those selected aspects of reality with which we shall be concerned , and they provide the terms in which problems are posed and answered." [6]

Levy Jr. provides some guidelines for dealing with concepts for empirical scientific purposes and enumerates his observations like this: "For empirical scientific purposes they (concepts) must first be precisely defined and precisely differentiated from other concepts. Second, they must be given empirical referents. Third, they are not more or less valid, but only more or less useful for a given purpose of analysis." [7] Sartori say "Whether concepts are theory-formed or theory-forming, in either case they are the basic units with which the social profession actually performs." [8]

A term is a work or phrase used to denote a concept. Sartori defines a term as "The form used to signify the concept-that is, a word allocated to a concept." [9] Explaining the relation between concepts and terms. Soergel says "In language, terms (single word terms or multi-word terms) are used to designate concepts. The relationships between concepts and terms are governed by the rules of terminology. However, as is well known, there is much confusion in this area. Firstly, there is not one-to-one relationship between concepts and terms. In the case of synonyms, several terms designate the same concept. for example, lawyer and attorney . . . . and place under government ownership and nationalization are synonyms. On the other hand, homonyms are terms, that correspond to different concepts (have different meanings) . . . socialization (economics) and socialization (social psychology) are examples. Secondly, different people use the same term with different meanings. Things are complicated even more by the well-known fact that different persons (or even the same person at different times) associate different concepts with one and the same term. It is therefore, necessary to control the relationship between concepts and terms. In most fields, this problem is far from solved. [10]

Sociological Concepts

Concepts in a discipline are useful for the formation of theories. Leslie *et al.* write "Whether we speak of men, tables, societies, cultures, or systems, the process is the same. We use abstract symbols to group things together, to distinguish one type of object from another and, ultimately, to see the world as orderly. Concepts enable man to classify, sub-classify and cross-classify the objects in the environment. They provide him with the flexibility to see connection among things, in ways that otherwise would be impossible. [11] Turner, emphasizing the importance of defining concepts unambiguously, writes under the heading `Concepts: the basic building blocks of theory' and says "Theories are build from concepts . . . concepts are constructed from definitions . . . concepts that are useful in building theory have a special characteristic. They strive to communicate a uniform meaning to all those who use them. However, since concepts are frequently expressed with the words of everyday language, it is difficult to avoid words that connote varied meanings- and hence point to different phenomena— for different groups of scientists. It is for this reason that many concepts in science are expressed in technical or more `natural' language, such as symbols of mathematics. In sociology, expression of concepts in such special languages is sometimes not only impossible, but also undesirable. Hence, the verbal symbols used to develop a concept must be defined as precisely as is possible, in order that they point to the same phenomena for all investigators. While perfect consensus may never be attained with conventional language, a body of theory rests on the premise that, scientists will do their best to define concepts unambiguously. Not to do so, or to give up because the task is difficult, is to invite conceptual chaos and thereby to preclude the accumulation of theoretical knowledge." [12]

Explaining the significance of concepts for sociology, Chinoy says "So significant a part of sociology are its concepts that the history of the discipline is in part a history of conceptual elaboration and refinement. Some have come into general use, whereas others have gained currency for a time, only to be displaced by more precise or more refined categories of observation and analysis." [13] Wallace and Wallace say "Concepts are categories of behavior, events, or characteristics that are considered similar for the sake of theory construction." [14]

Bibliographic Information Retrieval Tools

Bibliographic information retrieval languages use terms that represent concepts of specific fields of knowledge and disciplines. It is desired that a concept is represented by a single term by all those who deal with that concept, but generally it does not happen. According to the perception of an individual, he forms an image of an unit of thought, or an object, which we name concept and uses a term for it, many times quite different from what the concept in question should convey. As such, in specific disciplines, the concepts are given specific explanation, definition, and limiting boundaries, but in social sciences, the situation is not that much clear and several times, various terms are used to represent the same concept. Not only that, an individual object is also seen from different angles and different concepts are formed about it according to the cultural background.

Nedobity writing on the difference between common language and information languages, writes "In common language the specific meaning of a word is always dependent upon the context in which it is used. In special languages, a term is assigned to a distinct meaning, i.e. a defined concept. This concept, which is delimited from other concepts, is integrated in a system of concepts. It is dependent on this system, which is also9 indirectly true of the term. In indexing languages, a thesaurus word is assigned to a concept, which describes the contents of documents stored in an information retrieval system." [15] Nedobity further says "what is found in common in a set of individual objects is, summarized or abstracted mentally and expressed by a concept. In this way, the concept is an element of thinking, which comprises the characteristics common to a number of objects. The aggregate of characteristics of a concept is called its `intention '. Every concept is a member of a class of concepts and can itself form a class of concepts that are encompassed by it. The aggregate of all subordinate concepts (species) at the same level of abstraction or of all individual objects which belong to the concept in question, is called `extension'. The aggregate of all individual objects is also termed `class '. The characteristics of concepts help us classify concepts and construct systems of concepts." [15]

Organization of knowledge and its retrieval in libraries and information centers necessitates the grouping of concepts into classes, and arrangement of these classes in hierarchical relations. The first prerequisite to any classification and categorization is identification of the items to be classified. In a specific discipline, these items to be categorized can be named as concepts of that discipline. The delimitation of knowledge into specific compartments is not easy, as such, in many fields of knowledge, specifically in social sciences, where the same term is used in different discipline-specific contexts, the literature of that field provides the context in which a term is used and, to which concept a term represents. To find out the concepts used in a specific discipline, it's areas of interest are identified and some limits are drawn about its nature, perspectives, boundaries, range, field, scope, subject matter and coverage. The second aspect to be kept in mind in identifying the concepts related to a discipline is—to see what type of consensus is emerging about individual concepts with regard to their attributes, among the specialists of that discipline.

Organization of knowledge in libraries, is based on some systems of classification schemes, and use use of subject headings. The vocabulary or the terms used in these systems represent the concepts and categories used in the literature of that discipline. The success and effectiveness of any library's knowledge organization system depends on the extent to which the designers of the information retrieval tools have been able to identify the significant concepts of that discipline, and incorporate the terms representing them in the vocabulary of classification schemes and other bibliographic information retrieval tools.

Bliss says, classes are correlative to concepts and terms. In his words "In the multiplicity, diversity, and complexity of natural objects and their relations, we discern that individual things and events are discrete and that, tho (sic) they differ in their individualities and specific characteristics, we relate them in classes and in concepts, in primary learning and in mental comprehension. This is the process of classifying, of conceiving classes, and of relating them in mental comprehension. It is fundamental to generalization, to simplification, to classification, and to organization of knowledge, and thought. A class is denoted by one or more word or terms, which name it, signify it, and mean it. Such terms or class names are correlative to their classes and to the correlative concepts.[16]

On terms, Bliss says "Terms are definite as classes are, and they are correlative to the classes as the class names are. They should be distinctive and should be sued consistently. A class may however be denoted by several synonymous terms. The class-name may, moreover be composed of two or three terms together. In different languages the class names differ more or less, tho, they may be etymologically related." [17]

We have seen that concepts have been described as the building blocks of they and same relation exists between theories and a specific discipline like sociology. As such, it is essential for designing any type of bibliographic information retrieval tool to identify the concepts of a discipline. It may not be difficult to identify the concepts used in a discipline, but the real problem from the information retrieval point of view, it to adopt a methodology, through which, concepts are identified in such a way that, no significant concept is left un-represented in the retrieval tools. It is also essential to place the terms representing various concepts in relation to each other in such a manner that those concepts appear together, that have maximum interrelationship . Stressing this point Riggs says " The concepts used in a specialized field of knowledge are highly interdependent, as such, it it important that they are presented in systematic (i.e.) classified glossary, with inter-linked definitions, and comprehensive analytical index to all the terms, that can be used to designate each concept, given as an entry in the glossary." [18] However, the task of representing concepts in a systematic order in the form of terms is quite problematic and no arrangement can satisfy differing point of views. Highlighting this problem Coates writes " This would be very simple to achieve if there were an uncomplicated, one-to-one relationship between concepts and words: that is to say, if there were a single word corresponding to each concept and a single concept corresponding to each separate word. In fact, we have on the one hand, concepts that can be rendered by any one of a number of words, and on the other hand, concepts that can be rendered by any one of a number of words, and on the other hand, concepts for which no single word equivalent exists in the natural language." [19]

Sources of Data

To find out the terms used in sociology the following dictionaries and encyclopedias were used and the definition from these sources was used for arranging the concepts in a filiatory sequence:

1. 1955 Henry Part Fairchild, *Dictionary of sociology.*
2. 1964 Julius Gould; W L Kolb *Dictionary of social sciences.*
3. 1968 G D Mitchell *A Dictionary of sociology.*
4. 1968 *International Encyclopedia of Social Sciences.* by Sills.
5. 1969 Thomas Ford Hoult *Dictionary of modern sociology.*
6. 1983 Michael, Mann *Macmillan student encyclopedia of sociology.*
7. 1984 N. Abercrombie et al *Dictionary of sociology.*
8. 1985 Kuper; Kuper *Social science encyclopedia.*

To find out the main concepts of sociology on which introductory sociology textbooks include a chapter, 100 textbooks were used. The list of these books is provided in the appendix. Following bibliographical information retrieval tools were used for evaluating the provision in them for the main sociological concepts identified from the textbooks of sociology:-

1. *Dewey Decimal Classification.* 20th edition, 1989.
2. *Universal Decimal Classification.* International medium edition, 1985.

3. *Colon classification* 6th edition, 1960.
4. *Sociological Abstracts* scheme of arrangement from vol. 40, 1992.
5. *Library of Congress Subject Headings*, 12th edition, 1988.

Dictionaries of sociology were also evaluated for provisionin them, for the main concepts of sociology. Following two sources were very helpful in providing definition and guidelines for some of the concepts used in dealing with sociological concepts in the information retrieval tools:

1. Giovanni Sartori "Guidelines for concept analysis and glossary." in *Social science concepts: a systematic analysis.* 1984:p. 15-85
2. Gernot Wersig; Neveling Ulrich *eds. Terminology of documentation*. 1976: 275p.

It was decided to take a sufficiently large sample of textbooks, as such, 100 titles were selected and finally 87 books were included in the study for identifying main concepts from the terms used in the chapter headings. The textbooks included were published during the period 1939 to 1990, and the period coverage is also quite satisfactory. Thus, the sample represents the universe of sociology textbooks fairly well. for taking the terms from dictionaries, 5 dictionaries of sociology and 3 dictionaries / encyclopedias of social sciences published between 1955 and 1989 were taken. The sample appears to be quite sufficient. For evaluation of retrieval tools, with regard to the provision in them for the main sociological concepts, three general classification schemes, one subject specific classification scheme used in indexing, and one list of subject headings has been sued.

Thus, from the point of view of literature coverage, and period coverage, the scope of the study covers the filed of sociology fairly well. However, the study is not intended to be a study in the field of concept analysis, and touches the aspects of individual concepts only to the extent, that is helpful in understanding the scope of individual concepts, and to decide their interrelations and placement in a filiatory and helpful sequence for use in bibliographic information retrieval systems.

Presentation of the Study

The study has been divided into six chapters. The second chapter on literature survey provides a brief introduction to some of the theoretical as well as applied efforts to identify concepts pertaining to specific disciplines, mainly in the sociological literature. As there has not been many efforts to identify discipline-specific main concepts, mostly such studies are limited to individual suggestions and not based on any literature survey. The third chapter on methodology, includes data collection as well as the procedure adopted to analyze the data. The chapter also explains the reasons for adopting the chapter headings in the textbooks, as the basic source of identifying the main concepts of sociology.

The chapter on analysis and interpretation of data deals with identification and the basis of arrangement of the main concepts of sociology. Each one of the 100 concepts has been analyzed for arrangement, based on its definition, explanation and usage in the literature of sociology. The chapter also explains the methodology in detail, of categorization of main concepts, according to their relative significance. Fifth chapter tries to evaluate some of the bibliographic information retrieval tools as far as the provision for main sociological concepts in them is concerned. For this, various types of tools were selected, as such, three general classification schemes, the Sociological Abstracts classification scheme, and Library of Congress Subject Headings have been evaluated. The provision for these concepts in 8 dictionaries of sociology/ social sciences has also been seen. Finally, the main concepts are compared with the main concepts suggested by some sociologists. The last chapter summarizes the results of the whole study, which shows that main sociological concepts are not well represented in the various bibliographic information retrieval tools.

REFERENCES

1. E.W. Hulme, "Principles of book classification" *Library Association Record* 13, 1911: 354-358; 389-394; 444-49.
2. H. E. Bliss, *Organization of knowledge in libraries and subject approach to books*. 2nd ed. New York, H. W. Wilson, 1939.

3. J. Mills, "Library classification and subject analysis" in *Modern outline of library classification*. London, Chapman and Hall, 1968: p. 7,10.
4. *Ibid*.
5. Marion J. Levy Jr. "Some methodological problems" in *Structure of society*. Princeton, N. J. Princeton University Press, 1952: p. 227.
6. Ely Chinoy "Nature of concepts" *in Society: an introduction to sociology*. New York, Random House, (1961) 1967: p.11.
7. Marion J. Levy Jr. "The relationship between conceptual development and its corresponding theoretical development" *in op. cit.* p. 227.
8. Giovanni Sartori ed. *Social science concepts: a systematic analysis*. London, Sage, 1984: p. 9.
9. *Ibid*. p. 84.
10. Dagobert Soergel "Concepts and terms" *in Indexing languages and thesauri: construction and maintenance*. Los Angeles, CA., Melville, 1974: p.20 .
11. Gerald R. Leslie *et al*. "Concepts" *in Order and change: introductory sociology*, New York, Oxford University Press, 1973: p. 56.
12. Jonathan H. Turner "Sociological theorizing" in *Structure of sociological theory*. Homewood, Ill. Dorsey Press, 1978: p. 2-3.
13. Ely Chinoy, *op. cit.*, p. 15.
14. Richard C. Wallace; Wendy D. Wallace, "How is sociological theory constructed" in *Sociology*. London, Allen and Bacon, (1985) 1989: p. 13.
15. Wolfgang Nedobity, "Terminology and its application to classification, indexing and abstracting." *UNESCO Jl. of Inf. Sci.* 5(4), 1983: p. 27-34.
16. Henry Evelyn Bliss "A bibliographic classification: principles and definition." in *A bibliographic classification extended by systematic auxiliary schedules for composite specification and notation*. 2nd ed. New York, H. W. Wilson, 1952: p. 3-11.
17. *Ibid*.
18. F. W. Riggs, "Establishment of glossaries: their basic functions", *International Classification* 9(2), 1982:p.77.
19. E. J. Coates, *Subject catalogues: headings and structure*. London, Library Association, 1960: p. 19.

2
Literature Survey

Library Science Literature

Soergel [1] suggests some of the sources for collection of terms in connection with thesaurus construction and these sources can be used to identify the concepts used in various disciplines for representation in information retrieval tools. These are:

1. Treatises on terminology of a subject field for sub-field;
2. Encyclopedias, lexica, dictionaries, glossaries (universal or discipline oriented);
3. Tables of concepts and indexes of textbooks and handbooks;
4. Index of journals and abstracting journals;
5. Indexes of other publications in the field; and
6. Term association lists produced by subject experts in term association studies or similar experiments.

These are the possible sources for collection of terms related to specific disciplines, but we hardly come across any information retrieval tool that has tried to use all these sources to identify the terms used in a field of study. Identification of terms for use in the schedules of information retrieval tools pertaining to specific disciplines has been tried in some studies for preparation of depth schedules. The depth schedules for main subjects like computer science, economics, demography, social psychology, nuclear physics, political science, international relations etc. are available in published form.[2] Most of these studies identify some terms related to a discipline, categorize them into PMEST, and arrange these terms into a hierarchical and filiatory sequence according to the expertise of the individual trying to prepare the subject specific schedule.

As a standard procedure, it is generally suggested that, the subject experts be consulted to finalize the terms, form of the terms to be used, and also to decide the hierarchical and filiatory sequence for preparing a subject-specific schedule. But in practice, it is not practical to finalize the schedule with this procedure. A few experts can hardly decide a balanced picture of a vast discipline and also that, the search for consensus among sociologists about the status of a concept and its relationship with other terms is, many times unfruitful. Moreover, it may be possible to identify most of the concepts and the terms used for them in a discipline, but information retrieval tools can not accommodate all these terms in the classification schedule for that subject. As such, we require a methodology through which concepts of individual disciplines are represented in the subject-specific schedules according to their significance as main categories, and the capacity of a term to represent all the isolates falling within its purview.

While compiling *Thesaurus for information processing in sociology* Jean Viet [3] lists the sources for identification of terms. The sources consulted for constructing this thesaurus were, dictionaries of sociology, encyclopedias, *Sociological Abstracts,* and articles from some journals for over a period of time. About adoption of main sections, Viet writes in the introduction to the thesaurus as follows:

Jean Viet later on writes "In the disposition of sections, it was difficult to avoid using some presuppositions, but they reflect the manner in which the sociologists consider their own field there is quite a margin between a language aiming at the retrieval of documents and the specialist's conception of his subject matter." [3]

Ranganathan enumerates a few areas in the filed of fundamental research, and one of them is "break-even points between composite concepts and fundamental constituents in diverse regions of knowledge." [4] These observations show that in the filed of library science, or for that matter in the field of social sciences, there has not been any significant effort to identify the main concepts pertaining to a discipline.

Sociological Studies Suggesting Main Fields of Sociology

Division of sociology by Comte into statics and dynamics division into general sociology and special sociology by Tonnies and Durkheim's division into social morphology, social physiology, and general sociology, hardly helps to identify the main concepts of sociology or their arrangement into some categories. Moreover, the theoretical categories, and classification of concepts suggested by some sociologists is able to divide the field of sociology into limited categories, that are insufficient to arrange the documents related to the diverse areas of the subject.

Some sociologists have tried to identify or suggest some main areas/fields of sociology, but all these lists of terms are based on individual observation or preference and hardly any one on a detailed literature survey of the subject. Such lists of the main concepts of sociology suggested by a few sociologists are available. House (1936) suggested a list of 16 'sociological specialties' recognized in the united States.[5] He based his list on the areas of interest of the members of the American Sociological Society, and teaching and research positions in American universities during that period. Alex Inkeles reports a study by Hornell Hart (1959) in which 24 introductory textbooks of sociology were analyzed and 12 themes identified.[6] Alex inkeles (1971) suggests 33 'fields' in the form of a table under the heading 'A general outline of the subject matter of sociology' and claims 'on which almost every one would agree '.[7] In the same pattern, Smelser (1965) enumerates 11 areas under the heading 'Developing areas of sociology' [8]; Sergeant (1971) enumerates 16 aspects under the heading'Aspects of sociology which have yielded to empirical investigation' [9]; Leslie (1973)suggests 26 fields under the heading 'Among the areas of human society and behavior that sociologists study' [10]; and Horton (1980) includes 33 specialized fields with in the heading 'Sociology is divided into many specialized fields' [11] In addition to these, the field of studies of the 44 Research Committees of the International Sociological Association could also be taken as suggestive of the significant areas of sociology.

Table 2.1
Fields of Sociology suggested by some Sociologists

1. *Floyd Nelson House (1936) 'Sociological specialties'*

"A considerable number of specialized fields of research, teaching, and speculation, within or marginal to the larger field of sociology, are quite definitely recognized today, either by the existence of reputable literature dealing with these topics in a specialized way or by the fact that, individuals are restricting their efforts, more or less, to these specialties....

Following at least, may be enumerated as sociological specialties recognized in the United States at present (1936):

1. General theory and history of sociology and logic of the social sciences;
2. Historical sociology, theory of social evolution and progress;
3. Methods of sociological research (including statistical methods as a more or less distinct subspecialty, marginal to sociology and other social sciences);
4. Rural sociology;
5. Urban sociology;
6. Sociology and social work;
7. Criminology;
8. Child study, with special reference to 'problem-children ' and juvenile delinquency;
9. The family
10. 'Collective behavior'-crowd psychology and public opinion;
11. 'Cultural sociology' (marginal to the presumably distinct science of anthropology);
12. Educational sociology;
13. Population problem and social biology;
14. Race and nationalities, race relations, race prejudice;
15. Social psychology (marginal to sociology and psychology);

16. 'Human ecology', regional sociology and social geography.

Obviously, several of these categories can be sub-divided, and for some purposes they should be sub-divided obviously too, they are by no means distinctive categories they reflect strongly the tendency to specialize by 'problems' rather than on theoretical grounds."[5]

2. *Alex Inkeles (1965) 'Fields of Sociological concern'*

"Textbooks for introductory sociology courses, the rank-and-file membership of the American Sociological Association, and the leaders of the profession, all constitute the subject matter of sociology. We can therefore, construct a general outline of the field of sociology on which almost every one would agree.

A General outline of the Subject Matter of Sociology

I. Sociological analysis
   Human culture and society
   Sociological perspective
   Scientific method in social social science

II. Primary units of social life
   Social acts and social relationships
   Individual personality
   Groups (including ethnic and class)
   Communities urban and rural
   Associations and organisations
   Populations
   Society

III. Basic social institutions
   Family and kinship
   Economic
   Political and legal
   Religious
   Educational and scientific
   Recreational and welfare
   Aesthetic and expressive

Fundamental processes

IV. Differentiation and stratification
   Cooperative, accommodation assimilation
   Social conflict (including revolution and war)
   Communication (including opinion formation, expression and change)
   Socialisation and indoctrination
   Social evaluation (the study of values)
   Social control
   Social deviance (crime, suicide, etc.)
   Social integration
   Social change

It is doubtful if very many sociologists would challenge any item on the list as not deserving its position."[7]

3. *International Encyclopedia of Social Sciences (1968 p.5)*

"Sociology includes:
Economic, organizational, political, rural, and urban sociology
Sociologies of knowledge, law, religion, and medicine
Human ecology
History of social thought
Sociometry and other small group research
Survey research and
Such special fields as criminology and demography

4. *Neil J. Smelser (1969) " `Developing areas of sociology: '*

Research methods in sociology	Deviance and social control
Comparative study of societies	Social change
Demography	Political sociology
Social stratification	Sociology of education
Complex organizations	Medical sociology." [8]
Socialization	

5. *Graham Sergeant (1971) "`Aspects ofsociety which have yielded to empirical investigation:'*

Communication	Political sociology
Criminology	Social stratification-
Demography (population)	class and status
Family	Race relations
Industrial sociology	Sociology of religion,
Medical sociology	beliefs and ideologies
Sociology of education	Urban sociology. " [9]
Occupational sociology	

6. *Gerald R. Leslie et al (1973) "`Among the areas of human society and behavior that sociologists study are the following:*

Poverty	Migration	Hospitals
Family planning	Family life	Military
Social movements	Marriage	Student dissent
Urbanization	Personality formation	Social change
Race relations	Deviant behavior	Mobs
Ethnic relations	Religion	Crowds

Black power	Education	Riots
Social stratification	Language	Crime. [10]
Population growth	Labor unions	

7. *Paul B. Horton; Chester L Hunt (1980) "Sociology is subdivided into many specialized fields of which a partial list includes:*

Applied sociology	Military sociology
Collective behavior and mass communication	Political sociology
	Race and ethnic groups
Community	Rural sociology
Comparative sociology	Social change
Crime and delinquency	Social control
Cultural sociology	Social organization
Demography	Social psychology
Deviant behavior	Sociological theory
Formal and complex organizations	Sociology of education
	Sociology of knowledge, and science
Human ecology	Sociology of occupations and professions
Industrial sociology	
Law and society	Sociology of religion
Leisure, sports, recreation and the arts	Sociology of small groups
	Sociology of small
Marriage and family groups	Stratification and mobility
Mathematical sociology	
Medical sociology	Urban sociology." [11]
Methodology and statistics	

Some other titles also attracted attention, but none of them was suitable for the purpose of identifying the main concepts of sociology. Some of such attractive titles are ' The classification of the sciences of action' by Talcott Parsons (1949) [12]; 'Outlook for sociology at the beginning of the twentieth century' by Ginsberg (18961)[13]; 'Some observations on the scope of sociological analysis' by Naegele (1961) [14]; 'Divisions of sociology' by Tonnies (1971) [15]; 'The vocabulary of sociology' by Gould (1971) [16]; and 'Optimum scope of sociology' by Smelser (1980). [17]

The *International Encyclopedia of Social Sciences* (1968) enumerates 16 areas of sociology in it's introduction and writes " Sociology includes- economic, organizational, political, rural, and urban sociology, the sociologies of knowledge, law, religion, and medicine, human ecology, the history of social thought, socio-metry and other small group research, survey research, and such special fields as criminology and demography." At the end of volume 17, the encyclopedia classifies all the articles according to the disciplines. The alphabetical list includes 107 concepts of sociology, many of them further sub-divided and separate articles available on various discipline-specific aspects of the concept. However it is not possible for a general social science encyclopedia to include all the main concepts of a specific discipline.

Hoult (1969) in his *Dictionary of sociology* provides a classified list of the terms included in the dictionary under the heading 'entries classified in terms of specialties' and the specialties identified are as follows [18]:

1. Socio-cultural theory
2. Methodology and institutions
3. Demography and population
4. Rural-urban sociology disorganization
5. Social change, development
6. Socialorganization, structure,
7. Social problems,social
8. Social psychology

Ann K. Pasanella (1986) while surveying the field of sociology from the point of view of sources of information, enumerates the various fields as follows [19]:

1. What is sociology
2. Origins of sociology
3. Social theory
4. Methodology and empirical research
5. Sociology of science
6. Macro-sociology
7. Futurism
8. Stratification

9. Sex roles and social change
10. Sociology of medicine
11. Sociology of education
12. Organizational analysis
13. Mass communication
14. Social problems
15. Using sociology

'Significant Sociology Subject Headings'

Only one study could be identified , that suggests 'significant sociology subject headings. Baughman [20] has appended a list of 53 headings under the caption 'Listed below are most strongly related sociology subject headings from SSHI *(Social Sciences and Humanities Index)*, as determined by Goffman's indirect method.

Committee on Conceptual and Terminological Analysis (COCTA)

COCTA was formed in 1970, and is a joint committee of the International Political Science Association, and International Sociological Association (since 1978) and also one of the standing sub-committees of the International Social Science Council. The committee has in hand, a project on *International Conceptual encyclopedia for the social sciences*. The project envisages to bring out concept-wise volumes on social sciences and the first volume in the series is *INTERCOCTA glossary: Concepts and terms used in ethnicity research* published in 1988. [21]

Another contribution related to the field is the Social science Concepts: a systematic analysis (1984). The volume has individual chapters on the concepts of consensus, development, ethnicity, integration, political culture power, and revolution. Editor of the volume Sartori in his introductory chapter on 'Guidelines for concept analysis' writes "Single authors always have, and always shall engage in conceptual analysis. The point is, whether private fishing expeditions can be turned into a collective and systematic inquiry- where 'systematic' implied that a given procedure of analysis is replicated from concept to concept, thus following for a consistent and cumulative assessment of the state of a discipline (with respect to its building blocks). The novelty 9of this work is, then, that its contributors are engaged in a 'systematic inquiry' and do abide by a shared procedure of analysis- to wit, the 'guidelines' that constitute the first part of the volume. While no claim is made that the guidelines proposed in this work represent an exclusive method for the analysis of concepts, the claim that we do make is that without a method, the exercise is largely pointless." [22]

The studies mentioned above are aimed to an analyze the individual concepts, but do not mention the grounds on which only some concepts were selected, possibly on the availability of some experts willing to write on these concepts. The analysis of individual concepts is from the point of view of their application in the social sciences, but none of the contributors is from the field of sociology. The analysis can help in deciding about the scope and interrelationship of these concepts, but does not help in identifying discipline specific main concepts and their relative significance for use as main headings in the bibliographic information retrieval tools. As such , for designing bibliographic information retrieval tools, these studies can not be treated as relevant.

A concept in social sciences can be interpreted from various angles. Lane and Stenlund (1984) writing on the 'Power' say "The phenomena of power may be approached in terms of economic models of utility and exchange (Karlson, Harsanyi), psychological models of personality and communication (Lewin, French), sociological models of organizational hierarchy and work (Likert et al) and political science models of leadership and social choice (Dahl, March). [23] For designing information retrieval tools, related to the literature of specific disciplines, we are in search of discipline-specific definition, explanation and usage of individual concepts. Thus this literature survey indicates that, except for a few stray efforts to list some of the concepts of sociology, no systematic study is available that can help in identifying the main concepts of sociology, or any of the other social sciences.

REFERENCES

1. Dagobert Soergel "Flow of work in the construction of indexing languages and thesauri" *in Indexing languages and thesauri: construction and maintenance.* Los Angeles, Cal., Melville pub.(John Wiley), 1974: p. 355.
2. S. Seetharama " Library and information science research in India:

an analytical study based on the input to ISORID" *Lib. Sci.* 13(3-4), 1976: 121-36 .

3. Jean Viet *Thesaurus for information processing in sociology*. Paris, Mouton, 1971: p. 13.
4. S. R. Ranganathan "Depth classification, tools for retrieval and organization for research" *in Documentation and its facets*. Bombay, Asia, 1963: p. 612.
5. Floyd Nelson House "Differentiation of the sociological field" *in Development of sociology*. West Port, Conn., Greenwood Press, (1936) 1970: p.293-95.
6. Hornell Hart "Comparative coverage agreed on sociological topics" *in Project for comparative analysis of introductory sociology textbooks, 3rd report*. Florida, Southern college, 1959: p. 10 (unpublished).
7. Alex Inkeles "Fields of sociological concern" *in What is sociology*. New Delhi, Prentice Hall, 1971: p. 12.
8. Neil J. Smelser; James A Davis *eds*. "Developing areas of 1972: p 17-18.
9. Graham Sergeant "Aspects of sociology which have yielded to empirical investigation" *in A Textbook of sociology*. London, Macmillan, (1971) 1972: p.17-18.
10. Gerald R. Leslie et al "Field of sociology: among the areas of human society and behavior that sociologists study" *in Order and change: introductory sociology*. New York, Oxford University Press, 1973: p. 5.
11. Paul B Horton; Chester L Hunt "Sociology is divided into many specialized fields" *in Sociology*. New Delhi, McGraw Hill, 1980: p. 20-21.
12. Talcott Parsons " classification of the sciences of action"m in *Structure of social action"*. New Delhi, Amerind, (1949) 1974: p. 757-68.
13. Morris Ginsberg "Outlook for sociology at the beginning of Twentieth century" *Evolution and progress*. London, William Heinemann, 1961: p. 175-93.
14. Kasper Naegele "Some observations on the scope of sociological analysis" *in* T. Parsons et al, *eds. Theories of society*. New York, Free Press, (1961) 1965: p. 3-29.
15. Ferdinand Tonnies "Divisions of sociology" *in* Warner J. Cahnman; Rudolf Heberle *Ferdinand Tonnies on sociology, pure, applied and empirical*. Chicago, Univ. of California Press, 1971: p. 128-40.

16. Julius Gould "The vocabulary of sociology" in Edward A Tiryakiyan *ed. Phenomenon of sociology*. New York, Appleton, 1971: p. 313-324.
17. Neil J. Smelser "Optimum scope of sociology" in Gary T. Marx; N. Goodman *Sociology: classic and popular approaches*. New York, Random House, 1980: p. 2-13.
18. Thomas Ford Hoult *Dictionary of modern sociology*. Totowa, N.J., Littlefield Adams, 1969: p. 355-75.
19. Ann K Pasanella "Sociology: survey of the field" in William H Webb *Sources of information in the social sciences: a guide to the literature*. 3rd ed. New Delhi, Arnold Heinemann, 1986: p. 276-289.
20. James C. Baughman 'Most strongly related sociology subject headings' in " A structural analysis of the literature of sociology" *Library Quarterly* 44(4), Oct. 1974: p. 303-4.
21. Fred W. Riggs *Concepts and terms used in ethnicity research*. (International conceptual encyclopedia of the social sciences, INTERCOCTA glossary vol. 1.) Frankfurt, Indeks Verlag, 1988: 205p.
22. Giovanni Sartori *ed. Social science concepts: a systematic analysis*. London, Sage, 1984: p.10.
23. Jan-Erik Lane; Hans Stenlund "Power" *in ibid*. p. 318.

3
Data Collection and Analysis

Literature Survey and Analysis

The present study is based on the literature survey and analysis, as such, all the steps involved in a social survey are not applicable in this case. However, the methods adopted can not be termed fully descriptive, as instead of data collection from the social field, the data collection in this case is from the secondary sources. The secondary sources used as data, are dictionaries of sociology, textbooks of sociology, and bibliographic information retrieval tools. The remaining steps adopted in a research survey like- method of obtaining data, processing the data, comparative study of data, and descriptive analysis of the variables studied are similar.

Main concepts of sociology, identified with these methods can be deemed to have been collected through a questionnaire method, as it eliminates the bias, which the respondents might have shown, if they were served a questionnaire, since the respondents get the chance to reconsider their priorities. Secondly, the non-response possibility is also eliminated.

Alternative Sources Considered

Terms used in the Dictionaries

All the terms given in 5 dictionaries of sociology and 3 dictionaries of social sciences were taken and arranged in an alphabetical sequence. The arrangement shows, the number of dictionaries having a term, the form of the term used by them, and the scattering of terms in various dictionaries for a single concept on account of the use of synonymous terms. Each unadopted term along with 'see' reference, has also been shown in the index, such entries being shown in smalls. Second column of the alphabetical index shows the class number available for these terms in the sociology schedule of three general classification schemes: *Decimal Classification, Universal Decimal Classification,* and *Colon Classification.* Any significant term not used in any dictionary, but used in any classification scheme also appears in the index in smalls. A term not used directly against the class number, but shown among many other terms, in the scope note in the classification scheme is shown in italics to identify it. The arrangement in the alphabetical index is word by word. The subdivisions of a term are brought together and shown after the term with indention, however, in some cases, where the subdivisions run into several pages, all subdivisions carry the main term also for convenience of consultation, as in the case of terms starting with 'social'.

The alphabetical arrangement provides about 5000 terms. These terms represent the discipline of sociology to a great extent, and also represent some of the main concepts of allied disciplines used in sociology. The index tells the number of dictionaries that have provided a term. The terms commonly used by all the 8 dictionaries is not more than 20. The index shows the provision for each term in the classification schemes, and also the terms used in classification schemes but not provided in any of the 8 dictionaries consulted.

This term bank was, however, not found of much use, to decide the relative significance of the terms, that could be used as headings in the information retrieval tools, merely on the basis of the number of dictionaries having the provision for a term. On account of the use of many synonymous terms for a single concept by the authors, the terms for a single concept get scattered and any fruitful comparison is impossible, up to the time all the terms provided in all the dictionaries are classified. The effort provides a good amount of information about terms used in sociology, but mere identification of the terms used in a discipline can hardly help regarding the suitability of each one of them for use as main heading in the bibliographic information retrieval tools like classification schemes and indexing tools.

Sociological Abstracts as a Source of Terms

Sociological Abstracts includes a journal in it coverage, on the basis of some sociological article published in a journal. Once it gets included, all articles published in the journal get included in the abstracts. In this process, articles on other social sciences appearing in these journals also are also included. Moreover, the *Sociological Abstracts* represent the literature appearing during a certain period, that can not be treated as full representative of the main concepts of sociology.

Views of 'Founding Fathers'

This is a criterion considered among some other alternatives by Alex Inkeles. Even if some decision could be taken, as to whom to treat as founding fathers, it may not be easy to decide which concepts to be treated as the main concepts of sociology. The method is suitable to identify some individual aspects pertaining to sociology, but not for deciding the relative significance of the concepts.

Terms used in the Text book Chapter Headings

As the sources enumerated above were not found suitable, it was decided to use the chapter headings in the textbooks of sociology, for identifying the main concepts of sociology. For this one hundred introductory textbooks of sociology bearing the title, introductory sociology, basic sociology, principles of sociology, fundamentals of sociology, handbook of sociology, aspects of sociology, society and human society were selected. After screening the contents, 13 titles were not found relevant, and the chapter headings used in the remaining 87 titles were classified. All the chapter headings bearing a concept on which at least 3 authors has devoted some part of their book were taken into consideration. Thus, the chapter headings used by any one of the 87 authors on a specific concept were arranged chronologically, along with the surname of the author, the chapter number used for that concept and the total number of chapters in the textbook written by that author.

Reasons for Selecting the Textbooks as a Source

Textbooks generally try to represent the literature appearing in a discipline in the following way:

1. The textbooks include the concepts, that are generally prescribed in the syllabi of sociology courses in the academic institutions;
2. Textbooks assimilate and disseminate the ideas appearing in the form of articles in periodicals, and also in the form of books published in a field of study, on very specific topics;
3. Textbooks present a cumulative and consensual view of the field of study, and are generally supposed to represent all the main concepts of a discipline; and
4. Textbooks generally try to include the views of majority of the 'founding fathers' and the personal views of the author are subsidiary.

3.32 Implications of Classified Chapter Headings

The exercise helped in identifying 100 concepts, out of which some were used by up to 60 authors and others even only by 3 authors as chapter headings. The classification and arrangement of the chapter headings used in these 87 textbooks enabled to obtain the following information:

1. The number of textbooks having a chapter on a particular concept of sociology;
2. Various terms and their synonyms used by these authors for a concept in the chapter headings;
3. Consensus, uniformity, diversity and changes visible in the use of terms for a concept, over a period of time;
4. Some concepts are always used in pairs for use as headings by sociologists. Some of these are authority and power, status and role, values and norms, and evolution and progress. Such pairs have been identified and the information can be used for their placement in a filiatory sequence;and
5. The year when the textbooks started including a chapter on a particular concept, the period during which maximum authors include a chapter on a concept and the year after no author included a chapter on the concept can also be discerned.

While classifying the chapter headings, it was observed that in many cases, the textbook authors make a combined chapter heading for some concepts. Classifying such chapter headings posed some problems. Such headings have been repeated under all the significant terms appearing in the title. The terms included with other concepts also in this way have been shown with a star (*), as follows:

Social Differentation

9. 1959 Social Differentiation and Stratification Merton 19/25

As this chapter heading includes two concepts, it is included with both the terms and the star (*) above 'social differentiation' indicates that this heading is included there also. In case of division of a book by an author into major section and then into chapters, sections are shown distinctly in italics, to indicate that these chapter headings have been treated by the author as the topmost most significant terms in his book. For calculating the proportion of the book devoted to each concept, in the case of combined headings as above, half part of the heading is counted for each concept, i.e. in the example above half of 1/25th part of the book by Merton is devoted to the concept of 'stratification' and and another half of the 1/25th part for the concept 'social differentiation'.

Sources used to decide the Relative Placement of a Concept

The identified concepts were arranged and placed in relation to each other, on the basis of their definition, explanation and usage, and for this these sources were used:

a) *Dictionaries of the Subject*

Those definitions from 8 dictionaries of sociology or social sciences were taken into consideration, that provided scope of a term, use of other terms in explaining a term, and the views expressed by noted authors while defining or using a term.

b) *Analysis of Chapter Headings*

Most of the textbook authors divide their books first into some major sections and then these sections are sub-divided into chapters. How they subdivide a book into major sections, and these sections into chapters provides information about their views on broader and narrower terms for a concept. With this data, it was possible to show each concept how it has been treated by these authors as one of the main concepts or a part of a major concept.

c) Provision in the Library of Congress List of Subject Headings

Most of the libraries sued LCSH for deciding the subject headings in the catalogue. The list provides 'broader', 'narrower', 'related', 'use', and 'used for' terms for all the terms used in the catalogue of the Library of Congress. The list can not be treated as perfect guide, but in most of the cases, the relations of the concepts are well decided with the help of LCSH. Moreover, the results obtained from the literature analysis, can be compared with the list, to find out the difference and unanimity.

d) Related Terms used by Sociologists

Dictionaries of sociology provide 'see also ' terms at the definition a term. These 'see also' terms were collected from all the dictionaries for all the main concepts identified, and it was treated as the list of the terms shown by sociologists as related terms to a concept. It may be noted that, most of the contributions to dictionaries of sociology are generally by well known sociologists or the compilers themselves are sociologists.

Method used to decide the Relative Significance of a Concept

The number of chapters in the textbook written by an author and the chapter number for each heading was also noted while arranging the chapter headings under various concepts. This was deemed necessary, as some authors had devoted one fifth (1'5) part of his book to a section, thus giving it the position of a major concept, while on the other hand, some other author treats the same heading as one thirtieth (1/30) part of his book. While adding the proportion of a book devoted to a concept, the chapter or section heading shown as major section of a book has to be given more significance. Thus, the number of authors having a chapter on that concept, as well as the proportion of the book used by them for that concept is taken into account, while deciding the relative significance of a concept.

Scope including limitations of the Data used

The dictionaries included in the study were published during the period 1955 to 1989 and the textbook included were published during the period 1939 to 1990. Titles were not decided according to the eminence of the author, country of origin, or the type of presentation of the subject matter. The terms selected finally to represent the concept, among various synonyms, is not necessarily the one used by maximum number of authors, although it is so in a maximum number of cases. Out of various terms used in the headings for a concept by the textbook authors, a term has been selected that has been found to be most accepted or acceptable as heading. Most of the books included in the study have undergone several editions, and wherever available, latest edition was used, but for showing in the chronological list of books, the year of the first edition has been taken into consideration.

While calculating the proportion of books used for a concept by an author, it has been assumed that all the chapters in a book occupy equal number of pages, or have been give3n equal importance by an author, which may not be true. Generally textbook authors devote more pages to a chapter in the beginning of the book, and less number of pages to a chapter at the end of the book. The method of counting the number of pages for each chapter could be a further step to decide about the more accurate relative value. But the method adopted, also enables us to place all the concepts in the relative significance categories, and the concepts with less number of pages, automatically have shown lesser significance values. However, further studies could be taken up, to see whether counting the number of pages for a chapter or for a concept in these books changes the relative position of these concepts significantly from the one obtained through the present study.

4

Main Concepts, their Placement, and Relative Significance

Identification of Main Concepts

The main objective of this study has been to identify some main concepts of sociology. The collection of terms from the dictionaries of sociology/ social sciences helped in finding out the terminology used in the discipline, to a great extent, but it was not possible to identify main concepts with this method. In the same manner, it was also not found possible to identify the main concepts on the basis of literature on individual concepts that is appearing in the *Sociological Abstracts*. As such, the terms used in the chapter headings of the textbooks were adjudged to be the best source to identify the main concepts. Every author tries to provide the best and most significant term as chapter heading for the material he is presenting in his textbook. Bringing together all the chapter headings used in 87 textbooks on a concepts, automatically provides, as to what the most sociologists want to be the main concepts of sociology.

The main obstacle in identifying out some main concepts was the problem of synonyms used by the authors for a concept. To select a term out of several alternatives, for use in the information retrieval tools, some alternatives available are as follows:

1. To select a term that has been used by maximum number of authors;
2. To select a term that is used in the literature currently;

3. To select a term that can accommodate and has the capacity to express all the subordinate concepts within it;
4. To take a term as the first term and show other terms also with slash (/), when synonymous position of another term is not ascertainable.
5. To select a term as the first term and show other related or synonymous terms in the scope note as 'including....'; and
6. Use of 'see' or 'use' references for the terms not adopted as headings.

In the present study, all the synonymous terms used for a concept by all the authors could be brought together, but it was beyond the scope of this study, to find out, as to which term to be preferred out of many synonyms available. It was also a tedious task to find any consensus among sociologists about the use of a single term for a concept. In fact, some textbook authors appear to be trying to use an alternative an alternative or synonymous, but less popular term for a concept, in the chapter heading, so that they are not accused of adopting the heading term used by any other previous author, whose book is most popular or whose heading terms are widely used or most acceptable. In most of the cases, it was decided not to indulge or go into the question of the synonymous status of a term, instead, they have been presented separately, along with their definition, explanation, and usage and all other information that can help in any future decision about the most appropriate term among a few. But for inclusion in an information retrieval tool as a main heading, such terms need to be provided separately. For some terms, comparative table has been prepared in the next major section, which shows that, in most of the cases, an author has used only one out of many terms generally used. Some of these are:

a) Social differentiation, social stratification, social classes, social inequality;
b) Race, race relations, ethnic groups, minorities.

Table 4.1 : 100 Concepts of Sociology Identified from 87 Text books.

	Concept	*No. of authors*
0.	**Sociology, History, Theories, Research Methods**	
1.	Sociology/ scope	22/17
2.	History of Sociology	8
3.	Theories of Sociology	17
4.	Research Methods	34
5.	Scientific Method	8
I.	**Social Organization, Social Processes, group Formation**	
6.	Social Organization	31
7.	Social Systems	3
8.	Social Order	9
9.	Society/Social Life	22
10.	Socio-biology	12
11.	Sexuality	5
12.	Individual/	
13.	Personality	29
14.	Attitudes	6
15.	Social Processes	14
16.	Social Relations	12
17.	Social Interaction	24
18.	Groups	36
19.	Primary Groups	4
20.	Small Groups	8
21.	Associations	11
II.	**Social Institutions, Family, Political, Economic, Institutions**	
22.	Social Institutions	45
23.	Kinship	9
24.	Family	60
25.	Marriage	18
26.	Political Institutions	47
27.	Government	10
28.	Formal Organization	13
29.	Bureaucracy	12
30.	War	4
31.	Economic Institutions	39
32.	Capitalise	4
33.	Work	10
34.	Division of Labour	3
35.	Industrial Sociology	5
36.	Leisrue	7
III	**Cultural, Religion, Social Control, Education**	
37.	Culture	58
38.	Cuctoms	5
39.	Ideology	4
41.	Sociology of Religion	48
42.	Social Control	39
43.	Values	10
44	Noras	14
45	Morality	5
46.	Socialization	50
47.	Comforaity	11
48.	Deviance	46
49.	Sociology of Law	10
50.	Communication	16
51.	Public Opinon	6
52.	Sociologfy of Education	48
53.	Social. of Knowledge	3
54.	Sociology of Art	5
55.	Science and Technology	19
56.	Industrialisations	8
V	**Social Structure, Stratification, Race.**	
57.	Social Structure	23
58.	Social Differentiation	10
59.	Social Inequality	13
60	Social Stratification	51
61.	Social Classes	31
62.	Caste	4
63.	Social Status	15
64.	Role	17
65.	Power	20
66.	Authority	4
67.	Leadership	3
68.	Social Mobility	13
69.	Sociology of Gender	16
70.	Occupation	4
71.	Racil Groups	17
72.	Race Relations	25

73.	Ethnic Groups	10
74.	Minorities	22
V	**Social Disorganization, Conflict**	
75.	Social Conflict	9
76.	Social Disorg	11
77.	Revolution	4
78.	Crowd	6
79.	Collective Behavior	26
80.	Social Movements	16
VI	**Social Change**	
81.	Social Change	58
82.	Evolution	5
83.	Progress	7
VII	**Human Ecology, Communities**	
84.	Humanr Ecology 22	
85.	Environment	10
86.	Geographic Environ.	5
87.	Medical Sociology	7
88.	Community	26
89.	Rural Sociology	7
90.	Urbanization/	
91.	Urban Socioloy	28
VIII.	**Population**	
92.	Population	46
93.	Migration	4
X.	**Applied Sociology, Social problems**	
94.	Applied Sociology	7
95.	Social Planning	7
96.	Social Problems	12
97.	Crise	14
98.	Delinquency8	
99.	Poverty	4
100.	Sociology of aging	5

All such interrelated concepts need to be identified, and literature on them can be placed together, and provision in the information retrieval tools needs to be made accordingly. The textbook authors generally use a term or phrase or their choice for a concept, and to group them all into a common acceptable term, is only an effort to place a proposal before the designers of information retrieval tools. It has also to be observed that, we may classify a chapter heading according to the term used by an author, but he is in fact using it for some other concept. We can take the case of 'social order. Some authors use it for 'social organization' or 'social life' and others for 'social control '. All the synonyms can not be used to represent a concept in an information retrieval tool, an only one of them can be shown in the information retrieval tools as a leading term. The choice of this single term to represent all the synonyms used in the textbooks, is one of the most crucial decisions, and it is almost impossible to arrive at some unanimity, in case of most of the concepts of sociology, that can satisfy all the points of views,b schools of thoughts, or country-specific interpretations associated with some of terms. Under these circumstances, one term was selected, out of many, that was adjudged to be acceptable to maximum number of sociologists, conveys the meaning of the concept adequately with the use of minimum words, and generally in popular usage. However, it has to be accepted that there can be no guidelines for a strict compliance in this respect, and the individual understanding of the subject, of a designer of such a system has no alternative.

Basis for accepting these as the Main Concepts

The identified concepts appear to be main concepts of sociology on the basis of the following considerations:

1. The concepts selected are based on the terms used as chapter Headings by a large number of textbook authors;
2. Textbooks are generally written according to the syllabi prescribed in the academic institutions, and are expected to include all the main concepts of a discipline;
3. All the terms used in a discipline are not taken as chapter headings by the textbook authors, as can be seen from the present analysis that, not more than 100 concepts could be identified out of all the 87 textbooks seen, and many of these terms used by up to 60 authors;
4. A majority of these terms are used as main headings in some classification or the other, but not all in any single information retrieval tool;
5. Majority of these terms or their synonyms are provided in most of the dictionaries of sociology and also in the dictionaries of social sciences;
6. Sufficient amount of literature is appearing on these concepts as verified from the subject index to the *Sociological Abstracts*. Although, it also includes significant literature on some new fields and upcoming areas of interest of sociologists;
7. The concepts represent almost all the major areas on which 'masters of sociological thought' or 'founding fathers ' have written;
8. Main concepts identified, generally tally with the main fields or specialties suggested by some sociologists, who have tried to list some main fields of sociology;
9. The International Sociological Association has research committees on a number of significant aspects of sociology; and

10. Literature in the form of books also appears on most of these concepts.

Arrangement of Terms Representing the 100 Main Concepts

Knowledge is multi-dimensional and inter-related, and sociological concepts represent the borrowed terms from allied disciplines like philosophy, psychology, political science, anthropology, economics, geography and history. As such in most of the cases, the term used is the common in all these disciplines, but subject-specific interpretation differs. Mapping the fields of sociology and finding out the interrelationships of its main concepts has not been possible on account of the fact that most of the concepts used in sociology, pertain to the allied disciplines enumerated above. Over and above, the classificationists would like to see all concepts of a particular field and also all human knowledge in some linear sequence. But the problem is that no sociologist has tried to present the concepts of his discipline in any well thought out arrangement, or at least according to the major categories. The information retrieval tools in use also have not been able to solve the complexities that are faced in handling these concepts or the terms representing them for arrangement in a linear sequence.

It may be possible to trace some consensus among sociologists about the main concepts of sociology, and the scope of individual concepts, but it appears a difficult proposition to trace any agreement among them, regarding the use of a term among many synonyms, to represent a concept. Same is the case about the arrangement of sociological concepts in some categorized order, acceptable to all, even for presenting them in the textbooks. But the personnel that deal with the field of bibliographic information storage and retrieval have to present the literature of a subject in some order, that is helpful for easy retrieval of bibliographic material. For easy retrieval, major categories need to be identified, and individual concepts are required to be placed within these. A classifier is not expected to remember the relative location of each and every concepts, in a scheme of arrangement, but the major categories and their relative location is helpful even for the users of the system.

It has been tried in the present study, to arrange the main

concepts of sociology in a well thought out sequence and place them under some broad categories. The effort is first in this field, and no such arrangement can satisfy diverse points of views. In some cases, a number of main concepts have been placed together, when they are related to the maximum extent, so as to bring the major categories within a limited number. To arrange the identified 100 concepts in a filiatory and helpful sequence in relation to each other, definitions provided in 8 dictionaries of sociology/ social sciences were seen and the most relevant definition that was found helpful in understanding a concept in relation to other concepts have been quoted. Hoe the textbook authors divide their books into some major sections, that indicate the major categories and how they divide these major sections into individual chapters has been used to draw broader and narrower terms to a concept. The broader, narrower, and related terms provided in the LCSH for a term has also been taken into consideration, while arranging the terms representing the main concepts in relation to each other. The 'see' and 'see also' references provided at the end of the definition of a term show how sociologists relate a concept with other terms. This information has been collected from all the dictionaries and this gives a list of the terms related to a concept. The use of this source, has enabled to compare the related terms provided in the LCSH and that provided by sociologists.

How these sources help in the arrangement of the terms representing the main concepts of sociology, and what are the implications of compiling the information from these sources, is presented mostly in tabular format while analyzing the individual concepts. The compiled information, although collected to help in arranging the concepts in a helpful sequence, can be sued by the designers of the information retrieval tools to decide the relative placement of the terms representing these concepts. The information can also be sued by the users of the information retrieval tools, to decide the relative placement of literature on individual concepts , and also for making provision for headings that are most preferred by the clients of the retrieval systems.

Definition, Explanation, and Usage of the 100 main Concepts of Sociology

1. SOCIOLOGY

1.1 Definition, Explanation

Auguste Comte (1855)

1. "The statical study of sociology consists in the investigation of the laws of action and reaction of the different part's of the social system". [1]
2. "He (Comte) did propose and consistently treat sociology divided into two main parts, the social statics and social dynamics... In the first case the major social institutions or institutional complexes of society- such as economy , family, or polity are taken to be the major units for sociological analysis, and sociology is conceived of as the study of interrelations between such institutions.... The parts of society, he argued can not be understood separately "as if they had an independent existence" instead, they must be seen "as in mutual relation ... forming a whole which compels to treat them in combination." He referred to the principle of "universal social interconnection" as the "master thought " of his whole approach. If statics was to be the study of how the parts of societies interrelate, dynamics was to focus on whole societies as the unit of analysis, and to show how they developed and changed through time... Comte felt the comparative study of societies as wholes was the major subject for sociological analysis." [2]

Herbert Spencer (1910)

3. "The science of sociology has to give an account of (how) successive generations of units are produced, reared and fitted for cooperation. The development of the family, thus stands first in order... Sociology has next to describe and explain the rise and development of that political organization which in several ways regulates affairs- which combines the actions of individuals.. and which restrains them in certain of the dealings with one another... there has to be similarly

described the evolution of ecclesiastical structures and functions... the system of restraints, whereby the minor actions of citizens are regulated, has to be dealt with. The stages through which industrial part passes... have to be studied....(as well as) the growth of those regulative structures which the industrial part develops within itself." [3]

Emile Durkheim (1896)

4. "Durkheim divided the journal L'Annee' Sociologique into seven sections with numerous sub-sections under major headings... the major sections were general sociology- including a sub-section on personality in the individual and the collectivity sociology of religion sociology of law and morals, including sub-sections- political organization, social organization, and marriage and the family, the sociology of crime; economic sociology; including sub-sections on the measurement of value and on occupational groups; demography, including a sub-section on urban and rural communities; and one on sociology of aesthetics. This outline dating from 1896 could easily be used for a contemporary view of sociology." [4]

Max Weber (1864- 1920)

5. "Sociology is a science concerning itself with the interpretative understanding of social action and thereby with a causal explanation of its course and effects." [5]

6. "The subjects on which he (Weber) wrote extensively include religion, various aspects or economic life, including money and the division of labour; political parties and other forms of political organization and authority; bureaucracy and other variables of large scale organization; class and caste; the city; and music. [6]

Pitrim A. Sorokin (1928)

7. It (sociology) seems to be a study, first of the interrelationships and correlation between various classes of social phenomena (correlation between

economic and religious , family and morals, judicial, and economic, mobility and political phenomena and so on); second, that between the social and the non-social (geographical, biological etc.) phenomena, ; third, the study of the general characteristics common to all classes of social phenomena". [7]

J.W. Bennett; M. M. Tumin (1949)

8. "Sociology is the science of the structure and function of social life". [8]

Morris Ginsberg (1949)

9. "Sociology may be defined as the study of society". [9]

MacIver; Page (1952)

10. "Sociology is about social relationships, the network of relationships we call society". [10]

Nicholas S. Timasheff (1955)

11. "It (sociology) is interested in what happens when man meets man, when human beings from masses or groups; when they co-operate, fight, dominate one another, persuade or imitate others, develop or destroy culture. The unit of sociological study is never an individual, but always at least two individuals, somehow related to one another." [11]

Alfred McClung Lee (1958)

12. "The scientific study of the phenomena arising out of the group relations of human beings. The study of man and his human environment in their relations to each other. Different schools of sociology lay varying emphasis; upon the related factors, some stressing the relationships themselves, such as interaction, association, etc., others emphasizing the human beings in their relationships, focusing their attention upon the socius in his varying roles and functions. Whether, sociology as developed hitherto, is entitled to the rank of science, is still a matter of some disagreement, but it is uniformly recognized that the methods of sociology may be strictly scientific, and that the verified generalizations which are the earmark of true science, are being progressively built up out of

extensive and painstaking observation and analysis of the repetitious uniformities in group behavior. [12]

Hary M. Johnson (1960)

13. "Sociology is the science; that deals with social groups, their internal forms or modes of organization, the processes that tend to maintain or change these forms of organization, and the relations between groups. So complex a subject as social groups requires, for scientific treatment, precise concepts and carefully defined technical terms for them". [13]

T. B. Bottomore (1962)

14. "Sociology was , with social anthropology, the first science to concern itself explicitly with social life as a totality, with the whole intricate network of social institutions and groups which constitute a society, instead of singling out a particular aspect of society for study. The basic conception, or directing idea, of sociology is, therefore, that of social structure, systematic interrelation of forms of behavior or action in particular societies. From this follows the sociologist's interest in those aspects of social life which has previously been studies only in a desultory manner, or which had previously been the object of philosophical reflection rather than empirical enquiry: the family and kinship, religion and morals, social stratification, urban life." [14]

Edward A. Tiryakin (1962)

15. "Sociology is the science which seeks universal knowledge about man's social conditions, in their specific and general manifestations; it's raison d'etre is to investigate the implications of Aristotle's proposition that `man is a social animal' (or political in the sense that man is what he is because of his life in the polis." [15]

Young; Mack (1962)

16. "Sociology, then is the scientific study of the social aspects of human life. Moreover, sociology is the body of knowledge, compiled by scientific method about human interaction. By interaction we mean reciprocal

contact between two or more persons- interstimulation and response. Sociologists therefore, are concerned with man in society, with the human group". [16]

Bain; Kolb (1964)

17. "Sociology denotes the scientific study of the social behavior or social action of human beings. It can be defined as the science of social relations and processes, the science of society, if society is regarded as the totality of such relations and processes, or the science of culture, if the latter term is defined to denote the sum totality". [17]

Koller; Couse (1965)

18. "Sociology takes as its unit of study, the human group." [18]

Webster's Dictionary (1966)

19. "Sociology is the science of society, social institutions and social relationships. It is the systematic study of the development, structure, and function of human groups concerned as process of interaction or or as organized patterns of collective behavior." [19]

Alvin L. Bertrand (1967)

20. "Sociology may be defined as the scientific study of human relationships; or of systems of human interaction or of social groups; or of social structures; or of social systems including societies. Sociology ;studies man in relation to his fellow beings." [20]

21. Everyman' Encyclopedia (1967)

21. "Sociology is the name introduced by Comte (1798-1857) and increasingly used in systematic study of human society. Such study may be purely descriptive, assembling in some agreed order the main significant facts about some particular society, community, groups, or it may include interpretation of such facts and abstract generalization from them'"[21]

Albert J. Reiss (1968)

22. "Sociology is the study of social aggregates and groups in their institutional organization, and of the causes and consequences of changes in institutions and social organization."

22. "Sociologists are primarily interested in human beings as they appear in social interaction i.e. as actors taking account of one another in their behavior. The major systems or units of interaction as the family or peer group; social relationships, such as social roles and dyadic relationships; and social organizations, from such formal or bureaucratic organizations as government, corporations, and school systems, to such territorial organizations as communities. Although sociologists are principally concerned with human beings in social interaction, they are also concerned with social aggregates or population, in their institutional organization." [22]

Donald G. Macrae (1968)

23. "Sociology may be summarized as the study of 1. social structure; 2. the study of social composition, i.e. the nature, propositions, and diversities of the various groups, categories and classes in societies; 3. the constructing of accurate descriptive inventories of the social life of society; 4. the elaboration and testing of metnods of research, both, qualitative and statistical; 5. the; study of culture and life style in society. These are, of course all interconnected, and in total, comprise the enterprise of sociology at this point of time." [23]

Social Science Research Council, USA (1969)

24. "Sociology embraces a wide range of subject matter, including the family, rural and urban life, race relations, religion, crime, political parties, populations, and social stratification. Sociologists employ many concepts to lend coherence to their accounts of social phenomena; some of these concepts are now familiar to people outside the field- for example, concepts of role, institutions, social structure, norms, and conformity." [24]

Thomas Ford Hoult (1969)

25. "Sociology is the intellectual discipline concerned with developing systematic, reliable knowledge about human social relationships in general and about the products of such relationships... To other observers,

sociology is simply the social science specialty concerned with the study of social groups or social institutions, or ; social interaction patterns." [25]

Random House Dictionary (1970)

26. Sociological—"dealing with social questions or problems, especially focusing on cultural and environmental factors rather than on psychological or personal characteristics It is the scientific study of the origin, development, organization and function, of human society; the science of the fundamental laws of social relations, institutions etc." [26]

Alex Inkeles (1971)

27. "Sociology is the study of systems of social action and of their interrelations. Most prominent among these systems of action we find, in increasing order of size and complexity: social acts, social relationships, organizations and institutions, communities and societies [27]

Ronald Fletcher (1980)

28. "Sociology is the scientific study of social systems; the attempt to study as scientifically as possible, all forms of association known to us- their nature, functions, interconnections and patterns of continuity and change in various types of society." [28]

Michael Mann (1983)

29. "Defined in the dictionaries as the science or study of society. The term was coined by Comte (1830), linking the Latin socius (originally a people, tribe or city allied to Rome, but later a society) to the Greek Logos (reason or knowledge)... either social facts, or social processes or some combination of the two constitutes the subject matter of sociology." [29]

Nicholas Abercrombie (1984)

30. "Sociology- the term has two stems- the Latin socius (companion) and the logos (study of) and literally means the study of the bases of social membership. More technically, sociology is the analysis of the structure of social relationships as constituted by social interaction. [30]

Edward A. Sills (1985)

31. "The knowledge contained in sociology covers a very wide and differentiated range of phenomena, such as the conduct of individuals in institutions like families, churches and sects, workshops, armies, civic and political associations, territorial, ethnic and national communities; the patterns of relationship among individuals; the role of structure and authority in the working of institutions with respect to income; and status or deference; the role of cognitive and normative beliefs in the actions of individuals and in the functioning of ,communities, institutions, and societies." [31]

Joel M. Charon (1986)

32. "Sociology today is the study of society, interaction, institutions, social organization, and social problems Sociology is a perspective that tries to give a sophisticated and factual explanation at why people act as they do." [32]

Table 4.2

Major aspects of Sociology revealed by the Terms used in 32 Definitions

	Term	Source	Year
5.	Scientific method		
	Verified generalizations	Lee	1958
	Scientific method	Young; Mack	1962
	Abstract generalization	Everyman's encyclopedia	1967
	Systematic study	Everyman' Encyclopedia	1967
	Scientific study	Bertrand	1967
	Systematic and reliable knowledge	Hoult	1969
6.	Social organization		
	Comparative study of societies	Comte	1855
	Statical study	Comte	1855
	Interrelation of parts of society	Comte	1855
	Social organization	Durkheim	1896
	Forms or modes of organization	Johnson	1960
	Man's social condition	Bottomore	1962
	Social organization	Reiss	1968
	Organization of human society	R. H. Dictionary	1970

Organization	Inkeles	1971
All forms of association	Fletcher	1980
Social organization	Charon	1986
7. Social system		
Structure of human groups	Webster	1966
Social systems	Fletcher	1980
8. Social order		
Continuity in all forms of association	Fletcher	1980
9. Society		
Study of society	Ginsberg	1949
Human group	Young; Mack	1962
Social aspects of human life	Young; Mack	1962
Science of society	Bain; Kolb	1964
Human group	Koller; Cause	1965
Science of society	Webster	1966
Organized patterns of collective behavior	Webster	1966
Human society	Everyman"s Encyclopedia	1967
Social aggregates	Reiss	1968
Social phenomena	SSRC, US	1969
Function of human society	R H Dictionary	1970
Societies	Inkeles	1971
Nature and function of society	Fletcher	1980
Science of society	Mann	1983
Processes of companionship	Abercrombie	1984
Society	Charon	1986
9A. Social life		
Structure and function of social life	Bennet; Tumin	1949
Social life	Bottomore	1962
Man in society	Young; Mack	1962
Social life	MacRae	1968
Origin of human society	R H Dictionary	1970
Bases of social membership	Abercrombie	1984
10. Biological determinism		
Biological phenomena	Sorokin	1928
12. Personality		
Personality	Durkheim	1896
14. Attitudes		
Cognitive beliefs	Shils	1985

Concept	Author	Year
15. Social Processes		
Cooperation	Spencer	1910
Processes that tend to maintain organization	Johnson	1960
Social processes	Mann	1983
16. Social relations		
Network of social relationships	MacIver; Page	1952
Cooperation, fight, domination, persuation, imitation	Timasheff	1955
Human beings in their relationships	Lee	1958
Relation between groups	Johnson	1960
Science of social relations	Bain; Kolb	1964
Social relationships	Webster's Dictionary	1966
Behavior	Reiss	1968
Social relationships	Reiss	1968
Human social relations	Hoult	1969
Social relations	R H Dictionary	1970
Social relationship	Inkeles	1971
Social interrelations	Inkeles	1971
Structure of social relationships	Abercrombie	1984
Patterns of relationships	Shils	1985
17. Social interaction		
Laws of action, reaction of different parts of social systems	Comte	1855
Social action	Weber	1920
Interaction	Lee	1958
Repetitious uniformities in group behavior	Lee	1958
Systematic interrelation of Forms of behavior or action	Bottomore	1962
Human interaction	Young; Mack	1962
Interstimulation and response	Young; Mack	1962
Social behaviour or social sction	Bain; Kolb	1964
Function of human groups	Webster's Dictionary	1966
Process of interaction	Webster's Dictionary	1966
Dyadic relations	Reiss	1968
Social interaction	Reiss	1968
Social interaction patterns	Hoult	1969
Social acts	Inkeles	1971
Systems of social action	Inkeles	1971

	Social interaction	Abercrombie	1984
	Interaction	Charon	1986
18.	Groups		
	Groups	Timasheff	1955
	Group relations of human beings	Timasheff	1955
	Social groups	Johnson	1960
	Groups	Bottomore	1962
	Groups	Everyman's Encyclopedia	1967
	Groups	Reiss	1968
	Social groups	Reiss	1968
	Groups	MacRae	1968
	Social groups	Hoult	1969
20.	Small groups		
	Peer groups	Reiss	1968
21.	Association		
	Association	Lee	1958
22.	Social institutions		
	Institutions	Comte	1855
	Social institutions	Bottomore	1962
	Social institutions	Webster 's Dictionary	1966
	Institutional organization	Reiss	1968
	Institution	SSRC, US	1969
	Social institutions	Hoult	1969
	Institutions	R H Dictionary	1970
	Institutions	Inkeles	1971
	Institutions	Shils	1985
	Civic associations	Shils	1985
	Institutions	Charon	1986
23.	Kinship		
	Kinship	Bottomore	1962
24.	Family		
	Family	Comte	1855
	Family	Durkheim	1896
	Family	Spencer	1910
	Correlation between family and morals	Sorokin	1928
	Family	Bottomore	1962
	Family	Reiss	1968
	Family	SSRC, US	1969
	Family	Shils	1985
25.	Marriage		
	Marriage Durkheim	Durkheim	1896

26. Political institutions		
Polity	Comte	1855
Political organization	Durkheim	1896
Political organization for regulation of affairs	Spencer	1910
Political organization/ parties	Weber	1920
Political parties	SSRC,US	1969
Political associations	Shils	1985
28. Government		
Governments	Reiss	1968
29. Formal organizations		
Large scale organization	Weber	1920
Corporations	Reiss	1968
30. Bureaucracy		
Bureaucracy	Weber	1920
Formal or bureaucratic organization	Reiss	1968
31. War		
Armies	Shils	1985
32. Economic institutions		
Economy	Comte	1855
Economic sociology	Durkheim	1896
Economic life	Weber	1920
Money	Weber	1920
Correlation between economic and religious institutions	Sorokin	1928
34. Work		
Workshops	Shils	1985
35. Division of labor		
Division of labor	Weber	1920
36. Industrial sociology		
Factories	Reiss	1968
38. Culture		
Development and destruction of culture	Timasheff	1955
Science of culture	Bain; Kolb	1964
41. Sociology of religion		
Sociology of religion	Durkheim	1896
Ecclesiastical structures and functions	Spencer	1910
Religion	Weber	1920

Religion and morals	Bottomore	1962
Churches	Reiss	1968
Religion	SSRC, US	1969
Churches	Shils	1985
Sects	Shils	1985
43. Values		
Measurement of values	Durkheim	1896
44. Norms		
Norms	SSRC,US	1969
Normative beliefs	Shils	1985
45. Morality		
Sociology of morals	Durkheim	1896
Religion and morals	Bottomore	1962
47. Conformity		
Conformity	SSRC,US	1969
49. Sociology of law		
Sociology of law	Durkheim	1896
Restraints (of political organization)	Spencer	1910
Correlation between judicial and economic organization	Sorokin	1928
52. Sociology of education		
School system	Reiss	1968
Schools reiss	1968	
54. Sociology of art and aesthetics		
Sociology of aesthetics	Durkheim	1896
Music	Weber	1920
56. Industrialization		
Industrial stages	Spencer	1910
57. Social structure		
Social structure	Bottomore	1962
Social composition	MacRae	1968
Social structure	MacRae	1968
Social structure	SSRC,US	1969
Structure	Shils	1985
60. Social stratification		
Social stratification	Bottomore	1962
Categories	MacRae	1968
Social stratification	SSRC,US	1969
Stratification of societies	Shils	1985

61. Social classes		
Class	Weber	1920
Classes	MacRae	1968
Income stratification of societies	Shils	1985
62. Caste		
Caste	Weber	1920
63. Social status		
Status	Shils	1985
64. Role		
Role and functions	Lee	1958
Social roles	Reiss	1968
Role	SSRC,US	1969
66. Authority		
Authority	Weber	1920
Authority	Shils	1985
70. Occupation		
Occupational groups	Durkheim	1896
71. Race Relations		
Race relations	SSRC, US	1969
73. Ethnic groups		
Ethnic communities	Shils	1985
81. Social change		
Social dynamics	Comte	1855
Change in society	Comte	1855
Changes in institutions	Reiss	1968
Changes in social organization	Reiss	1968
Change in associations	Fletcher	1980
83. Progress		
Development of society	Comte	1855
Development of human groups	Webster's dictionary	1966
84. Human ecology		
Human environment	Timasheff	1958
85. Environment		
Environmental factors	R H Dictionary	1970
86. Geographic environment		
Geographic phenomena	Sorokin	1928
88. Community		
Community	Everyman's Encyclopedia	1967
Territorial organizations as communities	Reiss	1968

	Communities	Inkeles	1971
	National communities	Shils	1985
89.	Rural sociology		
	Rural communities	Durkheim	1896
	Rural life	SSRC, US	1969
90.	Urbanization		
	City	Weber	1920
91.	Urban sociology		
	Urban communities	Durkheim	1896
	Urban life	Bottomore	1962
	Urban life	SSRC,US	1969
92.	Population		
	Demography	Durkheim	1896
	Social aggregates or population	Reiss	1968
	Populations	SSRC,US	1969
93.	Migration		
	Mobility and political phenomena	Sorokin	1928
96.	Social problems		
	Social problems	Charon	1986
97.	Crime		
	Sociology of crime	Durkheim	1896
	Crime	SSRC,US	1969

Table 4.3

Terms used for Sociology in the Text-book titles: A case study of 100 titles

Terms used	*No. of authors*	*Terms used*	*No. of authors*
Social science	2	Sociological imagination	1
Sociology	78	Sociological perspective	1
Society	14	Change and conformity	1
Social system	1	sociology	24
Society in action	1	Society	15
Human societies	1	Social system	3
Social institutions	1	Human organization	1
Culture and society	1	Social organization	26
Man in society	1	Social life	6
Social order	1	Social order	8
Social web	1	Theories of society	1
Order and change	1	Dynamics of society	1
Social theories	1	Social processes and structures	1

Provision in the LCSH

Sociology

Here and with local subdivisions are entered works on the discipline of sociology. Works on the social condition of particular regions, countries, cities etc. are entered under the name of the place subdivided by social conditions.

UF Science, Social
Social science

BT Social sciences
in sociology

NT Anomy Knowledge
Aristocracy Sociology of Social groups
Chicago School of Leadership Social history
Sociology Macrosociology Social institutions
Clinical sociology Marginality, Social Social integration
Communication Mass society Social isolation

2. HISTORY OF SOCIOLOGY

1. Definition, Explanation

2.21 "The history of any science includes the history of the forming of its subject-matter, methods, conceptual apparatus, inner logical structures, the sphere of its practical application, its institutuionalization and relation with other disciplines, and the relations of the various schools and currents in the science itself. But interdisciplinary boundaries are mobile and shifting....One can list a number of principles underlying monographs and courses in the history of sociology:

1. a simple exposition of the views of various sociologists and schools in chronological order, with a minimum of analysis of their content;
2. organization of the material on a space-time principle, i.e., by separate countries and periods;
3. examination of sociological ideas and theories as an aspect and element of a broader history of sociol-political thought on a background of changes in socio-economic, political and ideological attitudes;

4. the history of the succession and development of sociological theory as a specialized system of knowledge, the various currents of sociological thought being treated either as a stage in the molding and preparation of an author's own conceptions, towards alternative, mutually supplanting streams;
5. a history of the shaping or manifestation in sociology of some definite, quite general philosophical orientation, for example, positivism;
6. the history of the evolution of certain fundamental sociological categories, whose content and functions have changed in the various stages of society's development;
7. a series of monographic essays on understanding sociologists of the past, each being studied in relation to the features of his time, personality, and scientific activity, and in a certain historical perspective;
8. a series of essays on separate, most important concrete studies, tracing the evolution of the relationship of theoretical conceptions and empirical methods of research;
9. the biographical approach, in which the content of sociological conceptions is deduced from a sociologist's personal features and life;
10. the history of empirical social studies, with reliance on the development of the methodology and technique of research;
11. the history of institutionalization of sociology and its conversion into a university discipline, the founding and development of scientific institutions, university chairs, journals etc.; and
12. a retrospective analysis of certain very important contemporary problems as they have been posed by major sociologists of the past." I.S. Kon ed. *A history of classical sociology*. Moscow, Progress Publishers, 1989: p. 6-7

2. Terms used in the Text-book Chapter-headings

Terms used	*No. of authors*
Origins of sociology	2
Social thought	1
Historical and analytical foundations	1
Social sciences; history	1
History	2
Historical foundations	1
Historical sociology	1
Development of sociology	1

3. Provision in the LCSH

Sociology - history

4. Related Terms used by Sociologists

RT Evolution
Interaction
Social institutions
Social structure
Society
Anthropology
Ecology
Economy and society
Functional analysis
History
Linguistics
Reference groups
Social control

5. Provision in the Classification Schemes

DC	301.09	Sociology: historical and geographical treatment
UDC	301.01	Nature and purpose of sociology...historical development of the phenomena of human communal life
CC	Yv	History of sociology

3. SOCIOLOGICAL THEORIES

3.1 Definition, Explanation

3.11 "inspection of the sociological theories of the past and present shows that they revolve around a few problems, the most important of which are indicated by the following questions:

1. What is society and culture ? ;
2. What are the basic units into which society and culture should be analyzed ? ;
3. What is the relationship between society, culture, and personality ? ;
4. What are the factors determining the state of a society and a culture, or change in society or culture ? ;
5. What is sociology and what are its appropriate methods ?" N. S. Timasheff *Sociological theory: its nature and growth.* NY, Doubleday, 1955. (quoted by Arnold M Rose in Gould (1964)

3.12 "In the joint statement by the authors of *Towards a general theory of action* (Cambridge, Mass., Harvard Univ. Press, 1951: p. 3) the following functions of theory in the social sciences are listed: codification of existing concrete knowledge guide to research facilitation of the control of biases of observation and interpretation.: Arnold M Rose in Gould (1964)

3.13 "A sociological theory is a statement, using abstract language, which seeks to explain a range -however broad or limited of phenomena defined as social. The field of sociology which has its task, the presentation of sociological theory, may, on the one extreme, be constituted by a historical survey of orientations or points of view towards social phenomena, or may, at the other extreme, consist of those logically integrated, conceptually well defined, sociological propositions for which a good deal of supporting evidence has already been accumulated." Arnold M Rose in Gould (1964)

3.14 "In general... the intention of a theory in modern science is to summarize existing knowledge, to provide an explanation for observed events and relationships on the basis of explanatory principles embodied in the theory." Claire Selltiz et al *Research methods in social relations.* New York, Holt Rinehart, 1959: p. 481 (quoted by Hoult (1969) in 'Theory'.

3. Chapter Headings used in the text-books of Sociology

Terms used for chapter headings are like this:

Terms used	*No. of authors*
Sociology theory	10
Theories	4
Theoretical perspectives	1
Theories about society	1
Models and theoreis	1
Analytical foundations	1

Other related terms used in the chapter headings along with Sociological theory:

Other terms used along with Sociological theory	*No. of authors*
Method	3
Methods	3
History of Sociology	2
Origins of Sociology	1
Historical foundations	1
Sociological thought	1
Origins	1
Models	1
Historical sociology	1
Methodology	1

3. Provision in the LCSH

Social theory

USE Social Sciences - philosophy

UF Social philosophy

Social theory

4. RT (Related Terms) used by Sociologists

RT Frame of reference

Methodology

Model

Theories of the middle range

5. Provision in the Classification Schemes

DC 301.01 Sociological theory

UDC 301.19 Sociological viewpoints and trends. Individual Sociologists and Schools

CC The term Sociological theory is not used in the Colon Classification.

4. RESEARCH METHODS, TECHNIQUES

4.1 Definition, explanation,

4.11 "In general, in respect to methods of research, sociological methods are substantially the same as those of any other branch of science, viz.:

1. giving attention to a subject arising as an unidentified and somewhat challenging or disturbing feature of the social situation;
2. construction of a working hypothesis as to its nature: that is, trying to identify it by trying to place it in its functional position in the more familiar background of experience as represented by a series of tentative predicates applied to it;
3. the validity of this placement aimed to give meaning to the subject is determined by a comprehensive search and experimentation: the assembly of data describing the phenomena known to be associated in objective relations with the subject, so as to throw light on its character, or meaning, as a functioning part of the community;
4. the result is an enlargement and better definition both of the particular subject and of the community life of which it is found to be a part. Charles J Bushnell in Fairchild (1955).

4.12 "T. Parsons... says that methodology does not refer `primarily to `methods ' of empirical research, such as statistics, case study, interview, and the like. These latter, it is preferable to call research techniques. Methodology is the consideration of the general grounds for the validity of scientific procedures and systems of them. It is, as such, neither a strictly scientific nor a strictly philosophical discipline.' *The structure of social action*. NY, Mcgraw-Hill, 1937: p. 23-4" Burkart Holzner "Methodology" in Gould (1964).

2. Chapter Headings used in the Text-books of sociology

A chapter on methods/research methods in provided in their books by 42 authors out of 87 books consulted. The topic is treated as a major section by 13 authors. Various terms used to represent this concept are as follows:

Term used	*No. of authors*
Method/Methods/Research methods	28
Sociology as a Science	4
Research Technique	3
Scientific method	3
Quantitiative methods	1
Empirical social research	1
Social research	1
Social investigation	1

Accompanying/related topics dealt along with methods/ research methods by these authors:

Term used	*No. of authors*	*Term used*	*No. of authors*
Sociological theory	6	Scientific approach	1
Perspectives	3	Statisitcal techniques	1
Fields	2	Logic	1
Data	2	Origins of sociology	1
Models	2	Nature of sociology	1
Field approach	1	Methodology	2
Scope	1	Collecting and interpreting the data	1

3. Provision in the LCSH

Scientific method

USE Science - Methodology

4. RT (Related Terms) used by Sociologists

Sociology as Science

RT	Causal explanation	RT	Neo-Kantianism
	Empathy		Objectivity
	Empiricism		Operationalisation
	Ethnomethodology		Phenomenological sociology
	Experimental method		positivism
	Falsification		Qualitative analysis
	Grounded theory		Realism
	Hermeneutics		Replication

Hypothesis	Understanding alien belief systems
Hypothetica-deductive method	Value freedom
Induction	Value neutrality
Methodenstreit	Value relevance
Naturalism	

5. Provision in the Classification Schemes

DC	001.42	Research methods. Class here research methods not otherwise provided for. Scientific method
UDC	303	Methods of Social Sciences
CC		The term methods or research methods not used in the Schedule of Sociology.
	9f	Research Methodology is enumerated as a basic subject in the schedule of basic subjects. (CC7th ed.)

5. SCIENTIFIC METHOD

5.1 Definition, Explanation

5.11 "in modern social science usage, the term `science' denotes the systematic, objective study of empirical phenomena and the resultant bodies of knowledge. It is believed by social scientists that their disciplines are themselves sciences in this sense, and that science as a human activity is itself an object of social investigation." William L Kolb in Gould (1964)

5.12 "The scientific method (some would prefer to say scientific methods) includes a great deal. The scientist must accumulate considerable background information on the problem. Then he/she formulates a hypotheses. This is a carefully considered theoretical statement which seeks to relate all the known facts to one another in a logical manner. The hypothesis is then tested by scientific research. Eventually, a hypothesis is confirmed, rejected, or revised, and in this manner a science grows. There are several steps in scientific research:

1. define the problem
2. Review the literature
3. Formulate the hypothesis
4. Plan the research design
5. Collect the data
6. Analyze the data
7. Draw conclusions."

Horton (1964: p. 8-9)

5.13 "Science deals with what is, what will be on the basis of what is, rather than , with what ought to be. At no time does the scientific investigator, at least in his function as scientist, state his own opinion of what ought to be or what is right, and what is wrong. His own biases or preferences do not enter the picture. He is neutral in the sense that he will accept without personal reservation, what his evidence has revealed. Objectivity is the willingness and ability to examine evidence dispassionately." Arnold W Green (1972: p. 6)

2. Terms used in the Chapter-headings in the Text-books of Sociology

Terms used	*No. of authors*
Sociology as a science	3
Sociology and Science	1
Empirical social research	1
Scientific method	1
Scientific approach	1
Scientific study of social life	1

3. Provision in the LCSH

Scientific method
USE
Science-Methodology

4. RT (Related terms) used by Sociologists

RT Causal explanation
Empathy
Empiricism
Ethnomethodology
Experimental method
Falsification
Grounded theory
Hermeneutics
Hypothesis
Hypothetico-deductive method
Induction
Methodenstreit
Naturalism
Neo-Kantianism
Objectivity
Operationalisation
Phenomenological sociology
positivism
Qualitative analysis
Realism
Replication
Understanding alien belief systems
Value freedon
Value neutrality
Value relevance

5. Provision in the Classification Schemes

DC	001.42	Scientific method
	303	Methods of social sciences
UDC	303.8	research organisation. Research procedure
CC	Y:(R17)	Scientific method

6. SOCIAL ORGANIZATION

6.1 Definition, Explanation and Usage

6.11 "Social organization denotes the totality of normatively regulated and patterned interrelationships among the sub-units of a group definitions in use include the idea that social organization is 1. the array of roles and statuses in a group, or 2. the system of norms and values prevailing in a group, or 3. a condition of value agreement among the participants of a given society, or 4. social accommodation to existing conditions , or 5. the organization consisting of a society's sub-groups. Often used synonymously with social structure and with social order. Sometimes contrasted with social disorganization and with social pathology. " Hoult (1969)

6.12 "The term means the interdependence of parts, which is essential characteristic of all enduring collective entities groups, communities and societies. These interdependent parts are... tasks and other activities relationships among roles values, norms and beliefs subgroups within a larger unit and (in societies) institutions... the interrelated parts of social systems are activities, interactions, and sentiments." Dorian A Sweetser in G D Mitchell (1968)

6.13 "All, society can be understood as a complex system of organizations. Organization, in general is a magnifier of power, and also the basis of much of the order and predictability in society. Social organization denotes a relatively stable set of functioning interrelations among component parts (persons or groups) which results in characteristics not present in the components and produce an entity sui generis." Robert E L Faris in Gould Kolb (1964)

6.2 Headings used in the Textbooks of Sociology

Altogether 27 authors use the heading and 21 of them treat it as a major section of the textbook. A detailed analysis of the 13 textbooks reveals that their authors include 35 diverse aspects of sociology within social organization. These aspects of sociology and the authors enumerating them as part of social organization are as follows.

Table 4.4

Aspects of Sociology enumerated within Social Organization

Aspect	Authors	Aspect	Authors
8. Social order*	Ogburn	44. Norms	Bierstedt; Gorman
15. Social processes	Koller	46. Socialization	Kenkel
17. Social action, interaction	Tischler; Charon	48. Deviance	Tischler
18. Groups	Bierstedt; Horton; Chinoy Hebding; Eshleman; Tischler	50. Communication	Koller
21. Associations	Bierstedt; Horton	52. Sociology of education	Horton; Eshleman
22. Social institutions	Bierstedt; Horton; Koller	58. Differentiation and leadership	Young
24. Family	Ogburn; Horton; Chinoy Koller; Eshleman	59. Inequality	Gorman
26. Political institutions	Gorman; Eshleman	60. Social stratification	Ogburn; Chinoy; Leslie; Kenkel
28. Government	Ogburn; Horton	61. Class	Koller
30. Bureaucracy	Chinoy; Gorman; Hebding	63. Statuses	Bierstedt; Young; Kenkel
31. International relations	Ogburn	65. Power	Bierstedt
32. Economic institutions	Ogburn; Horton; Eshleman	66. Authority	Bierstedt
38. Culture	Kenkel; Eshleman	68. Social mobility	Young
41. Sociology of religion	Ogburn; Horton; Eshleman	72. Racial-ethnic relations	Young; Chinoy
42. Social control	Tischler	74. Minorities	Leslie; Kenkel
		84. Ecology	Chinoy
		88. Community	Young; Chinoy; Tischler
		90. Cities	Leslie
		90. Urbanization	Chinoy
		92. Population	Young; Leslie

* = Serial number adopted here is taken from the arrangement of 100 main concepts of sociology.

3. Provision in the LCSH

Organisation, Social USE Social Strucutre
Organisations
Use Associations, institutions

4. RT (Related Terms) used by Sociologists

Bureaucracy	Social Order
Community	Social Strucutre
Organisation	Social System
Social Movement	

5. Provision in the Classification Schemes

Decimal Classification

No Provision for 'Social Organisation' in DC.

Universal Decimal Classification

The term Social Organisation is not used in UDC, however, the term is used at 304 'Social questions in general. Critiques of Social Organisation', which can not be used for Social Organisation.

Colon Classification

The term Social Organisation is not used in CC.

7. SOCIAL SYSTEM

7.1 Definition, Explanation, Usage

7.11 "A social system consists in a plurality of individual actors interacting with each other in a situation, which has at least a physical or environmental aspect, actors who are motivated in terms of a tendency to `optimization of gratification' and whose relation to their situations, including each is defined and mediated in terms of a system of culturally structured and shared symbols." T Parsons Social system. Glencoe, Ill. Free Press, 1951: p. 5-6

Guy Rocher "Classifications and types of social organisation." *in General introduction to sociology: a theoretical perspective.* Ontario, Macmillan, 1972: 580p.

7.12 "The defining properties of social systems are differentiation, organization, boundary maintenance and equilibrium tendency." J McIntyre "Structural functional approach to family study" in F I Nye; F Berardo eds. Emerging conceptual frameworks in family analysis. New York, Macmillan, 1966: p. 58

7.13 "It is analytically necessary to distinguish social from cultural and personality systems- although the term social system is sometimes for convenience, used to encompass all three. While personality system refers to those aspects of the human personality which affects the individual's social functioning and cultural system covers actual beliefs, concrete systems of values and symbolic means of communication, social system in this context refers to forms and modes of interaction and organization,such as the authority structure of an organization or the division of functions in a family." Ronald Robertson in G Duncan Mitchell (1968)

7.13 "The totality of the relationships of the involved individuals and groups often used synonymously with social organization." Hoult (1969)

2. **Terms used in the Chapter-headings in the Text-books of Sociology**

Terms used	*No. of authors*
Social system	3
Social life	6
Social order	8
Social order and disorder	1
Society	15
Human society	1
Life in the group	1
Society and culture	1

John Dewey "Social as a category" *Monist* 38, 1928: 161-78

Among the authors who have used the term 'Social System' Wilkins (1970) makes it a major section and includes most of the social institutions, and also social classes within it. Rocher (1972) places 'social system' within the major section 'Social organisation'. Leslie (1973) prefers to place it within the major section 'social life'.

3. Provision in the LCSH

Social Systems
Community
BT Sociology
System theory
NT Functionalism
(Social sciences)
Paternalism
Social institutions
-Growth
UF Societal growth
Social structure
BT Progress
Social evolution
Social stability
Social Structure

4. Related Terms used by Sociologists

RT Boundary maintenance

Function
Functional imperative
Functionalism
Holism
Organisation
Reciprocity
Role
Social organisation

Society
Sociologistic theorem
Status role
Systems theory

5. Provision in the Classification Schemes

DC	301	Sociology and anthropology Class here interdisciplinary works on Society
UDC		The terms social system or social organisaiton not used in UDC
CC		The term social system not used in CC

8. SOCIAL ORDER

8.1 Definition, Explanation

8.11 "In general, the term refers to the totality of human relationships and culture of any given area or time the constellation of social institutions. Critically, the reference is to a certain quality, namely, the smooth, efficient, logical, aesthetic and ethical interactional functioning of individuals and groups within any such totality; it is a condition comparable to health in the individual. It is not the same as peace, for conflict may be orderly; it is not the same as organization, for organization always implies an amount of complexity not necessarily found with order." Frederick E Lumley in Fairchild (1955)

8.12 "Social order refers to ascertainable patterns of regular structure, process, or change occurring in and resulting from interaction. This broader conception embraces regularities of what are often called pathology or disorganization the breakup of stable interaction may itself be orderly, i.e. it may take specific forms under given conditions." C Arnold Anderson in Gould (1964)

Term used	*No. of authors*
Social order	2
Basic patterns and order	1
Social control: Social order	1
Social order and social control	1
Social order and disorder	1

Terms used in the major section of the Book that includes a chapter on Social order	*Author*	*(Year)*
Social Organisation	Ogburn	(1947)
Culture and Personality	Biesanz	(1953)
Structural concepts	Scott	(1970)
Social Control	Bertrand	(1973)
Social Stability and Control	O' Donnell	(1985)
Society and Individual	Charon	(1986)

The position of the term 'social order' seems to be undecided. Many a times it is used to denote whole social system but several authors use it in the sense of social control. McNall (1968) includes culture, symbolic communication, socialization and interaction within it. 'Social order is used by various authors in diverse contexts as follows:

Social order and part of social organization	Ogburn	1947
Religion and social order come together	Biesanz	1953
Social order and disorder within structural concepts	Scott	1970
Uses it as 'problems of order:social control'	Worsley	1970
Uses it as 'social control: maintenance of social order	Bertrand	1973
Social order with stability and control	O'Donnell	1985
Brings together social order and social control	Charon	1986

McNall (1968) places culture, symbolic communication, socialization and interaction within 'images of order '.

3. Provision in the LCSH

The term social order is not used in LCSH

4. RT (Related Terms) used by Sociologists

RT	Authority	RT	Power
	Coercion		Social contract
	Conflict		Social control
	Consensus		Social intergration
	Dominant Ideology		Social organisation
	Thesis		Social structure
	hegemony		Value
	ideological State apparatus		

5. Provision in the Classification Schemes

DC	303.3	Coordination and control
	303.33	Social control
UDC	301.16	Social relationships
	301.18	Social structures. Groups. Society. Social sphare
	301.186	Rationally determined formations Society in the strict sense. Purposive groups. Organised structures
CC		The term social order is not used in CC Nearest it can be placed is : Y:1 Civilisation. Culture or Y 8 By association.

9. SOCIETY

9.1 Definition, Explanation

9.11 "the concept of society includes continuity, complex associational relationship and a composition including representatives of fundamental human types, men, women, and children." Fairchild (1955

9.12 "Each aggregate of human beings of both senses and all ages bound together into a self-perpetuating group and possessing its own more or less distinctive institutions and culture may be considered a society". Ely Chinoy in Gould (1964)

9.13 "The nineteenth-century sociologists tended to make a sharp distinction between the relatively simple, undifferentiated society and the mode5n complex industrial type thus the distinction between non-literate and literate societies. Durkheim contrasted what he called segmental and organic structures, the former being societies, where the parts are so many replicas of each other, the latter displaying complex differentiation with organic type relationships between the parts. A more recent kind of classification has been between open and closed societies . . . . A closed society is one illustrated by the totalitarian type, but also by the traditional simple society which resists change, where as an open society is one which admits changes in institutional structures especially those arising through free critical discussion." G Duncan Mitchell (1968).

9.14 "Usually denotes either:

1. human beings in general considered as a group, together with all the social relationships maintained among the persons and sub-groups making up the total or
2. any one of a number of relatively independent, self-perpetuating human groups each of which:
    a. has its own territory;
    b. is made of persons of both sexes and all ages; and
    c. maintains its own way of life in terms of a culture that is more less unique.

In some works denotes social relationships. Along with culture, one of the two basic concepts in sociology and in socio-cultural anthropology". Hoult (1969

9.15 "Social theorists have employed various strategies to conceptualize society, the most important of which are:

a. society as structure;

b. society as recurrence;

c. society as contradiction (Marxist view);

d. society as culture; and

e. society as process that is:

    1. recognizable network of interrelated institutions;
    2. social conduct reproduced;
    3. antagonistic social relations of production;
    4. ideas; and values; and
    5. interaction, negotiation and change."

Arthur Brittan in Kuper (1985)

2. Chapter Headings used in the text-books of Sociology

Terms used in the chapter headings to represent the concept of society are like this:

Term used	*No. of authors*
Society	15
Human society	1
Social life	6
Social system	3
Life in the group	1
Society and culture	1
(Social order)	8
(Social order and disorder)	1

Aspects of sociology which figure prominently within the major seciton society are discernible like this:

Aspects of sociology included as a chapter within the major section 'society'	*Authors*	*(year)*
Culture	Ogburn	(1947)
	Green	(1960)
Biological factor	Ogburn	
heredity	Ogburn Sachdeva	(1967)
Geographical factors	Ogburn	
Population	Biesanz	(1953)
Social stratification	Biesanz	
intergroup tensions	Biesanz	
interaction: social processes	Green	Sachdeva
Socialisation	Green	
personality	Green	
Groups	Tischler	(1983)
Communities	Tischler	
Social control and deviant behaviour	Tischler	

Wilkins (1970) provides chapters on individual, social classes, marriage and family, politicalsystem, economic system, industry, and religion and belief within 'social system.'

The broader terms within which some anthors like to place society, social system, are like this:

Broader section of the book	*Society/ Social system*	*Author*	*(year)*
Social organisation	Social system	Rocher	(1972)
Social organisation	Society	hebding	(1976)
Group	Society	Phillips	(1979)
Organisation of society	Society	Tischler	(1983)
Social organisation	Ssociety	Charon	(1986)

3. Provision in the LCSH

The term society as a separate heading is not used in LCSH.

4. RT (Related Terms) used by sociologists

RT	Cooperation	RT	Social contract
	Community		Social Darwinism
	Culture		Social structure
	Evolution		Social system
	Institutions		
	Integration		

5. Provison in the Classification Schemes

DC	301	Sociology and anthropology Class here interdisciplinary works on society
UDC	301.18	Social structures. Groups. Society. Social sphere
CC		The term society is not used in CC.

9.A1 SOCIAL LIFE

9.A11 Definition, Explanation

9.A111 "Social life, the object of study of sociology in its widest meaning, is explained by four factors: heredity, natural environment, culture and the group. But the variations in social life are explained rather inadequately by heredity and natural environment, for in these two factors, there is not much variation over time and not much hereditary variation for one large segment of population as compared with another. Variations in social life among human beings, and especially in the United States at the present time are explained largely by variations in culture and in the group, even though all four factors are essential to maintain human social life." Ogburn ; Nimkoff (1947:p. 22)

2. Terms used in the Chapter-headings in the Text-books of Sociology

Terms used	*No. of authors*
Social life	3
Composition of social life	1
Roots of social life	1
Foundations of social life	1
Life in the group	1

Eldridge (1950) seems to define sociology as social life by the use of the chapter heading 'scientific study of social life'. Gisbert (1957) calls social group and social institutions as roots of social life. Leslie (1978) lays emphasis on social institutions, social processes, values, norms and social system s within social life. Stewart (1978) believes culture, socialization and group interaction as the 'foundations of social life'. Larson (1982) divides his whole book into four major sections including one 'social life', others being perspectives and methods, social organization, and social institutions.

Aspects of sociology included as a chapter within the major secton 'social life'	*Author*	*(Year)*
Hereditary factors	Eldridge	(1950)
Social groups	Gisbert	(1957)
Social institutions	Gisbert	(1957)
Communication	Leslie	(1973)
Social interaction	Leslie	(1973)
Social processes	Leslie	(1973)
Values, norms	Leslie	(1973)
Social systems	Leslie	(1973)
Life in the group	Perry	(1973)
Culture	Stewart	(1972)
Socialisation	Stewart	(1972)
Group interaction	Stewart	(1972)

3. Provision in the LCSH

The term Social life is not used in LCSH.

Ssocial life and Customs

USE

Manners and Customs

4. RT (Related Terms) used by Sociologists

The term social life is not used in the eight sources (dictionaries) taken as source material for this analysis. The trm is in use as a synonym for society.

5. Provision in the Classificaiton Schemes

UDC	308	Political and social life in various countries (?)
DC	301	Sociology and anthropology Class here interdisciplinary works on society.
CC	G:56	Social life.

10. SOCIOBIOLOGY/BIOLOGICAL DETERMINISM

10.1 Definition, Explanation

10.11 "A school of thought whose proponents maintain that human behavior is basically a function of inborn physical characteristics." Hoult (1969)

10.12 Sociobiology—" Systematic study of the biological basis of all forms of social behavior, including sexual and parental behavior in all kinds of organisms, including man." Edward Wilson "What is sociobiology? " in Michael S Gregory et al Sociobiology and human nature. San Francisco, Jessy- Bass, 1978: p. 10

10.13 Biological sociology— " A somewhat ill-defined area of sociological inquiry centering in the study of the social correlatives and consequences of the biological processes of heredity, variation, selection and reproduction in human populations. In its broadest historical connotation this term includes the bio-organismic theories of society the anthropo-sociological, or social selectionist theories of racial and individual differences and their social effects `the struggle for existence' theories' with their emphasis on the role of war and even the demographic theories emphasizing the social effects of size and density of population." Frank H Hankins in Fairchild (1955)

10.14 Heredity—"The scientific study of genetic transmission of characteristics has resulted in the redefinition of the respective roles of heredity and environment, so that studies are increasingly concerned with the relative contributions of heredity and environment to the expression of physical traits and behavior rather than with dividing traits that are hereditary from those that are environmentally produced." L C Dunn

Heredity and evolution in human populations. Cambridge, Mass., Harvard Univ. Press, 1959: (quoted by William S Laughlin in Gould 1964)

10.15 "While biological heredity is sometimes defined as the tendency of like to beget like or the transmission of similarities, similarities are not inherited as such, but rather the genetic capabilities for their expression. Genes determine processes and they interact with the environment in which they are placed." William S Laughlin in Gould (1964)

10.16 "Systematic study of the biological basis of all forms of social behaviour, including sexual and parental behaviour in allkinds of organisms, including man." Edward Wilson "What is socio-biology?" in Michael S. Gregory *et al. Sociobiology and human nature.* San Francisco, Jossey-Base, 1978: p. 10.

2. Terms in the chapter Headings used in the Text-books of Sociology

a. *Terms used*	*No. of authors*
Biological aspects	2
Biological factor	1
Biological factors	1
Biological factros of social change	1
Biological structures	1
Biological development	1
Biology	1
Physical structures	1
Heredity and Environment	
Environment	4
Heredity	4
Hereditary makeup	1

Broader terms in the form of major section within which the chapter on Biological factors is placed

Society	Ogburn	(1947)
Social change	MacIver	(1950)
natural condition of human society	Bierstedt	(1957)

The chapter on Hereditary factors is placed within

Social life	Eldridge	(1950)
Social change	Gisbert	(1957)
Society	Sachdeva	(1967)
Individual	Shankar Rao	(1990)

Phillips makes a major section under the title 'Biological and physical structrues' but only population, and human ecology is included within it.

3. Provision in the LCSH

Sociobiology
BT Genetic psychology
Human bioligy-social aspoects
Human evolution
Man-animal nature
Psychology-comparative
Social evolution
NT Biopolitic
Law and sociobiology
Sexism in sociobiology

4. RT (Related Terms) used by Sociologists

Sociobiology
RT Altruism
Ecology
Ethology
Evolution
Organic analogy
Social Darwinism

5. Provision in the Classification Schemes

DC	304.5	Genetic factors Class here sociobiology (biosociology), the study of the genetic bases of human social behaviour. Class a specific aspect of sociobiology with the subject in sociology, e.g., the sociobiology of conflict 303.6
UDC		The term sociobiology or biological aspects of society not used in UDC
CC		The term sociobiology is not used in CC

3. Provision in the LCSH

Heredity, Human
UF heredity of man
BT Eugenics
Family

Man-Constitution
Prenatal influences
NT Deaf-Marriage
Degeneration
Education and heredity
Human genetics
Mentally-handicapped Mariage

4. RT (Related Terms) used by Sociologists

RT Biological herdity
Congenital
Culture
Inheritance
Physical anthropology
Socialisation

5. Provision in the Classification Schemes

DC	304	Factors affecting social behaviour
	304.5	Genetic Factors Class here sociobiology (biosociology), the study of the genetic bases of human social behaviour
UDC	575.1	Heredity
CC	G:61	Heredity

11. SEXUAL BEHAVIOR/ SEXUALITY

11.1 Definition, Explanation

11.11 "Sex is defined here as anything connected with genital stimulation, sexual gratification, reproduction, and the behavior that accompanies such stimulation, gratification and involvement. Kissing, petting, coitus and masturbation, for example, constitute forms of sexual behavior and are referred to, by the term sex and its derivatives, sexual and sexuality. Sexual behavior, when discussed within a particular social context such as premarital, marital, or extramarital sexual behavior, refers to those acts by an individual which involve another individual (imagined or real) and which center around sexual gratification." Graham B Spanier in Kuper (1985)

11.12 "The patterning of human sexual responses is learnt through symbolically mediated experience in particular groups every society embodies in its customs, institutions, and language, the biological distinction between the sexes, exemplified in the differentiation of social roles for the respective sexes the system of sexual social roles tends to change with socio-cultural change.

Human sexuality has six distinct characteristics:

1. it is contained within and controlled by a normatively governed process of selection;
2. emotionally intense and more or less permanent unions are formed;
3. human sexual behavior is not necessarily procreative;
4. human sexual behavior is partly rational rational in; that there is a decision to have or not to have sexual relations this sexual decision involves both parties;
5. human sexuality is subject to cultural variation among societies and subgroups of societies; and
6. in all human societies sexuality manifests itself to some degree in ways, which run counter to the values of the society." Frank E Hartung in Gould (1964).

2. Terms in the Chapter headings used in the Text-books of Sociology

Terms used	*No. of authors*
Sex	2
Sexuality	1
Sex and Sexuality	1

Broader terms used as secton-Headings that includes a chapter on sex/sexuality	*Autor*	*(Year)*
Culture and personality	Horton	(1964)
Applications of sociology	Sherman	(1979)
Contemporary areas of social Inquiry	Persell	(1984)

3. Provision in the LCSH

Sexuality
USE
Sex
UF Sex (Gender)
Sexology
Sexual behaviour
Sexuality
BT Reproduction
Love
NT Females
Homosexuality
Males
Parents

4. RT (Related Terms) used by Sociologists

RT Courtship
Endogamy
Family
Homosexuality
Libido
Marriage
Prostitution
Rape

5. Provision in the Classification Schemes

DC	306.7	Institutions pertaining to relations of the sexes Class here interdisciplinary works on sex, sexual live, sexual relations.
UDC	57.017.5	Sex and sexuality
	612.6.06	Sexuality
	591.551	Relation between the sexes
CC	S 5	Sex psychology Sociological aspects of sex and sexuality not available in the Sociology schedule.

12. INDIVIDUAL

12.1 Definition, Explanation

12.11 "The noun individual is a synonym for person or human being. As an adjective, individual denotes that the object modified is single, separate, distinguishable, as in the 'individual human being' Richard Dewey in Gould (1964).

12.12 Individualistic Psychology- "It is holistic ego-psychology and a social psychology which assumes that life is movement and must endlessly strive for better adaptation to the environment... The age old conflict as to the primacy of heredity or environment is resolved in this theory (which Adler calls 'striving for superiority')in his endeavor to construct his personality. Benjamin W Wolman in Dictionary of behavioral science. New York, Nostrand, 1973: p. 191

12.2 Usage of Terms in the Form of Chapter Headings

The term individual has been used in the chapter headings by 8 authors, one uses it in plural as individuals, and one each as individual and his personality and individualization. Society has been mentioned by 8 authors along with individual in the chapter headings, and 2 authors mention personality along with it.

2. Terms in the Chapter Headings used in the Text-books of Sociology

Term used	*No. of authors*	*Related terms used along with 'individual' in the title*	*No. of Authors*
Individual	8	Society	8
individual and his personality		personality	2
Individuals	1		
Individualisation	1		

3. Provision in the LCSH

Individual Not used in LCSH

Individuality

Works on the sum total of characteristics which distinguish an individual from all others. Works on the specific characteristics, qualities, or traits in which individuals differ are entered under Individual differences.

BT Psychology
RT Conformity
Personaity
Self
NT Identity

4. RT (Related Terms) used by Sociologists

RT Person
personality

5. Provision in the Classificaiton Schemes

DC	302.5	Relation of the individual to society
UDC	301.165	Relationship between groups and individual
CC	SN 14	Individualistic psychology

13. PERSONALITY

13.1 Definition, Explanation

13.11 "That dynamic organization of ideas, attitudes, and habits which is built upon the foundation of the biologically inherited psycho-physical mechanisms of a single organism and of socially transmitted culture patterns, and which embodies all the adjustments of this individuai's motives, desires, and purposes to the requirements and potentialities of his social and sub-social environments. The personality includes:

1. the focus of consciousness;
2. the pre-sensory area of sensory-motor experience and of unrepressed memories, ideas, wishes, and attitudes; and
3. the patterns of behavior which can be covertly observed and operated upon by others." Hornell Hart in Fairchild (1955)

13.12 "Personality is the totality of behavior of an individual with a given tendency system interacting with a sequence of situations." J Milton Yinger Towards a field theory of behavior. New York, McGraw Hill, 1965: p. 141

13.13 "A convenient rag bag shorthand way of referring individual's behavior, without reference to specific psychological processes, taking into account the continuing recognizable identity of the individual in the course of development. The term is best defined by context, as in Kurt Lewin's formula: `behavior is a function of the interaction of personality and environment.' That is individuals will behave differently in what appears the same environment. These differences may be attributable to differences in inborn stimulus-response characteristics and (or, interacting with) differences in the nature and organization of learned responses, which include differences in the way the environment is perceived." Josephine Klein in G D Mitchell (1968).

13.14 "The dominant use of the concept in sociology and social psychology is more specialized: it emphasizes those relatively stable characteristics of individuals which may underlie individual differences in behavior and may be used to predict or explain them. This view derives most immediately from the inter-war American social psychology of Allport and his students, who developed a view of personality in terms of traits and attitudes, neuro-psychic structures linked to repeated complexes of behavior. Some authors go further and define personality through the formula `behavior is a function of personality and situation' or B = f (P+S)." Joan Busfield in Michael Mann (1983)

13.14. Chapter Headings used in the text-books of Sociology

A chapter on personality or individual is provided by 29 authors out of 87 textbooks seen. The chapter on personality is placed under the major section individual by MacIver, (1950) and Perry (1973) under social differentiation by Bierstedt (1957), under group by Merton (1959), under social system by Wilkins (1970) and under Social relations by Young (1962).

Table 4.5

Who includes what within 'Personality'

Socialisation	Ogburn (1947); Young (1962); Phillips (1979) Eshleman (1983); and Rose (1976)
Conformity and deviance	Phillips (1979); Rose (1976)
Social deviation	Ogburn (1947)
Deviance an social control	Eshleman (1983)
Personality disorganisation	Merrill (1952)
Group influence on personality	Eldridge (1950)
Personality and civilisation	Eldridge (1950)
Culture and personality adjustment	Merrill (1952)
Culture conflict	Sutherland (1961)
Social interaction	Biesanz (1953); Phillips (1979)

E H lewis "Some definitions of individualisation" *Amer. Jl. of Sociol.* 18, 1912-13.

B D Smith: H J Vetter *Theoretical approaches to personality*. Englewood Cliffs, N J, 1982:

Associated/related terms used along with personality/individual in the headings:

Group	(Ogburn 1947)
Culture	(Ogburn 1947; Biesanz 1953; Sutherland 1973; Bertrand 1973)
Social interaction	(Biesanz 1953)
Social structure	(Merrill 1952; Gitler 1957; Merton 1959)
Socialisation	(Young 1962; Horton 1964; Bertrand 1973; McGee 1973; Tischler 1983)
Social system	(Parsons 1961)

3. Provision in the LCSH

Personality

UF Personality theory
Personality traits
Traits, Personality

BT Consciousness
Mental health
Psychology
Soul

RT Individuality
Persons
Self
Temperament

NT Adjustment (Psy.)
Character
Charisma
Ego (Psy.)
Humanistic Psy.
Identity (Psy.)
Introversion
Mood (Psy.)
Personality assessment
Personality change

4. RT (Related Terms used by Sociologists)

RT Attitude
Consciousness, focus of
Expanded personality
Ego
Id
Individuality
Internalisation
National character
Personality integration
Socialisation

5. Provision in the Classification Schemes

DC	The terms Individual or personality are not used in sociology schedule; perhaps it can be placed under: 302 Social interaction Class here psychological principles of sociology.
UDC 301.151	Socially significant characteristics of individuals
CC Y:7	Personality

14. ATTITUDES

14.1 Definition, Explanation

14.11 "An attitude is a mental and neural state of readiness, organized through experience, exerting a directive or dynamic influence upon individual's response to all objects and situations with which it is related." G W Allport in C Murchison ed. *Handbook of social psychology.* Worcestor, Mass. Clark Univ. Press, 1935: p. 810 (quoted by Newcomb in Gould (1964)

14.12 "An attitude can be defined as an enduring organization of motivational, emotional, perceptual, and cognitive processes with respect to some aspects of the individual's world." D Krech; R S Cruchfield *Theory and problems of social psychology* New York, McGraw Hill, 1945: p. 152 (quoted by Newcomb in Gould (1964)

14.13 "A general, learned and relatively enduring tendency on the part of the individuals to respond negatively or positively to a given phenomena, such response being based on the individual's evaluation of that which he believes about that phenomena—however, sociologists tend to view attitudes in relationship to social values (i.e. as the subjective aspect of values) ... usually differentiated from motive, the latter being regarded as less stable and inclusive (an enduring and relatively general motive being indistinguishable from an attitude) distinguished from belief on the dual ground that belief, in contrast to attitudes, do not:

1. imply anything about tendencies to act or
2. includes the positive-negative type of evaluation that constitutes the basis of attitudes;

Sometimes loosely used synonymously with opinion and with value, although usually distinguished from both on the grounds that neither involves tendencies to act and that, in addition, opinions are comparatively lightly held (i.e. not enduring)." Hoult (1969).

2. Terms in the Chapter-headings used in the Text-Books of Sociology

Terms used	*No. of authors*
Interests and attitudes	2
Psychology	1
Attitudes and beliefs	1
Psychology	1
Motivational system	1
Social psychology	1
Human nature	1
Mass mind	1
Psychic equipment	1
Prejudice	1

David J. Delevita *The Concept of Identity*. Tr. by Ian Finlay Paris, Moution, 1965.

Melvin L Defleur; Frank R Westie "Attitude as a scientific concept", *Social Forces* 42.

WJ McGuire "Nature of attitutde and attitude change." in *Handbook of Social Psychology* 2nd e. vol 3. Reading, Mass. 1969.

Parsons (1961) places the motivational system under the major section 'personality and social system'. Barnes associates the concepts of prejudice with it and thinks it as a factor in molding public opinion. Both of these concepts are placed by him within 'communication and formation of public opinion.

3. Provision in the LCSH

Attitude
UF Attitudes (Psychology)
BT Psychology
RT Public opinion
SA Subdivision attitudes under classes of persons and ethnic groups; and subdivision Views on (topic) and names of individual persons.
NT Affiliation (Psychology)
Attitude change
Conformity
Dogmatism
Empathy
Entitlement attitudes
Ethnic attitudes
Frustration
Health attitudes
Intention
Job satisfaction
Prejudices
Rejection (psychology)
Role expectation
Scale analysis
Sexism
Stereotype (psychology)

4. RT (Related Terms) used by Sociologists

RT Attitude research
Cognitive consistency theory
Ideology
Interview
Motivation
Personality
Reliability
Role
Sentiments

Systems of deprivation
Traits
Value

5. Provision in the Classification Schemes

DC	303.38	Public opinion Class here attitudes, attitude formation and change.
UDC	301.151	Socially significant characteristics of individuals. drives, propensities. Social psychology.
CC	S: 57	Sentiment, Interest

15. SOCIAL PROCESSES

15.1 Definition, Explanation

15.11 "Unfortunately one of the most vague terms in sociology. At on extreme, it is a general term which can denote almost any aspect of social interaction. At other extreme it can denote a continuous sequence of social activities rigorously defined on the basis of empirical research. In its most frequent use, the term means a transition or a entries of transitions between one social condition and another . . . . The social process is seen (by some sociologists) to be social interaction and is the pre-requisite for social activity of any sort. All of the other so called social processes are only more specific forms of interaction.

Gumplowicz's primary emphasis was on the social processes of conflict and competition... these two fundamentally different kinds of relationship became the base for a dichotomous classification of social processes, those which are associative or conjunctive and those which are dissociative or disjunctive. The former included such processes as cooperation, accommodation, and assimilation, while the latter included the processes of competition, contravention, and conflict. While some classifications embody only two categories, the associative and dissociative, others go into minute classification, and under contravention, for example, would further include rebuffing, venting, harassing and numerous other terms... In its fundamental aspects, social process is a concept of movement, change, flux." Russeel Langworthy in Gould; Kolb (1964)

15.12 "Any social change or interaction in which observer sees a consistent quality or direction to which a class name is given a class or social changes or interactions in which abstraction a common pattern can be observed and named (e.g. imitation, acculturation, conflict, social control, stratification)... social processes, like other processes, are changes in structure... Every social process has four or five possible forms: 1. interpersonal, when the interaction is between selves or complexes of a personality; 2. person to person; 3. a person to group; 3.b group to person; 4. group to group." Thomas Dawes Elliot in Fairchild (1955)

15.13 "An interaction pattern or social change involving particular repetitive features to such a degree that the pattern or change is classifiable as a distinctive type a pattern or interaction between aspects of a social system such interaction patterns often being viewed in terms of five major types, namely accommodation, assimilation, competition, conflict, and cooperation." Hoult (1969)

2. Chapter Headings used in the Text-books of Sociology

a.	*Terms used to represent the concept of social processes*	*No. of authors*
	Social processes	10
	processes	2
	Social process	2
b.	*Terms appearing in association with Social process/processes*	
	Social interaction	1
	Interaction	1
	Social roles	1
	Institutional structures	1
	Stability and change	1

3. Provision in the LCSH

Social processes

UF Processes

BT Social activities

RT Social interaction

NT Accommodation

Table 4.4

b. Who includes what within social processes? A tabular presentation

What are social processes	Authors	Eldridge (1950)	Mannheim (1957)	Green (1959)	Sutherland (1961)	Young (1965)	Goode (1966)	Muzumdar (1966)	Scott (1970)	Shapiro (1977)
Accommodation		*		*					*	
Adaptive processes										
Assimilation		*			*		*			
Acculturation										
Communication		*						*		
Competition		*	*			*		*		
Conflict		*								
Consensus										
Cooperation		*	*			*				
Deviance							*			
Individualisation			*							
Isolation			*							
Division of labour			*							
Integrative processes										
interaction				*	*			*	*	
Monopoly		*								
Opposition						*				
Power							*			

Contd...

What are social processes	Authors	Eldridge (1950)	Mannheim (1957)	Green (1959)	Sutherland (1961)	Young (1965)	Goode (1966)	Muzumdar (1966)	Scott (1970)	Shapiro (1977)
Social change		*			*					
Social contect										
Social control										
Social distance										
Socialisation										
Stability										
Stability										
Stress in Social system, management of-					*					
Status									*	

Assimilaiton
Competition
Conflict
Cooperation

4. RT (Related Terms) used by Sociologists

RT Accommodation
Assimilation
Competition
Conflict
Cooperation
Invesion
Situation process
Social
Structure-function
Succession

5. Provision in the Classification Schemes

DC	303	Social processes
	303.3	Coordination and control
	303.4	Social change
	303.6	Conflict
UDC	301.17	Social processes. Group formation
	301.171	Action and inaction in social processes
	301.172	Differentiating processes
	301.173	Integrating processes
	301.174	Disintegrating processes
	301.175	Transforming processes
CC		The term social processes is not used in the Colon Classification.

16. SOCIAL RELATIONS

16.1. Definition, Explanation

16.11 "Social relation (is) an inclusive term designating both social processes and social relationships. Social relationship (is) a form pattern of social conduct, i.e. interaction between persons and/or plurels in which space positions are more conspicuous than time sequences, andquiescence is more conspicuous than motion. The socialrelationship is one aspect of the graphic, the structural,the morphological patterning (???????) wedlock, kinship, citizenship, etc. Note the suffix—ship, denoting state or condition. This is not an essential feature of terms of social relationship, however, it is merely an occasional indication." Howard Becker in , Fairchild (12955)

16.12 " Among given persons and /or groups, a bond or connection based on the fact that such persons or groups take one another into account in orienting significant aspects of their behavior often used synonymously with interaction to denote reciprocal influence among the elements making a social system according to Timasheff, interaction from a static (i.e., structural in contrast to functional) point of view." N S Timasheff "Basic concepts of sociology." American Jl. of sociology 58(2), Sept. 1952: 176-86 (quoted by Hoult 1969)

16.13 "Social relationship consists entirely of the probability that individuals will behave in some meaningfully determinate way." Max Weber Basic concepts in sociology. New York, Citadel Press, 1964: p. 63 (quoted by Hoult 1969)

'Social relations' is used as a heading only by Young (1962), Potter (1974), Chambliss (1975), Rose (1976), and Sharma (1968). Hoult is of the opinion that the term social relationship is used synonymously with social interaction. By observing the textbook chapter headings it appears that those authors who have provided a chapter on social relations do not provide a separate chapter on social interaction. Young and Chambliss under social relationship and Gorman under individual integration include the following aspects under social relationship.

Aspects included within Social relations	*Young*	*Gorman (1971)*	*Chambliss*
Groups	*		
Culture variation	*		
Values and norms	*		
Social process		*	
Personality		*	
Roles and attitudes		*	
Friendship and association			*
Mass media and Mass mind			*
Power			*
Imperialism and industrialisation		*	
Bureaucratism			*
Deviant behaviour and social control			*
Social inequality			*

Young, and Chambliss under social relationship Gorman under individual integration include the following aspects by making these headings major sections.

3. Privision in the LCSH

The term social relations is not used in LCSH

4. R T (Related Terms) used by Sociologists

RT Groups
Interaction
Interaction process

5. Provision in the Classification Schemes

DC	302.5	Relation of the individual to society
UDC	301.16	Social relationships
CC		The term Social relations is not used in CC.

17. SOCIAL INTERACTION

17.1 Definition, Explanation

17.11 "The reciprocal influence of the social factors that result in human nature and... culture is.... social interaction." E B Reuter; C W Hart Introduction to sociology. New York, McGraw-Hill, 1937: p. 256 (quoted by Howard Becker in Gould (1964)

17.12 "Social processes when analyzed from the standpoint of the inter-stimulations and responses of the personalities and groups. The chief forms of social interaction are opposition (including competition and conflict) and cooperation. Accommodation and assimilation are often mentioned as cooperative forms of interaction, but they may be regarded even better as social processes related to social change and social adjustment. Isolation may be regarded as the zero degree of social interaction." Hornell Hart in Fairchild (1955)

Henry A Murray "Toward a classification of interaction." in Talcott Parsons; Edward A Shils (eds.) *Towards a General Theory of Action*. NY, Harper, 1951: 434-64.

P McHugh Defining the situation: the organisation of meaning in social interaction. Indianapolis, Bobbs-Merrill, 1968.

J C Mitchell "Concept and use of social network." in J C Mitchell ed. *Social networks in urban situations*. Manchester, 1969.

17.13 "(Often appearing as social interaction) usually denotes two or more persons, groups or social systems mutually influencing one another frequently used synonymously with social relationship to denote the connection between two social phenomena." Hoult (1969).

17.2 Usage of Terms in the Form of Chapter Headings

'Social interaction' has been used as a heading by 24 authors out of 87 textbooks seen.

Table 4.26

Terms used for Social Interaction

Terms used	*No. of authors*
Social interaction	6
Social interaction and social processes	3
Group interaction	2
Action/ social action	3
Social structure and interaction	2
Social interaction and personality	1
Social contact	1
Communication and social interaction	1
Individual and social interaction	1
Networks and interactions	1
Socialization and interaction	1
Social organization and interaction	1

Aspects included with Social Interaction or Associated with it	*Young*	*Gorman*	*Chambliss*
Communication	*		
Competition	*		
Conflict		*	
Cooperation	*		
Accommodation	*	*	
Assimilation	*		
Public opinion	*		
Role			*
Social class			*
Social mobility			*
Race and ethnic relations			*
Collective behavior			*

The chapter on social interaction is a part of the major section 'Social processes' in the books by Mannheim (1957), and Sutherland (1961), 'Group behaviour' in the book by Ogburn (1947), and 'Social organisation' in the text-book by Charon (1986). Some authors sub-divide the major section on social interaction and discuss the following aspects within it or associate the concept through their chapter headings:

3. Provision in the LCSH

Social interaction
UF Human interaction
Interaction, social
Symbolic interaction
BT Exchange theory (sociology)
Psychology
Social psychology
NT Apologizing Conflict
Attention seeking
Eye contact
Group relation training
Interaction analysis in training Networks
Inter-group relations
Prisoner's dilemma game
Self-presentation Role
Social acceptance Social contact
Social distance Social relationship
Social exchange
Social skills
Sociometry
Symbolic interactionism

4. Related Terms used by Sociologists

RT Action theory
Accommodation
Adjustment
Assimilation
Communication
Competition
Consensus
Cooperation
Exchange theory
Isolate
Opposition process
Public opinion

5. Provision in the Classification Schemes

DC	302	Social interaction Class here the psychological principles of sociology, interpersonal relations, social psychology
	302.1	Genral topics
	302.2	Communicaiton
	302.3	Social interaction within groups
	302.4	Social interaction between groups
	302.5	Relation of the individual to society
UDC	301.16	Social relationships
	301.165	Relationship between groups and individuals
CC		The term social interaction/socialrelations is not used in the Colon Classification.

18. GROUPS

18.1 Definition, Explanation

18.11 "A number of persons between whom exists a psychic interaction and who are set apart by that interaction in their own minds and in those of others as a recognized entity. The social group requires for its existence a durable contact between persons out of which conscious interaction may arise, a consciousness of sufficient likeness or common interest to establish some degree of identification of each with the group and some structure recognized by the members as essential to achieve its continued existence an an entity." Grace L Coyle in Fairchild (1955)

18.12 " Groups vary in size, duration, stability, mode of contact, objectives, manner of admission, sanctions, formality, role prescriptions, degree of acquaintance among members, and in many other ways." George A Lundberg et al. *Sociology.* 4th ed. New York, Harper, 1968: p. 73

18.13 "Collectivities of individuals who interact and form social relationships. Primary- are small, being defined by face to face interaction. They have their own norms of conduct and are solidaristic. Within this category may be included the family, group of friends and many work groups. Secondary- are larger and each member does not directly interact with every other . . . Social psychology of groups has been concerned with issues of group structure and cohesion, morale, group leadership, and the effects on the individual." Nicholas Abercrombie et al (1984).

2. Chapter headings used in the Text-books of Sociology

Number of authors who have used the category	34
Number of authors stating 'groups' as a major section	8

D Sanderson "A preliminary structural classification of groups." Social forces 17, 1938: 1-6

Frederick L bates "A conceptual analysis of group structure." *Social Forces* 36, 1957: 103-116.

a. Term used to represent the concept of Group

Term	*No. of authors*
Groups	17
Social groups	12
Human collectivities	1
Sociology of groups	1
Human groups	1
Group interaction	1
Group structure	1

b. Other related/associated terms used or discussed along with the heading group/groups

Term	*No. of authors*	*Term*	*No. of authors*
Organisations/ Social organisation	3	large fromal organisations	1
Small groups	2	Personality	1
Associations	1	Population	1
Conformity	1	Public	1
Crowd	1	Social categories	1
Group behaviour	1	Social institutions	1
Individual	1		

Table 4.7

c. Major section of the book under which the concept of 'Group' is discussed/included.

Major section	*Chapter heading used*	
Gisbert (1957)	Social organisation	Groups
Horton (1964)	Social organisation	Groups and associations
Hebding (1976)	Social organisation	Social groups
Goode (1977)	Social organisation	Groups: large & small
Eshleman (1983)	Social organisation	Social groups & Org.
Tischler (1983)	Organisation of society	Group structures
MacIver (1950)	Social structures	Social groups
Bertrand (1973)	Social structures and interaction	Structure of groups
Mannheim (1957)	Social integration	Sociology of groups
Young (1962)	Social relations	Social groups
Leslie (1973)	Social units	Groups
Perry (1973)	Sociology in principle	Group
Cole (1975)	Groups influencing	
behaviour	Groups and conformity	
Phillips (1979)	Groups Organisations,	Community, society
Persell (1984)	Social life	Groups and organisations.

3. Provision in the lCSH

Groups, Social
USE Social groups

Social groups
UF Association
Group dynamics
Groups, Social
BT Sociology
RT Social participation
NT Age groups
Coalition, Social sciences
Decision making, Group
Decision making, Group
Dominance (psychology)
Elite (social sciences)
Leadership
Neighbourhood
Polarisation (Social sciences)
Problem solving, Group
Reference groups
Small groups
Social isolation
Social mobility
Social psychology
Social values
Sub-culture
Work-groups

4. RT (Related Terms) used by Sociologists

RT Cohesion, Social
Community
Functional analysis
Group dynamics
Human relations
Idustrial relations
Leadership
Primary relationship
Reference group
Role
Social integration
Social psychology
Self

Society
Sociometry
Status, Social

5. Provision in the Classification Schemes

DC	305	Social groups General aspects: social status, role, interactions, problems of social groups Class here cluture and institutions of specific groups other than indigenous racial, ethnic, national groups (formerly also 306.08); subcultures of specific groups; consciousness-raising groups; social stratification, equality, inequality
	305.2	Age groups
	305.3	Men and women
	305.4	Women
	305.5	Social classes
	305.6	Religious groups
	305.7	Language groups
	305.8	Racial, ethnic, national groups
	305.9	Occupational and miscellaneous groups
UDC	301.18	Social structures. Groups. Society. Social sphere
CC		The term group or groups or social group is not used in the sociology schedule of Colon Classification.

19. PRIMARY GROUPS

19.1 Definition, Explanation

19.11 "The central sociological significance of the primary groupis its utility to bring about personal gratification and effective social control." G Lundberg *et al. Sociology*. 4th ed. New york, Harper, 1968: p. 76

19.12 "As suggested originally by C H Cooley, a relatively small group characterized by members who maintain intimate, cooperative and usually face to face relationship with one another and who treat one another as needs, not as means,for example, a family or a play group often used synonymously with gemeinschaft contrasted with secondary group and with gesellschaft." Hoult (1969)

2. Terms used in the Chapter-headings in the Text-books of Sociology

Terms used	*No. of authors*
Primary groups	2
Primary group	1
Groups in physical proximity	1
Disintegration of primary groups	1

Broader terms used as Section heading That includs a chapter on Primary Groups	*Author*	*(Year)*
Family and community Disorganisation (for Disintegration of primary groups)	Barnes	(1942)
Social Organisation	Chinoy	(1961)
Differentiation and variation in Social structures	Parsons	(1961)

Out of the 87 text-books studies on author has included a chapter on primary groups since 1967.

3. Provision in the LCSH

Primary groups

The term primary groups is not referred to in the LCSH.

4. RT (Related Terms) used by Sociologists

RT Gemeinschaft
Group
Social group
Contrasted with
Secondary group
Gesellschaft

5. Provision in the Classification Schemes

DC	302.3	Social interaction within groups
	302.34	In small (Primary) groups Groups small enough for all maembers to engage in face-to-face relationships at one time Examples: committees, gangs, play groups Class here friendship.
UDC		The term primary groups is not used in UDC
	301.183	Numerically small groups. Gangs, Circle, set
CC		The terms group or primary group are not used in CC.

20. SMALL GROUPS

20.1 Definition, Explanation

20.11 "A small group is a collection of people who meet more or less regularly in face-to-face interaction, who possess a common identity or exclusiveness of purpose, and who share a set of standards governing their activities." Wallace; Wallace (1989).

2. Terms used in the chapter-headings in the Text-books of Sociology

Terms used	*No. of authors*
Small groups	5
Small group	2
Near groups	1

Broader section which contains a chapter on small groups	*Author*	*(Year)*
Groups and the person	Merton	(1979)
Human collectivities	Sutherland	(1961)
Association	McNall	(1968)
Social units	Leslie	(1973)
Social Organisation	Goode	(1977)

No author has included a chapter on small groups in his text-book since 1977, out of the books included in this analysis.

3. Provision in the LCSH

Small groups
UF Groups, Small
BT Social groups
NT Communication in small groups
Group relations training SYMLOG system
-Research
USE
Small group research

4. RT (Related Terms) used by Sociologists

The term small groups has not been used by 8 authors consulted for finding out related terms used.

RT Friendship
Near groups
Neighbourhood

5. Provision in the Classification Schemes

DC	302.3	Social interaction within groups
	302.34	In small (Primary) groups
		Groups small enough for members to engage in face-to-face relationships at one time Examples: committees, gangs, play groups Class here friendship.
UDC	301.183	Numerically small groups. Gang, circle, set
CC		The tem Groups or small groups are not used in CC.

21. ASSOCIATIONS

21.1 Definition, Explanation

21.11 "The fundamental relationship which unites individuals into groups or societies. A comprehensive term for the relationships of inter-stimulation and response, usually of a somewhat enduring nature in contrast to mere contact." Fairchild (1955)

21.12 "A organized group formed in pursuit of some common interest with its own self-contained administrative structure and functionaries." Fairchild (1955)

21.12 "An group organized for the pursuit of an interest or group of interests in common." R M MacIver ; C H Page *Society*. London, Macmillan, 1955: p. 12 (quoted by C Madge in Gould (1964)

21.13 "An association... is any organized group, whether large or small... an institution on the other hand, is not a group at all, organized or unorganized." R Bierstedt *Social order.* 3rd ed. Bombay, Tata- McGraw Hill, 1970: p. 341

21.14 "The term describes either a process or an entity. The process is of a number of individuals interacting for a specific end or set of purposes. The entity is an organization or individuals who are held together by a recognized set of rules governing their behaviour to one another for a specific end or set of purposes." G Duncan Mitchell (1968)

21.15 "The term describes either a process or an entity. The process is of a number of individuals interacting for a specific end or set of purposes. The entity is an organization or individuals who are held together by a recognized set of rules governing their behavior to one another for a specific end or set of purposes." D Duncan Mitchell (1968)

21.16 "Association is defined as a general term inclusive of any group (formal or informal, passive or active), organized to pursue a special interest, whereas institution is defined as a process- but note that:

1. in a number of works the two terms, association and institution, are used interchangeably and
2. in works where the two terms are distinguished, some authorities assert or imply that associations as well as processes may become institutionalized." Hoult (1969)

2. Terms in the Chapter Headings used in the Text-books of Sociology

Terms used	*No. of Authors*	*Related Terms used along with Associations*	*No. of Authors*
Association	9	Institutions/Social institutions	4
Voluntary Associations	1	Groups/small groups	2
Great Associations	1	Friendship	1
		Interests	1
		Bureaucracies	1

Major section within which the chapter on Associations is placed	*Author*	*(Year)*
Social organisation	Bierstedt	(1957);
	Horton	(1964)
Forms of social structure	MacIver	(1950)
Groups	Muzumdar	(1966)
Associations	McNall	(1968)
Individual integration: alienation and belonging	Gorman	(1971)

Only two of the 11 authors who use the term as a heading treat it as a major section ans sub-divide into the chapters with the titles as follws:

	Broom (1955, 1977)	*Mcnall (1968)*
1.	Formal structure	Associations: small groups and bureaucracies
2.	Informal structure	Communities
3.	Cohesion and morale	Social stratification
4.	Communication and social status	Population

3. Provision in the LCSH

Associations, Institutions etc.

UF Institutions, Associaiton etc.
Network (Association, Institutions, etc.)
Organisations
Voluntary associations

RT Societies
Voluntarism
Associations, Institutions etc.

SA names of specific types of associations, institutions, etc. e.g. corporations; public institutions; trade and profession associations; also sub-divide societies etc. under appropriate subjects.

NT By-laws
Charities
Clubs
Committees
Community life
Cooption
Freedom of association
Meetings
Membership campaigns
Social group work

4. RT (Related Terms) used by Sociologists

RT Agglomerate
Aggregate
Community
Gesellschaft
Gemeinschaft
Group
Institutions
Institutionalisation

5. Provision in the Classification Schemes

DC	366	Association Organisation formed for common purposes of a fraternal nature or for mutual assistance
UDC	301.186.2	Voluntary associations. Cooperatives. Unions. Franternalism. Solidarity
CC	Y 8	By Association

22. SOCIAL INSTITUTIONS

22.1 Definition, Explanation

22.11 "R M MacIver and C H Page (*Society*. Rinehart, 1949: p. 15)understand by institutions, the established forms or conditions of procedure, characteristic of group activity. Associations in their conception are groups organized to pursue one or more interests, while institutions may be said in general, to represent the modus operandi' of the associations. In an illustrative charting of associations, characteristic institutions, and interest, these writers list marriage, the home, and inheritance, as institutions proper to the association known as the family collective bargaining, the strike, and picketing as proper to the trade union constitution, legal code, and forms of government as proper to the state." Louis Schneider in Gould (1964)

22.12 "An enduring, complex, integrated, organized behaviour pattern through which social control is exerted and by means of which the fundamental social desires or need sare met." Seldon C Menefee in Fairchild (1955)

22.13 "A process or an association that is highly

1. organized (i.e., there is a careful specification of the roles and role relationships of those involved);
2. systematized (i.e., there is a clear specification of what can and should be done by those involved) ; and
3. Stable (i.e. relative to any given group or process, there is no dependence upon the presence of any particular individuals, and the organization and systematization tend to remain relatively unchanged overtime)

But note that in some works (e.g. those of R MacIver, MGinsberg, R Bierstedt, etc.) only processes are termed institutions, groups being termed associations as used by those employing W Sumner's approach may be eithercrescive (i.e., grown unconsciously out of mores) orenacted (i.e., consciously created), an example of theformer being law and of the latter being constitutionallaw if related to an apparent basic need of society,often termed a major institution, five such institutions usually being designated (education, family, economy, government, religion)... in some works, used synonymously with norm to denote any standardized mode of activity." Hoult (1969)

22.14 "Five major complexes of institutions are convenientlyidentified: 1. economic institutions serve to produce and distribute goods and services; 2. political institutions regulate the use of, and access to power; 3. stratification institutions determine the distribution ofpositions and resources; 4. kinship institutions deal with marriage, the family and the socialization of the young; and 5. cultural institutions are concerned with religious, scientific and artistic activities." Abercrombie (1984)

22.15 "It is generally applied to aspects of social behavior regulated by well established, easily recognized and relatively stable norms, values and laws. Indeed, some sociologists have used it to designate the complexes of norms, values or laws, rather than the patterns of actual behaviour. Sometimes, it has been argued that, all societies can be analyzed into a handful of major institutional spheres, such as family and kinship, economic, political and cultural institutions and social stratification, each of which regulate important aspects of social life. (In this case, the idea of institution is linked to that of functional prerequisites of a society). But the word institution is also often used by sociologists in the looser, every day sense of a variety of patterns of social organization found in society."Stephen Mennell in Michael Mann (1983)

2. Headings as used in the Text-books of Sociology

'Social institution' or institution is used as a heading by 37 authors, 20 of them treating it as a major section. Out of these, 15 authors prefer to use the heading as 'institution'. MacIver (1950) introduces the concept but does not provide a separate chapter on social institutions. Horton (1964) and Eshleman (1983) discuss social institutions under the major section 'social organization'. Only Lee (1955) includes social control, Merton (1959) includes sociology of art, and Green (1960) includes crime and law as social institutions. A majority of the textbook authors include family, kinship and marriage, political institutions, religion and economic institutions under the major section social institutions. A tabulation of the views of 26 authors, as to which aspects of sociology they include as social institutions is presented separately in the following page.

Table 4.8

Aspects of Sociology Enumerated as Social Institutions' by Sociologists: Tabulation of the views of 26 text-book Authors (Chapters enumerated by these authors under the major section 'Social Institutions' in their text-books)

Text-book Author/ Year — Aspects of Sociology included as Social Institutions	Family (1)	Polit. Instts. (2)	Religion (3)	Education (4)	Eco. Instts. (5)	Kinship, Marriage (6)	Law (7)	Work, Leisure (8)	Science (9)	Health, Medicine (10)	Technology (11)	Power, Authority (12)	Leisure (13)	Labour (14)	Art (15)	Beliefs, Ritual (16)	Crime (17)	Civilization (18)	Stratification (19)	Occupation (20)	Aging (21)	Social Control (22)	Total Number of Institutions enume-rted by an author
1. Barnes (1942)		*	*	*	*		*						*										
2. Eldridge (1950)	*	*	*	*	*																		
3. O'Brien (1951)	*	*	*	*																			
4. Merrill (1952)	*	*	*	*	*									*									
5. Broom (1955)	*		*	*																			
6. Gisbert (1957)	*	*			*																		
7. Merton (1959)	*	*	*	*			*		*	*						*							
8. Mitchell (1959)	*	*				*	*																
9. Green (1960)	*	*	*	*		*	*						*					*					
10. Chinoy (1961)	*	*	*	*		*	*	*															
11. Sutherland (1961)	*	*	*	*	*					*													
12. Bottomore (1962)	*	*			*															*	*		

Text-book Author/ Year — Aspects of Sociology included as Social Institutions	Family (1)	Polit. Instts. (2)	Religion (3)	Education (4)	Eco. Instts. (5)	Kinship, Marriage (6)	Law (7)	Work, Leisure (8)	Science (9)	Health, Medicine (10)	Technology (11)	Power, Authority (12)	Leisure (13)	Labour (14)	Art (15)	Beliefs, Ritual (16)	Crime (17)	Civilization (18)	Stratification (19)	Occupation (20)	Aging (21)	Social Control (22)	Total Number of Institutions enume-rted by an author
13. Young (1962)	*	*	*	*	*																		
14. Goode (1966)	*	*	*	*																	*		
15. Bertrand (1967)	*	*	*	*	*	*																	
16. McNall (1968)	*	*	*	*	*																		
17. Leslie (1973)	*	*		*	*																		
18. kenkel (1975)	*	*	*	*	*																		
19. Warren (1977)	*		*	*	*				*														
20. Phillips (1979)	*	*	*	*		*		*															
21. Tischler (1983)	*	*	*	*	*	*																	
22. Persell (1984)	*	*	*	*	*			*	*		*	*											
23. Wallace (1985)	*		*			*	*			*													
24. S Rao (1990)	*		*	*			*	*															
25. Stewart (1978)	*	*	*	*		*		*															
26. Lee (1939)																						*	
No. of Authors	22	22	22	21	17	7	5	4	3	2	2	2	2	1	1	1	1	1	1	1	1	1	

* indicates the aspect enumerated by the author as a social institution.

3. Provision in the LCSH

Social institutions

Works on interrelated systems of social roles, norms, or processes organised for the satisfaction of an important need or function, e.g. family, economy, education.

UF Institutions, social
BT Social systems
Sociology
RT Social structure
NT Family
Institution building

4. RT (Related Terms) used by Sociologists

RT Association
Collectivity
Comparative method
Creative
Evolution
Folkways
Function
Groups
Institutionalisation
Institutions
Need
Norm
Organisations
Social Structure
Social System

5. Provision in the Classification Schemes

DC. The term 'social institutions' is not used in the Decimal Classification. However, most of the institutions are enumerated under the major heading. Culture and institutions.

306.1 Culture and institutions
Institutions: patterns of behaviour in social relationships.
General aspects: the roles, functions, and patterns within which the groups and members of a society conduct their lives.

306.2 Political institutions

306.3 Economic institutions

306.4 Cultural institutions

References on the concept of social institutions:

C Panunzio, *Major social institutions.* N Y, 1939. (MacIver refers it as an attempt to standardize sociological terms. MacIver, p. 636)

S N Eisenstadt "Social institutions: the concept." *Intl. Encyclo. of Social Sci.* vol 14, N Y, Macmillan, 1968: 409-21.

	306.5	Religious institutions
	306.6	Religious institutions
	306.7	Instituions pertaining the relations of the sexes
	306.8	Marriage and family
	306.9	Institutions pertaining to death
UDC		The term social institutions or institutions is not used to UDC, some of the social institutions are however, enumerated under the heading:
	301.18	Social structures. Grups. Society. Social sphere
CC		The term social institutions or institutions is not used in Colon Classification.

23. KINSHIP

23.1 Definition, Explanation

23.11 "A kinship system is usually taken to refer to the complex of rules in any one society (or section of a society) which, by governing descent, succession, inheritance, marriage, extra-marital sexual relations, and residence, determines the status of individuals and groups in respect of their ties or consanguinity and marriage. Maurice Freedman in Gould (1964)

23.12 "The central components of kinship studies are the questionof social paternity for the purpose of inheritance, thenature of marriage, and the varying social forms and behaviors of three biological pairs: parent/ child husband/wife and brother/sister (although relationships formed through marriage are often discussed as affinal, rather than kinship relations.) All types of kinship theory depend on the hypothesis that kinship and affinal relationship constitute coherent social institutions with related norms and behaviors." Judith Ennew in MichaelMann (1983)

A L Kroeber "Classificatory system of relationship." *Jl. of the Royal Anthrop. Instt.* 39, 1909:

Ernest Gellnar *Concept of kinship and other essay on anthropological method and explanation.* Oxford, Basil Blackwell, 1973: 228p.

A Kuper "Lineage theory: a critical retrospct." *Annual Rev. of Anthropology* 1982.

2. Terms in the Chapter-headings used in the Text-books

Terms used	*No. of authors*	*Related Terms used*	*No. of authors*
Kinship	7	Family	6
Kinship groups	1	Marriage	4
Clan	1	Neighbourhood	1
Spatial groups	1		

Terms used in the Major section of the book within which kinship is placed by some of the authors	*Author*	*(Year)*
Social institutions	Mitchell	(1959)
	Bottomore	(1961)
	Goldthorpe	(1968)
	Bertrand	(1973)
Kinship groups	Johnson	(1960)
Social organisation	Chinoy	(1967)
Differentiation in social structure	Parsons	(1961)

Only Johnson (1960) sub-divides the section on kinship into chapters and provides individual chapters for marriage, family, Consanguinal kin groups, class and kinship systems.

3. Provision in the LCSH

BT Ethnology
RT Clans
Consanguinity
Family
Tribes
SA Subdivision kinship under individual ethnic groups and groups of Indians
NT Double descent (kinship)
Joking relationship
Matrilineal kinship
Post-nuptial residence (ethnology)
— Terminology
UF Family-terminology

4. RT (Related Terms) used by Sociologists

RT Affinal lineage
Ambilateral
Bilateral
Clan
Cognate
Conjugal role
Consanguinity
Cross cousin
Descent
Descent groups
Endogamy
Exogamy
Extended family
Family
Filiation
Households
Inheritance
Kindred
Lineage
Marriage
Matrilineal
Moity
Nuclear family
Parallel cousins
Patrilineal
Sib
Succession

5. Provision in the Classification Schemes

DC	306.83	Types of kinship systems Examples: Matrilineal, patrilineal, totemic
	305.904	Persons by kinship characteristics
UDC	301.185.1	Blood-related groups. Consanguinity. racial, ethnic grouping
	17.023.32	Kinship
CC		The term Kinship is not used in CC
Y 2		Family

24. FAMILY

24.1 Definition, Explanation

24.11 "The human family may be defined as an institutionalized bio-social group, made up of adults (at least two of which, unrelated by blood and of the opposite sex, are married), and children, the offspring of the maritally related adults the minimal functions of which are theproviding of satisfactions and control of affectionalneeds, including sexual relations, and the provision of a socio-cultural situation for the procreation, care and socialization of the offspring." Weston La Barre in Gould (1964)

24.12 "Family is a group of persons united by the rites ofmarriage, blood, or adoption constituting a single household, interacting and intercommunicating with each other in their respective social role of husband and wife, mother, and father, brother and sister creating a common culture." E W Burgess H J Locke (1961) (quoted byG Duncan Mitchell ,1968)

Out of 87 textbooks seen, 60 contain a chapter on family. Merrill (1952) calls it a 'multi-functional institution.' Among social institutions, highest number of authors mention 'family, marriage and kinship' and family is named first among social institutions, by Eldridge, O'Brien, Green Young, Bertrand, Cole, Warren, Tischler and Phillips. Mannheim (1957) lists family within the major section 'major forms of social structure'. Biesanz (1953) makes a filiatory sequence of personality formation, family, education, and religion. Bierstedt (1957) discusses family within the major section 'social differentiation' and thus enumerates other types of differentiation with it like gender, rural-urban, and caste and class etc. . Gisbert (1957) highlights the socialization role of the family. Chinoy (1961) does not enumerate family under social institutions and instead, put it directly under 'social organization'. Wilkins (1970), instead of showing family under the heading social institutions or directly under social organization, prefers the major section as 'social system' Popenoe (1971) divides the discussion of family into the sub-headings as marriage, divorce and widow-hood. Eshleman (1983) does not provide a separate section as social institutions and instead makes family as the first chapter under social organization. On the whole, family is seem by most of the authors as a social institution, some describe it as the beginning of the organized way of life and still others see it as an institution for socialization of the child.

3. Provision in the LCSH

	Family	
UF	Families	
	Family relationships	
BT	Social institutions	
RT	Adult children	
	Domestic relations	
	Home	
	Households	
	Kinship	
	Marriage	
	Matriarchy	
	Patriarchy	
NT	Broken homes	Joint family
	Children	Parenthood
	Clans	Parents
	Divorce	Problem families
	Dual Career Families	Rural families
	Family size	Widows

4. RT (Related Terms) used by Sociologists

RT	Extended family
	Kinship
	Household
	Marriage
	Nuclear family
	Polygamy

5. Provision in the Classification Schemes

DC	306.8	Marriage and family
	306.81	Marriage
	306.82	Patterns in mate selecton
	306.83	Types of kinship systems
	306.84	Types of marriage
	306.85	The family Including the nonconsanguinal family. Class here interdisciplinary works on family

UDC17.023.32	Family
17.035.3	Family
301.185.1	Blood related groups. Consanguinity. Racial, ethnic grouping
CC Y 2	Family

25. MARRIAGE

25.1 Definition, Explanation

25.11 "Marriage denotes mating arrangements approved in society with special reference to the institutionalized relationships of husband and wife also the ceremonies which establish such relationships. In ordinary usage, marriage includes two distinct ideas: 1. that a man and a woman cohabit, generally with the intention of founding afamily and 2. that some distinction can be drawn betweenmarriage and other forms of sexual union, qualifiable as pre-marital, adulterous, etc." M Douglas in Gold (1964)

25.12 "The social institution that provides the recognized form for entering into matrimony or setting up a family unit...The marriage may indicate a customary legal or religious sanction of the provisions for forming a new family."Oscar Wesley in Fairchild (1955)

25.13 "A mere casual commerce, without the intention of cohabitation , and bringing up children would not constitute marriage under any supposition." R Barrowsed. "Marriage" in *Words and phrases judicially defined.* Vol. 3. London, Buttorworths, 1944: p. 331

25.2 Usage of Terms in the Form of Chapter Headings

25.3. Terms in the Chapter-Headings Used in the Text-books of Sociology.

There is no alternative to marriage as far as the use of a term is concerned, as all the 18 authors who included a chapter on marriage in their text-book, have used this term. However,

---

E R Leach "Polyyandry, inheritance and the definition of marriage." *Man* 54, 1955:

Mabel A Elliott "Scope and meaning of divorce." in H becker; R Hill eds. *Family, marriage and parenthood.* 2nd ed. Boston, D C Heath, 1955: 669-708p.

some related terms come out after analysis of the chapter headings, that have been used along with marriage and we can identify them as related terms:

Related terms along with mariage used in the chapter headings:	*No. of authors*
Family	13
Kinship	4
Courtship	2
Divorce	1
Sexual norms	1
Alternative life styles	1

Major section of the text-book within which the chapter on Family is placed by some authors	*Author*	
Social institution/Institutions	Green	(1960)
	Goldthorpe	(1968)
	Stewart	(1978)
	Tischler	(1983)
	Mitchell	(1959)
	Kinship groups	
	Johnson	(1960)
Social Organisation	Chinoy	(1961)
	Sachdeva	(1967)
Culture society and personality	Biesanz	(1967)
Socialisation of the individual	Lee	(1955)
Social system	Wilkins	(1970)
Applications of sociology	Sherman	(1979)
Contemporary society	Abrahamson	(1969)
Family and community disorganisation	Barnes	(1942)

3. Provision in the LCSH

Marriage
UF Matrimony
Nuptiality
Wedlock
BT Love
Sacraments
RT Betrothal
Courtship
Family
Home

NT Bigamy
Bisexuality i marriage
Bride price
Child marriage
Common law marriage
Communication marriage
Computer marriage
Concubinage
Divorce
Endogamy and exogamy
Fortune healer
Free love
Handicapped, Marriage
Honeymoon
Husbands
Inter-country marriage
Inter-marriage
Marital status
Married people
Mate selection
Matrimonial advertisements
Mentally hadicapped marriage
Polyandry
Posthumous marriage
Remarriage
Sex in marriage
Teenage marriage
Weddings
Wives
Wives-effects of husbands employment on.

4. RT (Related Terms) usd by Sociologists

RT Concubinage
Courtship
Divorce
Domestic labour
Endogamy
Exogamy
Family
Family History
Group marriage

Homogamy
Hypergamy
Kinship
Monogamy
Nuptiality
Polyandry
Polygamy
Women's studies

5. Provision in the Classification Schemes

DC	306.8	Marriage and family
	306.81	Marriage Class here interdisciplinary works on marriage
UDC	173.1	
	173.1	These places, marriage is mentioned
	340.61	in various contexts, but the term
	347.62	is not used in the sociology schedule
	392.5	
	613.89	
CC	Y 2	Family
	Y 217	Marriage

26. POLITICAL SOCIOLOGY/ POLITICAL INSTITUTIONS

26.1 Definition, Explanation

26.11 "This is the study of politics at four levels:

1. political conflicts and struggles between states, namely the sociology of international relations;
2. the nature and role of the state within societies;
3. the nature and organization of political movements and parties; and
4. the participation of individuals in politics, as shown for example in voting behavior." Abercrombie (1984)

26.12 Political institutions—"The social institution or complex or social norms and roles, that serves to maintain social order, to exercise power, to compel conformity to the existing system of authority, and to provide the means for

---

F Openheim *Political concepts: a reconstruction*. Chicago, University of Chicago Press, 1981.

changes in the legal or administrative systems. The political institution includes the tradition and laws by which a society is co-ordinated and administered and is the major repository of force. The modern state is one type of social structure in which the political institution finds much of its formal expression and codification." B B Sharma ed. *Encyclopedic dictionary of sociology.* New Delhi, Anmol, 1992: p. 674

26.2 Usage of Terms in the Form of Chapter Headings

b) Although 47 authors provide a chapter related to the concept of 'political instituions', only 10 have actually used the term 'political institutions.' Twenty two authors have given the chapter on political institutions under the major section 'social institutions'. It is worth noting that, along with family, religion, and education, political institution is enumerated by the highest number of authors under the major section social institutions. Various terms used in connection with the concept of political institutions are as follows:

Table 4.9

Various Terms used for political institutions

Terms used	*No. of authors*
1. Political institutions	10
2. Politics	8
3. Political systems/political organisation/ Political philosophies	8
4. Political sociology/Sciology of politics (1)	7
5. Political power/authority	7
6. Governing institutions/government	3
7. State	4
8. Polity	2
9. Political process	2
10. Political groups	1
11. political life	1

Other terms associated by these authors with political institutions or discussed along with it as indicated by the chapter headings is as follows:

1. Economic institutions	5
2. legal institutions	2
3. Political behaviour	1
4. Interest groups	1

Only Barnes (1942), Biesanz (1953), Johnson (1960), and O'Donnell (1985) make political institutions a major heading and provide several chapters under this major headings.

3. Provision in the LCSH

Political institutions

The heading is not used in the LCSH.

Political Sociology

UF Mass political behaviour
Political behaviour

BT Political science
Sociology

NT Political socialisation

4. RT (Related Terms) used by Sociologists

RT Authority
Citizenship
Civil society
Democracy
Dominant ideology thesis
Elite
Fascism
Gramsci
Ideological state apparatus
Incorporation
Labour movement
Leninism
Lipset
Marx
Marxist sociology
Michels
Miliband-Poulatzas debate
Mosca
Nationalism
Oligarchy
Pareto
Pluralism
Pluralism
Political behaviour
Political culture
Political participation

Political parties
Political process
Populism
Power
Psephology
Relative autonomy
Revolution
Socialist societies
State
Voluntary associations
Voting
Weber
Working class conservatism

5. Provision in the Classification Schemes

DC	306.2	Political institutions Institutions maintaining internal and external peace. Class here comprehensive works on patronage, on client relationships; political sociology
UDC		UDC does not use the term political institutions.
	301.188.2	Political groupings
	321	Forms of political organisation
CC	In CC	The term politcal institution is not used.

27. GOVERNMENT

27.1 Definition, Explanation

27.11 "A government is the association through which the politically organized society functions and works. A government is thus the instrumentality of the state, theagency by means of which the state is able to carry itsactivities at a given time." R Bierstdt *Social order*. (1970)

27.12 "Government plays a unique and indisputable part in society . . . . The main functions of government are, internally, the ultimate enforcement of norms, the final arbitration of conflicting interests, and the overall planning and direction of society and externally, the handling of war and diplomacy." Kingsley Davis, Wilbert E Moore "Some principles of stratification" *American Sociol. Rev.* 10, 1946: 245-6.

2. Terms used in the Chapter-headings in the Text-books of Sociology

Terms used	*No. of authors*
Government	4
Government institutions	1
government institutions	1
Governing of man	1
Government: Distributing power	1
Socio-state order	1
Unifunctional institutions: Government etc.	1

Most of the authors seem to use the term 'Government' in place of Political institutions', as the latter term is not used by them, if they have a chapter on 'Government'.

Broader terms used as seciton headings Which includes a chapter on government	*Authors*	*(Year)*
Social organisation	Ogburn	(1947);
	Horton	(1964)
Social institutions Merrill (1952);	Leslie	(1973)
	Kenkel	(1975)
Political system	O'Donnell	(1985)
Culture	Muzumdar	(1966)

Biesanz (1953) devotes a major section to 'governing of man' and has chpters on government, political systems and philisophies like democracy and communism within it.

3. Provision in the LCSH

Government
USE
Political science
UF Administration
Civil government
Commonwealth
Government
Political theory
Political thoght
Politics
Science, Political
BT History

RT Constitutional history
State

NT Authority
Bureaucracy
Citizenship
Communism
Conservatism
Democracy
Elections
Equality
Executive power
Ideology
Imperialism
Individualism
Internal organisation
Liberalism
Nationalism
Political parties
Political psychology
Power (Social sciences)
Pressure groups
Public administration
Public opinion
Radicalism
Revolution
Social contract
Socialism
Utopias
Village communities

4. RT (Related Terms) used by Sociologists

RT Political science
State

5. Provision in the Classification Schemes

DC	306.23-306.25	Governmental institutions
	306.2	Institutions maintaining internal and external peace . . . political sociology
UDC	342.51	Government
CC		The term is not used in sociology schedule.

28. FORMAL ORGANIZATIONS

28.1 Definition, Explanation

28.11 "Large-scale formal organizations typically have a bureaucratic structure, that is, they are formally and rationally organized with clearly defined patterns of activity that are related to the goals of the organization. Some of the major characteristics of these bureaucracies are elaborate division of labour, clear-cut hierarchical lines of authority and responsibility, technical and rational criteria for employment and promotion, and elaborate rules and regulations." Alvin L Bertrand *Basic sociology*. New York, Appleton, 1973: p.171

28.12 "Informal groups are easily distinguished from formal groups, which are found in complex organizations, such as government bureaucracies, large business and industrial enterprises, military establishments, and universities (p.162) Examples include large corporations, professional societies, and labour unions." (p.224) Alvin L Bertrand as above.

28.13 "A formal group usually has a definite purpose, explicit procedures, and a highly specialized division of labour. Agreements in formal groups normally are specific and written. Decisions are handed down from those in authority through a chain of command. The total structure of the group is formal, from the recruitment of members who have specialized abilities, to the rigid hierarchy of social positions." Peter M Blau; W Richard Scott *Formal organizations*. San Franscisco, Chandler, 1962: p. 5-8 (quoted by Alvin L Bertrand as above)

28.14 "The term formal organization is reserved for collectivities that have developed formal procedures for regulating relations between members and their activities. The sociological investigation of such collectivities is the domain of organization theory, which focuses primarily though not exclusively on economic and political or governmental formal organizations."Abercrombie (1984)

28.15 Organization—"Sometimes referred to as `formal' or 'complex organizations' these are deliberately created devices for coordinating human effort, marshaling solidarity or focusing

---

Renate Mayntz "Study of organisaitons." *Current Sociology* 13(3), 1964: 95-156.

sentiment and are manifested in a great variety of forms—as business corporations, government agencies, armies, churches, trade unions, political parties, schools, hospitals, charitable bodies, clubs etc. Four main features distinguish such entities from primary social groupings such as the family, the friendship clique, or the informal group of work-mates:

1. they were consciously established to marshal social power.
2. they possess relatively explicit aims and goals;
3. they are composed of functional positions and roles, that are distinct from the individuals occupying them; and
4. Explicit rules govern the relations between roles." Michael Rose in Michael Mann (1983)

2. Terms in the chapter headings used in the text-books of sociology

Term used	*No. of Authors*	*Related terms used*	*No. of used*
Formal organisation	8	Social groups	1
Organisations	3	Structure of groups	1
Large formal organisations	1	Bureaucracy	3
Organisational analysis	1		
Unifunctional institutions	1		
Organised groups	1		

Major section of the text-book within which the author places the chapter on formal organisation	*Author*	*(Year)*
Demographic social structure	Merton	(1959)
Polity	Johnson	(1960)
Social structure and interaction	Bertrand	(1973)
Groups and how they affect behaviour	Cole	(1975)
Social organisation	Hebding	(1976)
	Goode	(1977)

Only Scott (1970) in his text-book *Social Processes and Social Structure* devotes a major section to "Social processes in formal organisations" and five chapters in the section are 1. Integrative processes; 2. Socialisation processes; 3. Status processes;

4. Power processes; and 5. Adaptive processes, in the formal organisations.

3. Provision in the LCSH

The term formal organisations is not used in LCSH

4. RT (Related Terms) used by Sociologists

RT Bureaucracy
Organisation
Role
Social organisation
System

5. Provision in the Classification Schemes

DC	302.3	Social interaction within groups
	302.35	In hierarchically organised (complex) groups Class here bureaucracies, organisational behaviour
UDC	512.741	formal groups The term formal organisations is not used in UDC
CC		The term formal groups or formal organisations is not used in CC

29. BUREAUCRACY

29.1 Definition, Explanation

29.11 "Weber's set of structural characteristics of bureaucracy constitute a definition for taxonomic purposes, these are:

1. fixed and official areas of jurisdiction for members;
2. a graded system of centralized authority;
3. a system of central files;
4. a set of special skills called office management;
5. official activities which demand the full time of personnel, and as a corollary, the divorce of the official life of the employee from his personal life, particularly with reference to finances; and

---

M Crozier, *Bureaucratic phenomenon*. London 1964.

R H Hall "The concept of bureaucracy: an empirical assessment." *Am. Jl. of Social*, 69, 1963-64: 33-40.

6. systematic and general rules which define procedure and which are followed.

One of the recurring tendencies in bureaucratic organization is the development of red tape, rigid rules, and procedural emphasis. This tendency is also labeled bureaucracy." Robert C Stone in Gould (1964)

29.12 "Formal organization of the officialdom of large scale enterprise (e.g. government, military, economic, religious, educational), the ideal-type of such an organization being characterized by:

1. a clearly defined division of labour, including a careful specification of the decision-making power of particular individuals, so that there is an unambiguous chain-of-command among the hierarchy of officials;
2. rationality (i.e. a business-like attention to implementing the goals of the organization);
3. an impersonal application of rules that are regarded as all but inviolable; and
4. routinization of tasks to the degree that personnel are easily replaceable." Hoult (1969)

29.13 "An organization whose structure and operations aregoverned to a high degree by written rules. It's core is ahierarchy of 'offices', that is to say, of carefully defined functional roles, staffed by full-time salaried persons. Rules state the relationship of any one office to others, govern the administration of the business of any given office, and regulate the recruitment of staff to the bureaucracy and any later promotions. The logic behind bureaucratic structure is to produce entirely determinable, impartial, and impersonal operation.

Bureaucracy can equate with mis-government, incompetent administration, self-perpetuating administrative elite,obstructive officialdom, unnecessary paper-work, social parasitism or with similar pejorative meanings." Michael Rose in Michael Mann (1983)

2. Terms in the Chapter headings used in Text-books of Sociology

Terms used for Bureaucracy the chapter-headings	*No. of Authors*	*Terms related to Bureaucracy used in*	*No. of Authors*
Bureaucracy	10	Formal organisation	2
Buraucracies	1	Organisations	1
Buraucratism	1	Associations	1
Groups	1		

Major Section of the book within which Bureaucracy is a chapter	*Author*	*(Year)*
Social organisations	Chinoy	(1961);
	Hebding	(1976)
Strucutural patterns within society	Goode	(1966)
Association	McNall	(1968)
Social organisation; order and disorder	Gorman	(1971)
Invidivual in Greater culture	Acuff	(1973)
Social units	Leslie	(1973)
Social relations	Chambliss	(1975)

3. Provision in the LCSH

Bureaucracy

BT Interorganisational relations
Political science
Public administration

4. RT (Related Terms) used by Sociologists

RT Administration
Authority
Bounded rationality
Civil service
Decision making
Empires
Interest groups
Law: legal systems
legal-rational authority
Legitimacy
Management
Mass society
Organisational theory
Rationality

5. Provision in the Classification Schemes

DC	302.35	Social interaction within groups-in hierarchically organised (complex) gorups. Class here bureaucracies, organisational behaviour
UDC	301.188.5	Orderly, regular groupings. Groupings in a socially standardising order. Sociology of the state.
CC		The term bureaucracy is not used in CC
	Y 9(W8)	Civil service

30. WAR

30.1 Definition, Explanation

30.11 "Armed extensive conflict between organized bodies of people, regarding themselves as politically sovereign and ethically entitled to assert by force , their rights, which they claim to be blocked or invaded by their armed opponents. Charles J. Bushnell in Fairchild (1955)

30.12 "Relatively sustained and large-scale armed conflict between organized political units, international conflicts (i.e., between nation-states) usually being distinguished from civil (i.e. armed conflict between parts of nations). Hoult (1969)

2. Terms used in the Chapter-Headings in the Text-books of Sociology

Terms used	*No. of authors*
War	2
War as a social institution	1
War and international relations	1

Broader sections of the books which includes a chapter on war	*Author*	*(Year)*
Political and legal institutions in transition	Barnes	(1942)
Social organisaton	Ogburn	(1947)
Problem aras in contemporary society	Koller	(1965)

Out of the 87 books analysed no author has included a chapter on war in his text-book since 1965.

3. Provision in the LCSH

War
UF Fighting
Hostilities
Wars
BT International relations
RT Military art and science
Peace
S A Subdivision warfare under ethinc groups
NT Battles
Children and war
Civil war
Disarmament
Psychological warfare
Revolutions
Sociology, Military
Strategy
War and Society
Women and war
Women in war

4. RT (Related Terms) used by Sociologists

RT Conflict
Militarism
Pacifism
Peace

5. Provision in the Classification Schemes

DC	303.66	War Including pacifism, sociology of war
UDC	342.78	State of war
CC	Y:438	War

31. ECONOMIC INSTITUTIONS

31.1 Definition, and Explanation

ECONOMIC SYSTEM

31.11 "An economic system is a socially sanctioned group of people united for the purpose of producing, distributing, or consuming scarce goods and services, and who interact according to well-defined roles. Most individuals, especially in highly advanced societies are unable to produce by themselves all the things they need and want. The greater the division of labour, the more important economic systems become. All other institution—families, schools, government agencies, and churches—depend on the economy for survival, and all of them participate to some degree in the exchange of economic goods and services." Alvin L Bertrand (1973: p. 304)

31.12 "Economic system is (also) frequently used to denote the web of economic interaction controlled and regulated by institutions . . . work in economic systems as a sub-field tends to focus upon one or more of the following particular matters: Economic institutions, economic goals, comparative economic systems, the evaluation of the performance of economic systems, and the study of particular economic systems." C Addison Hickman in Gould(1964)

ECONOMY

31.13 "In any given society, the social and cultural components concerned with the production, distribution, and consumption of goods and services often termed one of the major institutionalized aspects of human society (the other aspects being the family, religion, education, and government.) Hoult (1969)

31.14 "Economists analyze production, markets, income, and distribution. They also study prices, wages, resources, money, banking, interest, investment, and trade. In doing so, they must make certain assumptions about the institutional framework of society, about people, and about the goals for which people strive. These assumptions are more sociological than economic obviously, sociology and economics overlap." Gerald R Leslie (1973: p. 587)

31.2 Usage of Terms in the Form of Chapter Headings

To represent the concepts related with economic institution, the textbook authors have used the term economic institution, economy, economies, or work. The term economic institution is included as a social institution by 17 authors,that is fifth highest, others at the top being family, political institutions, religion (22 authors each) and education (21 authors). Some authors however, have preferred other major aspects of sociology under which they place economic institution. Barnes

(1947), Horton (1964), and Eshleman (1983) place it directly under social organization, Parsons (1961) under socialstructure Muzumdar (1966) under culture and Wilkins (1970) under social system.'

Table 4.11

Terms used to represent the Concept of Economic Institutions

Terms used	*No. of Authors*	*Terms used*	*No. of Authors*
Economic institution/s	12	Economic association	1
Economy	10	Economic behaviour	1
Economic system	7	Economic groups	1
Economic order	3	Economic development	1
Economies	2	Corporate economy	1
Economic organisation	2	Economic life	1
Economic structure	1		

Other terms to reresent various aspects of economic institution are as follows, as used by authors in the chapter headings.

Term used	*No. of Authors*	*Term used*	*No. of Authors*
Work	11	Division of labour	3
Industry	4	Occupation	3
Capitalism	4	Occupational social.	1
Poverty	4	Profession	1
Industrial sociology	3	Wealth	2
Industrialisation	3	Property	2
Industry-social aspects	1	Income	1
Industrial society	1	Inheritance	1
Industrial worker	1	Resources	1
Farmers	1	Production and allocation	1
Underdeveloped countries	1		
Capitalist state	1	Competition and monopoly	1
Socialism	1		
Unemployment	1	Laissez faire	1
Conditions of employment	1	Cooperation	1
Exploitation	1		

Some other aspects of sociology, which the authors have included along with the heading economic institution, are like this:

Term used	*No. of Authors*	*Term used*	*No. of Authors*
Technology	3	Social structure	1
Education	1	Social class	1
Social change	1	Imperialism	1
Organisation	1	Urban community	1

3. Provision in the LCSH

The term economic institution is not used in LCSH.
Economics Sociological aspects

Here are entered works on sociological theories applied to economics.

UF Sociology of economics

4. RT (Related Terms) used by Sociologists

RT	Consumers	Industrial relations	System analysis: social systems
	Economic thought	Industrialisation	
	Economy: Dual	Peasantry	

5. Provision in the Classification Schemes

DC	306.3	Economic insitutions Social arrangements for production, distribution Class here economic anthropology; economic sociology; sociology of economic development, of consumption
UDC	301.188.1	Economic groupings
CC		The term economic institution is not used in Colon classification, either in sociology schedule or any where in the whole scheme.

32. CAPITALISM

32.1 Definition, Explanation

32.11 "Denotes an economic system in which the greater proportion of economic life, particularly ownership of and investment in production goods, is carried on under private (i.e.

J K Galbraith American capitalism: the concept of countervailing power, Oxford, 1952:

non-governmental) auspices through the process of economic competition and the avowed incentive of profit.... The word capitalism was largely popularized by sociologists as a name for the economic system they were attacking. By it they meant a system under which the means of production are mainly owned by private persons, who use them to extract profit by paying the laborers less than what the socialists considered the full value of their labour-power as determined under the conditions of private ownership of the means of production." G D H Cole in Gould (1964)

32.12 "The economic system- and or the related socialorganization and doctrine characterized particularly by

1. private ownership and control of the means of production and distribution (such means often being termed 'capital' ;
2. the competitive interchange of goods and services; and
3. the goal of profit for those who are owners and controllers sometimes termed profit system often termed welfare capitalism, when the system involves a measure of government intervention intended to protect the sell being of workers and dependent persons, orstate capitalism when the means of production and distribution are owned and controlled buy the government but are conducted in such a way as to return a profit to the government contrasted with communism and socialism." Hoult (1969)

2. Terms used in the Chapter-headings in the Text-books of Sociology

Terms used	*No. of authors*
Capitalism	3
Capitalist state	1

Barnes (1942) places capitalism under the major section economic institutions and Chambliss (1975) puts it within historical process along with social change etc.

3. Provision in the LCSH

Capitalism
BT Economics
Profit
RT Capital
NT Asiatic mode of production

Entrepreneurship
Mixed economy
propaganda, Capitalist
Technocracy

4. RT (Related Terms) used by Sociologists

RT Capital functions
Capital theory
Class
Convergence thesis
Democracy
Dual labour markets
Exploitation
Feudalism
Individualism
Industrial society
Labour process approach
Management
Managerial revolution
Marxist sociology
Marx's theory of history and society
Post-industrial society
Profit
Property
Relative autonomy
Socialism
State
Transnational
World system theory

5. Provision in the Classification Schemes

DC	306.342	Capitalism (free enterprise)
UDC	330.342.14	Capitalist economy
CC	X: 326	Capitalist

33. WORK

33.1 Definition, Explanation

33.11 "Most general term denoting exertion expended to some end often used synonymously with occupation and sometimes with career." Hoult (1969)

33.12 "Work can refer to any physical and /or manual

activities which transform natural materials into a more useful form, improve human knowledge and understanding of the world, and/or provide or distribute goods to others. The definition of work can not be limited to references to activities alone, however, but most also consider the purposes for which, and the social context within which, those activities are being carried out." Richard; K Brownin Kuper n (1985)

33.21 All the authors having a chapter on 'work and economy'do not provide a separate chapter for 'economy' or 'economic institution', and it shows that these authors have treated the economy as a whole and 'work' synonymously. Douglas (1964) uses the heading work and wealth in place of economy or economic institutions, along with other social institutions like family, religion, politics, law and education. Worsley (1970) also describes the topic under the title work, industry and organizations, and no other chapter on economic institutions is provided. Berger (1972) also does not provide a separate chapter on economic institutions and related aspects. Potter (1974) discusses two aspects of economic institutions under the title production and allocation and work. Warren (1977),Stewart (1978),Persell (1984), and Wallace (1985) enumerate work and economy or work and leisure under the broad term and section headings social institutions. Stewart (1978) names it as sociology of work and leisure. Haralambos (1985) and O'Donnell (1985) also use the heading work and leisure in place of economic institutions, and only O'Donnell (1985) makes the heading as a major section and subdivides the topic into three individual chapter like: meaning of work reward and conditions and changing conditions of employment.

3. Provision in the LCSH

Work
UF Industry (Psychology)
Method of work
NT Industrial sociology
Job satisfaction
Labour and labouring classes
Manual work
Performance
Quality of work life

Rest periods
Skilled labour
Vacation
Work ethic

4. RT(Related Terms) used by Sociologists

RT Affluent worker
Alienation
Automation
Bureaucracy
Capitalism
Career
Class imagery
Cooperative
Human capital
Labour movement
Occupation
Orientaton to work
Unemployment
Women and work

5. Provision in the Classification Schemes

DC	306.36	Systems of labour Class here the sociology of work, industrial sociology
UDC		No provision for sociological aspects of work.
CC		No provision for sociological aspects of work.

34. DIVISION OF LABOUR

34.1 Definition, Explanation

34.11 "The separation of a total work process—an industrial process, for example, or all the work needing to be done in a society- into a series of interdependent tasks, each task being assigned to a separate individual or group functional, and therefore role differentiation among the workers in a given system sometimes used synonymously with specialization, but in some contests,the two terms are distinguished from one another, specialization in such cases denoting the unique characteristics of any phenomenon whereas division of labour denotes task differentiation only." Hoult (1969)

34.12 "Originally a term used by economists to mean the process by which people come to perform more and more specialized tasks in social life. ... Division of Labour is one of several interconnected long term social processes—urbanization, population growth, and, of course, industrialization—which led to the emergence of the modern world." Stephen J Mennell in Michael Mann (1983).

2. Terms used in the Chapter-heading in the Text-books of Sociology

Freedman associates 'division of labour' with 'urban community'. Mannheim (1957) includes division of labour within 'elementary social processes' and treats it as a form of cooperation. Green (1960) thinks 'division of labour' as a form of organisation. Out of the 87 books used for this study, no author included a chapter on division of labour in his text-book on sociology, after 1960.

3. Provision in the LCSH

Division of labour
UF Labour, Division of
BT Economics
Labour and labouring classes
NT International division of labour
Job enrichment
Sexual division of labour work groups

4. RT (Related Terms) used by Sociologists

Deskilling
Differentiations
Domestic labour
Dual labour markets
Evolutionary theory
International Division of labour
Labour process approach
Occupation
Role
Specialisation

5. Provision in the Classification Schemes

DC 306.368 Non-agricultural occupations
Class here division of labour, occupations considered severally

UDC	330.341.42	Division of labour in society
	339.91	International division of labour
CC		The term division of labour or its equivalent, is not used in CC

35. INDUSTRIAL SOCIOLOGY

35.1 Definition, Explanation

35.11 "Systematic study of soçial relationships in work situations, of the social structures which arise in connection with work, and of the interrelationships between such relationships and structures with other aspects of society; although sometimes used synonymously with sociology of work, the two are usually distinguished on the grounds that industrial sociology is primarily concerned with the organizational aspects of work; situations, whereas in the sociology of work (often termed sociology of occupations) attention is focused on particular occupations as reflections of given social relations and cultural values." Hoult (1969)

35.12 "The sociology of industry has been concerned with thesocial structure of work organizations, with the roles andsocial relations within such milieus, and with the ways inwhich these roles and relations influence and areinfluenced by 'external' factors." Richard K Brown inKuper (1985)

2. Terms used in the Chapter-headings in the Text-books of Sociology

Terms used	*No. of authors*
Industrial sociology	3
Industrial managers and workers	2
Union	1

Sherman (1979) includes industrial sociology within 'applications of sociology'. Biesanz (1979) provides the broader section 'economy and society' for industrial sociology in which he discusses industrial managers and workers.

Works on social relations within industry, as distinguished from labour management relations. Works about the impact of industry on culture and societal changes, and works about the social responsibilities of businessmen are entered under Industry- social aspects.

3. Provision in the LCSH

Industrial sociology
Industrial sociology
UF Sociology, Industrial
BT Industrial management
Industrial relations
Personnel management
Psychology, Industrial
Sociology
Work
RT Industrial organisation
Industry-Social aspects
Industrial sociologists
Managing your boss
Office politics
Sex role in the work environment
-Research

4. RT (Related Terms) used by Sociologists

RT Affluent worker
Alienation
Automation
Capitalism
Collective bargaining
Human capital
Human relations
Industrial conflict
Labour movement
Labour relations
Management
Occupations privatisation
Sociology of work
Strikes
Trade unions
Unemployment

5. Provision in the Classification Schemes

DC	306.36	Systems of labour Class here systems of labour, industial sociology
UDC	331.1/ 658.31	Industrial relations The term industrial sociology is not used
CC	X: 97	Indusrial relations The term industrial sociology is not used in CC.

36. LEISURE

36.1 Definition, Explanation

36.11 "Either the time not needed for practical pursuits, or pleasurable activities engaged in, during such time."Hoult (1969)

36.12 "Free time after the practical necessities of life have been attended to... Connections of leisure vary from the arithmetical one, of time devoted to work, sleep and othernecessities, subtracted from 24 hours— which gives the surplus time- to the general notion of leisure, as the time which one uses as he pleases. Martin H Neumeyerin Fairchild (1955)

2. Terms used in the Chapter-headings in the Text-books of Sociology

Terms used	*No. of authors*
Work and Leisure	4
Work, Leisure and the arts	1
Leisure, Recreation and the Arts	1
Recreation	1
Sport and leisure	1
People at play	1

Headings of the major sections within which the chapter on Leisure is placed	*Author*	*Year*
Institutions promoting richer living	Barnes	(1942)
Social institutions	Green	(1960)
Social institutions and Organisations	Stewart	(1978)
Contemporary areas of social Inquiry	Persell	(1984)

O'Donnell has a major seciton devoted to work and leisure sub-divided into three chapters but no chapter on leisure.

3. Provision in the LCSH

Leisure

UF Free time (Leisure)
 Leisure time

RT Recreation

NT Amateurism
 Hobbies
 Retirement
 Language

4. RT (Related Terms) used by Sociologists

RT Automation
Communication, Mass
Employment and unemployment, Psychological aspects
Gambling
Industrial relations
Labour force, Hours of work
Lundberg
Marx
Time
Time budgets
Veblen
Workers

5. Provision in the Classification Schemes

DC	306.4	Cultural institutions
	306.48	Recreation
	306.481 2	Leisure
		Class here free time
UDC	331.811.8	leisure time
	377.4	time outside working hours, recreation and leisure
CC	MY	Physical training, sports, games, use of leisure, Hobby

37. CULTURE

37. CULTURE

37.1 Definition, Explanation

37.11 "A collective name for all behavior patterns socially transmitted by means of symbols hence a name for all the distinctive achievements of human groups, including not only such items as language, tool making, industry, art, science, law, government, morals and religion, but also the material instruments for artifacts in which cultural achievements are embodied and by which intellectual, cultural features are given practical effect, such as buildings, tools, machines, communication services, art objects, etc. The scientific meaning of the term is therefore quite different from its popular

---

E B Tylor, *Primitive Culture*, Vol. 1, 1871. (quoted by G. Duncan Mitchell)

connotation. It includes all that is learned through inter-communication. It covers all language, traditions, customs and institutions.

As culture is transmitted by processes of teaching and learning, whether formal or informal, by what has been called 'inter-learning ', the essential part of culture is to be found in the patterns embodied in the social traditions of the group, that is knowledge, ideas, beliefs, values, standards and sentiments prevailing in the group. The overt part of culture is to be found in the actual behavior of the group, usually in its usage, customs, and institutions." Charles A Ellwood in Fairchild (1955)

37.12 "Culture or civilization is that complex whole, which includes knowledge, belief, art, morals, law, custom, and other capabilities and habits acquired by man as a member of society." E B Tylor (1871)

37.13 "As a culture, the total, generally organized way of life, includes, values, norms, institutions, and artifacts, that is unique to a given people and that is passed on from generation to generation by learning alone along with society, one of the

---

References on the concept of culture:

C Wissler "Culture-area concept in social anthropology." *American Jl. of Sociol.* 32, 1927:

T S Eliot *Notes towards the definition of culture*. London, Faber and Faber, 1948: 124p.

James W Woodward "A new classification of culture and a restatement of the cultural lag theory" *Am. Sociol. Rev.* 1, Feb. 1936: 89-102

Leslie White "Concept of culture" *Amer. Anthropologist* 61(2), Apr. 1959: 227-51

E Hoyt "Integration of culture: a review of concepts." *Current Anthropology* 2, 1961.

A L Kroeber; Clyde Kluckhohn *Culture: a critical review of concepts and definitions*. N Y, Vintage, 1963:

Robert S Lynd "Concept of culture" in *Knowledge for what Princeton*, N J, Princeton Univ. Press, 1939: 11-53p.

R Williams *Key words: a vocabulary of Culture and Society*. London, 1976.

two basic concepts of sociology and of socio-cultural anthropology in England sometimes replaced by the term social structure." Thomas Ford Hoult (1969)

37.14 "Sociologists and anthropologists use `culture' as a collective noun for the symbolic and learned, non-biological aspects of human society, including language, custom and convention, by which human behavior can be distinguished from that of other primates. ... in the Anglo-French tradition, the concept of culture is often used synonymously with `civilization." Nicholas Abercrombie (1984)

37.21 Culture is used a heading by 58 authors and 22 of them use it a major section. Eldridge (1950) explains it as 'orderliness in human behavior '. O'Brien (1951) brings together the concepts of culture and that of normative order. Lee (1955) and Gitler (1957) discuss race and culture together. Bierstedt (1957), Johnson (1960), Bertrand (1973), Leslie (1973) and Rao (1990) make the chapter heading 'culture and socialization '. Parsons (1961) includes symbolism, communication, values and beliefs, knowledge and rationality, and religion and magic under the major section culture. Ogburn (1947), Biesanz (1953), Horton (1964), and Bertrand (1973) prefer the chapter heading as culture and personality. Koller (1965) brings the concept of social control with culture and discusses under the heading 'cultural values and social control'. Bertrand (1973) wants to make it clear that the goal of socialization is culture. Likewise, Hebding (1976) describes socialization as a means of acquiring culture.

3. **Provision in the LCSH**

Culture/Human culture

BT Historical sociology

RT Civilisation

Education

Learning and scholarship

NT Acculturation

Biculturalism

Cognition and culture

Communication and culture

Cross-cultural studies

Cross-cultural studies

Cultural lag
Cultural policy
Culture diffusion
Educational anthropology
Fascism and culture
Guilt and culture
Hinduism and culture
Intellectual life
Intercultural communication
International relations and culture
Language and culture
Material culture
Personality and culture
Political culture
Politics and culture
Psycho-analysis of culture
Religion and culture
Self-culture
Social evolution
Subculture

4. RT (Related Terms) used by Sociologists

RT Civilisation
Consensus
Custom
Diffusion
Dominant Ideology thesis
Evolution
Function
Hegemony
Language
Norm
Personality
Race
Social anthropology
Social structure
Society
Sociobiology
Sub-culture
Super-organic

5. **Parovision in the Classification Schemes**

DC

306	Culture and institutions. Culture: the aggregate of a society's beliefs, folkways, mores, science, technology, values, arts Class here mass culture, cultural and social anthropology

UDC

301.151.6	Mental, intellectual, cultural drives
303.446.2	cultural comparison. Cross-sectional study
17.023.36	Culture

CC

Y:1 Civilisation. culture

38. CUSTOMS

38.1 Definition, Explanation

38.11 "A socially prescribed mode of behaviour, carried by tradition and enforced by social disapproval of its violation. Custom lacks the coercive backing of the state, which characterizes the legal code or the extreme sanctions of the mores. Customs differ from institutions, among other ways, in their less definite recognition." Mirra Komarovsky in Fairchild (1969)

38.12 "Denotes the behavior patterns and thoughtways, that are traditional in a given group now particularly in sociology, largely supplanted by more technically precise terms such as norms, folkways, more and law." Hoult (1969)

2. **Terms used in the Chapter-headings in the Text-books of Sociology**

Title of the major section which includes a chapter on Custom	*Chapter heading*	*Author*	*(Year)*
Social structure	Social stratification: sustaining forces of code and custom	MacIver	(1950)
Forms of social control	Custom and law	Gisbert	(1957)
Regulation of behaviour	Custom and public opinion	Bottomore	(1962)
(Major headings not Provided) Douglas	Law, custom and morality (1964)		
Social control	Custom, law, fashion	S. Rao	(1990)

Here are entered general works on folkways, customs, ceremonies, festivals, popular traditions, etc. treated collectively.

3. Provision in the LCSH

Customs, Social
USE Manners and customs
UF Ceremonies
Customs, Social
Folkways
Social customs
Social life and customs
Traditions
Usages
BT Civilisation
Ethnology
RT Etiquette
Rites and ceremonies
SA Subdivision social life and customs under names of countries, cities, etc., and under classes of persons and ethnic groups
NT Birth customs
Caste
Dating
Festivals
Folklore
Foundaton Sacrifices
Funeral rites and ceremonies
Marriage customs and rites
Mourning customs
Sex customs
Social norms
Taboo

4. RT (Related Terms) used by Sociologists

RT Convention
Culture
Fashion
Folkways
Law
Mode
More

Norm
Tradition
Value

5. Provision in the Classification Schemes

DC	303.37	Normative methods Customs and belief systems Class here values, social ethics, social justice
UDC	301.153	Socially significant processes, norms. Reactions. Defences. Influence. Custom Convention. Public opinion. Fame. Ostracism.
CC	Y:356	custom

39 IDEOLOGY

39.1 Definition, Explanation

39.11 "The aggregate of ideas, beliefs, and modes of thinking, characteristic of a group, such as a nation, class, caste, profession or occupation, religious sect, political party etc. These ideologies are conditioned and determined by the geographical and climatic situation, habitual activities, and cultural environment of their respective groups. They are not necessarily mutually exclusive and may overlap. Thus, two individuals of the same nationality but different occupations may share their national ideology but differ in their respective occupational ideologies." Mourice Parmelee in Fairchild (1955)

39.12 "Ideology may be defined provisionally as beliefs, attitudes and opinions which form a set, whether tightly or loosely related. The term has been used in three important senses:

1. to refer to very specific kinds of belief;
2. to refer to beliefs that are in a sense distorted or false; and
3. to refer to any set of beliefs, covering everything from scientific knowledge, to religion, to everyday beliefs

---

G Lit Chtheim *Concept of ideology and other essays* NY, 1967.

C Geertz "ideology as a cultural system" in Interpretation of cultures. NY, 1973

J Larrain *The concept of ideology*. London, Hutchinson, 1979:

about proper conduct, irrespective of whether it is true or false." Abercrombie (1984)

2. Terms used in the Chapter-headings in the Text-books of Sociology

Title of the major section	*Chapter heading*	*Author*	*(Year)*
Social deviation and social control	Ideology	Johnson	(1960)
(does not provide major sections)	Sociology of Religion, beliefs and ideologies	Sergeant	(1971)
Social action	Culture, civilisation and ideology	Rocher	(1972)

The chapter headings shown against Sergeant is actually not a chapter heading but enumerated by him as 'aspects of society which have yielded to empirical investigation.'

3. Provision in the LCSH

Ideology

BT Knowledge, Theory of Philosophy
Political Science Psychology
Thought and Thinking-Religious aspects

4. RT(Related Terms) used by Sociologists

RT Alienation
Appearance and reality
Class consciousness
Consensus
Culture
Democracy
Determinism
Dominant ideology thesis
End of ideology theory
Fascism
Frankfurt School
Hegemony
Intellectuals
Interpellation
Marxism
Myth
Norms
Semiotics

Social movements
Social systems
Sociology of knowledge
Subjectivity
Utopia
Values
World view

5. Provision in the Classification Schemes

DC	320.5	Ideology (Political science)
	140	Ideology (philosophy)
UDC	301.152.4	Political ideology
CC	S: 44	Beliefs

40. MAGIC

40.1 Definition, Explanation

"Beliefs and practices concerned with producing effects by the coercion of supernatural forces or agents, as through the manipulation of fetishes or rituals, or by following out some mystical principle or association of ideas, e.g., that like effects like differentiated from religion by the absence or minimization of the element of propitiation, and from science, which has evolved from it by a process of refinement and correction, by its largely fallacious character called `black magic' when pursued for private or sinister ends hence by extension, sorcery or witchcraft in general." George Peter Murdock in Fairchild (1955)

40.12 "Magic is culturally finished defense against fear and the sense of powerlessness." J M Yinger *Religion, Society and Individual.* New York, Macmillan, 1957: (quoted by Hoult, 1969)

40.13 "A system of beliefs and practices centering around the idea that given rituals, properly performed, can control supernatural forces so that particular ends may be achieved closely related to religion, since the latter is also usually concerned with the supernatural, but the magical approach to the supernatural tends to be coercive in contrast to the generally propitiatory approach of religion types specified include `white magic' and `black magic', the latter, in contrast to the former, intended to do harm within some in-group to which the magician belongs." Hoult (1969)

40.13 "Tylor's study began the first phase in the modern scientific history of magic, which viewed magical ideas and practices as mistaken attempts by ignorant savages and backward and superstitious persons in European society to manipulate physical reality by non-physical means." Roy Wallis in Kuper (1985)

40.2 Usage of Terms in the Form of Chapter Headings

40.21 Only three text-book authors have a chapter on magic out of 87 seen. All these authors make a combined chapter for religion and magic.

40.3 Provision in the LCSH

Magic

Here are entered works on the use of charms, spells, etc. believed to have supernatural power to produce or prevent a particular result considered unobtainable by natural means.

UF Necromancy
Sorcery
Spells
BT Occultism
NT Amulets
Cabala
Charms
Idols and images
Incantations
Magic drawings
Magical thinking
Mana
Medicine, Magic
Mystic and sparigic
Science and magic
Symbolism of numbers
Talismans
Tantrism

4. RT (Related Terms) used by Sociologists

RT Black magic
Contagious magic
Imitative magic

Religion
Ritual
Sorcery
White magic

5. **Provision in the Classification Schemes**

DC	306.4	Cultural institutions Class here popular culture including the sociology of witch crazes, magic, symbols, eating habits, body shape
UDC	133.4	Magic
	291.62	Magicians
CC	Y : 87	Magic

41. SOCIOLOGY OF RELIGION

41.1 Definition, Explanation

41.11 "Under the heading, sociology of religion, we find researches and reflections concerned with or centering upon: general group influences on religion the function of ritual for societies typologies of religious organizations and of religious idea-systems on society and `components' or elements thereof (such as classes, nationality groups, ethnic groups) and of society on the idea-systems specific analysis of numbers of religious sects and movements . . . the interaction of significant religious entities at local or `community' level occasional self-consciousness appraisals by spokesmen for major religious groups of the social circumstances in which the groups find themselves." Louis Schneider in Gould (1964).

41.12 "The sociology of religion is the scientific study of the ways in which society, culture, and personality... influence religion... (as well as the ways in which religion affects society, culture, and personality)." J M Yinger *Religion, Society and Individual*. New York, Macmillan, 1957: p. 20-21 (quoted by Louis Schneider in Gould, 1964).

J. Goody "Religion and ritual: the definitional problem." *British Jl. Sociology*. 12, 1961.

Table 4.12

Major Sections which include a chapter on Religion

Author	*(year) Major section/ Heading under which religion is discussed*		*Chapter heading used for religion*
Barnes	1942	Institutions promoting richer living	Religion and morals
Ogburn	1947	Social organisation	Religious institution
Gisbert	1957	Social control	Morality and Religion
Bottomore	1962	Regulation of behaviour	Religion and Morality
Muzumdar	1966	Culture	Religion
Wilkins	1970	Social system	Religion and belief systems
Perry	1973	Sociology in practice	Religion
Eshleman	1983	Social organisation	Religious groups and systems
O'Donnell	1985	Social change	Religion

Authors use various terms to represent the concept of sociology of religion or religion. the terms used and the number of authors using a particular term is presented in the following table:

Term used	*No. of authors*	*Term used*	*No. of authors*
Religion	27	Religion and ritual	2
Religion and morals/ morality	5	Eligious grups	2
		Religon and social order	1
Religious institution	4		
Sociology of religion	4	Theology	1
Religious beliefs	4	Religion and social structure	1
Religion and magic	3		
Religious organisation	2	Religion and ideologies	1

3. Provision in the LCSH

Sociology of religion

USE

Religon and sociology

UF Religion and social problems

Religion and society

Religious sociology

Society and religion
Sociology, religious
Sociology and religion
Sociology of religion

BT Sociology

NT Buddhism and social problems
Irreligion and sociology
Religion and social status
Sociology, Biblical
Sociology, Christian
Sociology, Shinto

4. RT (Related Terms) used by Sociologists

RT Ancestor worship
Animism
Church
Consensus
Cult
Durkheim
Freud
Halevy thesis
Institution
Invisible religion
Magic
Mana
Millenarianism
Monotheism
Moral order
New religious movements
Non-empirical
Profane
Polytheism
Religion
Revitalisation movement
Ritual
Sacred
Sacrifice
Sect
Secularisation
Taboo

Theodicy
Value
Weber
Witchcraft

5. **Provision in the Classification Schemes**

DC	306.6	Religious institutions to be classed here, the institutions must be considered from a secular, nonreligious viewpoint Class here sociology of religion.
UDC	291.6	Religious organisation The terms, sociology of religion or religious institution not used in UDC
CC		The terms, sociology of religion or religious institution not used in Colon Classification.

42. SOCIAL CONTROL

42.1 Definition, Explanation

42.11 "The process by which, if a man departs from his existing degree of obedience to a norm, his behavior is brought back toward that degree, or would be brought back if he did depart." G C Homans *Human group*. New York, Harcourt,1950: p. 301 (quoted by Kurt H Wolff in Gould, 1964)

42.12 "The sum total of the processes whereby society or any sub-group within society, secures conformity to expectation on the part of its constituent units, individuals or groups. It exhibits two main forms:

1. Coercive control-emanates from the agencies of law and government and is accompanied by force or threat of force. The types of behavior specifically designated for coercive control fall under the general category of crime;
2. Persuasive control- operates through all the various agencies and instrumentalities that induce the individual to respond to the standards, wishes and imperatives of the larger social group. ... Law is the most concrete, explicit and obvious instrument of social control but by no means most powerful or comprehensive. Much the greater bulk of social control falls in the persuasive category, and is achieved by such agencies as suggestion, imitation, praise, blame, reward, recognition, and response." Fairchild (1955)

42.13 "Any social process (formal or informal, manifest or intent, coercive or persuasive) which conditions or limits the actions of individuals or groups— a definition which includes, among other conditioning-limiting factors, the socialization process whereby individuals internalizeprevailing norms and values and direct their behavior accordingly .....

Used synonymously with culture control, particularly in anthropology as formal social control, denotes institutionalized processes or associations such asadministrative law or police forces as informal social control, denotes sociology specialty concerned with the systematic study of the conditioning-limiting factors in human society." Hoult (1968)

42.14 "'Social control' refers promiscuously to all constraints and patterns which generate discipline and social order, and is virtually synonymous with social organization." Paul Rock in Michael Mann (1983).

42.15 "Majority of the sociologists argue that social control is achieved through a combination of compliance, coercion, and commitment to social values." Abercrombie (1984).

42.2 Usage of Terms in the Form of Chapter Headings

a) A chapter on social control is included in 39 books out of 87 textbooks taken for the present study.

Terms used to represent the concept of social control	*No. of Authors*
Social control	36
Social order	3
Discipline	1
Sanctions	1
Regulation of behaviour	1

Kurt H Wolff "Social control" in Joseph S Roucek (ed.) *Contemporary Sociology*. NY, Philosophical Library,

R Nett "Conformity-deviation and the social control concept." *Ethics* 64, 1953: p.41.

J R Pitts "Social control: the concept." in *Intl. Encycl. of Social Sci.* NY, 1968:

b) Other aspects of sociology which appear along with social control in the chapter headings used, showing relation with it:

Term used	*No. of authors*
Deviation/social deviation/ Deviance/deviant behaviour	17
Conformity	3
Aggression, conflict	1
Social problems	1
Social disorganisation	1
Social stability	1

Social control encompasses a large number of concepts within it, as such it was thought quite appropriate to find outwho includes what within social control.

Table 4.28

Who includes what within Social Control

1.	Custom	Gisbert (1957), Bottomore (1962), Sachdeva (1976)
2.	Law	Gisbert, Bottomore, Sachdeva
3.	Morality	Gisbert, Bottomore, Sachdeva
4.	Religion	Gisbert, Bottomore, Sachdeva
5.	Education	Gisbert, Bottomore, Sachdeva
6.	Public opinion	Bottomore, Sprott (1949)
7.	Norm	Shapiro (1977), Sachdeva, S Rao (1990)
8.	Values	Shapiro Sachdeva, S Rao
9.	Folkways	Sachdeva, S Rao
10.	Mores	Sachdeva, S Rao
11.	Fashion	Sachdeva
12.	Sanctions	Sahpiro S Rao
13.	conformity	Chinoy(1961), Ogburn (1947), S Rao
14.	Discipline	Spencer (1871)
15.	Regulation of behaviour	Bottomore
16.	Social Code	Sharma (1968)
17.	Socialisation	Gordon (1988), Haralambos (1988)
18.	Social Planning	Merrill (1952)
19.	Prestige	Goode (1977)

Table 4.29

Broader Sactions/headings used for Social Control'

Author	*Year*	*Majorheading/section title with which 'social control' is a chapter*
Ogburn	1947	Group behaviour
MacIver	1950	Code and custom
Lee	1955	Institutions
Johnson	1960	Social deviation and social change
Chinoy	1961	Social order
Young	1962	Social relations
Horton	1964	Culture and personality
Goode	1966	Social processes
Muzumdar	1966	Processes
Abrahamson	1969	Contemporary society
Scott	1970	Structural concepts
Chambliss	1975	Social relations
Eshleman	1983	Individuals
Tischler	1983	Organisation of society
Charon	1983	Indicidual
Wallace	1985	Groups

3. Provision in the LCSH

Social control
BT Social conflict
Sociology
RT Liberty
Pressure groups
NT Paternalism
Social engineering
Social norms

4. Related Terms used by Sociologists

RT Coercion
Conflict
Crime
Delinquency
Deviant behaviour
Drug addiction
Function
Law
Norm

Penology
Punishment
Religious
Organisation
Ritual
Sanctions
Sects and cults
Social movements
Social order
Socialisation
Society
Utilitarianism
Values

4. Related Terms used by Sociologists (contd.)

RT Criminal law
Community control
Criminology
Deviancy amplification
Internment and custody
Capital punishment
Gambling
Incest
Leadership
Legal systems
Police
Prostitution
Religious organisation

5. Provision in the Classification Schemes

DC	303.33	Social control
UDC		The term social control is not used in UDC
CC		The term cocial sontrol is not used in CC
Y:4:5		Prevention

43. VALUES

43.1 Definition, Explanation

43.11 "The term has come to denote the the shared cultural standards according to which the relevance— moral, aesthetic, or cognitive-of the objects of attitudes, desires, and needs can be compared and judged. There is the belief among those who share a set of such standards that they are valid and should be employed in valuing an object, i.e. relating it to needs, desires, or attitudes, and in evaluating an object, i.e. comparing its relevance with that of another object or other objects." Howard Becker in Gould (1964)

43.12 "Any phenomenon— that has some degree of worth positive or negative- (but in practice, usually the former) to the members of a given group ... a phenomenon's objective meaning to the members of a group, such objective meaning making the phenomenon an object of activity for the group members (attitudes, then being viewed as the subjective and individualized counterpart of value) often termed social value in a few works, used synonymously with interest in action theory, a conception of the desirable, that establishes a general direction of action, rather than a specific objective distinguished from belief on the grounds that values are preferences and beliefs are not distinguished from norm in the sense that norms are fairly precise rules for behavior, whereas values are general standards that are somewhat independent of specific situation." Hoult (1969)

2. Terms used as Chapter Headings in the Text-books of Sociology

Term used	*Number of authors*
Values, ideologies	1
Norms and values	2
Values and Norms	6
Values	1

Out of 10 authors having the term values in their chapter heading, 8 of them use it with Norms.

Table 4.30

Title of the Major section of the book which contains a Chapter on Values

Author	Year	Title of the Major section
Goode	1966	Social processes
Sachdeva	1967	Social control
Scott	1970	Structure
Gorman	1971	Social organisation; order and disorder
Acuff	1973	Development of social person
Leslie	1973	Social life

Rose	1976	Culture
Shapiro	1977	Social control
S Rao	1990	Social control

3. Provision in the LCSH

Social Values

BT Conformity
Quality of life
Social groups
Values

4. Related Terms (RT) used by Sociologists

RT Attitude
Coercion
Consensus
Motive
Norm
Social Order

5. Provision in the Classification Schemes

DC	303.372	Customs and belief systems. Class here values, social ethics, social justice.
UDC	364.122.8	Changes in social norms, patterns, values
	17.022.1	Standards, moral values
CC	R 3 7	Values

44. NORMS

44.1 Definition, Explanation

44.11 "A norm, then is an idea in the minds of members of a group, an idea that can be put in the form of a statement specifying what the members or other men would do, ought to do, are expected to do, under given circumstances."

GC Homans *Human group*. New York, Harcourt, 1950: p. 123

44.12 "1. Average or modal, i.e. most typical, behavior, attitude, opinion, or perception found in a social group;

2. A standard shared by the members of a social group to which the members are expected to conform, and conformity to which is enforced by positive and negative sanctions." William L Kolb in Gould (1964)

44.13 "M Sherif (Psychology of social norms, 1956 uses it to describe the common standards or ideas which guide members responses in all established groups. Social norms are thus, general precepts which being internalized or accepted by individuals, induce conformity in simple actions or in complex ethical judgments, thus increasing group unity." Briget A Pym in Duncan Mitchell (1968)

44.14 "A behavior expectation, four major types of such expectations being identified usually- i.e. 1. Folkways; 2. Laws; 3. Mores; and 4. Technicways, in any society at a given time, a prevailing expectation that particular people will act or think in a defined way in certain situations in contrast to the more general value, a fairly precise rule of conduct of thought, that prevails in a particular community in some works used synonymously with institution to denote any standardized mode of activity contrasted with cultural alternative, which is a tolerated variation in behavior." Hoult (1969)

2. Terms in the Chapter Headings used in the Text-books of Sociology

a.

Terms used	*No. of Authors*
Norms	9
Values/Social Values	10
Folkways	2
Codes	1
Social Codes	1
Norm	1
Social Norm	1
Normative order	1
Normative Integration	1

b.

Related Terms used in the Chapter headings along with Norm.	*No. of authors*
Custom	4
Customs	2
Law	3
Laws of Social Interaction	1
Mores	2

J P Gibbs Norms, *deviance and social control: conceptual matters.* N Y, 1981:

Morality	1
Modes	1
Modes of Social interaction	1
Social Control	1
Sanctions	2
Ideologies	1
Public Opinion	1
Social Systems	1
Culture	1
Fashion	1

c. *Title of the Major Section of the book within which some auhtors have placed Norm, Values, Custom (chapter on)* *author* *(Year)*

	author	(Year)
Social Control	Gisbert	(1957)
	Sachdeva	(1967)
	Shapiro	(1977)
Regulation of Behaviour	Shankar Rao	(1990)
	Bottomore	(1962)
Social Organisation	Bierstedt	(1957)
Social Organisation: order and disorder	Gorman	(1971)
Social Life	Leslie	(1973)
Structural concepts	Scott	(1970)
Culture	Rose	(1976)
Development of Social person (Socialisation?)	Accuf	(1973)

3. Provision in the LCSH

Social rules
USE Social norms
Social norms
UF folkways
Norms, Social
Social rules
BT Manners and Customs
Social Control
NT Customary law
Moral conditions

4. RT (Related Terms) used by Sociologists

Consensus	Anomie
Convention	Conflict
Custom	Social aspects
Folkways	Conformity
Institution	Control
Law	Deviance
Moral order	Deviant behaviour
Mores	
Normative order	
Role	Functional analysis
Sanction	
Taboo	Legal systems
Technic ways	
Tradition	Marxist
Value	Sociology

5. Provision in the Classification Schemes

DC	303.37	Normative methods Including perception of norms
	303.372	Customs and belief systems Class here values, social ethics, social justice
UDC	301.153	Socially significant processes, norms Reactions. Defences. Influence. Custom Convention. Public opinion. Fame. Ostracism
CC	R3 7	Value (in Metaphysics)

45. MORALITY

45.1 Definition, Explanation

45.11 "The essence of the moral code and conformity thereto. Specifically, morality as regards the members of a particular society, can be defined only in terms of the moral code of that society. There is no universal morality except in so far as certain items of behavior are similarly covered in the moral codes of all societies. Fairchild (1955)

MORALS

45.12 "Norms that are observed on the basis of conscience rather than because of some externally imposed sanction (i.e. norms that are accepted because it is believed that their conformity with 'right action' makes it unethical to deviate from them) sometimes used loosely as a synonym for mores." Hoult (1969).

2. Terms used in the Chapter Headings in the Text-books of Sociology

Terms used	*No. of authors*
Religion and morality	2
Morality and religion	1
Religion and morals	1
Religion, morality, magic	1

Terms used in the major section which includes a chapter on morality	*Author*	*(Year)*
Institutions promoting richer living	Barnes	(1942)
Forms of social control	Gisbert	(1957)
Regulation of behaviour	Bottomore	(1962)
Social control	Sachdeva(1967)	
Social institutions	Shankar Rao	(1990)

3. Provision in the LCSH

Moral conditions

UF Morals

BT Social history
Social norms

SA Subdivision Moral conditions under names of countries, cities etc.

4. RT (Related Terms) used by Sociologists

RT Culture
Custom
Folkways
More
Morals
Norm
Social norms

5. Provision in the Classification Schemes

DC	303.37	Normative methods Including perception of norms
UDC	301.153	Socially significant processes, norms. Reactions. Defences. Influence. Custom. Convention. Public opinion. fame. Ostracism
CC	Y:45R4	Moral

46. SOCIALIZATION

46.1 Definition, Explanation

46.11 "A socio-psychological process, whereby the personality is created under the influence of the educational institutions a process intertwined with 1. the institutions wherein the general conditioning process relates itself to the school process, the family, play groups, racial groups, community, church, motion pictures, and the like and 2. with some problems of the sociology of groups formed in the educational process, and of the groups engaged in education-teachers, administrators, school boards, statelegislatures, preachers, pressure groups." Joseph S Roucekin Fairchild (1955)

46.12 "The shaping of human behavior both mental and physical through experience in social situations. Socialization subsumes all the processes of enculturation, communication and learning, through which the individual human organism develops a social nature and is able to participate in social life. Some of these processes operate continuously throughout life, to shape and reshape attitudes, for example, the media and information services." Robert Witkin in G Duncan Mitchell (1968)

46.13 "Almost always the process whereby individuals learn to behave willingly in accordance with the prevailing standards of their culture although occasionally used synonymously with learning, usually reserved for the type of learning that bears on future role performance and that particularly involves group approval . . . in anthro-pology sometimes replaced by the term enculturation." Hoult (1969)

46.14 "Sociologists use this term to describe the process, whereby people learn to conform to social norms, a process that makes possible an enduring society and the transmission of its culture between generations. The process has been conceptualized in two ways:

1. Socialization may be conceived as the internalization of social norms social roles become internal to the individual, in the sense that they are thus part of the individual's own personality. The individual therefore feels a need to conform;

2. It may be conceived as an essential element of social interaction, on the assumption that people wish to enhance their own self-image by gaining acceptance and status in the eyes of others in this case, individuals become socialized as they guide their won actions to accord with the expectations of others. . . . It may be divided into three stages young child in the family, the school, adultsocialization." Abercrombie (1984)

46.15 "Socialization and social control go hand in hand they are complementary bases for social order and continuity, but they are by no means identical." John A Clausen *Socialization and society.* Boston, Mass. Little Brown, 1969: p. 6 (quoted by Hoult, 1969).

46.2 Usage of Terms in the Form of Chapter Headings

Bierstedt makes a major section 'culture and socialization' but discusses only meaning, content and acquisition of culture in three chapters under it. Parsons (1961) enumerates 'processes of socialization' under the main section 'culture and personality. Goode (1966), Muzumdar (1966) and Scott (1970) categorize socialization as a social process. Popenoe (1971) names life cycle, and sex roles related to socialization. Acuff (1973) places culture, socialization, values, and norms, and also roles in one sequence. Bertrand (1973) emphasizes that the goal of socialization is culture and discusses socialization, personality and culture together. Kenkel (1975) treats socialization as an aspect of social organization, and puts it together with culture, and position and roles. Stewart (1975) treats socialization as an essential aspect of preservation of societies. Hebding (1976) think socialization is 'acquisition of culture' and puts it under this broad section. Stewart (1978) calls it as he foundation of social life and places it between culture and group interaction. Sherman (1979) discusses socialization under the heading 'how society makes boys and girls into men and women', and treats it as a part of the family structure. Eshleman (1983) and Tischler (1983) both place socialization in between culture and social interaction. An analysis of the chapter headings used by these authors shows that most of them relate socialization with personality, culture, deviance and social control as follow:

Table 4.44
Who relates what with Socialization

Personality	
Socialization and personality	Young 1962
Personality and socialization	Horton 1964
Socialization and personality development	McGee 1973
Socialization, personality and culture	Bertrand 1973
Socialization and personality	Tischler 1983
Culture	
Culture and socialization	Bierstedt 1957
Culture and socialization	Johnson 1960
Socialization, personality and culture	Bertrand 1973
Culture and socialization	Leslie 1973
Socialization and culture	Rao 1990
Deviance	
Socialization and social deviation	Ogburn 1947
Socialization, conformity and deviance	Rocher 1972
Socialization and deviance	Perry 1973
Social order,socialization, deviance	Charon 1989
Social control	
Social control and socialization	Gordon 1988
Social control and socialization	Haralambos 1988

46.3 Provision in the LCSH

Socialization
Works dealing with the process by which individuals are taught to function in the group and share group values and pattern of behavior.

UF Child socialization
Children-socialization
Enculturation

BT Acculturation
Child rearing Sociology
Education

NT Assimilation (sociology)
Cognition and culture
Manchester scales of social adaptation
Military socialization
Political socialization
Professional socialization
Social learning
Social skills
Women- socialization
Ethnology Consensus
Culture and personality

46.4 Related terms used by Sociologists

RT Adolescence
Agency and structure
Consensus
Culture and personality
Deviant behavior
Imitation
Internalization
Role
Social control
Social interaction
Status

47. CONFORMITY

47.1 Definition, Explanation

47.11 "Correspondence of behavior or condition to some recognized pattern, norm or standard compliance to a cultural or other dominant standard or relatively rigid model. A policy of conformity, in social control, means a pattern of controls obviously or deliberately directed at bringing variants into line with the mode, or with some criterion, or at keeping in line those already conforming." Thomas Dowes Elliott in Fairchild (1955)

47.12 "For contemporary sociological application of the term (conformity), `to conform is to comply with any usage or practice'. Its simplest definition is implied in the words `we attempt to find out what is being done and we do it '. J J B Morgan *Psychology*. New York, Rinehart, 1947: p. 146 (quoted by P Halmos in Gould (1964)

47.13 "When a group of individuals react repeatedly in a characteristic way to a stimulus situation, we infer that the members of the group have an established social attitude in relation to it. This characteristic reaction of groups of people is sometimes called 'conforming behavior." M Sherif; H Cantril *Psychology of Ego-involvements* New York, Wiley, 1947: p. 29 (quoted by P Halmos in Gould , 1964)

47.14 "In any given society at a given time, thinking and doing, that is in accordance with relevant prevailing values suggested by R. Merton as one of five major adaptations to cultural values, such conformity adaptation being one of full acceptance of both the values and the institutionally approved means to achieve the values among social critiques, often used as pejorative." Hoult (1969)

47.2 Usage of Terms in the Form of Chapter Headings

Terms used	*No. of authors*	*Terms used*	*No. of authors*
Conformity and deviance	5	Groups and conformity	1
Social control and conformity	3	Conformity and deviant behavior	1
Conformity	1	Social conformity and deviance	1

Table 4.45

Major sections that include a chapter on conformity

Title of the major section	*Author*	*Year*
Group behavior	Ogburn	1947
Groups and their influence on behavior	Cole	1975
Individual integration: alienation and belonging	Gorman	1971
Individual in society	Rose	1976
Personality and social system	Parsons	1961
Personality structure	Phillips	1979
Personal and social dynamics	Goode	1977
Social action	Rocher	1972
Social control	S Rao	1990
Social deviation and social change	Johnson	1960
Social order, deviance and change	Chinoy	1961

47.3 Provision in the LCSH	**47.4 Related terms used by Sociologists**
Conformity	RT Adjustment
UF Counter-culture	RT Compliance Deviant behavior
Non-conformity Deviant behavior	Innovation
Rebels (Social Individuality psychology) Influence	Rebellion
Social conformity	Retreatism
	(Psychology) Ritualism
BT Attitude	NT Dissenters
(Psychology)	Persuasion
Liberty	(Psychology)
Social acceptance	Social values

48. DEVIANCE

48.1 Definition, Explanation

48.11 "The concept of deviance implies the concept of

order. We have at the back of our minds the notion of a social system with its normative regulations and deviance is the departure on the part of participants from culturally expected rules of conduct." W J H Sprott *Science and social action*. Glencoe, Ill. Fress Press, 1956: p. 104 (quoted by H Himmelweit in Gould (1964)

40.12 "Behavior which violates institutionalized expectations— that is, expectations which are shared and recognized as legitimate within a social system." A K Cohen "Study of social disorganization and deviant behavior" in R K Merton *et al* eds. *Sociology today*. New York, Basic Books,1959: p. 462 (quoted by Himmelweit in Gould, 1964)

48.13 "We must recognize that we can not know whether a given act will be categorized as deviant until the response of others has occurred. Deviance is not a quality that lies in the behavior itself, but in the interaction between the person who commits the act and those who respond to it." HS Becker *Outsiders: studies in the sociology of deviance*. Glencoe, Ill. Free Press, 1963: p. 130

48.14 "Behavior departs from, or conflicts with standards which are socially or culturally accepted within a social group or system." H Himmelweit in Gould (1964)

48.15 "A word without a single agreed meaning, though most sues center on deviation from social rules or norms which carries disrepute, stigma or disapproval and which therefore, evokes attempted social control over it." Paul Rock in Michael Mann (1983)

48.16 "Criminology has historically been largely concerned with the interaction of legal norms, whereas deviancy research has taken a much broader definition of deviance as any socially prescribed departure from normality. Thus, many different forms of behavior may be socially condemned or challenged even though the behavior is not specificallyillegal- e.g. 'foul language', 'bad company' etc. "Abercrombie (1984)

48.2 Usage of Terms in the Form of Chapter Headings

48.21 Terms related to the concept of deviance are used as chapter headings by 44 out of 87 textbooks seen. The terms used by these authors are as follows:

Terms used	*No. of authors*	*Terms used*	*No. of authors*
Deviance	30	Social deviation	5
Deviant behavior	14	Deviants	1
Conformity	6	Social deviance	1
Social conformity	2	Deviancy	1

Table 4.46: Related Terms used in combination with deviance

Headings used	*No. of authors*	*Headings used*	*No. of authors*
Social control	17	Social structure	1
Social change	4	Crime	1
Socialization	4	Roles and attitudes	1
Social disorganization	4	Norms	1
Social order	3	Resocialization	1
Social problems	2	Stigma	1

Major sections of sociology within which deviance is placed by authors is as follows:

Table 4.47

Major sections that include a chapter on Deviance

Title of the major section	*Chapter heading*	*Author*	*Year*
Personality	Socialization and social deviation	Ogburn	1947
Socialization	Deviants	Lee	1955
Culture and socialization	Deviance	Leslie	1973
Applications of sociology	Deviant behavior	Merton	1959
Social dynamics	Deviant behavior	Young	1962
Culture and personality	Social control and Social deviation	Horton	1964
Social processes	Deviance and social control	Goode	1966
Social change	Deviant behavior	Sachdeva	1967
Social change and Social conflict	Crime and deviance	McNall	1968
Social action	Deviance	Rocher	1972
Social relations	Deviant behavior	Chambliss	1975
Conflict	Deviancy	Kenkel	1975
Differences	Social deviance	Stewart	1975
Individual	Deviance	Charon	1986

Individual	Deviance	Rose	1976
Individual	Deviance	Eshleman	1983
Social disorganization	Deviance and stigma	Warren	1977
Organization of society	Deviant behaviour	Tischler	1983
Groups	Deviance	Wallace	1985
Social control	Deviance	S Rao	1990

48.3 Provision in the LCSH

Deviant behavior
UF Deviancy
Social deviance
RT Collective behavior
RT Conformity
Social adjustment
NT Crime and criminals
Criminal behavior

48.4 Related Terms used by Sociologists

Abnormal Norm
Addiction Deviancy
Adjustment Deviancy
Anomie amplification
Career Deviant
Collective
behavior association
Conformity Gang
Criminology Labeling theory
Delinquency Moral panic
Delinquent drift Social adjustment
Social integration
Social deviance
Social disorganization
Social pathology
Differential Social problems
Stereotype
Sub-culture
Symbolic interactionism
Vice

49. SOCIOLOGY OF LAW

49.1 Definition, Explanation

49.11 "The phrase 'sociology of law' means the study of law and legal institutions with their social context, as distinguished on the one hand, from a purely philosophical or sociological approach." W Friedman in Gould (1964)

49.12 "Involves the study of how social conditions influence the making and enforcement of law. For Marxist, the law ultimately serves the interests of the dominant class by, for example protecting property rights, whereas Weber argued that a stable system of abstract, general law was requirement of capitalism." Abercrombie (1964)

48.2 Usage of Terms in the Form of Chapter Headings

Terms used	*No. of authors*	*Terms used*	*No. of authors*
Law	5	Legal institutions	
Law and justice	1	in transition	1
Sociology of law	2	Judiciary	1
State	1		

Title of the major section of the textbook that includes a chapter on Sociology of law:

Title of the major section	*Author*	*Year*
Social institutions	Mitchell	1959
	Broom	1977
	Green	1959
Sociology of institutions	Merton	1959
Regulation of behavior	Bottomore	1962

49.3 Provision in the LCSH

Sociology of law

Use

Sociological jurisprudence

Law-sociology

Law and society

Society and law

Sociology of law

BT Jurisprudence

Sociology

Law

49.4 Related terms used by Sociologists

RT Criminal statistics

Criminology

Deviant behavior

Legitimacy

Property

State

Symbolic interactionism

50. COMMUNICATION

50.1 Definition, Explanation

50.11 "Process of making common or exchanging subjective states such as ideas, sentiments, beliefs, usually by means of language, though also by visual representation, imitation and suggestion. The process of social interaction in human groups is largely a process of communication usually through articulate speech or language. . . . Human groups have been able to share ideas, sentiments, and beliefs among all their members and to attain in this way like-mindedness and common activities.

Communication in human groups becomes the chief factor in their unity and continuity and the vehicle of culture." Charles A Ellwood in Fairchild (1955)

50.12 "The function of communication... has been to integrate, synthesize and consolidate the functions of individuals and groups into something like an organic or super-organic unit." R E Park, *Human communities*. Glencoe, Ill., Free Press, 21952: p. 120 (quoted by Hoult, 1969)

50.2 Usage of Terms in the Form of Chapter Headings

Terms used	*No. of authors*
Communication	10
Mass media	2
Mass communication	3
Symbolic interactionism	1

Table 4.48: Related terms used along with communication

Terms used	*No. of authors*	*Terms used*	*No. of authors*
Interaction/Language	1		
social interaction	2	Symbols	1
Collective behavior	1	Suggestion	1
Public opinion	1	Imitation	1
Mass mind	1	Sympathy	1
Consensus	1	Herd	1
Perception	1	Crowd	1
Social status	1	Propaganda	1
Symbolism	1		

Title of the major section	*Author*	*Year*
Forms of social structure	MacIver	1950
Applications of sociology	Merton	1959
Social organization	Koller	1965
Processes	Muzumdar	1966
Changing society	Wilkins	1970
Individual integration	Gorman	1971
Social life	Leslie	1973

50.3 Provision in the LCSH

Communication

Works on human communication including both the primary techniques of language, pictures etc. and the secondary techniques, such as the press and the radio. Works on the modern means of mass communication are entered under Mass media. Works on the communication industries treated collectively are entered under communication and traffic.

UF Mass communication

BT Sociology

NT Communication, primitive
Communicative competence
Information science
Inter-cultural communication
Knowledge, Sociology of
Language and languages
Mass media

NT Nonverbal communication
Oral communication
Popular culture
Symbolism in communication
Visual aids
Visual communication
Written communication

50.4 Related Terms used by Sociologists

Communication

RT Attitudes
Content analysis
Conversation analysis
Communication networks
Communication theory
Code
Critical theory
Discourse
Dominant ideology thesis
Film
Generalized media
Gesture
Gossip
Habermas
Ideological apparatus
Ideology
Information
Inter-communication
Language

RT McLuhan
Mathematical theory of
Communication
Mass communication, Media of
Meaning
Media studies
Non-verbal communication
Oral communication
Political communication
Public
Pragmatics
Propaganda
Semiotics
Sign
Sign language
Slogan
Social interaction
Social psychology of language
Sociolinguistics

Language and culture
Literature
Marcuse
Mass culture
Mass media
Mass society
Sociology of the mass media
Symbol
Symbolic interactionism
Symbolism
Written communication

50.A SYMBOLISM

50.A1 Definition, Explanation

50.A11 "The importance of symbolism in the social processes derives from the existence of collective symbols, rather than the individually developed symbols. Language, units of economic exchange and credit, flags, religious practices, all represent socially shared symbolism. Collective symbolism in the forms of language aids in the solution of problems by permitting various manipulations and by establishing means of communication in interpersonal contacts. Collective symbolism in the form of the use of emblems or of expressive actions aids in the maintenance of the collective, by arousing responses which increase solidarity and cohesion." Eugene L Hartley in Gould (1964)

SYMBOLS

50.A12 "A conventional sign a sign which can be used meaningfully in abstraction, from that which is signified and whose meaning is based on community consensus— for example flags, words, maps, insignia distinguished from signal." Hoult (1969)

SYMBOLISM

50.A13 "A symbol stands for a concept, general or particular. The person, thing, category, idea, or event evoked as a concept may be only imaginary, but may, along with other symbolized meanings in complex messages, bring about thoughts, feelings, or intentions in the decoders of the symbol. Every symbol is thus mental or intentional in itself, though its vehicle must of course be something physical such as marks on paper, as in writing. Harry M Johnson in Kuper (1985)

50.A2 Usage of Terms in the Form of Chapter Headings

Terms used	*No. of authors*
Symbolism and communication	1
Symbolic communication	1
Symbols	1
Language	1

Parsons (1961) and Rose (1976) place symbolism within the major section culture. While McNall (1968) includes symbolism within the major section 'basic patterns and images of order'

50.A3 Provision in the LCSH

Symbolism

BT	Mythology	Bangle (Sikkhism)	Idols and images
RT	Devices Language	Convenants	Religion, Primitive
	Emblems	Crosses	Ritual
	Signs and symbols	Cryptography	Sex symbolism
NT	Anthropomorphism	House marks	Sound symbolism

50.A4 Related Terms used by Sociologists

RT	Communication Meaning	Symbolic
	Culture	Semiotics interactionism
	Gesture	Sign Symbols
	Insignia	Signal

51. ATTITUDES

51.1 Definition, Explanation

51.11 "The attitude of a significant portion of a population toward any given proposition, based upon a measurable amount of factual evidence, and involving some degree of reflection, analysis and contradistinction to public sentiment, which is essentially a matter of emotion, and may and does exist without any factual basis whatsoever." Fairchild (1955)

51.12 "Public opinion is usually defined functionally as the opinion/s of a public, i.e. a group whose membership is defined only by a shared concern for the subject of the opinion/s." D C Watt in Gould (1964)

51.13 "Depending upon context and relative to given issues:

1. The variety of opinions expressed by members of a given public or 2. consensus on the part of a substantial number of people; or 3. a summarization of publicly expressed opinions." Hoult (1969)

51.2 The term public opinion has been used by only 5 text book authors.

51.22 Related Terms used in the chapter headings along with public opinion: The term public opinion has been associated through chapter headings to social control, communication, consensus, and customs by one author each.

Barnes (1942) highlights prejudice, propaganda, and censorship as key factors in molding public opinion. Sprott (1949) treats public opinion as a form of social control. Eldridge (1950) includes it within 'social interaction and social processes'. Bottomore (1962) includes customs and public opinion with the major section 'regulation of behavior '. It is worth to be noted that, out of the 87 textbooks considered , no author has included a chapter on public opinion in his textbook since 1965.

51.3 Provision in the LCSH

Public opinion

UF Opinion, Public

BT Liberty of conscience
Political psychology
Political science
Social psychology

RT Attitude (Psychology)
Press-Research
Propaganda use
Public relations
Publicity

A subdivision attitudes under classes of persons and ethnic groups

NT Knowledge, Sociology of
Polemics
Rumor
Social pressure

Public opinion polls

51.4 Related Terms used by Sociologists

RT Attitude research
Poll
Psephology
Public
Questionnaire
Sampling
Survey

52. SOCIOLOGY OF EDUCATION

52.1 Definition, Explanation

52.11 "Educational sociology is interested in the impact of the total cultural milieu in which and through which experience is acquired and organized. It is interested in the school, but recognizes it as small part of the total. Educational sociology is particularly interested in finding out how to manipulate the educational process (social control to achieve better personality development) " D W Dodson quoted by F J Brown in *Educational sociology*. New York, Prentice Hall, 1947: p. 36 (from Jean Floyd in Gould 1964)

52.12 "The sociology of education is concerned with the functional relationships between education and the other great institutional orders of society— the economy, the polity, religion and kinship. . . . The process of education is thought of sociologically, as the transmission of culture, with its elements of preservation, dissemination and innovation." A H Halsey in G D Mitchell (1968)

EDUCATION

52.13 "The acculturation of the newer and / or younger members of society by the older. The institution-process whereby the accumulated ideas, standards, knowledge and techniques of society are transferred to, or imposed upon, the rising generation. The essence of education, is the inculcation of one individual with the mental accumulations of another." Fairchild (1955)

52.2 Usage of Terms in the Form of Chapter Headings

52.21 Education is one of the concepts which is enumerated as a social institution by he highest number of sociologists (27 authors), along with family, political institutions, and religion (21 authors each), and economic institution (by 17 authors). Out of the 87 textbooks on sociology seen, 47 have a chapter on the concept of education, out of which only 7 use the term sociology of education or educational sociology in the chapter heading. Diverse terms used for this concept by these authors are as follows:

Terms used	*No. of authors*
Education	26
Sociology of education	7
Educational system	4
Education as an institution	4

52.22 Related Terms used in the Chapter headings along with education or sociology of education:

Table 4.50

Terms associated with education

Related terms used	*Author*	*Year*
Education in social crisis	Barnes	1947
Learning	Parsons	1961
Science and technology	Horton	1964
Work and social mobility	Abrahamson	1969
Social control	Berger	1972
Social mobility	Baldridge	1975
Educational process as transmission of cultural traditions	Stewart	1978
Formal and informal education	O'Donnell	1985
Economic system	S Rao	1990

Barnes (1942) discusses the concept of 'education in social crisis' under the interesting major section 'institutions promoting richer living' and includes religion, moral, recreation and arts along with education within it. Gisbert (1957) keeps 'educational system' under the major section 'forms of social control' along with custom, law, morality, and religion. Bottomore (1962) emphasizes the 'regulation of behavior' aspect of education. Horton (1964) makes a combined heading for 'education and science and technology'. Wilkins (1970) places the chapter on education under the major section 'social system'. Eshleman (1983) places 'educational groups and systems' under social organization. Wallace (1985) includes education within the major section 'social change', other headings discussed within it being political institutions, and population and environment.

52.3 Provision in the LCSH

The term 'sociology of education' is not used in the LCSH.

52.4 Related Terms used by Sociologists

RT		
RT	Class	Intelligence
	Classroom interaction	Life chances
	Classroom knowledge	Nature-nurture debate
	Cultural capital	Pedagogical practices
	Cultural deprivation	Restricted code
	Cultural reproduction	Sponsored mobility
	Educational attainment	Stereotypes
	Hidden curriculum	

53. SOCIOLOGY OF KNOWLEDGE

53.1 Definition, Explanation

53.11 "Sociology of knowledge is the analysis of the functional interrelations of social processes and structures on the one end and the patterns of intellectual life, including the modes of knowing, on the other." H Becker; H O Dahlke "Max Scheler's sociology of knowledge" in Philosophy and phenomenological research 2, 1941-42: p. 310 (quoted by Stark in W Gould, 1964)

53.12 "The sociology of knowledge is concerned with the way in which systems of thought . . . are conditioned by other social facts." W J H Sprott *Science and social action.* London, Watts, 1954: p. 141 (quoted by W Stark in Gould , 1964)

53.13 "The first aim of the sociology of knowledge, conceived as a branch of learning is to understand the origin of ideas, not to judge of their political bearing/ and/or their validity. . . . Second, if it is to be a scholarly discipline, must avoid dogmatic pronouncements about the problem of determinism and freedom in thought and constitute itself as method for the interpretation of the meaning of ideas in the light of their (social) parent situation. Third, ... the provision of a clear definition of what is to be meant by social sub-structure, i.e., the social circumstances within which ideas some into being and in the light of which they can be interpreted." W Stark in Gould (1964)

53.14 "The idea that man, through the exercise of reason, can achieve knowledge of eternal truth except to the degree that reasoning are limited by social and cultural factors (not to speak of other impediments to reasoning) or 2. The substantive and/ or methodological implications of the idea that knowledge is a function of culture and social structure." Hoult (1969)

The term sociology of knowledge has been made a chapter heading by only 2 authors and one another author uses it as knowledge and rationality.

Parsons (1961) and Muzumdar (1966) place the chapter on sociology of knowledge within the major section 'culture'.

53.3 Provision in the LCSH

Knowledge, Sociology of

UF	Knowledge, Theory of	BT	Communication
	(sociology) Knowledge,		Theory of
	Sociology of knowledge		Public opinion
	Sociology		

53.4 Related Terms used by Sociologists

RT	Alienation Ideology	Social structure:	
	Bacon	James social structural	
	Base and	Mannheim analysis	
	superstructure	Marx Sociology of	
	Critical theory	Marxist sociology literature	
	DeweyPierce	Sorokin	
	Discourse	Scheler	Veblen
	Durkheim	Science,	Weber
	Frankfurt school	Sociology of World view	
	Halbwachs	Semiotics	Znaniecki
	Historicism		

54. SOCIOLOGY OF ART

54.1 Definition, Explanation

54.11 "Science concerned with the definition, classification, and interpretation of artworks and artists in their effect on society and society's effect on them." Joseph H Bunzel in Fairchild (1955)

54.12 "The strengths of the sociology of art to date, particularly in the United States and in Britain, have been, first the development of a methodology for the study of the institutions and practices of cultural production and, second, the analysis of culture as a part of a wider social and historical framework. The sociology of cultural production and the sociology of text, as complementary analyses, provide a valuable corrective to the traditional, uncritical approaches to the arts dominant in art history, literary criticism, and aesthetics." Janet Wolff in Kuper (1985)

54.2 Usage of Terms in the Form of Chapter Headings

Terms used	*No. of authors*
Arts	2
Art	1
Sociology of art and music	1
Sociology of art	1

Title of the major section of the text book that includes a chapter on sociology of art:

Title of the major section	*Author*	*Year*
Sociology of institutions	Merton	1959
	Warren	1977
Institutions promoting richer living	Barnes	1942

54.3 Provision in the LCSH
Sociology of art

Use
Art and society
UF Art and sociology
Society and art
Sociology and art
NT Art and state
Folk art
Street art

54.4 Related terms used by Sociologists

RT Aesthetics
Art, Anthropology of
Anthropology of hermeneutics
Hermeneutics
Semiotics

55. SOCIOLOGY OF SCIENCE AND TECHNOLOGY

55.1 Definition, Explanation

55.11 "Technology is the combination or totality of techniques employed by a people or at a given period for the purpose of adaptation to their bio-physical environment. More broadly, it includes elements of social organization such as cooperation, division of labour, management etc. . . . Technological change is shown to be an enduring force of history, through the increasing differentiation in the form of tools and implements used by man, the constant additions to the range of inventions, the gradual increase in empirical knowledge and the resulting greater ability in utilizing and exploiting the natural environment for his needs. Factors making for technological change may be migration, or change of locality, and changes in techniques, and knowledge, through inventions within the group, or the introduction of new techniques from without." Samuel Joseph in Fairchild (1955)

55.12 "Science is the institutionalized search for truth, while, technology is practical application of discoveries. There is constant interaction between science and other institutions. Attitudes and policies of government, business, education, and religion determine the level of support of scientific work. Meanwhile, developments drastically modify all other institutions." Horton (1964: p. 282)

55.2 Usage of Terms in the Form of Chapter Headings

Table 4.51

Terms used for sociology of Science and Technology

Terms used	*No. of authors*	*Terms used*	*No. of authors*
Technological factors of social change	1	Science and technology	1
Technology and social change	1	Sociology of science	1
Technology, Economy	1	Science	1
Technology	1	Innovation	1
Technological society	1	Industrialization	1
Technology and civilization	1	Industrialization and social change	1
		Industry and social change	1

55.22 Related Terms used in the chapter headings along with science and technology:

Terms used	*No. of authors*
Education	1
Transformation from traditional to modern society	1
Traditional society	1
Population, resources	1
Urbanization and social change	1

Title of the major section	*Author*	*Year*
Social change	MacIver	1950
Social change	Gisbert	1957
Social change	Rocher	1972
Social change	Goode	1977
Social institutions	Chinoy	1961
Social institutions	Goldthorpe	1968
Social institutions	Persell	1984
Social organization	Horton	1964
Social organization	Rocher	1972
Sociology of institutions	Merton	1959
Socio-cultural change	Ogburn	1947
Economy	Biesanz	1953

55.3 Provision in the LCSH

Sociology of science

use

Science- social aspects

Works on the impact of science on modern society and the sociology of science. Works on the role of science in the history and development of civilization are entered under science and civilization. UF Science and society

Sociology of science

NT Science indicators

Science and civilization

Works on the role of science in the history and development of civilization. Works on the impact of science on modern society and the sociology of science are entered under Science- social aspects.

UF Civilization and science BT Progress

History and science

Science and history

Science and society

55.4 Related Terms used by Sociologists

Science/ Sociology of science

RT Diffusion

Ethno-medicine

Innovation

Knowledge, Sociology of

Technology

56. INDUSTRIALIZATION

56.1 Definition, Explanation

56.11 "In any given society, a stage of social-technological development—or movement toward such a stage- characterized particularly by assembly-line mass production in large factories employing extensive power-driven machinery and a specialized work force with a finely wrought division of labour, and characterized also by urbanization and by highly mechanized methods of communication and transportation." Hoult (1969)

56.12 " Industrialization is meant to denote a phase in economic development in which capital and labour resources shift both relatively and absolutely from agricultural activities into industry, especially manufacturing. The rise in the factory system, increasing urbanization, and movement from rural areas, partly describe the nature of the absolute decline as he rapid growth of productivity, coupled with the relatively slow growth in demand for agricultural output, generate `surplus labor' in the agricultural sector. The expanding industrial sector in turn, pulls in the surplus agricultural employment as the output of industry takes on increasing importance." John Cornwall in Kuper (1985)

56.2 Usage of Terms in the Form of Chapter Headings

Terms used	*No. of authors*
Industry	1
Industry and social change	1
Industrialization and social change	1
Industrialization	1
Industrialization and imperialism	1
Industrial man	1
Evolution of industry	1
Social aspects of industry	1
Related terms used along with industrialization: Industrial sociology	3

Title of the major section of the textbook that includes a chapter on industrialization:

Title of the major section	*Author*	*Year*
Economic institutions	Barnes	1947
Social change	Gisbert	1957
Social change	Goode	1977
Social relations	Chambliss	1975
Social system	Wilkins	1970

The chapter on industrial sociology is placed within 'applications of sociology' by Sherman (1979).

56.3 Provision in the LCSH

Industrialization
Works on the industrialization of individual countries or regions are entered under the name of the area followed by the subdivision industry.
UF Industrial development
BT Economic development
Economic policy
Industry
Underdeveloped countries
RT Technical assistance
Workers
NT Developing countries
United Nations economic
Space industrialization assistance
Territorial production
United Nations technical complexes assistance

56.4 Related terms used by Sociologists

RT Automation
De-industrialization
Division of labour
Economic growth
Entrepreneurship
Industrial revolution
Industrial society
Labour force
Modernization
Post-industrial society

Urbanization

57. SOCIAL STRUCTURE

57.1 Definition, Explanation

57.11 "The structure or organization of a society consists of statuses, such as occupations, offices, classes, age and sex distributions and other circumstance-occasioned reciprocities and rules of conduct." E H Tiller *Social relations and social structure*. New York, Harper, 1947: p. 330 (quoted by Gould (1964)

57.12 "Often used loosely as a synonym for social organization, for social order and for social system in England, sometimes used to denote culture." Hoult (1969)

57.13 "Many familiar sociological concepts are used to denote aspects of social structure. Parsons defined the components of social structure as being roles, norms and values, together with collectivities (i.e. groups of people sharing common values). Sociologists, less tied to a consensual view of social order regard social classes, elites, patterns of social conflict, and mechanisms for the unequal allocation of scarce resources as basic components of the social structure of societies. Formal and informal organizations and institutions also fall within the broad notion of social structure." Stephen J Mennell in Michael Mann (1983)

57.2 Usage of Terms in the Form of Chapter Headings

Out of 87 textbooks consulted, only 22 authors use the term social structure for a chapter or section heading. MacIver (1950) divides his book into 3 main sections and one of these is social structure. He includes diverse aspects of sociology within social structure as social codes, groups, family, community, class and caste, ethnic racial groups, crowd, and mass communication, and also political, economic and cultural association. Parsons (1961) includes kinship, ethnic solidarity, primary groups, territorial community, economic institutions, economic development, political organization and authority, and religion and social structure within 'differentiation and variation in social structures. An analysis of, who includes what within social structure indicates that only 5 authors agree and mention social stratification as a part of social structure. On other aspects of sociology, to be included as part of social structure, hardly few authors agree on a single point. A summary of the various aspects of sociological concepts included as parts of social structure is as follows:

Table 4.53
Constituents of social structure

Social stratification	O'Brien	1956	Rose	1976
Social stratification and mobility	Parsons	1961	Goode	1966
			Bertrand	1973
Status and role	Merrill	1952	Popenoe	1971
Roles and relationship			Rose	1976
Culture O'Brien 1951			Phillips	1979
Social interaction	Popenoe	1971	Bertrand	1973
Structure of groups and organizations	O'Brien	1951	Bertrand	1973
Religion and social structure			Parsons	1961
Race and ethnicity			Rose	1976
Social institutions			Rose	1976
Types of societies			Popenoe	1971
Occupation			Goode	1966
Bureaucracy			Goode	1966
Social power			Bertrand	1973

Bottomore (1962) includes social structure within social institutions, Young (1967) within social relations, Popenoe(1971), and Persell (1964) within social life, Tischler (1983)within social interaction, and Charon (1989) within social patterns. Terms appearing along with or in association with social structure in the chapter headings are as follows:

57.3 Provision in the LCSH

Social structure

UF Organization, Social
Social organization

BT Psychiatry
Sociology

RT Social institutions

NT Social systems— growth

57.4. Related Terms used by Sociologists

RT Agency and structure
Culture
Function
Functional analysis
Functionalism
Graph theory

RT Phenomenological sociology
Realism
Semiology
Social anthropology
Social institutions
Social interaction

Groups
Hermeneutics
Interaction
Mathematical sociology
Methodological anthropological individualism
Norms
Organic analogy
Perception
Social order
Social organization
Social system
Social structure-approaches
Sociology- development of social thought
Structuralism

58. SOCIAL DIFFERENTIATION

58.1 Definition, Explanation

58.11 "Social differentiation is a general term used to denote: 1. the process whereby individuals or groups acquire more or less distinct and/or specialized roles and the accompanying statuses and 2. the results of such a process. The classic work in this area is C C North (Social differentiation. Chapel Hill, Univ. of North Carolina Press, 1926: p. 5) North argues that 'the significant social differences . . . fall into four types: namely a. differences of function; b. differences of rank;c. differences of culture; and d. differences of interests." J Gould in Gould (1964)

58.12 "The process, or the results of the process, whereby persons or groups acquire characteristics— including roles and statuses— that tend to make each of them unique in function and/ or form as social differentiation, sometimes used synonymously with social stratification, although the two terms have traditionally been distinguished from one another on the grounds that stratification, unlike differentiation, necessarily- by definition- involves collectivities of people, who, together with their immediate forebears and descendants, have generally the same relative privileges, power, and esteem." Hoult (1969)

58.13 "The organs, functions, groups and categories which are made, or become, different in the course of social development take countless forms. Some of the difference sinvolve ranking and hierarchy and therefore, social stratification, but differentiation need not be hierarchical, and indeed some sociologists use it only to indicate non-hierarchical differences . . . . Vertical differentiation characterizes ethnic, religious, linguistic or other distinctions playing a major part in the structuring of social relations where the ethnic, religious and linguistic communities concerned are not ranked or ordered in hierarchy."

58.2 Usage of Terms in the Form of Chapter Headings

Terms used	*No. of authors*
Social differentiation	4
Social differentiation and stratification	3
Differentiation and variation in social structures	1
Differentiation and leadership	1
Differences within societies	1

Table 4.55

Terms used by 65 sociologists for Differentiation, Social Stratification, Class and Mobility

Textbook Year classes author		Differentiation/Social stratification Social Social mobility inequality
Spencer	1871	Class bias
Ogburn	1947	Social stratification
MacIver	1950	Social class and caste
O'Brien	1951	Groups and organizations: Social stratification
Freedman	1952	Rank stratification Class stratification
Merrill	1952	Social stratification: Social stratification: caste class
Biesanz	1953	Social stratification
Weinberg	1956	Equality Social class
Bierstedt	1957	Social differentiation Class and caste
Gisbert	1957	Social stratification
Gitler	1957	Social stratification
Mannheim	1957	Class problem
Merton	1959	Social differentiation Social stratification
Mitchell	1959	Social stratification
Green	1960	Class Mobility
Johnson	1960	Social stratification Social ranking
Chinoy	1961	Social stratification
Parsons	1961	Differentiation in Stratification Mobility social structures

Sutherland	1961	Stratification Mobility
Bottomore	1962	Social stratification
Young	1962	Differentiation and Minorities in theSocial class and its leadership stratification systemconsequences
Horton	1964	Social class Social mobility
Kar	1964	Social stratification
Koller	1965	Social class system
Vales	1965	Stratification
Goode	1966	Stratification
Muzumdar	1966	Class groupings
Basu	1967	Social strataClass and caste
Sachdeva	1967	Social stratification
Goldthorpe	1968	Social class
McNall	1968	Social stratification
Sharma	1968	Caste and social class
Abrahamson	1969	Social stratification Social mobility
Smelser	1969	Social stratification
Mercer	1970	Social classes
Wilkins	1970	Social classes
Worsley	1970	Social stratification Class, status, power
Gorman	1971	Inequality
Popenoe	1971	Social stratification Social classes
Sergeant	1971	Social differentiation Social stratification Class and status
Berger	1972	Stratified society Stratified community: class and status
McGee	1972	Social class
Acuff	1973	Social stratification Social mobility
Bertrand	1973	Social stratification Social mobility
Leslie	1973	Social stratification
Perry	1973	Stratification
Baldridge	1975	Stratification Social mobility
dynamics		Social class system
Chambliss	1975	Social inequality: sources of conflict and change
Cole	1975	Types of inequality
Denisoff	1975	Social stratification
Kenkel	1975	Social stratification
Hebding	1976	Social differentiation Stratification

Stewart	1976	Differences within Stratification Classes Mobility societies
Broom	1977	Social stratification
Goode	1977	Equality and inequality Stratification system
Shapiro	1977	Stratification
Warren	1977	Inequality Social hierarchies: stratification, class and society
Szymanski	1979	Class society
Marx, G	1980	Inequality Stratification
Eshleman	1983	Social differentiation Social stratification Social inequality
Tischler	1983	Social inequality Social stratification
Persell	1984	Social inequality Social stratificationSocial class
O'Donnell	1985	Social differentiation Social mobility
Wallace	1985	Social inequality Social stratification Social mobility
Charon	1986	Social inequality Social class

Major section of the text books that includes a chapter on social differentiation

Title of the major section	*Author*	*Year*
Social differentiation	Eshleman	1983
	S Rao	1990
Demographic social structure	Merton	1959
Social dynamics	Young	1962

Out of 10 authors who provide a chapter on social differentiation do not provide a separate chapter on social stratification. The analysis shows that most of the authors have a chapter either on social differentiation or social stratification or social classes, thus showing the synonymous, and filiatory relation among these terms.

Table 4.56
Sub-divisions of the major section Social differentiation

Title of the individual chapter within social differentiation	Author				
	Bertrand	O'Donnell	Parsons	Stewart	Hebding
Women and men	*				
Family	*				
City, country and suburb	*				
Class	*			*	
Caste	*			*	
Color and creed	*				
Minority group relations			*		
Society and individual	*				
Kinship		*			
Ethnic solidarity		*			
Primary group		*			
Territorial community		*			
Economic institutions		*			
Stratification/social stratification			*	*	*
Mobility/social mobility		*		*	
Social structure	*		*		
Political organization and authority	* *				
Power	*				
Religion	*				
Deviance			*		
Wealth and income				*	

58.3 Provision in the LCSH

The term social differentiation is not used in the Library of Congress Subject Headings.

58.4 Related Terms used by Sociologists

RT Caste
Community- society continuum
Conflict- social aspects
Culture
International division of labor
Kinship
Lenin
Lowie
Malinowski
Social institutions
Social status
Sorokin
Spencer
State
Thomas

Democracy
Discrimination
Division of labor
Durkheim
Ethnic group
Evolutionary theory
Family
Integration
Occupations and careers
Organic analogy
Political parties
Reference groups
Religious organization
Ross
Simmel
Thurnwald
Tonnies
Totalitarianism
Znaniecki

59. SOCIAL INEQUALITY

59.1 Definition, Explanation

59.11 "Differences in social prestige, based chiefly on differences in family backgrounds, social conventions, wealth, income, political influence, education, manners, and morals, in a homogeneous society. Possession of differing degrees of social poser, privilege, and influence by the diverse social groupings in society indicate the extent and kinds of social inequality. These differences in degrees of social prestige are largely transmissible from parent to children through family institutions, contacts with other persons in the same social class, and institutions of property ownership and inheritance. Racial and religious differences are of another order and typically do not correlate with social inequality. William Cecil Headrick in Fairchild (1955)

59.21 The term inequality has been used by 11 authors,equality by 2 and social inequality by one author.

59.22 Title of the major section of the textbook that includes a chapter on Social inequality:

Title of the major section	*Author*	*Year*
Social organization	Gorman	1971
Social relations	Chambliss	1975
Stratification and inequality	Cole	1975
Social hierarchies	Warren	1977

Table 4.57
Subdivisions of the major section Social Inequality

Inequalities	*Goode*	*Eshleman*	*Tischler*	*Charon*	*Persell*	*Wallace*
Stratification system	*		*	*		*
Race and ethnic inequality	*	*	*			*
Gender role/ women and men	*	*	*	*		*
Social differentiation and stratification	*					
Age inequality	*		*			
Social class inequality				*	*	*
Minority groups				*	*	
Social power					*	
Mobility						*

59.3 Provision in ĹCSH

Equality
Caste
UF Inequality Class
Social equality
Competition
BT Political science
Sociology
Deprivation
RT Democracy
Liberty and wealth
Socialism
Dual consciousness
NT Aristocracy
Individualism
Social justice

59.4 Related terms used by Sociologists

RT Capitalism Hierarchy
Industrial democracy
Industrial society
Commune Justice
Life chances
Cultural deprivation Progress
Democracy Stratification
Distributionof income
Distributive justice
Educational attainment
Equalitarianism
Estates

60.1 Definition, Explanation

60.11 "Social stratification is manifestation of the sociologist's general interest in the basic principles of social organization. It is a particular kind of social differentiation and necessarily conveys the notion of hierarchical ranking, a ranking which produces strata into one of which there are recognized and sanctioneddifferences, which place one higher, or lower, than another in the admitted social order." Margaret Hewitt DDuncan Mitchell in Duncan Mitchell (1968)

60.12 "The process and/ or the results of the process, wherebyfamilies in a given society become differentiated from one another in terms of power, privileges, and prestige, and-in all relatively large and complex societies— become grouped, along with like families, into ranked strata. Various forms of social stratification are distinguishedfrom one another in terms of a number of criteria such as:

1. the basis of differentiation (family connection, wealth, occupation, education, etc.);

2. the basis of stratum membership (achievement or ascription); and

3. intra- and inter-stratum mobility possibilities specific major types termed caste, class, and estate."Hoult (1969)

60.2 Usage of Terms in the Form of Chapter Headings

Title of the major section	*Authors*	*Year*	*Author*	*Year*
Agencies of social change			Gisbert	1957
Social organization	Chinoy	1961	Sachdeva	1967
	Leslie	1973	Kenkel	1975
			Ogburn	1947
Association			NcNall	1968
Social differentiation	O'Donnell	1985	Hebding	1976
Equality and inequality	Goode	1977	Eshleman	1983
	Tischler	1983	Persell	1984
			Wallace	1985
Social hierarchies			Warren	1977
Social structure	O'Brien	1951	Merrill	1952
	Bertrand	1973	Rose	1976
Problems of demographic social structure			Merton	1959
Structural patterns			Goode	1966
Diversity			Stewart	1978
Theory and methods			Sherman	1979

60.3 Provision in the LCSH

Social stratification
use Social classes

60.4 Related terms used by Sociologists

RT Bureaucracy Functionalism
Caste Gender
Class, Social Hierarchy
Differentiation
Equality Marxist sociology
Estate Prestige
Ethnic groups
Functional theory
of social Social conflict
stratification Social differentiation
Social mobility
Social status
Social structure
Leisure Status
Status
Status inconsistency
Power
Professions

61. SOCIAL CLASSES

61.1 Definition, Explanation

61.11 "In its association with stratification, it has sometimes been loosely used to denote all those individuals (or families) who possess within the framework of some societyor community, relatively same amount of power, income, wealth, or prestige or some loosely formulated combinationof these elements. . . . Marxists, taking economic power based on the social relations related to the means of material production as the central variable, have assimilated market chances, other modes of power, occupational prestige, and style of life to class. . . . Some investigators may speak of a simple income category as a class, a social class, or an index of either, while others may use the term class to denote a stratum of position, whose members enjoy common life chances, common styles of life, common attitudes and ideologies towards self and society, consciousness of kind, and a sense of fundamental antagonism to other strata."

Among the consequences of social class position which have been studied among various kinds of population are: child-rearing practices mental health and the treatment of mental illness physical health infant mortality general demographic rates various pathologies, such as drug addiction, alcoholism, prostitution educational facilities and accomplishments; voting behavior consumer preferences marriage, divorce, and desertion rates organizational membership racial and religious prejudice and discrimination national and international political attitudes and preferences.

Studies in political behavior, particularly voting, organizational participation, party activities, etc. have shown considerable sensitivity to class positionas a major independent variable." Melvin M Tumin in Gould(1964)

61.12 "class came to refer to large categories of population:

1. distinct from other categories in respect of wealthand related social position;

2. deriving their distinctive status mainly from theirlocation in the production and distribution of socialwealth;

3. sharing accordingly in distinctive interests eitheropposing or complementing other group's interests; and

4. consequently displaying a tendency to a group-distinctive political, cultural and social attitudes and behavior. " Zygmunt Bauman in Kuper (1985)

61.13 "A social class is a group of people who share the same level of resources, such as education, income, prestige, and poser, or work in the same occupational category (such as the blue collar jobs). According to another view, asocial class is constituted by persons who hold similar positions in the process of production (workers, employers). Since social classes are groups of unequal statuses, and ethnic groups are descent groups, they can cross-out each other. A social class may include membersof different ethnic groups, and en ethnic group mayinclude members of different social classes." Sammy Smooha "Ethnic groups" in Kuper (1985)

61.2 Usage of Terms in the Form of Chapter Headings

Table 4.59

Terms used for social classes

Terms used	*No. of authors*	*Terms used*	*No. of authors*
Social class	12	Class problem	1
Social classes	3	Class grouping	1
Social stratification:		Social class system	1
Class	3	Class society	1
Classes	1	Class struggle	1
Class	1	Class consciousness	1
Class bias	1	Stratified society: class	1
Class stratification	1	Stratification dynamics	1

Headings used	*No. of authors*	*Heading used*	*No. of authors*
Caste	2	Social stratification: caste	1
Castes	1	Social stratification: Castes	1
Caste- estates	1	Social status	1
Culture	1	Social stratification: status	1
Mobility	2	Social stratification: power	1
Poverty	1	Stratified community	1
Social hierarchies	1	Stratified society: status	1
Social ranking	1	Stratification	1

Title of the major section			*Author*	*Year*
Forms of social structure			MacIver	1950
Social structure			Merrill	1952
Social differentiation			Bierstedt	1957
Social integration			Mannheim	1957
Stratification			Johnson	1960
Social organization	Young	1962	Koller	1965
			Goldthorpe	1968
Social interaction			Horton	1964
Groups			Muzumdar	1966
Social system			Wilkins	1970
Social inequality	Persell	1984	Wallace	1985
	Charon	1986	S Rao	1990

61.3 Provision in the LCSH

Social classes NT Class consciousness
UF Class distinction Elite (social sciences)
Classes, Social Labor and laboring
Rank classes
Social stratificationLeisure class
Stratification, social Middle classes

BT Caste Paternalism
Estates (social order)Poor
Social status Upper classes
Working class whites
Working class women

61.4 Related Terms used by Sociologists

RT Bourgeoisie Hierarchy Proletarianization
Caste Life style Social closure
Class consciousness Marxist sociology Social mobility
Class imagery Occupation Status inconsistency
Division of labor Prestige Stratification.
Equality Profession

62. CASTE

62.1 Definition, Explanation

62.11 "G S Ghurye in his caste and race in India. (London, Routledge, 1932) discerns six fundamental characteristics of the Indian caste system:

1. the segmental division of society into distinct groups with membership determined by birth;

2. hierarchy according to a definite scheme of social precedence with the Brahmin as the head of the hierarchy;

3. restriction on inter-dining and social intercourse arising out of notions of ritual pollution;

4. varying civil and religious disabilities and privileges of the different segments;

5. restrictions on occupation; and

6. endogamy." K C Rosser in Gould (1964)

62.12 "A form of social stratification characteriszed by:

1. a number of strata- generically called castes or sub-castes- which in terms of power, privilege, and esteemof stratum members, constitute a rigid hierarchy;

2. virtual absence of inter-stratum vertical mobility; and

3. restrictions on social interaction between the members of particular different strata, including enforced endogamy among, and generally ascribed occupations (andsometimes even prescribed clothing and ornamentation) for given stratum members." Hoult (1969)

62.13 "It includes endogamous marriage, strict rules regardingsocial and personal contacts, occupational homogeneity, and structured economic and ritual practices within each caste." Christopher Bryant *et al.* in Michel Mann (1983)

62.2 Usage of Terms in the Form of Chapter Headings

Title of the major section	*Chapter heading*	*Author*	*Year*
Forms of social structure	Social class and caste	MacIver	1950
Social structure and personality Social stratification caste		Merrill	1952
Social differentiation	Class and caste	Bierstedt	1957
Groups	Caste groupings	Muzumdar	1966
Social strata: classes and castes		Basu	1967
Social inequality	Castes- estates and classes	S Rao	1990

62.3 Provision in the LCSH

Caste

BT Manners and customs
Brahmanism
Hinduism
Social classes
- India Social closure

RT Ethnology- India

NT India- denotified tribes
Untouchables

62.4 Related terms used by Sociologists

RT Class system
Endogamy
Ethnic group
Hierarchy
Stratification

63. SOCIAL STATUS

63.1 Definition, Explanation

63.11 "A position in a social group or in society. Relative position, rank, or standing. Locus in the social scale of an individual or group. Within the limits prescribed by an individual's status in society generally, he may occupy different statuses in different groups and institutions.The assignment of statuses and the definition of their duties and rewards are crystallized in, and sanctioned by the folkways and mores. . . . Persons occupying social statuses in which they are instruments of group action, policy, ritual, or leadership are called social functionaries. Some of the criteria by which status is judged are leadership, dominance, ability, accomplishment, occupation, or other means of recognition designated by title, degree, membership, dress, behavior, or other devices for securing attention." Alfred McClung Lee; Oscar Wesley in Fairchild (1955)

63.12 "Status (very occasionally described as social status), role, and social position are often used inter-changeably. . . . Status is sometimes used as synonym for prestige or honor, and by loose implication is sometimes used to denote the power, authority, rights and obligations associated with prestige." Dorrian Apple Sweetser in Gould (1964)

63.13 "Social status has a hierarchical distribution in which a few persons occupy the highest positions. The simplest theoretical model of the status system would be a distribution in which position was determined competitively by the possession of abilities relative to the demand for abilities in society. The institution ofprivate property, inheritance, differential taxation, and social services all modify the form of the distribution of statuses. ... Social status; is determined by education, income, possessions and the social valuation of occupation and of other activities in society." Dennis Chapman in G Duncan Mitchell (1968)

63.14 "Esteem is sometimes used synonymously with status but is better reserved for the evaluation of personal qualities and the quality of role performances people, not positions, are held in high esteem. . . . Evaluation and ranking of social positions follow definite principles,and reproduce a status system. The stable systems of traditional societies are called status orders. In such orders, titles, decorations, speech, and accent, education, privileges and property are testimony to then iceties of ranking, and underwrite status distinctions."Christopher Bryant in Michael Mann (1983)

63.15 "Ascribed status is that which is inherited, such as sex, race, or ethnicity, or over time age, and is crucial to defining the basic patterns of people's lives. Achieved status, on the other hand, is acquired through personal effort or chance, possibly from occupational or educational attainment. Both of these types are bases for the formation of status communities." Charlotte Wolf in Kuper (1985)

63.2 Usage of Terms in the Form of Chapter Headings

Terms used	*No. of authors*	*Terms used*	*No. of authors*
Status	11	Position	1
Statuses	2	Positions	1
Social status	2	Relationships	1
Social ranking	1	Prestige	1
Ranking	1		

Table 4.63
Related Terms used along with Social Status

Terms used	*No. of authors*	*Terms used*	*No. of authors*
Social stratification/ Social processes	1	Authority	1
Stratification	3	Control systems	1
Class	3	Culture	1
Social classes	2	Culture conflict	1
Social hierarchies	1	Communication	1
Stratified society	1	Self	1
Power	2	Identity	1

Table 4.64
Major sections that include a chapter on Social Status

Major section	*Author*	*Year*
Social organization	Bierstedt	1957
	Young	1962
	Sachdeva	1967
Social structure	Kenkel	1975
	Merrill	1952
	Rose	1976
Stratification	Johnson	1960
Structural concepts	Scott	1970
Socialization	Lee	1955
Personality	Sutherland	1961
Culture and personality	Horton	1964
Development of social person	Acuff	1973
Personal and social dynamics	Goode	1977
Internalisation of institution	Warren	1967
Sociology in principle	Perry	1973
Complex society	Mitchell	1959

63.3 Provision in the LCSH

	Social status	NT	Fascism and social status
UF	Socio-economic status		Marital status Status, social
			Social classes
BT	Power (Social sciences)		Social role
	Prestige		Speech and social status
SA	Subdivision social-condition		Wit and social status
	under classes of persons e.g.		
	Student- social conditions		

63.4 Related terms used by Sociologists

RT	Bernard Interaction	Simmel
	Class	Linton Social class
	Class, Office	Social mobility
	Weber on	Ordinal scale Social
	Cooley	Position stratification
	Esteem Prestige	Social structure
	Equality	Rank Status
	Group	Role inconsistency
	Influence	Role structure

64. ROLE

64.1 Definition, Explanation

64.11 "A role is a category of persons distinguished by a normative set of personal and behavioral attributes. Role marks the distribution of activities and of socially recognized characteristics (such as age, kinship, or lunacy) among other members of a society." S F Nadel'sviews in Theory of social structure Glencoe, Ill. Free Press, 1957: p. 20-44 (quoted by Dorrian A Sweetser in Gould (1964)

64.12 "A social role is the expected behavior associated with asocial position. A position is simply the label or themeans of identifying a particular social role, and often in the literature on the subject, the two terms are used interchangeably. ... To define a social position is tostate the essential or minimal features of the expected behavior or role. . . . Role concept is one at theindividual level, the level of interaction. It isindividuals, not organizations, institutions, or sub-systems, who play roles and occupy positions." D J A Woodland in G D Mitchell (1968)

64.13 "When role and status are distinguished, various specific types and aspects of role are often delineated as follows:

1. achieved and ascribed (the former being the behavioral manifestation of a status, that can be assumed only after a potential incumbent meets particular requirements, the latter being arbitrarily assigned to an individual, frequently at birth, irrespective of desire or accomplishment);

2. role playing (actual manifestation of behavior associated with a status);

3. role taking (emphatic understanding of the behavior associated with a status);

4. playing-at-a-role (engaging in a behavior associated with a given status without, in reality, having an ordinary, illegitimate claim to the status- as in a theatrical performance);

5. role-making (acting as if a particular role exists when, in reality, it is not yet well-defined);

6. reciprocal roles (complementary behaviors such as those of the ideal type husband-wife);

7. role-set (the array of roles associated with a given position);

8. role-strain (difficulty, individuals experience in meeting their role obligations); and

9. role vs. role behavior (the two terms when used incontrast- denoting, respectively, the a. behavior expected versus the b. behavior actually manifested, by a person having a given status." Hoult (1969)

64.14 "When people occupy social positions their behavior isdetermined mainly by what is expected of that position, rather than by their own individual characteristics- roles are bundles of socially defined attributes and expectations associated with social positions. Role is sociologically important because it demonstrates how individual activity is socially influenced and thus follows regular patterns. Sociologists use role as the units from which social institutions are constructed."Abercrombie (1984)

64.2 Usage of Terms in the Form of Chapter Headings

64.21 Role has been used as chapter heading by 7 authors, roles by 4, social roles by 3, and one each uses the term social role; and role conflict.

64.22 Related Terms used in the chapter headings along with social role:

Terms used	*No. of authors*	*Terms used*	*No. of authors*
Status	7	Social processes	1
Positions	2	Relationships	1
Culture	1	Self	1
Culture conflict	1	Identity	1

64.3 Provision in the LCSH

Role- sociological aspects
Role, Social
use Institution
Social role
UF Role, Social
BT Social psychology
Social status
NT Role conflict
Role playing
Sex role
Socialization
Status, Social

64.4 Related terms used by Sociologists

RT Consensus
Culture

Interaction
Norms
Position
Rank
Reference group
Self
Social structure

65. POWER

65.1 Definition, Explanation

65.11 "The general term denoting all the means whereby people control aspects of their environment, including one another— a conception that is usually distinguished from:

1. force (on the grounds that force, but not power, always involves physical coercion);

2. Prestige (Being conceived as a consequence of power); and

3. authority and influence (both of which are viewed as types of power- but note that in some works power is seen as a form of influence, a usage that is illustrated herein in the definition of prestige).

In a few works (e.g. R MacIver *The web ofgovernment.)* power is defined as the ability to control people against their will, a conception that distinguishes sharply between power and authority (the latter being defined as the established and widely accepted right tocontrol others." Hoult (1969)

65.12 "Anything which gives one person or group a degree of control over what others want or need can be seen as power resource. Among resources discussed by sociologists are ownership of the means of production, income, status-honor, sacramental and magical capacities, scarce skills or knowledge, and charisma." Stephen J Mennell in Michael Mann (1983)

65.13 "For Max Weber power has the following characteristics:

1. power is exercised by individuals and therefore involves choice, agency and intention;

2. it involves the notion of agency, that is, an individual achieving or bringing about goals which are desirable;

3. power is exercised over other individuals and may involve resistance and conflict;

4. it implies that there are differences in interests between the powerful and powerless;

5. power is negative , involving restrictions and deprivations for those subjected to domination.

Weber argued that, when the exercise of power was regarded by people as legitimate, it became authority." Abercrombie (1984)

65.14 "Different disciplines within the social sciences emphasize different bases of power (for example,wealth, status, knowledge, charisma, force, authority) different forms of power (such as influence, coercion, control); and different uses of power (such as individual or community ends, political ends, economic ends)."m Mark Philp in Kuper (1983)

65.21 The term power has been used as a chapter heading by 14 out of 87 authors, 3 use it as social power, and one as political power and 4 use the term authority.

65.22 Related Terms used :

Terms used	*No. of authors*	*Terms used*	*No. of authors*
Politics	4	Interest groups	1
Status	2	Leadership	1
Social stratification	1	Government	1
Class	1	Political institutions	1
Pressure groups	1	Political organizations	1

Table 4.65
Major Sections that include a chapter on Power

Title of the major section	*Author*	*Year*	*Author*	*Year*
Social organization	Bierstedt	1957	Sachdeva	1967
Social institutions	Chinoy	1961	Kenkel	1975
	Persell	1984		
Social stratification	Worsley	1970		
Social structure and interaction	Bertrand	1973		
Social hierarchies	Warren	1977		
Differentiation and variation social structures (for authority)	Parsons	1961		
Social inequality	Charon	1986		
Social institutions and organizations	Stewart	1978		
Political system (for pressure and interest groups)	O'Donnell	1985		
Social relations	Chambliss	1975		
Politics and power	Popenoe	1971		
Social change (for pressure groups)			Rocher	1972

65.3 Provision in the LCSH

Power, social sciences NT Coalition (Social sciences)
BT Exchange theory (sociology) Community power
Political science Countervailing power
Sociology Elite (social sciences)
RT Consensus (Social sciences) Law and politics
Politics and war
Social status
Sociologists
RT Authority Influence Ruling class
Coercion Leadership Sanction
Conflict theory Marxist sociology Social control
Elite Pluralism State
Force Prestige
Hegemony Privilege

66. AUTHORITY

66.1 Definition, Explanation

66.11 "Authority is that form of power, which orders or articulates the actions or other actors through commands which are effective because those who are commanded, regard the commands as legitimate. Authority differs from coercive control, since the latter elicits conformity withits commands and prescriptions through its capacity toreward or punish. The distinction is an analytical one, since empirically, authority and coercive control exist together in many combinations. Authority is therefore, by definition, legitimate authority." Edward A. Shils in G Duncan Mitchell (1968)

66.12 **"A special form of power, either:**

1. power which is function of legitimate position, knowledge, or respect (power being defined as the ability of persons to have their will obeyed) hence power, whose possession by given persons or groups is willingly accepted by relevant others; or

2. persons or groups possessing such power- in either case, similar to, but subtly differ from, influence, the latter involving less legitimacy and formality in comparison with authority." Hoult (1969)

Terms used	*No. of authors*
Authority	1
Power, authority, and political institutions	1
Power, status, authority	1
Political organization and authority	1

66.22 Title of the major section of the textbook that includes achapter on authority:

Title of the major section	*Author*	*Year*
Social organization	Bierstedt	1957
Social institutions	Chinoy	1961
Differentiation and variation in social structures	Parsons	1961
Basic sociological terms	S Rao	1990

66.3 Provision in the LCSH 66.4 Related terms used by Authority **Sociologists**

BT	Political science	BT	Bureaucracy
RT	Authoritarianism		Charisma
	Consensus (social sciences)		Force

	Despotism	Freedom
		Influence
NT	Divine right of king	Leadership
	Example	Legal- rational authority
	General will	Legitimacy
	Power (Philosophy)	Legitimacy of authority
		Power

67. LEADERSHIP

67.1 Definition, Explanation

67.11 "A situation-process in which a person (or persons)because of his actual or supposed ability to solve problems in the field of current group interests, is followed by others in the group and influences their behavior. (In a leadership situation, the character of`followers' is equally important). Leadership may be based on spontaneous personal ascendancy (physical, courageous, congenial), or upon a combination." Charles J Bushnell in Fairchild (1955)

67.12 "Weberian sociology has identified three types of leadership, corresponding to the different forms of authority:

1. charismatic leaders lead by virtue of their extra-ordinary powers attributed to them by their followers;

2. traditional leaders lead by virtue of custom and practice, because a certain family or class has alwaysled; and

3. Legal leadership based on expertise andimplemented according to formal rules is typicallyfound in public administration and modern business enterprises. From this perspective, modern management represents the exercise of leadership on the basis of technical or professional competence." Abercrombie(1984)

67.2 Usage of Terms in the Form of Chapter Headings

67.3 Provision in the LCSH

Leadership

Works on the quality, power, or ability to lead others founded upon the prestige of position or upon ability and qualities of character. Exercise or military leadership under Command of troops.

BT	Ability	RT	Command of troops
	Executive ability		Meetings
	Psychology, Military	RTN	Community leadership
	Social groups		Elites
	Social psychology		Political leadership
	Sociology		Recreation leadership

67.4 Related Terms used by Sociologists

Administration	Democracy	Influentials
Authority	Democracy	Legitimacy
Bigman	Group	Organizations
Charisma	Human relations	Prestige
Decision making	Influence	Power

68. SOCIAL MOBILITY

68.1 Definition, Explanation

68.11 "A concept used in the sociological investigation of inequality, social mobility refers to the movement of individuals between different levels of the social hierarchy, usually defined occupationally. The study of mobility looks at mobility rates, mobility patterns, (whether short-range between adjacent hierarchical levels or long-range between widely separated levels), who is recruited to various positions and the determinants of this selection. Inter-generational mobility, compares the present position of individuals with those of their parents, intra-generational mobility compares the positions attained by the same individual at different moments in the course of his or her work-life. Abercrombie (1984)

68.12 "Movement within the system of stratification . . . represents a change of status and role, particularly in the occupational realm, without a change in social class position, it is called horizontal mobility. If such a change in status and role involves a change in social class position, it is called vertical mobility, with the sub-classes of upward mobility and downward mobility." William L Kolb in Gould (1964)

68.13 "In modern industrial societies, there is a hierarchical arrangement of statuses in which advantages in wealth, power and esteem increase as the hierarchy is ascended. Unlike the situation in caste, estate, and earlier class systems, movement from status to status can be achieved by means, which are in the control of the person. . . . Within broad occupation groups there are rankings which correspond to the extent of power and responsibility and are differentially rewarded. Positions are achieved by competition, modified by patronage and nepotism." Dennis Chapman in G Duncan Mitchell (1968)

68.2 Usage of Terms in the Form of Chapter Headings

68.21 Terms used	*No. of authors*
Social mobility	5
Stratification and mobility	3
Social stratification and mobility	3
Stratification and social mobility	1

68.22 Related Terms used in the chapter headings along with social mobility:

Terms used	*No. of authors*
Education	2
Work	1
Class	1

mobility

Title of the major section	*Author*	*Year*
Social structure	Parsons	1961
	Bertrand	1973
Human collectivities	Sutherland	1961
Social interaction	Horton	1964
Structural patterns	Goode	1966
Social organization	Kenkel	1975
Diversity and strain	Stewart	1978
Social differentiation	O'Donnell	1985
Social inequality	Wallace	1985

68.3 Provision in the LCSH

Social mobility
Bureaucracy Migration
UF Mobility
Caste
BT Social groups
Social history
Sociology
Elites

68.4 Related terms used by Sociologists

RT Anticipatory socialization
Career
Occupational mobility
Occupations and careers
Class Service class
Educational attainment
Educational mobility
Social stratification

NT Occupational mobility
Middle class
Fluidity Sponsored mobility
Gender stratification
Stratification

69. SOCIOLOGY OF GENDER

69.1 Definition, Explanation

69.11 "The sociology of gender considers the ways in which the physical differences between men and women are mediated by culture and social structure. These differences are culturally and socially elaborated so that:-

1. women are ascribed specific feminine personalities and a gender identity through specialization;

2. women are often secluded from public activities in industrial societies by their relegation to the private domain of the home;

3. women are subjected to stereotypical ideologies which define women as weak and emotionally dependent on men."

Abercrombie (1984)

SEXISM

69.12 "Sexist attitudes or actions are those that discriminate against men or women purely on grounds of their gender. While these may often be explicit, they may be implicit, being an assumed and unrecognized part of culture. For example, sociological studies of stratification have been accused of being sexist because they do not take account of women's place in the class structure." Abercrombie (1984)

SEXUAL DIVISIONS

69.13 "Sociologists increasingly investigate the manner in which the chances and opportunities available to women differ from those open to men. In the jobs taken by men and women, for example, there is a clear division between the sexes. . . . Furthermore, women tend to occupy the lower reaches of the occupational hierarchy. ... Women are themselves socialized to believe that they are bettersuited to being housewives than seeking equality with men in employment." Abercrombie (1984)

Table 4.67

Terms used for Gender Differentiation and Sex Roles

Terms used	*No. of authors*	*Terms used*	*No. of authors*
Sex roles	3	Gender inequality	1
Sexism	1	Gender role inequalities	1
Sex stratification	1	Stratification: women and men	1
Social stratification: sex	1	Inequality: women and men	1
Sexual barriers to social mobility	1	Discrimination against women	1
		Women and society	1
Gender differentiation	1	Women's studies	1
Gender roles	2		

69.22 Related Terms used in the chapter headings along with gender differentiation:

Terms used	*No. of authors*	*Terms used*	*No. of authors*
Sexuality	2	Social mobility	1
Sex	1	Age stratification	1
Social differentiation	1	Age differentiation	1

Title of the major section	*Author*	*Year*
Social differentiation	Bierstedt	1957
Culture and personality	Horton	1964
Social stratification and inequality	Cole	1975
Equality and inequality	Goode	1977
Diversity and strain	Stewart	1978
Stratification	Phillips	1979
Applications of sociology	Sherman	1979
Social inequality	Tischler	1983
Social inequality	Persell	1984
Social inequality	Wallace	1985

69.3 Provision in the LCSH

Gender discrimination

use Sex discrimination

Sex discrimination

Here are entered works dealing solely with discriminatory behavior directed toward both of the sexes.

69.4 Related terms used by Sociologists

BT Class

Division of labor

Domestic labor

Domestic mode of production

Dual labor markets

Educational attainment

Feminism

UF Discrimination, Sexual
Gender discrimination
Sexual discrimination
BT Discrimination
Sexism
NT Radical therapy
Sex discrimination against men
Sex discrimination against women
Sex discrimination in employment
Sex of children, Parental preferences for
Gender
Maternal deprivation
Orientation to work
Patriarchy
Sexism
Sexual divisions
Sexuality
Social reproduction
Sociology of gender
Sociology of the family
Stereotypes
Symbolism
Women and work

70. SOCIOLOGY OF OCCUPATIONS

70.1 Definition, Explanation

70.11 "The principal usage in the social sciences (e.g. in the preparation of census data and in the study of the labor market) follows closely the common usages which take an occupation to denote an employment, business, or calling. 'The occupation is the kind of work performed and of the status of employment of the individual'. Intl. Standard Classification of Occupations, 1949, Geneva, ILO, 1949: p.14) H H Smith in Gould (1964)

70.12 "The term refers not to a clearly delineated field of sociological inquiry, but to a heterogeneous range ofstudies dealing with the problem of how the occupationalstructure and particular occupations articulate with othersegments of society life family, the economy, theeducational system, the political system, and the systemof social stratification. Investigation center upon the following themes:

1. the division of labor, its causes and consequences;

2. the function and meaning of work and related phenomena such as leisure, employment and retirement;

3. the study of specific occupations as diverse as the hobo, the prostitute, the dock worker, the clerk, the architect and the physician.

Research has concentrated on such topics as the amount and method of remuneration, recruitment and training, career patterns, conflict inherent in the role, the relation between personality and occupation, inter-personal relations at work, the public image of the occupation, and the distribution of power and prestige within the occupation." S W F Holloway in Duncan Mitchell (1968)

70.2 Usage of Terms in the Form of Chapter Headings

Terms used	*No. of authors*
Occupation	1
Occupations	1
Occupational sociology	1
Occupations and professions	1

Most of the authors see occupation in the context of socialdifferentiation and social stratification, except Goode (1977) who likes to place it within social institutions.

70.3 Provision in the LCSH

Occupations

UF Career patterns
Careers
Jobs
Trades

BT Business
Labor and laboring classes

RT Handicrafts
Vocational guidance

S A subdivision Vocational guidance under subjects e.g. Agriculture-vocational guidance

NT Civil service positions
Invalids-occupations
Job description
Job evaluation
Life-span,Productive
Occupational mobility
Occupations and race
Personality and occupation
Professions
Vocation
Vocational interests
Vocational qualification

70.4 Related Terms used by Sociologists

RT Career
Division of labour
Hobby
Industrial sociology
Professions
Social closure
Social mobility
Social status
Work
Workers

71. RACIAL GROUPS

71.1 Definition, Explanation

71.11 "A biological subdivision, based upon similarity of ancestry and consequent physical kinship. ... A variety of species. The ideal race is a group of organisms all descended from a single ancestor, or pair of ancestors, without the introduction of any external germ plasm during the entire series of generations." Fairchild (1955)

71.12 "A race is a sub-group of people possessing a definite combination of physical characters, of genetic origin; this combination serves, in varying degree, to distinguish the sub-group from the other sub-groups of mankind, and the combination is transmitted in descent, providing all conditions which originally gave rise to the definite combination, remain relatively unaltered as a rule, the sub-group inhabits, or did inhabit, a more or less restricted region." M Crogman "What do we know about race" *Scientific Monthly* 57, 1943: p. 97-104(quoted by Munro S Edmonson in Gould (1964)

71.13 "Physical anthropologists, relying on morphological traits, have long divided, living mankind into great geographical races (also called major races, sub-species and constellations of races). Most classifications recognized three major such divisions, the Negroid, Mongoloid and Caucasoid Some investigators designated other major races, such as the Amerind and the Oceanian. . . . As with other living groups, historically the classification of living Homo sapiens was based on morphological traits, such as skin color, hair form, and body size." Phillip V Tobias in Kuper (1985)

71.2 Usage of Terms in the Form of Chapter Headings

Race and race related terms are used by 48 out of 87 authors' text books used in this study. These terms have beenclassified into 6 groups like this:

Table 4.69
Terms used for Racial/ethnic groups by 48 authors

	Terms used	*No. of authors*
1.	Race/ racial groups/ racial minorities	20
2.	Race relations/ race discrimination/ racism/ race conscious groups	14
3.	Ethnic groups/ ethnic minorities	9
4.	Ethnic relations/ ethnic solidarity/ ethnicity	11
5.	Minorities/ minority groups/ minority relations	17
6.	Inter-group relations/ inter-group tension/ prejudice	7

Table 4.70
Terms used by 48 authors for Racial, Ethnic, and Minority Groups and Inter-group Relations

Author	*Year*	*Race* *Race relations*	*Ethnic groups/* *Relations*	*Minorities*	*Inter-group relations*
MacIver	1950	Racial groups	Ethnic groups		
Merrill	1952	Race and social structure			
Biesanz	1953	Multi-group society			Inter-group tensions
Lee	1955		Ethnic minorities	Racial minorities	
FISR	1956				Prejudice
Weinberg	1956	Racial discrimination			
Bierstedt	1957	Color	Creed		
Gisbert	1957	Race problem			
Gitler	1957	Race relations			Cultural relations
Merton	1959	Race relations	Ethnic relations		
Green	1960			America's minorities	
Chinoy	1961	Racial groups	Ethnic groups Ethnic solidarity		
Sutherland	1961	Race/race conscious groups			
Young	1962			Minorities in the stratification system	
Douglas	1964	Physical differences			
Horton	1964	Race relations	Ethnic relations		
Kar	1964	Race			
Koller	1965			Minority groups	
Goode	1966		Ethnic relations		
Muzumdar	1966	Racial groups			
McNall	1968			Minority relations	

Sharma	1968	Race/ racism			
Mercer	1970			Minority group relations	
Wilkins	1970			Minority groups and social organization	
Popenoe	1971			Racial minorities Ethnic minorities	Inter-group
Sergeant	1971	Race relations		Minority problems	relations
Acuff	1973			Minorities- social adjustment	
Leslie	1973			Minorities	
Perry	1973			Majority and minorities	
Cole	1975				Discrimination against blacks
Denisoff	1975				Inter group relations
Kenkel	1975			Minority group relations	
Hebding	1976			Minority group relations	
Rose	1976	Race	ethnicity		
Stewart	1976	Racial groups	Ethnic groups	Racial and ethnic minorities	
Broom	1977		Race Ethnicity		
Goode	1977	Race relations	Ethnic relations		
Shapiro	1977		Minority relations: prejudice and discrimination		
Phillips	1979	Biological structures	Ethnic groups		
Sherman	1979	Race /Racism	Ethnicity		
Szymanski	1979	Racism and Capitalism			
Eshleman	1983	Racial differentiation	Ethnic differentiation		
Tischler	1983	Ethnic minorities		Racial minorities	
Persell	1984			Minority groups	
Wallace	1985	Race relations	Ethnic relations		
Charon	1986			Minorities and social structure	
Gordon	1988	Race	Ethnicity		
Total 47		26	17	17	5

Table 4.71

Major sections that include a chapter on racial groups etc.

Title of the major section	*Chapter heading*	*Author*	*Year*
Major forms of social Structure	Racial and ethnic groups	MacIver	1950
Culture and personality	Inter-group tensions	Biesanz	1953
Race and culture	Racial, ethnic minorities	Lee	1955
Social differentiation	Color and creed	Bierstedt	1957

Agencies of social change	Race problem	Gisbert	1957
Demographic social structure	Sociology of race and ethnic relations	Merton	1959
Numbers and organization	American minorities	Green	1960
Social organization	Racial and ethnic groups	Chinoy	1961
Human collectivities	Race and race conscious groups	Sutherland	1961
Social interaction	Race and ethnic relations	Horton	1964
Problem areas in contemporary society	Minority groups, race relations	Koller	1965
Groups	race groups	Muzumdar	1966
Social change and social conflict	Minority relations	McNall	1968
Changing society	Minority groups	Wilkins	1970
Social organization	Minorities	Leslie	1973
Social stratification and inequality	Discrimination against blacks	Cole	1975
Conflict and change	Minority group relations	Kenkel	1975
Differences within societies	Racial and ethnic minorities	Stewart	1976
Social differentiation	Minority group relations	Hebding	1976
Social structure	Race and ethnicity	Rose	1976
Equality and inequality	Race and ethnic relations	Goode	1977
Stratification	Ethnic groups	Phillips	1979
Applications of sociology	Race, ethnicity, racism	Sherman	1979
Social inequality	Racial and ethnic differentiation	Eshleman	1983
Social inequality	Racial and ethnic minorities	Tischler	1983
Social inequality	Minority groups	Persell	1984
Social inequality	Minorities	Charon	1986
Social inequality	Race and ethnic relations	Wallace	1985

71.3 Provision in the LCSH

Race

BT Physical anthropology

NT Black race
Mongoloid race
Caucasian race
Mortality and race
Ethnocentrism
Occupations and race
Health and race

71.4 Related Terms used by Sociologists

RT Accommodation
Assimilation Ghetto
Caste Ghetto
Colonialism
Dual labour markets
Ethnic groups
Ethnicity Intelligence testing
Ethnocentrism
Ethnos
Evolution Plural societies
Prejudice
Racism
Heredity Slavery
Imperialism Social closure
Intelligence Social stratification
Stereotypes
Internal colonialism Stigma
Nationality Under-class

72. RACE RELATIONS

72.1 Definition, Explanation

72.11 "Cultural contacts between people of different races, involving different degrees of prejudice and conflict and often a condition of subordination, as well as the process of toleration, accommodation and possible assimilation."Ray E Baber in Fairchild (1955)

72.12 "The field of race and minority group relations is constituted by the study of social contact, conflict, and accommodation among racial, nationality, religious, and language groups, with particular reference to prejudiceand discrimination and their causes and consequences."Arnold M Rose in Gould (1964)

72.13 "Interaction between ethnic groups, particularly but not exclusively racial groups in technical publications, gradually being supplanted by the term ethnic grouprelations or minority group relations." Hoult (1969)

72.14 "The sociology of race relations comprises the following issues:

1. the study of racialist ideologies which suggest that social inequality between ethnic groups is caused by genetic endowment;

2. the analysis of the structures which support racism and racialist ideologies;

3. the study of the interaction between social classethnicity in social stratification, giving rise to both vertical and horizontal segments in the social structure of societies;

4. the historical inquiry into the origins of race and racism, with special reference to colonialism and anti-colonialism;

5. the study of the location of ethnic groups within the labour market;

6. the contribution of these social, historical and cultural factors to the contemporary inequality between ethnic communities within industrial societies." Abercrombie (1984)

72.15 "The usual topics dealt with under this approach are economic, political, legal, and social discrimination race prejudice minority group relations (accommodation and protest) and institutional adjustment to discrimination and prejudice and minority group solidarity." (topics suggested by G Myrdal in *the American dilemma.* New York, Harper, 1944 and quoted by A M Rose "race and minority group relations" in Gould (1964)

72.3 Provision in the LCSH

Race Relations

UF Integration, Social
Race problems
Race question
Relations, Race

BT Acculturation
Assimilation
Ethnic groups
Ethnology
Social problems
Sociology

RT Ethnic relations
Minorities
Racism

NT Anti-Semitism
Blacks- relocation
Culture conflict
East Indian- relocation
Genocide
Inter-cultural education
Interracial adoption
Mass media and race relations
Race discrimination
Social service and race relations
Whites- relocation

72.4 Related Terms used by Sociologists

Accommodation
Apartheid
Assimilation
Black
Black power
Caste
Civil rights
Colonialism
Conflict relations
Competition
Contact
Discrimination
Ethnic groups
Ethnicity
Ethnocentrism
Minorities
Minority group
Plural society
Prejudice
Race
Segregation
Slavery
Stereotype
Stratification

73. ETHNIC GROUPS

73.1 Definition, Explanation

73.11 "A social group which, within a larger cultural and social system, claims or is accorded a special status in terms of a complex of traits (ethnic traits) which it exhibits or is believed to exhibit. Such traits are diverse,... prominent among them are those drawn from the religious and linguistic characteristics of the social group, the distinctive skin-pigmentation of itsmembers, their national or geographic origins or those oftheir forebears." Melvin M Tumin in Gould (1964)

73.12 "Characteristics identifying an ethnic group oraggregate may include a common language, common customs and beliefs and certainly a cultural tradition, but whilst it may be a racial group, an ethnic group is not to be confused with such a nation may consist of several ethnic groups." G Duncan Mitchell (1968)

73.13 "Segment of a population form ethnic groups by virtue of sharing the combination of:

1. common descent (real or supposed);
2. a socially relevant cultural or physical characteristic; and
3. a set of attitudes and behaviors. . . .

A primary basis for differentiation between ethnic groups can be either cultural— such as a language, a nationality and a religion- or physical- such as skin pigmentation and body shape- or both. The distinguishing feature is considered significant in the society, and people use it in differentiating themselves from others. . . . Members of an ethnic group also share certain feelings, ideas, and behaviors." Sammy Smooha in Kooper(1985)

73.14 "A group characterized by unity of both, race and culture now, often denotes any social group which, as part of a larger system, is perceived as being somewhat distinctive because its members adhere to a religion that is more-or-less unique to them, because of some special national origin or language, or because they are racially different from the majority." Hoult (1969)

73.15 "In anthropology, ethnic group is sometimes used to designate a culturally distinctive, autonomous group, but more general application is to a distinct category of the population, also sharing common cultural features and social institutions as a group." Michael P Banton in Michael Mann (1983)

Ethnic groups

Theoretical works on the concept of groups of people who are bound to gether by common ties of ancestry and culture. Works on the subjective sense of belonging to an individual ethnic group are entered under ethnicity. Works on the discipline of ethnology, and works on the origin, distribution, and characteristics of the elements of the population of a particular region or country are entered under ethnology with appropriate local subdivision. General works on racial, religious, ethnic, or other minority groups are entered under minorities.

UF Groups, Ethnic NT Ethnic art
Ethnic relations
BT Ethnology Minorities
Race relations

73.4 Related Terms used by Sociologists

RT Accommodation Ethnic relations Nationalism
Assimilation EthnicityPlural society
Black power Ethnos Racism
Caste Group Social classes
Conflict Internal colonialism
Stratification

74. MINORITIES

74.1 Definition, Explanation

74.11 "Minorities are sub-groups within a culture which are distinguished from the dominant group by reason of differences in physiognomy, language, customs or cultural pattern (including combination of any of these factors). Such sub-groups are regarded as inherently different and`not belonging' to the dominant group. For this reason they are consciously or unconsciously excluded from full participation in the life of the culture." R A Schermerhorn These our people Boston, D C Heath, 1949: p. 5 (quoted by Preston Valien in Gould, 1964)

74.12 "A group is a minority group if it is the object of prejudice and discrimination from the dominant group, and if the members think of themselves as a minority. It is not a minority, because its members have a distinctive racial or nationality background, or because its members adopt a certain religion or language although, minority status is attached to at least one of these four characteristics." A M Rose *Race, prejudice and discrimination.* New York, Knoff, 1951: p. 5

74.13 "The term minority group, sometimes minority is often used as a synonym for ethnic, racial, and religious groups." Preston Valien in Gould (1964)

74.14 "A minority is a group which, regardless of where U is on the class ladder, faces barriers to the pursuit of life's values that are greater than the barriers faced by persons otherwise equally qualified." J M Yinger A minoritygroup in American society. New York, McGraw-Hill, 1965: p. 22 (quoted by Hoult (1969)

74.15 "In any society, a group that, because it is made up of persons having particular biological or social characteristics is an object of prejudice and/or is subjected to negative discriminatory treatment. . . similar to caste- in terms of privilege often used synonymously with ethnic group." Hoult (1969)

74.3 Provision in the LCSH

Minorities

General works on racial, religious, ethnic and otherminority groups.

UF Ethnic minorities SA Individual races, ethnic
Foreign population groups or other minority
Minority groups groups and subdivisions.
Ethnic relations under

BT Ethnic groups individual countries,
cities etc.

RT	Assimilation (psychology)		Plebiscite
	Discrimination		Race relations
	Ethnic relations		Segregation
	Majorities		Self-determination-
	Nationalism national		
NT	Children of minorities	NT	Linguistic minorities
	Church and minorities		Mass media and minorities
	Ethnic attitudes		Muslim- non-Muslim countries
	Ethnic mass media		Nationalities, Principles of
	Ethnic press		Population transfer
	Ethnic theatre		Race discrimination
	International materials center,		Social work with minorities

Services to minorities
Minorities
RT Anti-Semitism Race
Assimilation Race and minority group
Caste relations
Constitutional lawRace relations
Ethnic groups Sects and cults
Prejudice

75. SOCIAL CONFLICT

75.1 Definition, Explanation

75.11 "A process-situation in which two or more human beings or groups seek actively to thwart each other's purposes, to prevent satisfaction of each other's interests, even to the extent of injuring or destroying the other. . . . Conflict may exist in varying degrees of intensity and severity, and with reference to objects of varying degrees of importance. It may be organized or unorganized, transitory or enduring, physical intellectual, orspiritual. Fairchild (1955)

75.12 "Both, conflict and competition, are forms of interaction, but competition is a struggle between individuals, or groups or individuals, who are not necessarily in contact and communication, while conflict is a contest in which contact is an indispensable condition. Competition is unconscious, conflict is always conscious. Both competition and conflict are forms of struggle. Competition, however is continuous and impersonal, conflict is intermittent and personal." R E Park; E W Burgess *Introduction to the science of sociology*. Chicago, Univ. of Chicago Press, 1921: p. 574 (quoted inGould ,1964)

75.13 "Conflict may be defined as `a struggle over values and claims to scarce status, power and resources in which the aim of the opponents are to neutralize, injure oreliminate their rivals '. Louis A Coser Functions of social conflict. Glencoe, Ill., Free Press, 1956: p. 8 (quoted by Gould, 1964)

75.14 "The social interaction process wherein two or more individuals or groups seek consciously either to block one another in reaching a goal or to injure, defeat, or even annihilate one another often viewed as a particularly severe form of competition, although the latter is morenormatively regulated and, by definition, can not involvethe use of force or violence contrasted withcooperation." Hoult (1969)

75.15 "Social scientists are interested in two aspects of conflict: how conflict relations permeate and shape all aspects of human interaction and social structure (thatis, a conflict perspective to social life) and how a conflict or other theoretical perspective helps elucidate the genesis, escalation, de-escalation, strikes and uprisings." Louis Kriesberg in Kuper (1983)

75.21 Calverton (1937) thought social conflict as a major section of sociology and used it in the modern usage of social disorganization. Goode (1966) makes the heading as 'management of stress in social systems'. McNall (1968) associates social conflict with social change and social movements. Kenkel (1975) relates it to minority group relations and deviancy. Charon (1986) shows relation between social conflict and social change and social movements. A summary of the terms used by some of the authors is presented as follows :

Terms used	*No. of authors*	*Terms used*	*No. of authors*
Social conflict	3	Contradictions	1
Conflict	3	Stress in social systems	1
Conflict and tension	1		

75.22 Related Terms used in the chapter headings along with social conflict:

Terms used	*No. of authors*	*Terms used*	*No. of authors*
Revolution	4	Aggression	1
Change/social change	2	Social control	1
Social movements	2		

As stated above, Kenkel sub-divides social conflict and includes 1. minority group relations and 2. deviancy: going beyond the norm, within conflict.

75.23 **Title of the major section of the textbook that includes a chapter on Social conflict:**

Title of the major section	*Author*	*Year*
Social processes	Goode	1966
Social change and social conflict	McNall	1968
Historical process	Chambliss	1975
Dynamic nature of society	Charon	1986

75.3 Provision in the LCSH

Conflict, Ethnic use Ethnic relations
Conflict, Inter-group use Inter-group relations
Conflict, Interpersonal use Interpersonal conflict
Conflict, Social use Social conflict
Social conflict

UF	Class conflict	RT	Interpersonal conflict
	Class struggle	NT	Conflict management
	Conflict, Social		Conflict of generations
	Social tensions		Social control
BT	Social psychology		Social Darwinism
	Sociology		

75.4 Related Terms used by Sociologists

RT	Competition	Game theory
	Conflict- political aspects	Marx's theory of history and society
	Conflict resolution	Marxism
	Cooperation	Social control
	Development of sociological thought	Social process
		War

76. SOCIAL DISORGANIZATION

76.1 Definition, Explanation

76.11 "A decrease of the influence of existing rules of social behaviour upon members of the group." W T Thomas; FZnaniecki *Polish peasant in Europe and America.* Boston, Badger, 1920: p.2

76.12 "Any disturbance, disruption, conflict, or lack of consensus within a social group or given society, which affects established social habits or behaviour, social institutions, or social control, so as to make relatively harmoniously functioning impossible without some significant intermediate adjustments. . . A certain amount of social disorganization is present at all times, but in general sociological practice, the concept (social disorganization) is applied, whenever these disrupting forces exceed or threaten those making for social stability. The term is also applicable to ideational conflict. These in turn, may be considered as the counterpart of other cultural disturbances. Since old habits and institutions become vested with sanctity, any social change is certain to divide society into conflicting groups, those who believe in the validity of the status quoand those which insist upon altering old institutions to meet present needs. The division of opinion or lack of consensus is in itself a disruptive force as well as, an evidence of lack of harmony or of social disorganization." Mabel A Elliott in Fairchild (1955)

76.13 "It is any kind or degree of weakening or disruption of the pattern of social relations which constitute a society, an association, or any social system." Robert EL Faris in Gould (1964)

76.14 "Social disorganization is the condition which prevails to the degree that a group loses control over its subparts; sometimes briefly defined as a disruption in a community's established social relationships; sometimes appears as the name for the sociology specialty concerned with the study of social problems, . . . contrasted with social organization, when the latter is defined as a condition of value agreement among the participants of a given society;sometimes used synonymously with social pathology andwith social problems." Hoult (1969)

76.15 "Often cited as an implicit or explicit cause of delinquency, crime and other forms of pathology. Generally, it refers to the disturbance of pattern, tradition and discipline which accompanies or composes social change. ... Disorganization is akin to anomie, its the result of social displacement, a new brutality, unfamiliar practices and a dislocation between economic and social life. It leads to drunkenness, crime, cruelty and the breakdown of stable family life." Paul Rock in Michael Mann (1983)

76.2 Usage of Terms in the Form of Chapter Headings

76.21 Terms used in the chapter headings for social disorganization:

Terms used	*No. of authors*	*Terms used*	*No. of authors*
Social disorganization	8	Deviant behaviour	3
Disorganization	1	Social problems	3
Social disorder	1	Social deviation	1
Family and community disorganization	1	Social control	1
		Social order	1

76.22 Title of the major section of the textbook that includes a chapter on social disorganization :

Title of the major section	*Author*	*Year*
Socio-cultural change	Ogburn	1947
Applications of sociology	Merton	1959
Deviance	Chinoy	1961
Social change	Sachdeva	1967

Very few authors make social disorganization a major section and Barnes and Warren discuss following aspects within it

Barnes (1942)	*Warren (1977)*
Marriage disorganization	Deviance
Family disorganization	Stigma
Primary group disintegration	Crime
Community disorganization	Delinquency

76.3 Provision in the LCSH

The term social disorganization is not used in LCSH.

76.4 Related Terms used by Sociologists

RT	Anomy	Function Disorganization
	Degeneration	Organic analogy Social pathology
	Disintegration	Social deterioration Social problems
	Deviance	Social disintegration Suicide
	Deviant	Social deviance

77. REVOLUTION

77.1 Definition, Explanation

77.11 "The term is used by most modern authors to denote: sudden, radical changes which take place both in political and social conditions, that is when an 'established' government (as well as a social and legal order) is suddenly sometimes violently, replaced by new law." J S Eros in Gould (1964)

77.12 "A relatively complete and usually sudden, change in a total system, especially a social system or in some major part of such a system in strict usage a radical altercation in the bases of legality; sometimes denotes virtually total change in a particular area of social life, e.g. the sexual revolution contrasted with the selected change associated with social reform and with the orderly change associated with evolution." Hoult (1969)

77.13 "In everyday usage, a revolution is any sudden, usually violent change in the government of a society. However, social scientists regard such events as `palacer evolutions ' or `coup d'etat ' reserving the term `revolution ' for a total change in the social structure, of which political changes in the government are only manifestation. The explanation of revolution may be political (for example, the failure of government to fulfill electoral commitments or to function adequately) economic for example the combination of long-term poverty and short-term failures); or sociological (for example, the curtailment of social mobility." Abercrombie (1984)

Only four out of eighty-seven authors devote a chapter to revolution in their sociology text books. Sociologists associate revolution with social movements and social change.

77.3 Provision in the LCSH

	Revolution/s	NT	Civil war
	Counter revolution		
UF	Insurrections		Coups de tat
	Political science		De facto doctrine
	Rebellions		Europe- history- 1848-1849
BT	History		Imaginary revolutions
	Political science		Insurgency
	War		Legitimacy of governments
	National liberation movements		
RT	Government, resistance		Peasant uprisings
	Permanent revolution theory		
SA	Subdivision History- revolution		Revolutionary ballads
	(date) under names of place and		songs
	e.g. France- history-		Revolutionary poetry
	revolution 1789-1799		State of siege
	-Philosophy		

77.4 Related Terms used by Sociologists

RT	Citizenship	Peasants
	Conflict theory	Political violence
	Contradiction	Purges and terror
	Evolution	Radicalism
	Institutionalization	Rebellion
	of conflict	Relative deprivation
	Marxist sociology	

78. CROWD

78.1 Definition, Explanation

78.11 "A crowd is a relatively unstructured and temporary aggregation of people who: 1. are in physical proximity; 2. have a common focus of attention; and 3. engage in much interaction with one another. All of which lead crowd members, relative to one another, to feel close rapport and to be highly suggestible and therefore strongly inclined to engage mutually and spontaneously in non-rational action. In Some analysis, types of crowds are delineated- namely a. the active crowd; b. the expressive crowd, often dancing crowd; c. the casual crowd; d. the conventional crowd. Sometimes used as a general term inclusive of all human aggregations such as the audience, mob, public, social movement, and unorganized masses." Hoult (1969)

78.2 Usage of Terms in the Form of Chapter Headings

Terms used	*No. of authors*
Crowds and publics	1
Herd, crowd	1
Crowd as collective behaviour	1
Sociology of groups: crowd	1
Crowd behaviour	1
Masses	1

71.22 Title of the major section of the textbook that includes a chapter on crowd:

Title of the major section	*Author*	*Year*
Group behaviour	Ogburn	1947
Forms of social structure	MacIver	1950
Social integration	Mannheim	1957
Crowd	Merrill	1952

78.3 Provision in the LCSH

BT Social psychology

RT Collective behaviour

Riots

NT Demonstration

Mob

78.4 Related terms used by Crowds Sociologists

RT Audience

Collective behaviour

Mass

Mass society

Mob

Spectator control	Public
-psychology use	Social movements
Collective behaviour	Milling

79. COLLECTIVE BEHAVIOR

79.1 Definition, Explanation

79.11 "The behaviour of a group, when it is of such a nature as to give the appearance of arising from unity of attitude, feeling and motivation. The type of behaviour consistent with the analogical concept of the group as an organism." Fairchild (1955)

79.12 "1. A particular type of relatively spontaneous group action; 2. The essence of collective behaviour as a sociological phenomenon, is the emotionalized mass attempt to resolve widespread feelings of dissatisfaction, such attempts being exemplified in crazes, fads, panics, mobs, riots, and revolutions; considerable agreement that, given types of group behaviour are properly classifiable as collective behaviour only to the degree that they are -among other characteristics- uninstitutionalized, although some observers include, as legitimate examples of the phenomenon, organized social movements and conventionalized crowds such as audiences; some authors , following the lead of H Blumer, differentiate between the less structured and the more structured forms of collective behaviour, terming the two terms, respectively, elementary collective behaviour and social movements; sometimes used synonymously with terms collective dynamics, mass behaviour, and mass phenomena." Hoult (1969)

79.13 "By `collective behaviour ' sociologists now mean the mobilization of a mass of people to change the general structure of society. Such movements to change society as a whole include both secular movements of social protest and religious attempts to change society, for example millenarianism. The most influential general theory of collective behaviour is that of N J Smelser (Theory of collective behaviour. New York, Free Press, 1962), which draws particular attention to the importance of `generalized belief ' and values in directing social movements in periods of rapid social change and political disruption." Abercrombie (1984)

79.2 Usage of Terms in the Form of Chapter Headings

Out of 87 textbooks seen only 26 have a chapter related to the concept of collective behaviour. The terms used for the concept are as follows:

Terms used	*No. of authors*
Collective behaviour	15
Collective behaviour and social movements	6
Group behaviour/ group mind	3
Crowd as collective behaviour/ crowd behaviour	2
Collective behaviour and mass communication	1
Human nature and collective behaviour	1
Near groups and collective behaviour	1
Collective behaviour as social change	1

Table 4.73

Individual chapters within the major section collective Behaviour

Social interaction	Ogburn 1947
Crowds and public	Merrill 1952 Ogburn 1947 Popenoe 1971
Social control and conformity	Ogburn 1947
Public opinion	Broom 1977 Eldridge 1950 Popenoe 1971
Social movements	Merrill 1952 Lee 1955 Popenoe 1971
Social movements as social change	Broom 1977
Collective groupings	Lee 1955
Propaganda	Broom 1977

79.3 Provision in the LCSH

Collective behaviour

UF	Behaviour, collective	RT	Crowds
	Crowd behaviour		Deviant behaviour
	Crowds, psychology		Violence
	Mass UNT		Demonstration
BT	Disasters		Mass suicide
	Social action		Panic
	Social psychology		

79.4 Related Terms used by Sociologists

RT	Attitude change	Mass behaviour
	Brain washing	Mass phenomena
	Cohesion	Mass society

Collective dynamics
Crowds
Crowd behaviour
Demonstration
Deviant behaviour
Fad Social psychology
Fashion Violence
Social action
Social control
Social interaction
Social movements
Social organization

80. SOCIAL MOVEMENTS

80.1 Definition, Explanation

80.11 "Collective enterprises to establish a new order of life. They have their inception in a condition of unrest, and derive their motive power on one hand from dissatisfaction with the current from of life, and on the other hand, from wishes and hopes for a new scheme or system of living. . . . As a social movement develops, it takes on the character of a society. It requires organization and form, a body of customs and traditions, established leadership and enduring division of Labour, social rules and social values— in short, a culture, a social organization and a new scheme of life." B H Blumer "Collective behaviour" in A M Lee ed. *A new outline of the principles of sociology.* New York, Barnes and Noble, 1946: p. 199 (quoted by Preston Valien in Gould, 1964)

80.12 "Denotes a concerted and continued effort by a social group aimed at reaching a goal/s common to its members. More specifically, the effort is directed at modifying, maintaining, replacing or destroying an existing social institution. The term is also used to denote the groups engaged. This general information leaves open the question, e.g. of degrees of organization and continuity or of clarity of purpose-all of which may vary from one social movement to another or within any one social movement in the course of its history." Preston Valien in Gould (1964)

80.13 "Scholarship in the twentieth century has pluralized the term, removed its historical connotation and applied it to a variety of social phenomena, from unstructured collective behaviour, to cults and religious sects, to issue oriented protest movements all the way to organized revolutionary groups. The only common denominators in the variety of definitions employed is that social movements are un-institutionalized groups in some insurgent relationship to existing society, involving unmediated bonds between leaders and followers." Sidney Tarrow in Kuper (1985)

80.21 A chapter on 'social movements is included in the sociology textbooks by 16 authors. Diverse terms used by these authors to represent the concept of social movements are as follows:

Terms used	*No. of authors*
Social movement	4
Social movement and/or collective behaviour	6
Social conflict and social movements	2
Social movement and pressure groups	1
Social movements and revolution	2
Protest movements	1
Social change and social movement	1

Title of the major section	*Author/Year Author/Year Author/Year*
Social change	McNall 1968 Rocher 1972 Rose 1976 Tischler 1983 Persell 1984
Dynamic society	Charon 1986
Collective behaviour	Merrill 1952 Lee 1955 Popenoe 1971
Social disorganization	Sachdeva 1967
Deviance	Hebding 1976
Living in groups	Wallace 1983

80.3 Provision in the LCSH

Social movements

BT Social history
Social psychology

NT Anti-imperialist movement New age movement
Anti-nuclear movement Peace movements
Anti-smoking movement Survivalism
Civil rights movement Welfare rights movements
Gay liberation movement White supremacy movements

80.4 Related Terms used by Sociologists

RT	Anarchism	RT	Nationalism
	Civil disobedience		Nativism and revivalism
	Collective behaviour		Norm oriented movement
	Communism, International movement		Organizations
			Pacifism

Conservation
Crowd
Falangism (Spanish Fascist group)
Fascism
Ideology
Imperialism
Interest groups
International relations, Ideological aspects
Latin-American political movements
Mass phenomena
Mass society
Militarism
Millenarianism
National socialism
Pan movements
Political participation
Political parties
Political sociology
Radicalism
Religion
Revolution
Sects and cults
Social organization
Social reform
Socialism
Syndicalism
Totalitarianism
Urban social movement
Utopianism
Voluntary associations
Zionism

81. SOCIAL CHANGE

81.1 Definition, Explanation

81.11 "Social change denotes an observed difference from antecedent states of the social structure, institutions, habits, or equipment of a society insofar as it is:

1. the outcome of legislative or other overt measures to control conduct; or

2. the product of a change either in a specified substructure or dominant sector of social existence,

or in the physical or social environment; or

3. the repercussive effect of social actions pursued in conformity with the systematically related modes of fulfilling needs and meeting expectations which prevail in a society." Tom Burns in Gould (1964)

81.12 "Usually applied to modifications in social relationships or in culture, the former often being termed 'social change ' and the latter 'cultural change '— but since the two types of changes are interdependent, the term socio-cultural change is increasingly used both in sociology and anthropology; as social change, the sociology specialty particularly concerned with the systematic study of variation in social and cultural systems." Hoult (1969)

Acuff, Ogburn, Young, Horton, Valdes, Abrahamson, Perry, and Kenkel use the chapter heading as 'social and cultural change' and O'Brien, Merrill and Mercer as 'social change and social planning '. The term social change is used as a major heading by the highest number of textbooks (35 authors) and 25 of them placing it as a last section of the textbook. Ogburn uses heading 'socio-cultural change' and includes innovation, social disorganization and adjustment within it. MacIver treats it as one of the two main parts of sociology, the other being social structure and includes biological (that includes demographic), technological, cultural factors, and evolution and progress within it. Chambliss divides social change into evolution, revolution, and social movements. Cole thinks it is the change from simple to complex societies. Kenkel brings the concepts of conflict and change together. Goode explains it in the form of urbanization, population growth, industrialization, and socio-political changes. Phillips thinks collective behaviour has a major part of social change. Tischler places social movements, collective behaviour, demography and ecology within social change. Wallace enumerates political institutions, education, population and environment, and urbanization and modernization within the major heading social change.

81.3 Provision in the LCSH

Social change

Here are entered works on the theory of social change. Works on the history of social structure, institution, interaction, stability, problems, change etc. treated collectively are entered under social history.

UF Change, Social

Cultural change
Cultural evolution
Cultural transformation

BT Anthropology
Progress
Social sciences
Historical materialism

81.4 Related Terms used by Sociologists

RT Automation
Conflict theory
Cooperation
Coup
Culture change
Elitism Sociology Evolutionism

RT Social evolution — Industrialization
Innovation

NT Agriculture-social aspects — Marx
Community development — Mode of production
Cultural lag — Modernization
Culture diffusion — Protestant ethic thesis
Economic development-Revolution
Social aspects — Science, sociology of
Industry- Social aspects — Secularization
Institution building — Transportation
Social Darwinism — Under-development

82. EVOLUTION

82.1 Definition, Explanation

82.11 "The development, planned and unplanned, of culture and forms of social relationships or social interaction. The processes of social revolution are conceived to be more or less analogous to those of biological evolution...i.e., variation, struggle for existence, selection and adaptation but they are identical with these processes. The term evolution differs from progress in that the former does not necessarily imply change for the better, or even increase in complexity. It is usually understood to refer, but not exclusively, to the long run aspects and consequences of social change, and to those which may be regarded as cumulative or irreversible, rather than repetitive." Floyd Nelson House in Fairchild (1955)

82.12 "The term comes to denote movement of an orderly nature which is productive of change of a novel kind. More specifically, it denotes the process of change through which something new is produced in a continuous ways not to violate the identity or individuality of the originalentity." R V Sampson in Gould (1964)

82.13 "Orderly change, or a process of growth, in which each new stage of a phenomena is a further development, but not adenial, of that which preceded it inclusive of changed eliberately brought precipitous change associated with revolution in some works general evolutionary theory is distinguished from special or particular theories." Hoult (1969).

82.21 The term social evolution has been used in the chapter headings by 4 and the term evolution by 1 author.

82.22 Title of the major section of the textbook that includes a chapter on evolution:

The chapter on evolution is included in the major section social change by MacIver (1950), Gisbert (1957), Bottomore (1962), and Parsons (1961).

82.3 Provision in the LCSH

Evolution
BT Heredity Culture
RT Man-origin Differentiation
NT Behaviour evolution
Human evolution
Social evolution
Women evolution
-Religious aspects
UF Evolution and religion
Religion and evolution
BT Religion and science
NT Bible and evolution

82.4 Related terms used by

RT **Sociologists**
Progress
Race
Division of labour Revolution
Ecology (contrasted to)
Genetics Social change
Integration Social Darwinism
Intelligence Social reform
Man, Origin Sociobiology
Organic analogy Urban ecology
Population genetics

83. PROGRESS/SOCIAL PROGRESS

83.1 Definition, Explanation

83.11 Social progress- "Social change or movement in the direction of some recognized and approved goal. . . . Sheer change, even though of an evolutionary character is not necessarily progress. ... Nearly all sociologists hold that social progress must be defined in terms of control—control over physical nature, on the one hand, and controlover human nature and human relations, on the other. Theonly improvement in human relations which man knows evidently must come though the improvement of culture. Whether anything like general progress is possible, depends upon our answer to the question, whether a general high level of culture is possible for the whole of mankind." Fairchild (1955)

PROGRESS

83.12 "Change in a desired direction change that produces a condition or a phenomenon defined as an improvement over a previous condition or phenomenon." Hoult (1969)

83.13 "If progress means development in a desirable direction, then, what seems desirable to some, may seem undesirable to others. Although several attempts were made to define 'progress' objectively, the concept had to be abandoned for sociological use." R Bierstedt Social order. Bombay, Tata-McGraw Hill, 1957: p. 557

83.14 "Key elements in this tradition (of evolution and progress) were the beliefs that organisms were intrinsically bound to improve themselves, that changes were progressive and often radical and sudden, and that acquired characters could be transmitted genetically." Adam Kuper in Kuper (1985)

83.2 Usage of Terms in the Form of Chapter Headings

83.21 The term progress. Social progress, change development and progress has been used in the chapter headings by 2 authors each and one author uses it as social change and progress.

83.3 Provision in the LCSH

Progress
UF Social progress
BT Civilization
RT Regression (civilization)
Social stability
NT Cultural lag
Science and civilization
Social change
Social systems-growth

83.4 Related terms used by Sociologists

RT Civilization
Cultural evolution
Evolution
Evolutionary theory
Social telesis

84. HUMAN ECOLOGY

84.1 Definition, Explanation

84.11 "Human ecology may be defined as the study of relations between human groups (or populations) and their environments.... most definitions agree that human ecology includes the study of two aspects of group structure, both of which depend strongly on sustenance relations between man and physical environment, namely spatial structure and the division of labour." James A Quinn in Gould (1964).

84.12 "It explores how man distributes himself in geographic space. Ecological units such as cities are formed when men distribute themselves over land areas to realize some advantage. These advantages are economic (to be near a supply of a natural resource), health and recreational (a salubrious climate), transportation (a natural crossroads), and the like." Alvin L Bertrand *Basic sociology*. (1967).

84.13 "In sociology, the specialty concerned with the systematic study of the spatial aspects of human life, with particular reference to the effects of competitive processes on the distribution and organization of physical phenomena such as neighborhoods, streets, shopping areas, churches, and the like; sometimes termed 'social ecology.' Hoult (1969).

84.2 Usage of Terms in the Form of Chapter Headings

Table 4.76
Terms used for human ecology

Terms used	*No. of authors*
Human ecology	6
Demography/population and ecology	4
Human ecology and population/demography	3
Ecological aspects of community	2
Community and human ecology	1
Man and ecology	1
Human ecology and change	1
Ecology and urbanization	1
Population, urbanization and ecology	1
Human ecology and environmental problems	1

Title of the major section	*Chapter heading*	*Author Year*
Community	Ecological aspects	Merrill 1952
Social organization	Ecology	Chinoy 1961
Human ecology		Young 1962
Social change	Heredity and environment	Gisbert 1957
Demography and ecology		Tischler 1983
Population and environment		Wallace 1985
Social problems	Human ecology and environmental problems	Bertrand 1973
Physical structure within human ecology	Human ecology	Phillips 1979
Ogburn Lee Young		Horton Eshleman

Communities	*		*	*
Ecology		*		
Population		*	*	*
Dominance		*		
Migration and mobility		*		
Succession		*		
Rural (human ecology)			*	
Urban (human ecology)		*		

84.3 Provision in the LCSH

Human ecology

UF Ecology- social aspects
Ecology, Human
Ecology, Social
Environment
Environment, Human
Human environment
Social ecology environments
Survival (human ecology)
Landscape assessment

NT Closed ecological systems
Community life
Environmental archaeology
Environmental health
Environmental indexes
Hazardous geographic
Human settlements

BT Ecology Man- influence of environment
Human biology Man- influence of nature
Social sciences Population
Quality of life

RT Anthropo-geography
Conservation of natural resources
Environmental policy-moral and ethical aspects
Social psychology
Survival skills
War- environmental aspects

84.4 Related Terms used by Sociologists

RT Balance of nature
Cities
Commensalism
Dominance
Environment
Epidemiology
Hunting and gathering
Invasion
Succession
Suicide
Urban ecology
Zonal hypothesis

85. ENVIRONMENT

85.1 Definition, Explanation

85.11 "The individual's environment has been classified as

physiographic, bionomic, economic, cultural (material and non-material, institutional and symbolic), and personal-social. In groups, each person is part of each other person's personal-social environment. A group as a whole is environed as is an individual, and also by other groups. Environment is also definable as the field of adjustment of any responsive organism from molecule to United Nations. As such, it merges with the ecological idea of habitat." Thomas Dowes Elliott in Fairchild (1955)

85.12 "All the external conditions, physical and socio-cultural, which can influence an individual or a group; sometimes used to denote physical surroundings as distinguished from the socio-cultural when employed in the general sense, often used synonymously with milieu." Hoult (1969)

85.2 Usage of Terms in the Form of Chapter Headings

85.21 Terms used	*No. of authors*
Society and environment	2
Heredity and environment	4
Society and environment	2
Total environment and accommodation	1
Organism and its physical environment	1
Human ecology and environmental problems	1
Population and environment	1

MacIver (1950) includes adaptation, heredity, geography, and land within the major section society and environment. Gisbert (1957) places heredity and environment within the major section agencies of social change. Wallace (1985) also thinks population and environment a part of social change or factors of social change. Bertrand (1973) enumerates human ecology and environmental problems within the broader section social problems.

85.3 Provision in the LCSH

Environment
use
Ecology

UF	Balance of nature	NT	Human ecology
	Environment Urban ecology		

85.4 Related Terms used by Sociologists

Ecology and also environment

RT Balance of nature
Commensalism
Cities gathering
Dominance Invasion
Epidemiology Milieu
Habitat
HereditySocial situation
Hunting and Succession
Suicide
Urban ecology
Zonal hypothesis

86. GEOGRAPHIC ENVIRONMENT

86.1 Definition, Explanation

86.11 "Those natural phenomena that affect the origin or development of physical or social life, such as climate, temperature, seasons, sunshine, rainfall, floods, droughts, soil, minerals, topography, land or water formations, altitude, latitude, longitude. Recent knowledge concerning the mechanism of heredity shows that some factors in the geographic environment assist and that others harm or prevent the development of hereditary traits." Oscar Wesley in Fairchild (1955)

86.2 Usage of Terms in the Form of Chapter Headings

Terms used	*No. of authors*
Geographical factors	2
Geography	2
Natural condition of human society	1

Ogburn (1942) enumerates culture, biological factors and geographical factors as the three main aspects of society. Bierstedt (1957) also includes geographical, biological, and also demographic factors as the main three natural conditions of human society. Eldridge (1950) highlights the near relation of geographical factors and culture. Goode (1977) considers geography as a significant aspect of social life and thinks it a deciding factor for the type of social organization.

86.3 Provision in the LCSH

Human geography
use
Anthropo-geography RT Human ecology

UF Cultural geography
Environment
Geography, Cultural
Geographical distribution
of manMan- influence of climate
Geography, Human
Geography, Social
Human geography
Social

RT Geography, Political
Human settlements
Land settlement patterns
Man- migration
Population geography
Regionalism
geography

BT Geography

86.4 Related Terms used by Sociologists

Out of the eight dictionaries consulted only Fairchild (1955) has used the term geographic environment, as such terms related to it are not available through these sources.

87. MEDICAL SOCIOLOGY

87.1 Definition, Explanation

87.11 "Medical sociology covers a variety of topics:

1. the sociology of the healing professions;

2. the sociology of illness, illness behavior, and help seeking behavior;

3. medical institutions and health service organizations;

4. social factors in the aetiology of illness and disease

5. social factors in fertility and mortality;

6. social factors influencing the demand for and use of medical facilities;

7. the sociology of doctor-patient interaction;

8. the social effects of different medical systems, such as between private and public provision of health care; and

9. international pattern of illness and health services." Abercrombie (1984)

87.12 "Medicine, sociology of; medical sociology: the study of the form and influence of medicine as ideology and of its practitioners as a powerful professional organization enjoying a privileged status in the process of constructing knowledge of what constitutes health and illness in society. It overlaps with the sociologies of knowledge, power and occupations. . . . A more subversive set of concerns, perhaps more appropriately incorporated within the sociology of health, is the development of alternative accounts of the causes, form and nature of sickness in society." Nicky Hart in Michael Mann (1983).

87.2 Usage of Terms in the Form of Chapter Headings

Terms used	*No. of authors*
Medical sociology	3
Sociology of medicine	1
Population and health	2
Health and welfare	1

Merton (1959) includes sociology of medicine within sociology of institutions.

87.3 Provision in the LCSH

Sociology of medicine not used in the LCSH.

Medicine, Social SA subdivisions Patients-social
use conditions and social aspects
Social medicine under individual diseases, UFMedical care- e.g.
Cancer patients-social
Medical sociology conditions and subdivisions
Medicine- social social aspects and sociological
aspects aspects under medical topics
Medical, Sociale. g. Heart transplantation

BT Public health social aspects
Public welfare Hospitals- sociological
Sociology aspects.

RT Medical ethics

87.4 Related terms used by Sociologists

NT		RT	
NT	Family- health and hygiene	RT	Clinical sociology
	Medical cooperation		Demography
	Medical social work		Epidemiology
	Medical sociologists		Gerontology
	Social psychiatry		Health care systems
	Trans-cultural medical care		Medical anthropology
	Sick		Morbidity
	Sociology of health and illness		Public health
			role

88. COMMUNITY

88.1 Definition, Explanation

88.11 "A community is not only a collection of people, but it is a collection of institutions. Not people, but institutions, are final and decisive in distinguishing the community from other social constellations." Robert E Park *Human communities.* Glencoe, Ill., Free Press, 1952: p. 66 (quoted in Hoult, 1969)

88.12 "A sub-group having many of the characteristics of society, but on a smaller scale, and with less extensive and coordinated common interests. Implicit in the concept of `community ' is a territorial area, a considerable degree of interpersonal acquaintance and contact, and some special basis of coherence that separates it from neighbouring groups. The community has more limited self-sufficiency than society, but within those limits has closer association and deeper sympathy. There may be some special bond of unity, such as race, national origin, or religious affiliation." Fairchild (1955)

88.13 "A community is functionally related aggregate of people, who live in a particular geographical locality at a particular time, share a common culture, are arranged in social structure, and exhibit an awareness of their uniqueness and separate identity as a group." D E Mercer *American community.* New York, Random House, 1956: p. 27

88.14 "An interdependent collectivity of persons living permanently in a geographically limited area which serves as a focus for a major portion of the residents' daily life; usually involves people who share a common culture, although sometimes applied to collectivities- e.g. the prison community- where the cultural similarity of the participants may be minimal; although sometimes used to denote entire nations, usually applied only to relatively small areas and numbers of people, the maximum of the latter sometimes being designated as the number who can maintain face-to-face relationships with one another; sometimes denotes specialized groupings (i.e., the academic community) set off from society at large by the unique ways of doing and thinking hat are maintained by the group members; although sometimes loosely used synonymously with group, society, social organization, and social system, usually differentiated from such terms on the grounds that they do not, as community almost always does—by definition—necessarily involve a limited territorial setting." Hoult (1969)

88.15 "1. The quality of appertaining to or being held by all in common joint or common ownership, tenure, liability, etc.;

2. common character quality in common; commonness; agreement; identity;

3. a body of people organized in a political, municipal or social unity; and

4. the body of those having common or equal rights or ranks as distinguished from the privileged class; the body of commons the commonality." *Oxford English Dictionary.*

A total of 28 authors devote a chapter or section of chapter to the concepts related to community/communities.

Table 4.79
Terms used for community

Terms used	*No. of authors*	*Terms used*	*No. of authors*
Community	9	Community organization and behavior	1
Communities	5	Rural community	1
Community and Ecology	4	Urban community	1
Social institutions	2	Folk society	1
Individual	1	Societies- comparative study	1
Geography	1	Community organization	1
Human ecology	1	Social processes in communities	1
Population	1	Tribal community	1
Urbanization	1	Community power	1
Urban development	1		

Title of the major section	*Author*	*Year*
Human ecology and population	Ogburn	1947
Social structure	MacIver	1950
Social organization	Chinoy	1961
	Young	1962
	Tischler	1983
Human ecology	Horton	1964
	Eshleman	1983
Continuity and change	Rose	1976
	Groups Phillips	1979

Chapter heading into which the major section on community/ communities is sub-divided

Chapter Heading within	*MacIver*	*O'Brien*	*Merrill*	*Chinoy*	*Southerland*	*Scott*
Community as place	*					
Community as settlement	*					
Inter-communal differences	*					
Social system		*				
Urbanization		*		*		
Ecological aspects			*	*	*	
Integrative processes						*
Socialization processes						*
Status processes						*
Power processes						*
Adaptive processes						*

88.3 Provision in the LCSH

Community

Here are entered works on geographically defined social units within a larger society, served by an aggregate of institutions, economically self-sufficient, and characterized by close contacts and common interests and activities.

BT **Cities and towns**
Human settlements
Sociology
Sociology, rural
Conflict
BT Artists and community

Community life
Community organization
Gemeins

88.4 Related terms used by Sociologists

RT Association Group
City Neighborhood
Norm
Deviant behavior Social organization
Disasters Social system
Ecology Society
chaft

89. RURAL SOCIOLOGY

89.1 Definition, Explanation

89.11 "Rural sociology has been regarded as somewhat marginal to the main theoretical interests of both sociology and anthropology, until recently. It seemed of little interest to general sociology. Rural sociology has, it seems, lost the grounds for claiming to be a distinctive discipline with its own special objects of investigation and mode of explanation." Norman Long in Kuper (1985)

89.12 "The sociology specialty concerned particularly with the systematic study of human life in rural areas and with the ruralization process, in some senses, contrasted with urban sociology." Hoult (1969)

89.2 Usage of Terms in the Form of Chapter Headings

89.21

Terms used	*No. of authors*	*Terms used*	*No. of authors*
Rural community	2	Modern farmer	1
Rural sociology	1	Farmer in an industrializing world	1
Village community	1		
Folk communities	1		

89.3 Provision in the LCSH

Rural sociology

use

Sociology,

Works on the social organization of rural areas.

UF Rural sociology

BT Sociology

NT Agriculture-social aspects

Community

Rural development- social aspects

Rural population

Urbanization

89.4 Related terms used by Sociologists

Agricultural economics

Rural Agriculture

Cooperatives

Modernization

Peasants

Rural planning and development

Rural communities

Ruralization

Urban sociology

90. URBANIZATION

90.1 Definition, Explanation

90.11 "When non-urban persons acquire the roles, style of life, symbols, forms of organization, and cultural artifacts, characteristic of the city, and when they come to share the meanings, values, and perspectives that are characteristically urban, we can say that they are experiencing the process of urbanization." Noel P Gist; Sylvia Fleis Fava *Urban society*. 5th ed. New York, Thomas Y Crowell, 1964: p. 271 (Quoted by Hoult, 1969)

90.12 "The sociological use of the term is broader, encompassing the notion of a social process which at once is the cause and consequence of a change in man's ways of life, as in which conscious and deliberate planning assumes a greater and greater role. ... Louis Wirth argues that the city, characterized by size, density, and heterogeneity is the main determinant of various kinds of social behavior. In the urban areas, we find increasing secondary group relationships, voluntary associations, a plurality of norms and vagueness with respect to their definition, increasing secularization and segmentary roles." G Duncan Mitchell (1968)

90.13 "Refers properly to a growth in the proportion of a country's population living in urban centers of a particular size." Abercrombie (1984)

90.21 Usage of Terms in the Form of Chapter Headings

Terms used	*No. of authors*	*Terms used*	*No. of authors*
Urbanization	13	Urban sociology	2
Urban community	5	Urban living	1
City	4	Urban development	1
Cities	1	Suburbanization	1
City planning	1	Rural- urban continuum	2

90.22 Related terms used in the chapter headings along with urbanization:

Terms used	*No. of authors*	*Terms used*	*No. of authors*
Social change	3	Industrialization	1
Population/demography	3	Modernization	1
Ecology	2	Region	1
Community change	1	Rural trade area	1
Folk	1	Stratification	1

Table 4.82

Major sections that include a chapter on urbanization

Title of the major section	*Author*	*Year*
Social structure	MacIver	1950
Social planning	Merrill	1952
Social differentiation	Bierstedt	1957
Demographic social structure	Merton	1959
Communities	Sutherland	1961
Human ecology	Sachdeva	1967
Social organization Chinoy 1961	Leslie	1973
Changing society	Wilkins	1970

Conflict and change	Kenkel	1975
Sources of change	Stewart	1978
Social change	Goode	1975
	Persell	1984
	Wallace	1985

Urbanization sociologists
UF Cities and towns, movement to
Urban development Community
BT Cities and towns
Social history transition continuum
Sociology, Rural Ecology
Sociology, Urban Human settlements
Urban policy
RT Rural- urban Migration migration Modernization
NT Detribalization
Urban geography

RT Residential
City mobility
Rural sociology
Demographic Rural- urban
Urban areas
Urban community
Industrial society Urban planning
Urban society
Urban sociology
Residential analysis Urbanism

91. URBAN SOCIOLOGY

91.1 Definition, Explanation

91.11 "The scientific study of the socio-economic adaptations and adjustments induced by the concentration of population within limited geographical area." Fairchild (1955)

91.12 "Urban sociology is the sociological study of cities, city life or urbanism or selected topics in this field." Giden Sjoberg in Gould (1964)

91.13 "A branch of sociological studies focusing primarily on urban aspects of man's social life and thus related to most other branches of the subject without always very clear distinctions. It ranges from studies, of city life, ancient, medieval, and modern often comparative studies, to small scale studies of human interaction in urban communities." G Duncan Mitchell (1968)

91.14 "Sociology specialty concerned particularly with the systematic study of human life in cities and with the urbanization process in some senses, contrasted with rural sociology." Hoult (1969)

91.2 Usage of Terms in the Form of Chapter Headings

The term urban sociology is used as chapter heading only by two authors out of 87 textbooks seen. The terms used to express this concept are as follows:

Terms used	*No. of authors*	*Terms used*	*No. of authors*
Urban community	5	Rural- urban contrast	2
Urban sociology	2	Urban development	1
Urban living	1		

Merton includes the article by Sjoberg on 'comparative urban sociology' in the book edited by him. Sergeant merely mentions urban sociology under the list of items which he describes as 'aspects of society which have yielded to empirical investigation.

91.3 Provision in the LCSH 91.4 Related terms used by Sociologists

UF	Urban sociology		
RT	Cities and towns	RT	Ecology
NT	Aerial photography in urban sociology urban sociology		Interviewing in Rural
	City and town life Urban ecology		Rural sociology
	Community development, urban		Urban community
	Community power		Urban policy Urban society
			Urban renewal Urbanism
			Urbanization Urbanization

92. POPULATION

92.1 Definition, Explanation

92.11 "Demography is the size, territorial distribution, and composition of population, changes therein, and the components of such changes, which may be identified as natality, mortality, territorial movement (migration) and social mobility (change of status)." P M Hauser; O D Duncan *Study of population*. Chicago, Univ. of Chicago Press, 1959: p. 31

92.12 "Demographic analysis is confined to the study of components of population variation and change. Population studies are concerned not only with population variables but also with relationships between population changes and other variables—social, economic, political, biological, genetic, geographical and the like. The field of population studies is at least as broad as interest in the determinants and consequences of population trends." P M Houser; O D Duncan *ibid.* p. 2

92.13 "Demography is concerned with the number of populations, changes in numbers, and the way in which such changes come about, e.g. by an excess of births over deaths, or by migration. It also deals with the division of populations into certain sub-groups, by sex, age, and marital status and changes in these structures. The methods used are primarily quantitative and statistical, and special techniques have been evolved to deal with demographic data. However, demography is sometimes taken to include the study of long-term population movements and theoretical speculations about the causes of such movements." E Grebenik in Gould (1964)

92.14 "Intellectual discipline whose practitioners are concerned with the statistical study of population, special emphasis being given to birth, death, and migration rites; compound phrases are used to designate special aspects of demography—e.g., in descriptive demography the geographical distribution of aspects of population are described, and in formal demography (also termed pure demography, theoretical demography, or population analysis) the statistics of population change are studied in abstraction from concomitant social factors, interaction between such factors and population being the concern of what is sometimes termed economic demography, social demography, or population study; a specialty discipline in sociology and statistics." Hoult (1969)

92.15 "Demography is a very technical and highly mathematical; study of the vital statistics of human population (specially birth, death, and migration) as well as of the characteristics of population structure (including age, sex, and marital status) as they contribute to an understanding of population change." H Stanford ed. *World's population: problems and growth*. New York, Oxford Univ. Press, 1972: p. 4.

92.2 Usage of Terms in the Form of Chapter Headings

The term population has been used as heading by 34 authors, while 11 prefer to use the term demography. Eight of these authors bring the concept of population and ecology together and make the heading as population and ecology or demography and ecology. Other terms used as headings along with population/ demography are social structure, communities, social groupings, resources, urbanization, technology, wealth, environment, and also beggary. Eldridge (1950), Merton (1959), Broom (1955), Sutherland (1961), and O'Donnell (1985) treat the heading as a major section and subdivide it into chapters. A large number of textbook authors place the chapter on population under the major section social change or change as follows:

Title of the major section	*Chapter heading*	*Author*	*Year*
Social change	Population	Gisbert	1957
Conflict and change	Social demography	Kenkel	1975
Social change	Population growth	Goode	1977
Sources of change	Population trends and consequences	Stewart	1978
Human ecology and change	Population and health	Eshleman	1983
Social change	Demography and ecology	Tischler	1983
Social change	Population and health	Persell	1984
Social change	Population and environment	Wallace	1085

Table 4.84

Major sections that include a chapter on Population

Title of the major section	*Chapter heading*	*Author*	*Year*
Human ecology	Population	Lee	1955
Human ecology	Population	Horton	1964
Human ecology	Population	Sachdeva	1967
Natural conditions of human society	Demographic	Bierstedt	1957
Social organization	Population and resources	Young	1962
Problem areas in contemporary societies	Demography	Koller	1965
Social problems	Demography and population problems	Bertrand	1964
Association	Population	McNall	1968

92.3 Provision in the LCSH

Population
Here are entered works on the caracteristics of human population, especially with reference to the size and density,

Demography
UF Historical demography the
BT Social Sciences
RT Population
Vital statistics

growth, distribution, migration, and vital statistics, and effects of these on social and economic conditions.

UF Population, Human
BT Economics
Human ecology
Sociology
RT Demography
Malthusianism
NT Baby boom generation
Birth intervals
Census
Cities and towns, growth
Contraception
Demographic transition
Education, Demographic aspects
Households
Human population genetics
Human settlements
Man- migrations
Migration, Internal
Mortality
Population biology
Rural population
Stable population model

SA subdivision population under names of countries cities etc.

NT Cohort analysis
Communication in demography
Demographers
Demographic anthropology
Demographic transition
Education- demographic aspects
Family demography
Fertility, Human
Linguistic demography
Mortality
Population density
Population geography
Population policy
Population psychology
Sex distribution (Demography)
Stable population model
Technological innovations demographic aspects
War- casualties (statistics etc.)

92.4 Related Terms used by Sociologists

RT Aging
Birth rate
Cohort
Census of population
Death rate
Demographic transition
Demography
Fertility
Mortality
Nuclear family
Population and resources
Population study
Population policy
Population projections

93. MIGRATION

93.1 Definition, Explanation

93.11 "Migration manifests four distinct forms—invasion, conquest, colonization, and immigration." Fairchild (1955)

93.12 "Denotes geographical movement of relatively settled people, especially those making a comparatively permanent change of residence; two major forms, internal (migration within the boundaries of a nation) and external or international (migration across the boundary of a nation); called emigration if viewed in terms of the place or nation of origin, and immigration if viewed in terms of the place of destination; differentiated from horizontal mobility, the ecological concept denoting more or less daily movement between place of residence and job location." Hoult (1969)

93.2 Usage of Terms in the Form of Chapter Headings

93.21 The terms migration has been used by 2 authors, and one each of the authors uses the term migration and mobility, and man as a migrant.

Eldridge (1950) places migration within the major section 'population traits and trends'. Lee (1955) names the broader section human ecology. O'Donnell (1985) calls migration as social aspects of population.

93.3 Provision in the LCSH

Migration

Works on the movement of population from one section to another section of the same country. Works dealing with migration from one country to another or from one section of a country to another country or to a section of another country are entered under Emigration and immigration.

UF	Internal migration	NT	Cities and towns- growth
	Mobility Forced migration		
BT	Colonization		Labor mobility
	Emigration and immigration		Residential mobility
	Man- migrations		Rural- urban migration
	Migrant labor		Student mobility
	Population		Urban- rural migration
	Population geography-sex differences		

93.4 Related Terms used by Sociologists

RT Assimilation Refugees
Mobility Residential mobility
Movement Urbanization
Population distribution

94. APPLIED SOCIOLOGY

94.1 Definition, Explanation

94.11 "The deductive phase of scientific sociology. The accurate and precise use of sociological generalizations to assist in the solution of social problems. The application of sociological laws and principles to particular cases. Applied sociology may be an instrument of either social reform or social engineering." Fairchild (1955)

94.12 "Using the findings of sociological inquiry to help in implementing given policy or to achieve desired social change most efficaciously." Hoult

94.2 Usage of Terms in the Form of Chapter Headings

94.21

Terms used	*Authors*	*Year*
Applied sociology	Valdes	1965
	Bottomore	1979
	S Rao	1990
Applications of sociology	Merton	1959
Uses of sociology	Cole	1975
Role of sociologists	Cole	1975

Table 4.85

Subdivisions of the major section Applied Sociology

Heading used	*Merton*	*Bottomore*	*S Rao*	*Cole*
Social disorganization	*			
Deviant behavior	*			
Mental illness	*			
Criminological research	*			
Mass communication	*			
Social system	*			
Sociology as a teaching profession	*			
Social policy		*		
Social planning		*		
Social problems		*		
Problems of order			*	
Uses of sociology				*

94.3 Provision in the LCSH

The term applied sociology is not used in the LCSH.

94.44 Related terms used by Sociologists

RT Social engineering Social reform

95. SOCIAL PLANNING

95.1 Definition, Explanation

95.11 "The interactional process— investigation, discussion, agreement— of projecting order upon human relationships; it involves a number of people reaching agreement as to what may be in human relations to prepare a program for any body or organization." Frederick E Lumley in Fairchild (1955)

SOCIAL POLICY

95.12 "The term social policy is not used technically, but rather merely describes the policies of governments in respect to a range of social services. Thus, matters pertaining to health, education, housing, social insurance and national assistance are to be included under this description." G Duncan Mitchell (1968)

95.2 Usage of Terms in the Form of Chapter Headings

Terms used	*No. of authors*
Social change and social planning	3
Societal planning	1
Social control and social planning	1
Social policy and social planning	1
Social policy	1

Bottomore (1962) treats social planning as a part of applied sociology and places along with social problems.

95.3 Provision in the LCSH

Social planning NT Aged- government policy
use Christian- democracy
Social policy Deaf-government policy

UF National planning Economic security
Social planning Education and state
State planning Housing policy
Institution building

BT Planning Land reform
Social history Medical policy
Nutrition policy

RT Economic policy
Family policy
Social legislation
Population policy
Social action

SA Social policy under names of countries, cities etc.Welfare state
Urban policy
Welfare economics

95.4 Related Terms used by Sociologists

RT Idealization Social administration Social engineering

96. SOCIAL PROBLEMS

96.1 Definition, Explanation

96.11 "The most general, formal and stable patterns of behavior are called social institutions. Accordingly, social problems may be conveniently classified in terms of disapproved deviant behavior in each institution." G Lundberg *et al. Sociology* 3rd ed. New York, Harper, 1963: p. 649

96.12 "Any situation which is regarded by significant number of the members of a group, as a threat to one or more of the group's basic values and which is believed to be remediable by collective action as social problems, often appears as the name for the sociology specialty concerned with the study of problem areas such as crime, war, disease, poverty, race relations; sometimes used synonymously with social disorganization and with social pathology." Hoult (1969)

96.13 "Sociology of social problems attempts to describe and explain how new definitions of social problems emerge, how troublesome persons or social arrangements are identified, how institutions are created to deal with them. The field has largely abandoned the attempt to explain deviant behavior and social disorganization. Rather, it is attempting to explain how society through an essentially political process, discovers and invents its problems." Malcolm Spector in Kuper (1983)

96.2 Usage of Terms in the Form of Chapter Headings

Out of the 87 textbooks studied, only 11 authors include a chapter on social problems in the textbook authored by them. Out of them 10 use the term social problems and only one expresses it as the problem of problems. Some of the related terms used by these authors along with social problems are social disorganization (3 authors), deviant behavior/deviance (2 authors), and social change (1 author).

Table 4.86

Subdivisions of the section on Social problems

Chapter heading within the major section	*Lee*	*Koller*
Social problems		
Problem families	*	*
Children	*	
Youth	*	
Adults	*	
Minorities: racial, ethnic, class	*	*
Community problems	*	
Social planning		*
Society problems		*
Demography		*
Gerontology		*
Crime		*
Urbanization		*

96.21 Title of the major section of the textbook that includes a chapter on social problems :

Title of the major section	*Author*	*Year*
Social change	Merrill	1955
	Sachdeva	1967
Applied sociology	Bottomore	1962
Social disorganization	Bertrand	1973

96.3 Provision in the LCSH

Social problems
Alcoholism
UF Reforms, Social
Social reforms
Social welfare
Delinquency
BT Social history
Sociology
Divorce
NT Buddhism and social problems
Parasitism (social sciences)
Race relations
Social action
Social ethics

96.4 Related terms used by Sociologists

RT Addiction
Anomy
Conflict
Criminology
Deviancy amplification
Deviant behavior
Labeling theory
Mental health
Poverty
Social disorganization
Symbolic interactionism
Unemployment

97. CRIME

97.1 Definition, Explanation

97.11 "The study of crime and delinquency is an interdisciplinary inquiry which brings together the theoretical and methodological insights of sociology, economics, political science, psychology, and law. The field consists of two interrelated but separable areas of concern: 1. the development and implementation of laws which define acts and people as criminal or delinquent; and 2. the social, psychological and biological forces that cause people to commit acts of crime and delinquency. William J Chambliss in Kuper (1985)

97.12 "Any behavior which, in a given time and place is prohibited by applicable statutory law." Hoult (1969)

97.13 "No matter what the degree of immorality, reprehensibility, or indecency of an act, it is not a crime unless it is prohibited by the criminal law." E Sutherland; D Cressey Principles of criminology. 7th ed., Chicago, Phil., J B Lippincott, 1966: p. 4 (quoted by Hoult (1969).

97.2 Usage of Terms in the Form of Chapter Headings

Terms used	*No. of authors*	*Terms used*	*No. of authors*
Crime and delinquency	4	Crime and punishment	1
Criminology/Crime and	1	Criminological research	3
Crime and the state	1		
Crime	2	Social pathology	1
Crime and law	1		

97.22 Related Terms used along with crime in the chapter headings:

Delinquency	1
Delinquency and anti-social behavior	1
Juvenile delinquency	1

Table 4.87

Major section that includes a chapter on crime

Title of the major section	*Author*	*Year*
Applications of sociology	Merton	1959
Social institutions	Green	1960
Social problems	Koller	1965
Social conflict	McNall	1968
Changing society	Wilkins	1970

Social, Deviation	Bertrand	1973
Social disorganization	Warren	1977
Social control	O'Donnell	1985

Crime and criminals

UF City crime
Criminals
Criminology
Urban crime
Female offenders

NT Conspiracies
Crime and superstition
Crime prevention
Delinquents

BT Criminal justice, Gangs
administration of Hoodlums
Deviant behavior
Social ethics
Sociology
Vice Organized crime
Prostitution

Illegitimacy and crime
Juvenile delinquency
Narcotics and crime

SA headings beginning with
the word Criminal
Rural crimes

Rehabilitation of criminals
Rogues and vagabond

NT Aged offenders
Alcoholism and crime
Alien labor criminals
Assassins
Atrocities
Bravos
Commercial criminals
Computer crimes

Sex offenders
Smugglers
Suburban crimes
Swindlers and swinging
Thieves
Violent crimes
War and crime
War criminals

97.4 Related Terms used by Sociologists

RT Criminal law
Criminal responsibility
Criminology
Delinquency
Deviance

Labeling theory
Punishment
Social control
White collar crime

98. DELINQUENCY

98.1 Definition, Explanation

98.11 "Failure of an individual to perform a socially designated task violation of a social obligation. The judicially accepted distinction between a criminal act and a delinquent act is inherent in the theory that juveniles are not motivated by the same responsible considerations as are assumed to actuate adults. Legally and sociologically the distinction is justified by a recognition of the need for differential treatment of juvenile offenders." James M Reinhardt in Fairchild (1955)

98.12 "In the most general sense, any behavior which, although prohibited by applicable statutory law in a given time and place, is regarded as less serious than behavior classifiable as crime usually appears as juvenile delinquency and, as such, denotes legal violations by children or youths, such violations consisting of behaviors which be punishable as crime if they were committed by adults sometimes used in a way which implies inclusion of violations— by children or youth— of all prevailing norms, whether or not such norms may be embodied in statutory law." Hoult (1969)

98.2 Usage of Terms in the Form of Chapter Headings

98.21 Terms used	*No. of authors*
Delinquency	5
Sociology of delinquency	1
Juvenile delinquency	1

98.22 Title of the major section of the textbook that includes a chapter on delinquency:

Title of the major section	*Author*	*Year*
Changing society	Wilkins	1970
Social disorganization and social deviation	Bertrand	1973
Social disorganization	Warren	1977
Social stability and control	O'Donnell	1985
Social disorganization and social problems	S Rao	1990

98.3 Provision in the LCSH

Delinquency the term is not used in the LCSH

Delinquents

UF Delinquent classes

BT Crime and criminals

NT Delinquent girls

Education and crime

Incorrigibles (juvenile delinquency)

Social work with delinquents and criminals -Education

98.4 Related terms used by Sociologists

RT Adolescence

Crime

Criminology

Delinquent area

Deviant behavior

Differential association

Pachuco

Gang

Labeling theory

Social problems

Sub-culture

99. POVERTY

99.1 Definition, Explanation

99.11 "The state of being (relatively) poor more specifically a situation in which a given presence's or family's plane of living, or a given group's level of living, seems to be below the standard of normal living of whatever community, is used as the basis of reference. Lack of goods and services enough to cause misery if not provided from the sources outside the channels of income considered normal for the given culture. Distinguished from dependency and pauperism." Thomas Dowes Elliott in Fairchild (1955)

99.12 "In the most general sense, a scarcity of the means of subsistence; more specifically, in any given society, a level of living that is below a particular minimum standard, such standards being relative to time and culture (one current suggestion being the idea that poverty in any given nation should be defined as the economic condition of a family having an income less than one-half the median family income for the nation)." Hoult (1969)

99.2 Usage of Terms in the Form of Chapter Headings

Terms used	*No. of authors*
Poverty	2
Poverty and social class	1
Poverty in America	1

Sherman (1979) enumerates poverty, and exploitation as the basic issues of sociology. Baldridge (1975) devotes his attention to poverty in the United States. Sharma (1968) provides a sequence of chapters as social disorganization, crime, unemployment, and poverty.

99.3 Provision in the LCSH 99.4 Related terms used by Sociologists

Poverty
UF Destitution
BT Evangelical Counsels
Wealth and wealth
RT Basic needs Human needs
Poor Poverty trap
Subsistence economy

RT Culture of poverty
Deprivation
Distribution of income
Relative deprivation

SA	subdivision Economic condition and social condition under names of countries e.g. India-Economic conditions, India-conditions Welfare state	Social engineering Social reform Social welfare policy Social Under class Unemployment

100. SOCIAL GERONTOLOGY

100.1 Definition, Explanation

100.11 "The intellectual discipline concerned with the systematic study of the social and psychological aspects of the aging process in man term suggested by C Tibbits to denote the specialty which concentrates on studying the changes of status and role- and the personal and social adjustments thereto - experienced by individuals who are undergoing the aging process in a given socio-cultural setting....; often simply referred to as gerontology." Hoult (1969)

AGING

100.12 "Current interest in aging and gerontology has been stimulated by the growing proportion of the aged in the population of industrialized societies and by the public concern with the aged as a social problem. ...Social gerontology is concerned with aging as:

1. a contingent process relating to the social and demographic structure of human groups;
2. as an aspect of personal status in the life cycle;
3. as the dynamic component of stratification in terms of generational membership;
4. as a contemporary social problem raising questions about exploitation, victimization and stigmatization."

Terms used	*No. of authors*	*Terms used*	*No. of authors*
Gerontology	1	Aging	1
Old age	1	Aged	1
Agism	1		

100.22 Title of the major section of the textbook that includes a chapter on aging or gerontology:

Title of the major section	*Author*	*Year*
Problem areas in contemporary society	Koller	1965
Applications of sociology	Sherman	1979
Social institutions	Wallace	1985
Social problems	S Rao	1990

100.3 Provision in the LCSH

Aged

Here and with local RT Age organization subdivision are entered works on Demographic transition the condition of the aged in Demography general and in particular places. Generation Works on the discipline of Health care systems gerontology are entered under Life cycle gerontology. Nuclear family

UF	Aging persons	RT	Old age
	Elderly persons	NT	Aging
	Old persons		Old age assistance
	Senior citizens		Social problems
BT	Adulthood		Sociology of medicine

100.4 Related Terms used by Sociologists

RT	Age organization	Life cycle
	Demographic transition	Nuclear family
	Demography	Old age assistance
	Generation	Social problems
	Health care systems	Sociology of medicine

4.4 Justification for Relative Placement

The arrangement of the main concepts of sociology has been made by considering a number of factors, like arrangement of the terms representing these concepts in textbooks, and the general tradition of their placement in relation to other concepts. As far as possible, the actual literature in the field of sociology has been used to reach an arrangement, so that the arrangement can be compared with that adopted in the existing information retrieval tools. The sections that follow explain the scope of each major category and all the 100 main concepts of sociology, and tries to explain their relationship with the categories and concepts placed immediately before and after them. The short note against each category and concept provides some of the broad considerations on the grounds of which the relative placement has been proposed.

4.41 RELATIVE PLACEMENT CRITERIA FOR 100 MAIN CONCEPTS

0. Sociology, History, Theories, and Research Methods

History, theories and methods constitute the basic background for understanding a discipline and its concepts. Most of the sociologists and some bibliographic information retrieval tools agree about the placement of these major categories in the beginning of any arrangement of the terms representing sociological concepts.

1. *Sociology/Scope:* In an arrangement of the main concepts of a subject, general aspects of the subject have to be dealt in the beginning. Some sociologists term these aspects as the perspectives, nature, or range of sociology. The section also includes how sociology differs from other disciplines in social sciences. Scope is also expressed in the form of terms like field, coverage, subject matter, boundaries etc.

2. *History of sociology:* When we discuss scope, it is not complete, unless history of the discipline is also traced. Scope emerges in the early developmental stages of a discipline and goes on changing continuously. We conceptualize the present status of a discipline by evaluating the contributions made by the 'masters' of the subject in its various developmental stages.

3. *Theories of Sociology:* History of a subject is the history of the theoretical development in it, as such, theories form part of the history of a subject. Timasheff writes "A science is mature if it has a solid foundation for the construction of theories. This solid foundation is a set of commonly accepted and well defined concepts, in terms of which the theories could be couched." [33] Selltiz *et al.* say "the intention of a theory in modern science is to summarize existing knowledge, to provide an explanation for observed events and relationships, and to predict the occurrence of as yet un-observed events and

relationships on the basis of explanatory principles embodied in theory." [34]

4-5. Research Methods/Scientific Method: An analysis of chapter headings shows that many authors make sociological theory and research methods a combined heading. Theories and methods are closely linked, as without the use a scientific method, neither the theories can be generalized nor their verification is possible.

I. Social Organization, Social Processes, Group Formation

The prerequisites of organization and basic forms of organization have been placed within this category. Some of the constituents of social organization are individual, personality biological, and sexual factors which shape the form of organization. Organization is manifested in the form of social processes, like social relations, interaction, and formation of groups and organizations. Out of 32 definitions of sociology examined in this study earlier, 11 authors mention organization, or social organization, 15 include society, 7 include social life, 14 include social relations, 17 include social interaction, and 9 include groups. Social organization encompasses all these concepts.

6. Social Organization: Social organization has been treated as a synonymous term to sociology by a number of sociologists and authors like Inkeles, Johnson, Charon, Durkheim, and others include social organization as the main factor in the study of sociology, while defining it. It is the broadest concept among sociological concepts and encompasses all other concepts which are generally included in the mainstream sociology. All those concepts of sociology, which can be grouped with some major categories like social institutions, education, culture, religion, social control and deviance, and social structure can be treated as forms of social organization in some form or the other. Thus, all these major categories follow social organization in the arrangement.

Hoult defines organization as "the totality of normatively regulated and patterned interrelationships among the sub-unit of a group." [35] Faris explains social organization as " it denotes a relatively stable set of functioning interrelations among component parts (persons or groups)... [36]

Organization includes process of organization, components of organization, factors that influence organization and some preliminary forms of organization like groups and associations. However, we study the individual groups and associations under 'social institutions'; 'cultural and religious groups'; and class groups and racial groups under 'social structure'.

7. Social system: For a large number of sociologists social system and social organization are synonymous terms. Some authors use it from the system point of view. It may not be possible to differentiate social system from social organization, but it is proper to provide a category for the literature appearing on society as a system. Parsons (*Social system,* 1951) uses social system for social organization or society. J McIntyre (1966) sees social system from the system point of view. Roland Robertson (1968) distinguishes social system from cultural system and personality system, and Hoult (1969) is of the opinion that the term is used synonymously with social organization.

8-9. Social Order: Society/Social Life Organization and system are a prerequisite for society, which is also termed as social life and social order. Various authors include, culture, social interaction, groups, etc. within society, but the term society, social life, social order still remain demarcated, as such, are deemed to a great extent synonymous, that even the LCSH has avoided these terms for being used as subject headings. Some authors use social order in the sense of social control also. C Arnold Anderson (1964) calls social order as patterns of regular structure occurring or resulting from human interaction.

10. Biological Determinism: Biological determinism has been defined as 'the biological basis of all forms of social behavior, including sexual... behavior.' (Gregory 1978). Hoult (1969) sums up the views of biological determinants that 'human behavior is basically a function of inborn physical characteristics'. Many authors prefer to use the term heredity in place of biological aspects. Heredity and environment are given equal importance in shaping the individual personality and resultant social organization.

11. Sexuality: The biological aspects of sexuality are a part of individual and his personality. Sexuality is seen as a psychobiological aspect of an individual's inherent instinct to propagate the generations to come, and this instinct takes the shape of family, the basic form of association and the beginning of social organization. Formation of pairs formation of family, and the customs regarding partner selection are a form of social organization and many a social institutions take shape to regulate biological sexuality.

12. *Individual:* Individual to individual interaction is the basis of social relations of all types called social processes. It is the psychological needs of the individual, which make to lead social life, as such individual is the basis of social organization, society and social life.

13. *Personality:* When we consider individual as a concept in social organization, we are mainly concerned with personality aspect, and that also in two ways. First, how personality is shaped within the social organization and culture of which he is a part, and second, how the psychological aspects of individual and his personality, form the basis of social interaction as well as, whole social organization.

14. *Attitude:* Attitude can be seen in two ways in sociological context. First, attitude of the individual which is a part of personality, and the second, the attitude of the group as a whole. Forms of social interaction mainly depends on the psychological make-up of the individuals. Out of the 87 textbook's contents classified, only one author has a chapter on social psychology. Other authors include these aspects within the headings like, attitudes, motivation, human nature, mass mind, motivational system etc. Attitude of the groups in various situations is to be placed with that category, like racial attitudes in race relations group attitudes in public opinion and group behavior related to conflict, in social disorganization.

15. *Social Processes:* Russell L Langworthy (1964) thinks, social processes denote social interaction. All forms of interaction are grouped under the broad category social processes, and these interactions are the basic requirement of any organized life called social organization.

16. *Social relations:* All social processes involve social interaction, but interaction is only one aspect of social relations. Non-interaction is also a relation, hence, social relations is a

broader term and precedes social interaction. For some authors, it is synonymous with social interaction, and they use either of the two terms. An observation of the aspects included within social relations by sociologists shows that they include groups, values, roles, association, deviance, social control and social inequality. Out of these aspects, deviance and social control are included by some authors within social interaction.

17. Social Interaction Some of the major aspects of social interaction are communication, cooperation, conflict, competition etc. Social interaction is also a broad concept, and groups, associations, family, role, culture, social control, disorganization, and social conflict are associated with social interaction.

18. Groups: Fairchild (1955) defines groups as 'persons between whom exists a psychic interaction' thus showing the relation of group with social interaction. Abercrombie (1984) defines groups as 'collectivities of individuals who interact and form social relationships.' Gisbert, Horton, Hebding, Goode, Eshleman, and Tischler include groups within social organization. MacIver, and Bertrand include it within social structures, Young within social relations, and Persell within social life.

19-20. Primary groups/Small groups: Hoult defines primary groups as 'members who maintain intimate, cooperative, and usually face to face relationships with one another.' Small groups and primary groups are treated by many as synonymous. Family is a primary group and play group can be called a small group, as an example.

21. Associations: Fairchild defines associations as 'fundamental relationship which unites individuals into groups', but MacIver says 'it is a group organized for the pursuit of an interest.' Hoult says 'association is defined as a general term inclusive of any group, organized to pursue a special interest.' Some authors, however, use associations and groups synonymously, while for others associations and institutions are synonymous.

Institutions

Many sociologists define sociology as the study of social institutions. Many a times, social organizations and institutions are used as synonymous terms. The category has been given the second highest significance by the textbook authors, which is only next to social organization. A number of categories shown separately after this section are also deemed a part of social institutions, but need to be enumerated separately for showing in a classified order, although most of the concepts used in sociology can be enumerated within social institutions.

22. *Social Institutions:* Social organization is a broader concept and social institutions are a part of it. Organization is visualized in the form of social institutions. Louis Schneider (1964) says 'institutions may be said in general, to represent the modus operandi of associations.' Organization is an abstract concept like social system, groups and associations, but these are seen in the form of social institutions like family, political institutions, and economic institutions, social structure and social control. Social institutions constitute most of the subject matter of sociology, that is why, most of the sociologists , while defining sociology, say it is he study of society or social system or social organization, and a major part of these are social institutions.

23. *Kinship:* Ely Chinoy (1967) says 'the family must be seen as part of a larger whole, the kinship system. The latter consists of a structure of roles and relationships based upon blood ties (consanguinity) and marriage (affinity) that bind men, women, and children into an organized whole.' Kinship involves rules of descent, succession, inheritance, marriage and family norms and behavior.

24. *Family:* Family is the basic multi-functional social institution. While discussing social institutions, kinship, family, and marriage is dealt first by most of the sociologists. In fact, family represents political, economic, cultural, and educational institutions in one, on a smaller scale. It also represents social structure and social control.

25. *Marriage:* Family system came into existence long before any social system. Marriage system evolved quite late chronologically. The system can be seen in two ways, first is to give stability to the family system, and the other to regulate sexual relations in the family.

26. *Political Institutions:* Political institutions are a larger

unit than the family and regulate and control most of the other type of social institutions.

27. Government: Many sociologists use the term government in place of political institutions. Among the political institutions, government is the first concept that is dealt by sociologists.

28. Formal Organizations: Formal organizations are also termed complex organization, 'Formal groups are found in complex organizations such as government bureaucracies, large business and industrial enterprises, military establishments and universities.'

29. Bureaucracy: Bureaucracy is a formal organization. It is defined as 'organization whose structure and operations are governed to a high degree by written rules'.

30. War: War is seen as conflict between nations, and the concept for it is international relations. Koller (1965) treats war among the 'problem areas in contemporary society.'

31. Economic Institutions: 'Economic system is . . . frequently used to denote the web of economic interaction controlled and regulated by institutions'—often termed one of the major institutionalized aspects of human society (the other aspects being the family, religion, education, and government).'

32. Capitalism: Defined as 'private ownership and control of the means of production (capital) and distribution', capitalism, can be described as the product of division of labor and industrialization.

33. Work: Analysis of textbook chapter headings in sociology shows that, some authors use the chapter headings as economic institutions and other use the term 'work'. It appears, by work they mean economic activity.

34. Division of labor: Division of labor denotes specialization, and task differentiation. Work organization in modern industrial societies is governed by division of labor.

35. Industrial Sociology: Industrial sociology is defined as 'social relationship in work situations'. It is also explained as the study of social structure of work organizations.

36. Leisure: Most of the sociology textbook authors prefer to make a combined chapter-heading as 'work and leisure'. Leisure includes within it, recreation, sports etc. It is considered as part of economic activities, as leisure activities are supposed to re-energize the work-force for increased production.

III. Culture, Religion, Social Control, and Education

In an arrangement of the major categories of sociology, social institutions include family, political and economic institutions, and also culture, religion, social control and education. Culture, religion, and education have been placed together, as culture and religion form a major part of education, education is deemed to be a form of acculturation and socialization, and religious beliefs are formed and molded very much, in the cultural and educational environment an individual gets. The level of education, cultural variation, and religious beliefs also contribute to social differentiation and inequality, which is a part of social structure. Education, culture and religion also play their part in social control. For example, out of the 87 textbooks examined to see the social institutions enumerated by these authors, 22 include religion, and 21 include education as a social institution. However, it is helpful to make a separate category for these, as both are closely related to culture also. Thus, this major category is placed immediately by the category on social institutions.

37. Culture: Tylor (1871) says 'Culture includes knowledge, belief, art, morals, law, customs and any other capabilities and habits acquired by man as a member of society' Thomas Ford includes values, norms, institutions, and artifacts within culture. Generally, social institutions, and social control are also treated as part of culture.

38. Customs: Customs are defined as 'socially prescribed mode of behavior, carried by tradition and enforced by social disapproval of its violation.' The concept of custom is related to culture and religion and also to deviance if violated norms are a part of customs.

39. Ideology: The aggregate of ideas, beliefs and modes of thinking, characteristic of a group' is termed ideology. Beliefs, attitudes, and opinion which form a set are called ideology. Ideology can be deemed a part of the theory of knowledge.

40. Magic: Magic and religion both are concerned with supernatural forces, and both are based on beliefs and practices.

Magic is treated as precursor to religious beliefs, thus associated with the animistic stage of belief in the supernatural.

41. *Sociology of Religion:* Sociology of religion is explained as 'the scientific study of the ways in which society, culture, and personality influence religion (as well as the ways in which religion affects society, culture and personality)'. Religion is also a factor when we consider it in the context of social control, socialization, regulation of behavior and social change.

42. *Social Control:* 'Social control refers to all constraints and patterns which generate discipline and social order, and is virtually synonymous with social organization' Socialization process, communication, social institutions, education, culture, religion, and morality, values, norms, custom, and public opinion, all are forms of social control, in addition to formal laws. Enforcement of discipline, sanctions and other types of regulation or behaviour in various forms is termed social control. Social control is patterned according to education, culture and religion in a society, and intensity of social control depends on the volume of deviance and disorganization prevalent in a social system.

43. *Values:* Social control has been used a broader section for values by the maximum number of sociologists, and most of them use the heading as values and norms. This shows the relation of values with social control and norms. Values are general standards whereas, norms are fairly precise rules for behavior,.

44. *Norms:* To understand the scope of norms, the scope of values also needs to be kept in mind. 'What the members would do, ought to do, are expected to do, under given circumstances, are norms. Norms induce conformity according to norms, members are expected to conform as such, norms are a form of social control. Most of the authors, associate norms with customs, and social control.

45. *Morality:* Morals are defined as 'norms that are observed on the basis of conscience. Textbook authors place morality within social control, or regulation of behavior. The concept is closely related to religion also, as such, most of the authors title their chapter headings as 'religion and morals.' LCSH uses social norms as the broader term for moral conditions.

46. Socialization: Most of the text books author associate socialization with personality, but it is more associated with acquisition of culture, and its various forms like, customs, norms, and values. It is also associated with family as the primary institution associated with socialization. Education treated as formation socialization, and socialization by family as non-formal. Socialization is related to sexuality also as a means of regulating it. Individual is prepared through socialization for an organized life called social organization.

47. Conformity: Thinking and doing according to the relevant prevailing values is conformity. Conforming behavior is regulated behavior and non-conforming behavior labeled as deviance. Conformity is also regarded as the success of socialization. In social psychology, conformity is associated with attitudes.

48. Deviance: 'Deviance is departure from culturally expected rules of conduct'. It is also called behavior which violates institutionalized expectations. Deviance is also explained as 'deviation from social rules or norms which carries disrepute, stigma or disapproval and which therefore, evokes attempted social control over it. Some sociologists call it 'socially prescribed departure from normality.' Thus, the concept of social control and deviance are closely inter-linked.

49. Sociology of Law: Sociology of law is defined as 'the study of how social conditions influence the making and enforcement of law.' Sociology of law also tries to see how the formal control in the form of law is a reflection of the informal controls of customs, values and norms. Sociology of law is also associated with the control of crime and social disorganization.

50. Communication: Communication is seen in the context of socialization and education and is a part of individual's interaction with others as an expression of social life. Culture and customs and other organized ways of life are communicated from generation to generation and from one individual to another, which give birth to social relations, social interaction, and social organization. It could well be treated a part of individual personality also, but it appears to be more appropriate with public opinion, education and culture.

50. A Symbolism: Symbols are a medium of communication,

thus related to cultural institutions and language. 'Use of emblems or expressive actions aids in the maintenance of the collective, by arousing responses which increase solidarity and cohesion', solidarity and cohesion being part of organization and also of culture.

51. Public Opinion: Public opinion in the sociological context is concerned with its impact on individual's decision for a particular action, when it acts as the regulation of behavior. Individual behavior is shaped, or postponed for fear of public opinion. All these factors suggest that public opinion forms a part of social control as far as its use in sociology is concerned.

52. Sociology of Education: 'The process of education is thought of sociologically as the transmission of culture, with its elements of preservation, dissemination and innovation.' It is also described as 'the acculturation of the newer and/or younger members of society by the elder.' Education is seen sociologically as 'social control to achieve better personality development.'

53. Sociology of Knowledge: 'Sociology of knowledge is concerned with the way in which systems of thought . . . are conditioned by other social facts'.

54. Sociology of Art: Sociology of art involves the 'development of a methodology for the study of the institutions and practices of cultural production.'

55. Sociology of Science and Technology: Science and technology has been associated in most sociological works to education, culture, knowledge, and sometimes seen in contrast to religious beliefs. It is also seen from the point of view of its impact on socio-economic changes. 'Attitude, and policies of government, business, education, and religion determine the level of support of scientific work. Meanwhile developments drastically modify all other institutions.' Scientific and technological change is seen from the sociological point of view with special reference to cooperation, division of labor, social classes, alienation, and urbanization.

IV. Social Structure, Stratification, Race

Organization of the constituents of society into a hierarchical pattern is termed as social structure, but sociologists are not unanimous about the scope and appropriate usage. Some of them have included organization, institutions, stratification, social control and even conflict within it. To some extent, deviance, disorganization, and conflict are also deemed to be manifestations of dissatisfaction by individuals or groups, with the existing social structure of differentiation and inequality. Culture, religion and education also contribute in creating hierarchical or differentiating structures and social control in various forms is the vehicle for maintaining the status quo. Keeping these points in view, social structure has been placed in between education, culture, and religion on the one side, and social conflict and disorganization on the other. Social structure is deemed by many , as the initiator of social change and progress also, hence the category also follows these sections.

57. *Social Structure:* Not many sociologists agree on the scope and exact meaning of the term social structure in sociology. In defining it, they show its relation with occupations, offices, inequality, classes, age and sex distributions, roles, norms and values, elites, and patterns of social conflict. The concept is treated so broadly by many sociologists that even social organization, social order, social system, formal and informal organizations and institutions are also included as part of social structure. The LCSH uses social structure for social organization. Culture, religion and social control are deemed to maintain stability in the social structure, and disequilibrium is termed disorganization, conflict etc.

58. *Social Differentiation:* Non-hierarchical differences among the populations such as ethnic, religious, and linguistic are termed social differentiation. But many sociologists use social differentiation and social stratification interchangeably. Parsons and Stewart show social structure as a part of social differentiation.

59. *Social Inequality:* Social inequality is explained as 'differences in social prestige, based chiefly on differences in family backgrounds, social conventions, wealth, income, political influence, education, manners and morals' These, parent to child transmissible attributes make diverse social groupings in society, to possess 'differing degrees of social power, privilege, and influence.'

60. Social Stratification: Social stratification is hierarchical ranking in terms of power, privilege, and prestige. Three major types of stratification generally identified are: class, estate, and caste. LCSH uses social classes for social stratification. Decimal classification also treats stratification as a sub-heading of social classes.

61. Social Classes: Social classes are identified on the basis of power, income, wealth, prestige, occupational prestige, style of life, and educational level. 'A social class may include members of different ethnic groups, and an ethnic group may include members of different social classes.' A majority of the textbook authors use the heading 'stratification: class, status, power', but many others make it a sub-heading of special organization or social inequality . LCSH makes it a sub-heading of social status.

62. Caste: Caste is defined as the 'segmental division of society into distinct groups with membership determined by birth.' It is a form of social stratification, and social classes are formed on the basis of caste. LCSH treats caste a part of manners and customs.

63. Social Status: 'Some of the criteria by which status is judged are, leadership, dominance, ability and accomplishment, occupation, or other means of recognition designated by title, degree, membership, dress, behavior, or other devices for securing attention'. It is also explained as denoting 'the power, authority, rights and obligations associated with prestige'.

64. Role: 'A social role is the expected behavior associated with a social position.' Roles are bundles of socially defined attributes and expectations associated with social positions. Social status decides the role, and most of the sociologists use these terms together as status and role. Role is also associated with social control, as each individual abides by the role of his position, and 'it demonstrates how individual activity is socially influenced and thus follows regular patterns.'

65-66. Power/Authority: Not many explanations are available as to whether, authority bestows power or power bestows authority. Bureaucracy exhibits power and authority as the executive wing of the government. Power and authority are mainly discussed in the context of status and role as part of social structure.

67. *Leadership:* Leadership is associated with groups, elites, authority, decision making, power, status and role. Many authors prefer to associate the concept of leadership with social psychological aspects only. Some other see it in the form of role of the individual in the group. Leadership defines the role and status of a person as such it would be appropriate to place it within social structure.

68. *Social mobility:* A concept used in the sociological investigation of inequality, social mobility refers to the movement of individuals between different levels of social hierarchy, usually defined occupationally'. It is also explained as 'movement within the system of social stratification'.

69. *Sociology of Gender:* 'Sociology of gender considers the ways in which the physical differences between men and women are delineated by culture and social structure'. The discrimination or differentiation against men or women purely on grounds of gender, is the subject mater of sociology of gender. It is also expressed as sex roles and gender roles, sexism, and sexual divisions.

70. *Sociology of Occupations:* Sociology of occupations relates to the 'studies dealing with the problem of how occupational structure and particular occupations articulate with other aspects of society, like family, the economy, the educational system and social stratification.

71. *Racial Groups:* 'A biological subdivision, based upon similarity of ancestry and consequent physical kinship' or 'a group of organism all descended from a single ancestor, or pair of ancestors' is called a racial group. It is also explained as 'classification of living homo-sapiens on the grounds of morphological traits, such as skin color, hair from and body size'. Many sociologists consider race differences as a part of social inequality. Sociologists provide a heading as race or racial groups in their textbooks, but race, as such is not the main concern of sociologists, instead they are mainly concerned with the impact of racial differences on social organization, and race relations.

72. *Race relations:* 'Race and minority relations is the study of social contact, conflict, and accommodation among racial, national, religious, and language groups with particular

reference to prejudice and discrimination, and other causes and consequences.' Race relations is also treated by some sociologists as a social problem.

73. Ethnic Groups: 'A primary basis for differentiation between ethnic groups can be either cultural or physical, such as skin pigmentation, and body shape or both'. Other criteria on which ethnic groups are classified are religion or linguistic groups, national or geographic origin etc.

74. Minorities: 'A minority is a group, regardless of where it is, on the class ladder, faces barriers to the pursuit of life's values.' 'A group is minority group if it is the object of prejudice and discrimination for the dominant group.' The term is often used as a synonym for ethnic, racial, and religious groups.'

V. Social Conflict, Disorganization

The mechanism of social control is created and enlarged to contain or eliminate disorganization, deviance, and conflict. Conflict, and disorganization are also treated as precursor to social change, revolution and progress. Social disorganizations is included as a social problems by some sociologists, but generally these are not placed within this category of disorganization, for the simple reason that, while social disorganization is one of the major concerns of sociologists, social problems is not.

75. Social conflict: Social disorganization may be reflected in various forms and one of these is social conflict. Wars, revolutions, strikes, uprisings, struggle, tension, and stress in social system are grouped under the broad term social conflict. Like social disorganization, some sociologists place social conflict under the major heading 'social problem' also.

76. Social Disorganization: 'Disruption in a community's established social relationship' or 'any disturbance, disruption, conflict, or lack of consensus within a social group' is termed as social disorganization. 'Often called as an implicit or explicit cause of delinquency, crime, and other forms of pathology.' social disorganization leads to drunkenness, crime, cruelty, and the breakdown of stable family life'. The term is used synonymously with social pathology or social problems. While social disorganization is one of the major concerns of the sociologists, social problems are of marginal interest to them.

77. Revolution: 'Revolution is generally associated with political revolution, but in sociological context it is defined 'a relatively complete and usually sudden change in a total system, especially a social system or in some major part of such a system.' Sometimes used for sudden political changes only, but usually taken to be change in a total system. Occasionally war is associated with revolution and made a broader concept to it, as done in LCSH.

78. Crowd: 'Crowd is a general term inclusive of all human aggregations such as the audience, mob, public, social movement, and unorganized masses.' Crowd and collective behavior are used sometimes interchangeably.

79. Collective Behavior: Collective behavior is expressed in the form of crazes, fads, panics, mobs, riots and revolutions. It is also explained as 'mobilization of a mass of people to change the general structure of society. Crowd behavior is seen from the point of view of social psychology, social action, and social change.

80. Social Movements: Social movements are a form of collective behavior. In it 'the effort is directed at modifying, maintaining, replacing, or destroying an existing social institution.' It is also explained as 'collective enterprises to establish a new order of life.' Social movements may result in disorganization, conflict or bring change and progress. It is also associated with change in religious beliefs and practices, revolution, and also as a part of social problems and social planning.

VI. Social Change

Social change may involve change in any aspect of the social system, like change in social institutions, change in social structure, or change in social control. Cultural change is sometimes mentioned separately from other changes, and if both are to be mentioned together, the term socio-cultural change is preferred.

81. Social Change: 'Social change involves an observed difference from antecedent states of the social structure, institutions, habits or equipment of a society, social relationship or in culture.' Thus, social change may involve, change in any major aspect of organization, culture, institutions etc., but it is directly related to progress, social planning, social control, disorganization, conflict, and social movements.

82. Evolution: 'Evolution is change, but not necessarily for the better, or even increase in complexity.' It may be regarded a change which is 'cumulative, or irreversible, rather than repetitive.' Conceived to be more or less analogous to that of biological evolution: i.e. variation, struggle for existence, selection and adaptation.

83. Social Progress: 'Progress is a change in the desired direction change that produces a condition or a phenomenon defined as an improvement over a previous condition or phenomenon.' Progress is also associated with civilization, industrialization and urbanization. It may be considered in the context of social planning also.

VII. Human Ecology and Communities

Human ecology affects almost all other aspects of social organization. This major category of sociology is neither a part of organization, institutions, social structure, social control or even disorganization. However, to some extent, it is associated by sociologists with social problems and also with social disorganization and conflict. Human ecology, and urbanization, bring changes in cultural values, religious beliefs, and also may be responsible for deviance, crime and delinquency. Keeping these points in view, the major category on applied sociology and social problems, follows later.

84. Human Ecology: Human ecology is the 'study of relations between human groups (or populations) and their environments.' It is 'concerned with spatial aspects of human life . . . effect of competition and cooperative processes on the distribution and organization of physical phenomena, such as neighborhoods, streets, shopping areas, churches, and the like.' Some textbook authors like Gisbert, Tischler, and Wallace treat human ecology as a part of social change. Some sociologists associate it with population by making a combined chapter heading as 'population and environment'.

85. *Environment:* 'All the external conditions, physical and socio-cultural, which can influence an individual or group' is considered as environment. Sociologists study environment in the context of human ecology, and this aspect includes socio-cultural and man-made environment, like urban growth, industrialization, and social conflict resulting in deviance, alienation and crime etc.

86. *Geographic Environment:* Geographical factors that influence human social organization and institutions, as well as social behavior is included in the geographic environment. It is regarded as one of the three main factors which shape a particular society, other being biological and demographic factors.

87. *Medical Sociology:* Some of the major concerns of medical sociology are the study of 'medical institutions and health service organizations.' It also concentrates its attention on 'sociology of doctor-patient interaction' and 'development of alternative accounts of the causes, form and nature of sickness in society.' For these reasons, medical sociology has direct relation with human ecology, and population (including social factors in fertility and mortality).

88. *Community:* Community is identified by a geographical or territorial area, common culture, and face to face relationships among members. In individual gets the environment of the community he is socialized. This environment differs from community to community. Each community has a specific type of social organization, which is the result of spatial human settlements.

89. *Rural Sociology:* Rural sociology is 'concerned with... human life in rural areas and with the ruralization process.' It is also termed as rural community studies, village community, folk community, and also peasants and farmers study.

90. *Urbanization:* 'Growth in the population of a country's population living in urban centers' and the consequent 'increasing secondary group relationships, voluntary associations, a plurality of norms....(and) increasing secularization and segmentary roles' is called urbanization. In the recent literature in sociology, urbanization is deemed as a part of social change. Urbanization includes urban growth and its social consequences.

91. Urban Sociology: Urban sociology is best described as 'human interaction in urban communities' and also as 'urban aspects of man's social life'. It is also called study of urban communities. Urban growth and its regulation is also studied by geographical point of view, and city planning point of view, but human interaction and the development of new type of social structure, and norms and values, quite different from rural societies is the concern of sociologists only.

VIII. Population

Population studies although now a separate discipline, it could be treated as part of human ecology, and also seen by many sociologists as social problem, as such, this category is placed in-between these two major categories.

92. Population: 'Population studies are concerned with the relationship between population changes and other variables—social, economic, political, biological, genetic, geographical and the like'. A majority of the sociologists deal with population as a part of social change and also of human ecology. Textbook authors generally place human ecology and population together and use the chapter headings like 'ecology and population' or 'demography and ecology' etc.

93. Migration: Migration 'denotes geographical movement of relatively settled people', in this way, it is the concern of population geographers also. Political scientists are interested in the political migration and the problem of refugees, invasion, conquest, colonization and immigration. Sociologists are interested in the causes and consequences of migration, problems of assimilation, the question of minorities in the place of settlement, and social adjustment of immigrants. Population experts are interested in migration as far as it affects the balance of population in some areas and concentration in some others. migration

IX. Applied Sociology, Social Problems

Sociologist's concern is limited to- how social problems are designated under what type of social conditions social problems arise how social systems deal with social problems and not the problems themselves or the ways of their solution. A number of social problems are associated with and enumerated under various major categories- like social inequality and race relations within social structure. Some sociologists however, would prefer these aspects of sociology within social problems. It appears for want of some agreement on the interest of sociologists about the status of social problems in sociology, the concept is always relegated to the position of last section in the sociology textbooks and given meager space, as seen in the present study that only 11 out of 87 textbooks seen, taken for the study have a chapter on social problems.

94. *Applied Sociology:* Use of sociological generalizations to assist in the solution of social problems is the field of study, called applied sociology. It may be an instrument of either social reform or social engineering. Applied sociology uses sociological generalizations to deal with the problems of social disorganization, deviant behavior and social conflict. It also helps in framing social policies and social planning.

95. *Social Planning:* Social planning is associated with social control, social policy and social change. It is explained as ' projecting order upon human relationships'. Social planning is also termed social engineering, and is associated with welfare economics, welfare state, urban policy, social legislation, population policy, state planning, and social innovation etc.

96. *Social Problems:* 'Social problems' is explained as the 'sociological specialty concerned with the study of problem areas as crime, war, disease, poverty, race relations.' Some sociologists define it as 'disapproved deviant behavior in each institution'. But the recent view is that 'the field has largely abandoned the attempt to explain deviant behavior and social disorganization. Rather it is attempting to explain how society through an essentially political process, discovers and invents its social problems'. Sociologists generally treat social problems as a part of social change, social disorganization or applied sociology.

97. *Crime:* Deviance is related to crime on account of the fact that, any 'departure from culturally expected rules of conduct is deviance, but it is not a crime unless it is prohibited by applicable statutory law'. The concept of crime is closely related to social control and also to social dis-organization and conflict.

98. Delinquency: Violation of law by children and youth is termed delinquency, and is treated as deviance. The violation of law in this case is 'regarded as less serious than behavior classifiable as crime.' Delinquency is also associated with social disorganization. Like crime, it is also placed by some sociologists under the major section social problems.

99. Poverty: Explained as 'scarcity of the means of subsistence' poverty, is related to wealth. Possession of wealth is prosperity, and non-possession by an individual or society is termed poverty. Some sociologists would like to include within social inequality but it would be appropriate to place it with social problems, as it is the context in which sociologists like to see the concept.

100. Social Gerontology: Social gerontology is the study of the social and psychological aspects of the aging process in man, and the personal and social adjustment problems experienced by the aged, such as exploitation, victimization and stigmatization. It is also considered as one of the social problems and also an an aspect of applications of sociology.

4.5 Relative Significance Categorization

Collection of terms provided in 8 dictionaries of sociology/ social sciences enabled to get about 5000 terms, but it is not possible to include all the terms used in a discipline, in any information retrieval tool. As such, the designers of information retrieval tools are required to identify some concepts of each discipline, that need to be included as major categories or main headings in these tools. This identification also ensures that no significant concept remains un-included in the information retrieval tools. In the present study, main concepts of sociology were identified on the basis of the terms used for them in the chapter headings by at least three authors. This enabled to obtain a list of 100 main concepts used in sociology. But even in this case, it may be required to identify some concepts that can be adopted as main headings and others that can be accommodated as subordinate headings according to their importance as heading. As such, it was felt necessary to devise a method, through some concepts could be identified as relatively more significant than others. The second objective of this identification was to evaluate some of the existing bibliographic information retrieval tools, with regard to the provision in them, for some relatively more significant concepts of sociology.

While classifying the chapter headings used in 87 textbooks, it was observed that some concepts are used by up to sixty authors, while others by only three. Treating the terms or their synonyms used by only a few authors , equivalent to the terms or their synonyms used by even up to 60 authors, was felt improper. In the same way merely counting the number of authors having a chapter on a concept, and deciding its significance on this basis was also was not found appropriate. In this case, an author devoting one/fifth (1/5) part of his textbook to a concept and another having devoted one thirtieth (1/30) part of his book to the concept would have been counted equal. Thus, merely counting the number of authors having a chapter on a concept was adjudged a crude method to decide the popularity or significance of that concept, among sociology textbook authors, and it was decided to take into account the proportion of the textbook, that has been devoted to a concept by all the authors under consideration.

4.51 Explanation of Some Terms Used

Categories: Broad areas/ specialties/fields of studies having an independent status within sociology, and also include one or more sub-areas or individual concepts within it. It may not be possible to delineate the exact number of categories within a subject, however, for purposes of the present study, main concepts of sociology have been arranged into 10 sections containing 27 categories, e.g. social organization, social institutions, social structure, social change etc.

Main concepts: Concepts dealt in the chapter headings of 87 introductory textbooks of sociology, on which at least three authors had devoted a chapter heading. All synonymous terms used for a concept by various authors were grouped together to identify 100 main concepts dealt in all the chapter headings.

Relative Significance: Each one of the 100 concepts has been given a significance value, based on the proportion of chapter headings devoted to a concept in 87 books. All these concepts have been grouped into three categories according to this proportion and termed as 'relative significance categories'.

Core Concepts: The most significant concepts of sociology, which have been given highest cumulative importance by 87 authors. When one hundred main concepts were arranged in descending order of this significance, the concepts with highest value appear on top of the list, and have been termed as 'core concepts '. Although the list could be extended to any extent in the decreasing order, in the present study 50 out of 100 main concepts are being treated as 'core', to evaluate their representation in some BIRTs in the field of sociology.

4.52 Identification of Main Concepts

Concepts discussed in the form of chapter headings adopted in eighty-seven textbooks of sociology, published between 1939 and 1990 were classified according to the most substantive terms contained in them. Terms for the concepts on which at least three authors had devoted a chapter heading or part of it, in the textbook, authored by them were taken into consideration. As every author tries to provide the best and the most significant term as heading for the material he is presenting in the chapters of the books authored by him, the terms used by such a large number of authors can be treated to represent the most significant concepts of sociology. Why chapter headings of the textbooks were considered a better alternative to identify the main concepts, and on what basis these concepts were arranged in a filiatory and helpful sequence within ten major sections is explained elsewhere. (3)

4.53 Method used for Categorization of Main Concepts

Out of one hundred concepts identified from the terms used in the chapter headings adopted in the eighty-seven textbooks, it was observed that, while terms representing some concepts were used as chapter headings by up to 60 authors, on the other hand, even only three authors adopted some other terms as headings. As such, it was deemed appropriate, to categorize these concepts according to the number of authors having a chapter on it, as well as, the total number of chapter headings devoted to a concept, out of all these books. To obtain the proportionate value for each concept, the data on chapter headings was tabulated in the following format:

Table 4.88
Sample data sheet on 'Social differentiation'

58. Social Differentiation

Sl. No.	*Year*	*Title of Chapter Heading*	*Author Chapter no./ Total chapters*
1.	1957	Social Differentiation	Bierstedt 5/6
2.	1959	Social differentiation and Stratification	* Merton 19/26
3.	1962	Differentiation and Leadership	* Young 25/26
4.	1965	Differentiation and variation in Social structures*	Parsons 2/5
5.	1971	Social Differentiation	Sergeant 2/6
6.	1976	Social Differentiation	Hebding 4/5
7.	1976	Differences within Societies	Stewart 2/5
8.	1983	Social differentiation and Stratification *	Eshleman 8/20
9.	1985	Social Differentiation	O'Donnell 4/9
10.	1990	Social Differentiation and Stratification*	S. Rao 13/30

Note: Headings containing more than one concept have been marked with a star (*) and included in the data sheet of the Respective concepts also. As such, only half proportion of the chapter is being counted for 'social differentiation' here.

The chapter headings on a concept arranged in the above format can be interpreted in the following way:

1. Out of 87 textbooks seen, only 10 have a chapter on social differentiation;

2. Out of 10 authors, 6 make the concept, heading of a major section, thus dividing it into further chapters (shown in bold above);

3. The chapter heading number one above, is the 5th major section in the textbook by Bierstedt, published in 1967 and one sixth (1/6) part of the book is devoted to the concept of 'social differentiation';

4. Some headings that include more than one concept together in a heading indicate the preference of these authors for keeping the concept of social differentiation with, stratification, social structure, and leadership;

5. Out of 10 authors, 7 use the term 'Social differentiation', 2 use 'Differentiation' and one uses ' Differences within societies';

6. The total proportion of books devoted to the concept 'Social differentiation' is 1.0253 (1/6+ 1/52+ 1/10+ 1/6+ 1/5+ 1/5+ 1/40+ 1/9+ 1/60) out of total proportion of all chapter headings for all concepts in the 87 books, that is 114.3602, implying that 0.8966 per cent of the headings in the 87 textbooks of sociology have been used for 'social differentiation'; and

7. We can infer that out of total chapter headings in the 87 textbooks of sociology, social differentiation has been given the significance of 1.0253 and all the concepts can be categorized according to these values representing the views of a large number of sociologists.

4.54 Arrangement in Descending Order of Significance

Arrangement of main concepts of sociology in a descending order of relative significance, provides a better picture for viewing them in relation to each other from the significance point of view. However, the arrangement on the basis of these values is tentative and suggestive only, as it is nearly impossible to see concepts in a quantifiable form. Moreover, a number of terms could be regrouped and the values combined together on account of the use of synonymous terms by the authors. To explain it further, some authors use the term 'racial groups' and others 'race relations', which are shown in table 3 separately. If the significance values of both of these terms is clubbed together, the concept of 'race and race race relations' will gain higher rank among other concepts of sociology, according to the significance value. However, such clubbing can be done only by rearranging all the chapter headings containing both of these terms in one sequence, from the data available separately and shown in the appendix, and clubbing of significance values presented in the table 2 will not provide the exact rank of this concept, as such it is not recommended.

4.55 Implications of Significance Categorization

Bibliographic information storage and retrieval tools are required to represent the concepts of individual discipline or a field of knowledge to the best extent possible, but it becomes difficult to include all the concepts in the form of terms representing them in the subject-specific schedule itself. As such, categorization of concepts into significance level groups, enables to identify, those core concepts of a discipline, that need to be included invariably in the discipline-specific schedule. With this categorization, most of the core concepts of sociology, automatically fall in the first category and only a few in the second category. The categorization implies that, no bibliographic information retrieval tool, that deals with sociology, is complete, unless it includes all the core concepts of sociology in the form of some terms in the sociology schedule itself. Some concepts showing lower significance values can be shown within some main categories as sub-headings. If the subject-specific schedule is required to be made very brief, as in the case of Colon Classification, concepts falling in the lower significance categories in sociology, can be shown in the schedules of the respective subjects and used in sociology, through subject device, if required.

Relative Significance

Sl. No.	*Sociological concepts*	*Relative Significance*	*Sl. No.*	*Sociological concepts*	*Relative Significance*
1	2	3	1	2	3
1.	Social change	9.0708	53.	Attitudes	0.5638
2.	Social institutions	5.5380	54.	Norms	0.5505
3.	Culture	4.9952	55.	Biological determinism	0.5428
4.	Social organization	4.7906	56.	Social order	0.5243
5.	Socialization	7.7337	57.	Ethnic groups	0.4977
6.	Family	3.2195	58.	Social mobility	0.4865
7.	Population	3.0431	59.	Sociology of law	0.4856
8.	Sociology/ Scope	3.0277	60.	Scientific method	0.4699
9.	Political institutions	2.9881	61.	Kinship	0.4660
10.	Social stratification	2.9682	62.	Small groups	0.4625
11.	Sociology of education	2.8657	63.	Government	0.4525
12.	Sociology of religion	2.7768	64.	Sociology of work	0.4492
13.	Groups	2.7087	65	Environment	0.4181
14/15	Individual/Personality	2.6977	66.	Social system	0.4160

16.	Research methods	2.6350	67.	Medical sociology	0.3994
17.	Social control	2.3428	68.	Crowd	0.3564
18.	Economic institutions	2.3235	69.	Role	0.3514
19.	Social structure	2.1703	70.	Social planning	0.3359
20.	Deviance	2.1384	71.	Industrialization	0.3161
21.	Society/ Social life	1.9610	72	Leisure	0.3074
22.	Collective behavior	1.9044	73.	Values	0.2982
23.	Social interaction	1.8078	74.	Industrial sociology	0.2977
24.	Community	1.6993	75.	Customs	0.2931
25.	Human ecology	1.6740	76	Conformity	0.2804
26/27	Urban sociol./Urbaniz	1.5310	77.	Public opinion	0.2787
28.	Theories of sociology	1.5087	78	Rural sociology	0.2728
29.	Social inequality	1.4898	79.	Sociology of art	0.2455
31.	Social relations	1.1410	80.	Sociol. of occupations	0.2424
32.	Race relations	1.0559	81.	Evolution	0.2323
33.	Social differentiation	1.0253	82.	Geographic environment	0.2320
34.	Communication	0.9487	83.	Capitalism	0.2186
35.	Racial groups	0.9153	84.	Social gerontology	0.2171
36.	Social classes	0.9125	85.	Revolution	0.2081
37.	Power	0.8614	86.	Poverty	0.2068
38.	Minorities	0.8391	87.	Delinquency	0.1986
39.	Social status	0.8382	88.	Ideology	0.1867
40.	History of sociology	0.8310	89.	Primary groups	0.1744
41.	Social problems	0.8299	90.	Migration	0.1734
42.	Social movements	0.7419	91.	Sociology of war	0.1723
43.	Social conflict	0.7417	92.	Sociology of knowledge	0.1686
44.	Science, technology	0.7316	93.	Division of labor	0.1560
45.	Formal Organizations	0.6928	94.	Sexuality	0.1542
46.	Association	0.6832	95.	Progress	0.1313
47.	Crime	0.6522	96.	Morality	0.1097
48.	Social disorganization	0.6262	97.	Leadership	0.0959
49.	Applied sociology	0.6161	98.	Authority	0.0939
50.	Bureaucracy	0.5823	99.	Caste	0.0902
51.	Marriage	0.5757	100.	Magic	0.0875
52.	Sociology of gender	0.5698			

Note: 1. NA = not available in the sociology schedule.

2. Class numbers within brackets indicate the availability of the term in the scope note or in other than sociology schedule.

4.6 Distribution into Relative Significance Categories

Table 2 shows one hundred main concepts of sociology, arranged in a filiatory order, as well as grouped into three relative significance categories, while retaining them within 10 major sections of sociology. The number of authors using the concept as chapter heading and the proportion of chapter headingsdevoted to a concept is shown against each concept. The categories adopted are: 1. concepts of highest relativesignificance; 2. medium significance; and 3. lower significancein sociology. The table also indicates that, in case of a large number of concepts, although higher number of authors have a chapter heading on them, but the net proportion of all the textbooks devoted to the concept is proportionately notsignificant. The fact justifies, taking the cumulative proportion of the books devoted to a concept is a better measure than merely counting the number of authors, having a chapter on that concept, although the former automatically takes into account, the latter also. The relative significance value for each concept, fall within a range between highest 8.0708 (for social change) and lowest 0.0875 (for magic) among 100 main concepts of sociology. Distribution of 100 main concepts into three 'level-of-significance' categories enables to draw these conclusions:

1. Almost all the core concepts of sociology fall in the firstcategory, having a significance value in the range between8.0708 and 0.7316;

2. The second category contains the concepts with a value rangebetween 0.6928 and 0.3074. This category has mixed type ofconcepts, some core concepts with slightly less significantvalues, and some concepts of allied disciplines, also studiedin sociology, but can not be called the core concepts ofsociology;

3. Sociological concepts falling in the third category, with asignificance value of less than 0.3, mostly appear to be themain concepts of other disciplines, but indicatesociologist's interest in them. The concepts also indicate aneffort tc give sociological explanation to the main conceptsof allied disciplines; and

4. The concepts which appear to be the main concepts of other disciplines, and appear to be among the main concepts of sociology also, automatically fall in the second and the third category of relatively significant concepts.

Table 4.90

100 Main Concepts in Classified Order Grouped into three Relative Significance Categories

Significance Level Categories											
I Category : above 0.7				II Category : between 0.3 to 0.7				III Category : Below 0.3			
Sl. No.	Concept	No. of Authors	Significance	Sl. No.	Concept	No. of Authors	Significance	Sl. No.	Concept	No. of Authors	Significance
1	2	3	4	5	6	7	8	9	10	11	12
01	**Sociology, History, Theories, Research methods**										
1.	Sociology/scope	22/17	3.0277								
2.	History of Sociology	8	0.8310								
3.	Theories of Sociology	17	1.5087								
4.	Research Methods	34	2.6350	5.	Scientific Method	8	0.4699				
I.	**Social organisation, social process, group formation**										
6.	Social Organisation	31	4.7906	7.	Social System	3	0.4160				
				8.	Social Order	9	0.5243				
9.	Society/ Social Life	22	1.9610	10.	Socio-biology	12	0.5428	11.	Sexuality	5	0.1542
12.	Individual/13.Personality	29.	2.6977	14.	Attitudes	6	0.5638				
15.	Social Processes	14	1.4594								
16.	Social Relation	12	1.1410								
17.	Social Interaction	24	1.8078								
18.	Groups	36	2.7087					19.	Primary Groups	4	0.1744
				20.	Small Groups	8	0.4625				
				21.	Associations	11	0.6832				
II.	**Social institutions, Family, Political, Economic, Institutions**										
22.	Social Institutions	45	5.5380	23.	Kinship	9	0.4660				
24.	Family	60	3.2195	25.	Marriage	18	0.5757				
26.	Political Institutions	47	2.9881	27.	Government	10	0.4525				
				28.	Formal Organizations	13	0.6928				
				29.	Bureaucracy	12	0.5823	30.	War	4	0.1723

1	2	3	4	5	6	7	8	9	10	11	12
31.	Economic Institutions	39	2.3235					32.	Capitalism	4	0.2186
				33.	Work	10	0.4492	34.	Division of Labour	3	0.1560
								35.	Industrial Sociology	5	0.2977
				36.	Leisure	7	0.3074				
III.	**Culture, Religion, Social Control, Education**										
37.	Culture	58	4.9952					38.	Customs	5	0.2931
								39.	Ideology	4	0.1967
								40.	Magic	3	0.0875
41.	Sociology of Religion	48	2.7768								
42.	Social Control	39	2.3428					43.	Values	10	0.2982
				44.	Norms	14	0.5505	45.	Morality	5	0.1097
46.	Socialization	50	3.7337					47.	Conformity	11	0.2804
48.	Deviance	46	2.1384	49.	Sociology of Law	10	0.4856				
50.	Communication	16	0.9487					51.	Public Opinion	6	0.2787
52.	Sociology of Education	48	2.8657					53.	Social of Knowledge	3	0.1686
								54.	Sociology of Art	5	0.2455
55.	Science and Technology	19	0.7316	56.	Industrialization	8	0.3161				
IV.	Social Structure, Stratification, Race										
57.	Social Structure	23	2.1703								
58.	Social Differentiation	10	1.0253								
59.	Social Inequality	13	1.4898								
60.	Social Stratification	51	2.9682								
61.	Social Classes	31	0.9125					62.	Caste	4	0.0902
63.	Social Status	15	0.8382	64.	Role	17	0.3514				
65.	Power	20	0.8614					66.	Authority	4	0.0939
				67.	Leadership	3	0.0959				
				68.	Social Mobility	13	0.4865				
				69.	Sociology of Gender	16	0.5698	70.	Occupation	4	0.2424

1	2	3	4	5	6	7	8	9	10	11	12
71.	Racial Groups	17	0.9153								
72.	Race Relations	25	1.0559	73.	Ethnic Group	10	0.4977				
74.	Minorities	22.	0.8391								
V.	**Social Disorganization, Conflict**										
75.	Social Conflict	9	0.7417	76.	Social Disorg.	11	0.6262				
								77.	Revolution	4	0.2081
				78.	Crowd	6	0.3564				
79.	Collective Behavior	26	1.9044								
80.	Social Movements	16	0.7419								
VI.	**Social Change**										
81.	Social Change	58	8.0708					82.	Evolution	5	0.2323
								83.	Progress	7	0.1313
VII.	**Human Ecology, Communities**										
84.	Human Ecology	22	1.6740	85.	Environment	10	0.4181	86.	Geographic Environ.	5	0.2320
				87.	Medical Sociology	7	0.3994				
88.	Community	26	1.6993					89.	Rural Sociology	7	0.2728
90.	Urbanization/										
91.	Urba Sociology	28	1.5310								
VIII.	Population										
92.	Population	46	3.0431					93.	Migration	4	0.1734
IX.	**Applied Sociology, Social Problems**										
				94.	Applied Sociology	7	0.6131				
				95.	Social Planning	7	0.3359				
96.	Social Problems	12	0.8299	97.	Crime	14	0.6522	98.	Delinquency	8	0.1986
								99.	Poverty	4	0.2068
								100.	Sociology of aging	5	0.2171
Total		44	92.4827			28	13.8473			28	5.4512
Miscellaneous concepts not enumerated above										56	2.5790
Cumulative Total										156	114.3602

Table 4.91

Significance of Major Sociological Categories, Calculated on the basic of importance given to them 87 text-book authors

Sl.No	Major Category	Proportion of Significance	Per-centage	Radius value* for circular Representation
0.	Sociology- History, Thedries, Research Mehtods	8.4723	7.4	1.64
I.	Social Organization	20.0874	17.6	2.52
II.	Social Institutions	18.4396	16.1	2.42
III.	Culture, Religion, Social Control, Education	23.8435	20.8	2.75
IV.	Social Structure, Stratification, Race	15.5038	13.6	2.22
V.	Social Disorganization, Conflict	4.5787	4.0	1.21
VI.	Social Change	8.4344	7.4	1.64
VII.	Human Ecology, Communities	6.2266	5.4	1.41
VIII.	Population	3.2165	2.8	1.01
IX.	Social Problems	3.0536	2.7	0.99
X.	Miscellaneous concepts not enumerated above	2.5038	2.2	0.89
	Grand Total	111.3602	100.0	6.03

$*r = \sqrt{\frac{area}{\pi}}$ Where proportion of significance assumed as area of that category for circular representation

Table 4.92
Some less significant Concepts of Sociology pertaining to allied disciplines

Disciplines allied to Sociology Second level of Significance	*Concepts related to them used in Sociology but falling in*	
	Third level of	*Significance*
Psychology	Attitudes	Leadership, Sexuality
Biology		Sexuality
		Evolution
Political Science	Government	Authority
	Formal Organization	War
	Bureaucracy	Ideology
Economics	Work	Division of labor
	Leisure	Occupations
	Industrialization	Industrial sociology
		Capitalism, Poverty
		Progress
Religion		Magic
Ethics	Norms	Values, Morality
		Conformity
Law	Sociology of law	Delinquency
	Crime	
History,		
Political Science		Revolution
Geography		Geographic environment
		Migration
Social Welfare	Applied sociology	Social Gerontology
	Social planning	

REFERENCES

1. Auguste Comte, *Positive Philosophy of Auguste Comte.* tr. byH. Martineau. New York, Blanchard, 1855: 442 p.
2. Alex Inkeles, *What is sociology? an introduction to the discipline and profession.* Englewood Cliffs, N.J.,Prentice Hall, 1964 : p. 3-4
3. Herbert Spencer *Principles of sociology.* 3rd ed. Vol. 1.New york, D. Appleton, 1910:pp. 437-40
4. Inkeles *op. cit.* p. 6
5. Max Weber, *Theory of social and economic organization* tr. byA. Henderson and T. Parsons. New York, OUP, 1947:p. 88

6. Inkeles op., *cit. p.* 7
7. Pitrim A Sorokin, *Contemporary sociological theories*. NewYork, Harper, 1928: pp. 760-61
8. J.W. Bennett; M.M. Tunin, *Social life: an introductory sociology*. New York, Alfred A Knopf, 1949: p. 196
9. Morris Ginsberg, *The study of society*. London, Routledge,1949: p. 436
10. R. M. MacIver and C. H. Page *Society: an introductory analysis*. London, Macmillan, 1952: p. 5
11. Nicholas S Timasheff, *Sociological theory: its nature and growth*. New York, Random House, (1955) 1967: p. 4
12. Alfred McClung Lee in Henry Pratt Fairchild ed. *Dictionary of sociology*. London, Vision Press, 1958: p. 302
13. Harry M. Johnson *Sociology: a systematic introduction*. NewYork, Harcourt Bruce and World, (1960) 1973, p. 2
14. T. B. Bottomore *Sociology: a guide to problems and literature*. London, Blackie, (1962) 1971:. p. 25
15. Edward A Tiryakin *Sociologism and existentialism: two perspectives on the individual and society*. Englewood Cliffs, N.J. Prentice Hall, 1962: p. viii
16. Kimball Young; Raymond W Mack *Sociology and social life*. Affiliated East-West Press, 1962: p. 8
17. Read Bain; William L Kolb in Gould and Kolb eds. *A dictionary of sociology*. London, Tavistock, 1964: pp.676, 678
18. Marvin R. Koller; Harold C Couse *Modern Sociology London*, Holt Rinehart, (1965) 1969: p. 3
19. Webster *Webster's third new international dictionary of English language*. Vol. 3, 1966: p. 213
20. Alvin L. Bertrand *Basic sociology* 2nd ed. New York, Appleton Century-Crofts, (1967) 1973: p. 3
21. *Everyman's encyclopedia* Vol. 2 London, J.M. Dent, 1967: p.277
22. Albert J. Reiss "Sociology: the field" in *International Encyclopedia of social sciences*. Vol. 15. New York, Macmillan, Free Press, 1968:p. 1
23. Donald G. MacRae in D Duncan Michael ed. *A new dictionary of sociology*. London, Routledge, 1968: p. 210
24. Social Science Research Council, U.S.A. *Behavioral and social sciences*. New Jersey, Prentice Hall, 1969: p. 307

25. Thomas Ford Hoult *Dictionary of modern sociology*. NewYork, Littlefield Adam, 1969: p. 307
26. *Random House dictionary of english language*. New York, Random House, 1970: p. 1351
27. Alex Inkeles *What is sociology: an introduction to the discipline and the profession*. New Delhi, PrenticeHall, (1964) 1971: p. 16
28. Ronald Fletcher *Sociology: its nature,; scope and elements*. London, Batsford Academic, 1980: p. 31
29. Michael Mann Macmillan *Student encyclopedia of sociology*. London, Macmillan, 1983: p. 110
30. Nicholas Abercrombie; Stephen Hill; Bryan S. Turner *Penguin dictionary of of sociology*. London, Penguin, (1984)1988: p. 232
31. Edward Shils in Adam Kuper; Jessica Kuper (eds.) *Social science encyclopedia*. London, Routledge, (1985), 1989: p. 799
32. Joel M. Charon *Sociology: a conceptual approach*. London, Allyn and Bacon, (1986), 1989: p. 24
33. N S Timasheff "Basic concepts of sociology" *American Jl.of Sociology* 58(2), Sept. 1952: p. 176 (quoted by Hoult,1969)
34. Clare Selltiz *et al*. *Research methods in social relations*. New York, Holt Rinehart, 1959: p. 481 (quoted by Hoult,1969)
35. Thomas Ford Hoult "social organization" in *Dictionary of modern sociology* Totowa, NJ., Littlefield Adams, 1969.
36. Robert E L Faris "Social organization (sociology)" in Gould; Kolb eds. *Dictionary of social sciences*. London,Tavistock, 1964: p. 661

5

Representation in Information Retrieval Tools

Guidelines and Criteria for Evaluation

Representation of the universe of knowledge and its concepts in the information retrieval tools and the form of the terms to be used, has been of constant concern of classificationists and other individuals and groups working in this field. Ranganathan defined the terminology of a scheme for classification as "the system of terms in a language, denoting or meaning the classes of the scheme, the language being the nature alone or the jargon of a profession or trade".[1] Again he writes "terminology is the system of terms used to denote- that is to name - the classes or ranked isolates in a scheme for classification."[2] from the terminological point of view Riggswrites "Although a word may have several senses, only one of them is intended, when it is used as a term. Hence, a word is termonly when it designates one of it's possible meanings."[3]

Ranganathan suggested four canons for terminology and these are: 1. Canon of currency (the use of terms which are incurrent use among the specialists of the field); 2. Canon of reticence (are uncritical); 3. Canon of enumeration (express ordenote the link of a term with other terms in the chain) and 4. Canon of context (enumeration of terms in specific context, leading to non-repetition of terms already enumerated in the hierarchy above, thus satisfying the law of parsimony).

According to Classification Research Group (CRG) [5] an essential tool in constructing any retrieval system is a classification of knowledge. The purpose of this classification is to provide schedules in which the most useful genericrelations of each unit term are displayed. The main interest of CRG has been to consider how such a classification should be constructed. The CRG commenting on the existing general classification schemes writes:

1. The schedules provide insufficient details;
2. Revision and extension are too slow;
3. The schemes often disagree as to the correct placing of subjects;
4. Many classes are heterogeneous jumble of tenuously related items;
5. The occurrence of subjects in more than one class is not satisfactorily dealt;
6. Phenomena, whose relations with existing knowledge are uncertain, can not readily be accommodated; and
7. New classes or knowledge, which developed from new phenomena or by growth within existing class can not readily be accommodated.

CRG is of the view that, "taking all such criticism into account, there is no existing set of general schedules which is satisfactory, nor is there, which can be made satisfactory by a simple process of extension or revision. The Group has found the need for a prior discussion of principles by which classification schedules may be constructed to serve the purpose defined above. . . . The group, after a long period of theoretical discussion , is now undertaking a detailed practical examination of a series of subject fields. In doing this, we will have the double purpose of further developing principles, and of constructing satisfactory schedules. The CRG is convinced that many weaknesses of existing classifications and other methods of information retrieval are due to an insufficiently searching consideration of principles on the part of their makers." [6]

Commenting on the situation Grolier writes "one must have a unified terminology and this terminology does not exist even now. Almost every author has his own terminology and to reconcile these terminologies and to say what is hidden behind the various terms which have been adopted, is not easy thing. So, in this respect we have no science: we are in the situation of chemistry before Lavoisier or physics before Newton." [7]

Lancaster provides some requirements that seem to be of most importance in a controlled vocabulary for information retrieval, some of which are as follows:

1. It should have 'warrant' derived from the terminology of the literature and the information needs of the actual users or potential users;

2. It should promote consistency in indexing and searching by the control of synonyms, near synonyms, and quasi-synonyms;

3. It should reduce terminological ambiguity through these paration of homographs and through the definition of terms whose meaning or scope would otherwise be unclear;

4. It should also assist the indexer and searcher in these election of the most appropriate terms needed to represent a particular subject through its hierarchical and cross-reference structure. [8]

The points raised above by various authors are also enumerated by Susan Bury in connection with the various criteria for evaluation of classification schemes. Writing on the criteria to judge a successful classification scheme, from the terminology aspects, Wynar writes "It (the scheme) must employ terminology that is clear and descriptive, with consistent meaning for the user and the classifier. The arrangement of terms in the schedule and the index should themselves should beunambiguous and reasonably current, correctly identifying the concepts and characteristics present in the material being classified. [10} Kaula also emphasizes the use of current terms in classification schemes.[11]

In the light of the guidelines about the terminological aspects of a scheme for classification, some of the points have been isolated, on the basis of which some major schemes taken for the present study, have been scrutinized.

Criteria adopted in this study for evaluation of the schedule for sociology in some of the schemes for classification with regard to the terms used and the major categories and headings adopted are as follows:

1. Arrangement of major categories;

2. Coverage of main concepts as headings in the schedule and number of headings adopted as direct headings, i.e. not just mentioned in the scope note only;

3. Main concepts of sociology available for provision has been made in the schedules of other subjects;

4. Terms used and the use of singular or plurals;

5. Use of phrases or single terms;

6. Treatment and placement of terms generally appearing as pairs in the literature;

7. Scattering of related concepts;

8. Provision for main concepts in the scope notes only;

9. Placement of multiple concepts within the same class;

10. Hospitality through gap device;

11. Scheme's suitability for classifying micro-documents; and

12. non-specific headings.

5.21 Arrangement of Major Categories

302 *Social Interaction:* The first major section in 300 social sciences is : '302 Social interaction. Sociology and anthropology is 301, and sub-divided into 302 to 307. Leaving apart the section on 'History, theory, and methods' in any arrangement of the major sections/categories of a subject, like sociology, it is appropriate to enumerate or place the most significant aspect of the subject first. In sociology, society, social life, social organization, are the basic aspects of the subject. Sociologists generally define sociology as the study of social organization. Other aspects like social interaction, social relations, individual and personality, and the process of formation of groups are contributory factors to social organization. Thus social organization is heading in sociology that needs to be placed first in a schedule, than 'social interaction' as adopted in DC. Even if we go through sociology textbooks, 51 chapters are devoted to social organization and society and only 24 to social interaction, out of 87 books seen.

303 *Social Processes:* Social processes is the second major category, adopted in DC. Accommodation, assimilation, competition, cooperation and conflict are generally described as the form of social processes. Russell Langworthy [12] says "Social process is seen (by some sociologists) to be social interaction." DC includes control, social change and conflict, the three major sections of sociology within social processes, although they themselves are major categories of sociology. Even if we go by the relative significance calculated in the previous chapter for each of the 100 concepts, we can decide whether' social processes' can be made a significant major category?

Conc pt	*No. of chapter*	*Significance*
Social change	59	8.07
Social control	41	2.34
Social processes	15	1.46
Social conflict	9	0.74

Thus, it does not seem proper to place high significance value headings like social control, and social change within acomparatively less significant heading like social processes.

304 *Factors affecting social behaviour:* The heading adopted in DC is so ambiguous that one can include any aspect of sociology or for that matter, any other subject within it. In sociological literature, human ecology and communities form distinct categories and at least 54 authors out of 87 have a chapter on human ecology and communities, but we do not find a single author adopting a heading like 'factors affecting social behaviour. Moreover, the main concept on population included as 304.6 can be treated as a factor related to economic institutions, and resources, but not directly affecting social behaviour, as treated in the DC.

305 *Social\Groups:* Major a major category for all types of groups does not appear to be reasonable. Sociologists discuss more about group interaction, structure, group behaviour, and social interaction etc. than the various types of groups of men and women, except a few like religious groups and occupational groups.

Table 5.1
Placement of various types of groups in the DDC

Class no. and heading within Social groups	*Section or Category where in DDC can fit better*
305.2 Age groups	Social structure or population
305.4 Men and women	Sociology of gender and social structure
305.5 Social classes	Social structure, social stratification
305.6 Religious groups	Education, culture, religion
305.7 Language groups	Racial, ethnic, and minority groups
305.8 Racial, ethnic, national groups	Social structure
305.9 Occupational and misc. groups	Social structure

306 *Culture and institutions:* Social institutions is a major category of sociology, and in the same way culture also. In the literature of sociology, we find the headings placed together like culture and normative order (O'Brien), culture and personality (Biesanz), race and culture (Lee), culture and socialization (Bierstedt), social organization and culture (Abrahamson), and social structure and culture (Cole), but nota single headings as culture and institutions., which places two major categories of sociology with class number. Within culture and institutions, 306.1 sub-culture is the first heading, which could easily be accommodated within social disorganization, social problem etc. Sub-culture is not the main part of culturė to deserve the first heading while discussing culture. Among institutions, family is the first and the foremost, that shapes the individual personality through socialization, so as to make him a useful part of the organization. As such, family deserves to be mentioned as the first among social institutions. Incoining the heading marriage and family, it appears as if only marriage leads to family, but in fact, family as in institution came into existence far earlier than marriage institution, as such, in such heading, family should have been placed first. In DC, 306.9 is institutions pertaining to death. The concept does not possess the amount of literature to warrant a main section like this and could have been placed with customs and beliefs i.e. at 303.372. Religious groups and religious institutions are placed separately at 305.6 and 306.6 respectively. As far as literature suggests, study of religious groups is not a major concern of sociologists, but sociological study of religious institutions, beliefs and practices as far they affect the social organization is a part of sociological literature. Thus devoting two major sections to religion at different places is unjustifiable.

307 *Communities:* Planning and development has been provided at 307.1. Sociologists talk about social planning and they do not deal separately with general social planning and community planning, as such, the heading social planning, would have been better, but not within communities. Rural communities and urban communities have been placed within 307.7, but generally, sociologists prefer the terms rural sociology and urban sociology. The analysis above shows that the major categories in DC are not properly identified and their sequence is also not satisfactory.

5.22 Provision for Main Concepts in the Sociology Schedule

Table 5.2

Main concepts of Sociology	Class no.	Headings used in DC (20th ed.)
0. SOCIOLOGY, HISTORY, THEORIES AND METHODS		
1. Sociology/Scope	301.00	Sociology and anthropology class here inter-disciplinary works on society
2. History	301.09	History of sociology
3. Theories	301.01	Theories of sociology
4. Research Methods, Techniques	001.42	Research methods. Class here research methods not otherwise
5. Scientific Method		provided for scientific method
I. SOCIAL ORGANIZATION, SOCIAL PROCESSES, GROUP FORMATION		
6. Social Organization		
7. Social System		
8. Social order		
9. Society/ Social life	301	Sociology and anthropology class here interdisciplinary works on society
10. Socio-biology		
11. Sexuality	306.7	Class here interdisciplinary works on sex, sexual love, sexual relations
12. Individual/		
13. Personality		
14. Attitudes	303.38	Attitudes, attitude formation and change

15. Social Processes		
16. Social relations	302.5	Relation of the individual to society
17. Social interaction	302.3	Social interaction within groups
	302.4	Social interaction between groups
18. Groups	305	Social groups general aspects: social status. role, interaction, problems of groups discrimination against and conflict involving social groups
19. Primary groups	302.34	Social interaction in small (primary) groups Groups small enough for all members to engage in face to face relationships at one time
20. Small groups		
21. Associations		
II. SOCIAL INSTITUTIONS, FAMILY, POLITICAL, ECONOMIC INSTITUTIONS		
22. Social Institutions	306	Culture and institutions Institutions: patterns of behaviour in social relationships
23. Kinship	306.83	Types of kinship systems Examples: Matrilineal, patrilineal, totemic
	305.9	(groups of) Persons by kinship characteristics
24. Family	306.8	Marriage and family
	306.85	The family Including then on-consanguinal family Class here interdisciplinary works on the family
25. Marriage	306.81	Marriage Class here inter-disciplinary works on marriage
	306.7	Institutions pertaining to relation of the sexes Class here inter-disciplinary works on sex, sexual love, sexual relations
26. Political Institutions	306.2	Political institutions Institutions maintaining internal and external peace
27. Government	306.23	Governmental institutions
28. Formal Organizations	302.35	Interaction in hierarchically organized (complex) groups Class here
29. Bureaucracy		bureaucracies, organizational behaviour
30. War	303.66	War including pacifism, sociology of war
31. Economic institutions	306.3	Economic institutions Social arrange-ments for production, distribution consumption here

		economic anthropology, economic sociology, sociology of economic development, of consumption
32. Capitalism	306.342	Capitalism (free enterprise)
33. Work	306.36	Systems of labor Class here sociology of work, industrial sociology
34. Division of labor	306.368	Non-agricultural occupations class here division of labor
35. Industrial sociology	306.36	Systems of labor Class here sociology of work, industrial sociology
36. Leisure	306.4812	Leisure Class here free time
III. CULTURE, RELIGION, SOCIAL CONTROL, EDUCATION		
37. Culture	306	Culture and institutions Culture: the
38. Customs		aggregate of society's beliefs, folkways, mores, science, technology, values, arts
39. Ideology	320.5	Political ideologies
40. Magic	306.4	Cultural institutions Class here popular culture including
41. Sociology of religion		the sociology of the sociology of
42. Social control		witch crazes, magic symbols, eating habits, body shape
43. Values	303.372	Customs and belief systems Class here values, social ethics, social justice
44. Norms	303.37	Coordination and control Normative methods
45. Morality		
46. Socialization	303.32	Socialization including social learning Class here
47. Conformity		conformity
48. Deviance	302.542	Deviation Class here madness considered as a form of interaction of individuals with society
49. Sociology of law	306.25	Judicial institutions
50. Communication	302.2	Communication Class here inter-disciplinary works on communication, mass communication
51. Public opinion	303.38	Coordination and control Public opinion Class here attitudes, attitude formation and change
52. Sociology of education	306.4	Cultural institutions
53. Social. of knowledge	306.42	Sociology of knowledge Class here the sociology of intellectual life, of

		information
54. Sociology of art	306.489	Sociology of arts and crafts
55. Science and Technology	303.483	Development of science and technology
	306.45	Science and technology as cultural institutions
56. Industrialization		

IV. SOCIAL STRUCTURE, STRATIFICATION, RACE

57. Social Structure		
58. Social differentiation		
59. Social inequality	305	Social groups Class here . . . social stratification, equality, inequality
60. Social stratification	305.512	Principles of stratification
61. Social classes	305.5	Social classes Class here class struggle
62. Caste	305.5122	Social classes Principles of stratification caste system
63. Social status	305	Social classes General aspects: social status, role . . .
64. Role	302.15	Social role, role theory
65. Power	303.3	Coordination and control Class here power, policy formulation
66. Authority	303.36	Coercion Examples: authority, punishment, restraint, threat
67. Leadership	303.34	Coordination and control Leadership including influence, cooperation
68. Social mobility	305.413	Social mobility
69. Sociology of gender	305.3	Men and women
	305.4	Women
	305.2	Age groups
70. Sociol. of occupations	305.9	Occupational and miscellaneous groups
71. Racial groups	305.8	Racial, ethnic, national groups
72. Race relations		
73. Ethnic groups	305.8	Racial, ethnic, national groups
74. Minorities		
	305.7	Language groups
	305.8	Religious groups

V. SOCIAL CONFLICT, DISORGANIZATION

75. Social Conflict	303.63	Conflict
	303.69	Conflict resolution
76. Social Disorganization	302.17	Social dysfunctions Dysfunctions affecting a substantial part of society e.g. mass hysteria, crazes examples apathy, fear, panic Class here social psycho-analysis

77. Revolution	303.64	Conflict- civil war and revolution
78. Crowd	302.33	Crowds, mobs
79. Collective behaviour		
80. Social movements	303.484	Purposefully induced change Including dissent, radicalism Class here social innovation, social reform, social reform movements
VI. SOCIAL CHANGE		
81. Social change	303.4	Social change
82. Evolution	303.42	Gradual (evolutionary) change
83. Progress	303.44	Growth and development Class here progress, specialization
VII. HUMAN ECOLOGY, COMMUNITIES		
84. Human Ecology	304	Factors affecting social behaviour
	304.2	Human ecology
85. Environment		
86. Geographic environment	304.22	Geographic, space, time factors
87. Medical Sociology	306.461	Medicine Class here the sociology of medicine, of health, of illness
88. Community	307	Communities
	307.1	Planning and development
	307.2	Population
	307.3	Structure
	307.7	Specific kinds of communities
89. Rural sociology	307.72	Rural communities Class here rural sociology, rural villages
90. Urbanization	307.76	Urban communities Class here urban sociology, interdisciplinary works on cities
91. Urban Sociology		
VIII. POPULATION		
92. Population	304.6	Population Class here demography, demographic anthropology, population geography
93. Migration	304.8	Movement of people
IX. APPLIED SOCIOLOGY, SOCIAL PROBLEMS		
94. Applied sociology		
95. Social planning	361.25	Class here policy, planning
96. Social problems	362	Social problems
97. Crime	364	Crime
98. Delinquency	364.36	Delinquent children
99. Poverty	305.569	The impoverished
	362.5	Poor
100. Sociology of aging	362.6	Social gerontology

Some of the main concepts of Sociology not provided in DDC and their relative significance is as follows:

Headings not used in DDC	Relative significance	Headings not used in DC	Relative significance
Research methods	2.64	Social structure	2.17
Social organization	4.79	Social differentiation	1.03
Society, social life	1.96	Minorities	0.84
Individual, Personality	2.70	Collective behaviour	1.90
Associations	0.68	Industrialization	0.32

5.23 Multiple Concepts within One Class and Use of Scope Notes

As mentioned earlier, headings with a relative value of 0.3 are less significant, as shown in the previous chapter. For purposes of this table provision in the sociology schedule only has been considered. A large number of headings do not appear as direct headings but appear in the scope note or under the direction 'class here'. As the adoption of the headings is not based on any significance criteria, all the headings can not be accommodated as the first term against a class number. Theproblem has been resolved by placing a large number of headings in the scope note, e.g. 306.36 Systems of labor class here sociology of work, industrial sociology. Some of the main concepts, not provided as direct headings, and only shown in the scope note in the form of 'class here' 'including', 'examples' and 'general aspects' etc. are as follows:

Table 5.3

Some of the main concepts not adoped as main heading in the DDC

Class no. and the Main heading adopted		Term mentioned in the scope-note or 'class here'
301	Sociology and Anthropology	Society
302.3	Social interaction in hierarchically organized (complex) groups	Bureaucracies
303.36	Coercion	Authority
303.3	Coordination and control	Power
303.36	Systems of labor	Sociology of work Industrial sociology
306.368	Non-agricultural occupations	Division of labor

306.4	Cultural institutions	Magic
305	Social groups	Inequality
305	Social classes	Social status
303.372	Customs and belief systems	Values
303.38	Public opinion	Attitudes
303.32	Socialization	Conformity
303.484	Purposefully induced change	Social reform movements
303.44	Growth and development	Progress
307.72	Rural communities	Rural sociology
307.76	Urban communities	Urban sociology
306.461	Medicine	Sociology of medicine
361.25	Social problems and social welfare	Policy, planning

5.4 Main Concepts represented in the Schedule of other Subjects

Only a few concepts of sociology are enumerated in the schedule of other subjects. Educational institutions, sociology of education is placed at 370.19 in education. Ideology is placed as political ideology in 320.5. Crime is placed at 364 and delinquent children at 364.36. Social problem is placed at 362, social gerontology at 362.6 and social policy and planning at 361.25.

5.25 Terms used- Singular or Plural and Phrased Headings

Most of the terms used in DDC are in plurals, as social processes, genetic factors, age groups, social classes, religious groups, language groups, institutions, sub-cultures and communitics.

Table 5.4

Headings used for some main concepts in the DDC

Social relations	302.5	Relation of the individual to society
Social interaction	302.3	Social interaction within groups
	302.4	Social interaction between groups
Sexuality	306.7	Sex
Groups	305	Social groups
Social institutions	306	Culture and institutions
Kinship	306.83	Types of kinship systems
Family	306.8	Marriage and family
Formal organizations	302.35	Hierarchically organized (complex) groups
Work	306.36	Systems of labor

Division of labor	306.368	Non-agricultural occupations class here division of labor
Occupations	305.9	Occupational groups
Poverty	305.569	The impoverished
	362.5	Poor
Sociology of religion	306.6	Religious institutions
Social stratification	305.512	Principles of stratification
Sociology of gender	305.3	Men and women
Sociology of law	306.25	Judicial institutions
Social conflict	303.6	Conflict
Social disorganization	301.12	Social dysfunctions
Crowd	303.33	Crowds, mobs
Social movements	303.484	Social reform movements
Evolution	303.42	Gradual evolutionary change
Community	307	Communities
Migration	304.8	Movement of people
Social policy	361.25	Policy, planning
Delinquency	354.35	Delinquent children

5.251 Use of Phrases or Single-word Headings

Phrases have been preferred to single word headings in DC. Some of the phrases used instead of single word terms are like this:

302.3	Social interaction within groups
302.4	Social interaction between groups
302.5	Relation of the individual to society
304	Factors affecting social behaviour
304.8	Movement of people
306.7	Institutions pertaining to the relations of the sexes
306.88	Alteration of family arrangements
306.9	Institutions pertaining to death
307.7	Specific kinds of communities

Table 5.5
Scattering of related concepts in the DDC

Paired-terms used by Text-book authors		*Placement in DC*
History and theories	301.09	History of sociology
	301.01	Theories of sociology
Individual and personality to society	302.5	Relation of the individual
	302	Social interaction psychological principles of sociology — Personality not used in the sociology schedule
Family, kinship, marriage	306.8	Marriage and family
	306.83	Types of kinship systems
Power and authority	303.3	Coordination and control class here power,...
	303.36	Systems of labor class here sociology of work
	306.4812	Cultural institutions-recreation, leisure
Knowledge and ideology	306.42	Sociology of knowledge
	320.5	Political ideologies Differentiation and — not used in DC stratification
	505.512	Principles of stratification
Status and role	305	Social groups general aspects: social status, role,...
	305.523	By economic status
	305.524	By political status
	302.15	Social role, role theory
Racial and ethnicgroups	305.8	Racial, ethnic, national groups
Values and norms class here values, . . .	303.372	Customs and belief systems
	303.37	Normative methods including perception of norms
Conformity and deviance	303.32	Socialization class here conformity
	302.542	Deviation
Conflict and collective	303.6	Conflict

behaviour	—	Collective behavior not used
Crowd and collective	302.33	Social interaction examples
		behavior crowds, mobs
Evolution and progress	303.42	Gradual (evolutionary) change
	303.44	Growth and development
		class here , progress,...

Table 5.6
Another view of Scattering of related concepts in DDC

Related concepts	*Class number in DC*
Religious groups	305.6
Religious institutions	306.6
Types of kinship systems	306.83
Persons by kinship characteristics	305.9
Population	304.6
Population of communities	307.2
Culture and institutions	306.4
Sociology of education	370.19
Customs and beliefs	303.372
Institutions pertaining to death	306.9
Conformity	303.32
Deviance	302.542
Development of science and technology	303.483
Science and technology as cultural institutions	306.45-46
Social dysfunctions	302.17
Social conflict	303.6
Social role (role theory)	302.15
Social groups: social status, role..	305
Social interaction class here psychological principles of sociology	302
Public opinion class here attitudes, attitude formation and change	303.38
Language groups	305.7
Cultural institutions- language	306.44

5.27 Hospitality through Gap Device

A number of places have been left un-assigned. In the class 301 only .7 stands assigned. In 303 also only .3, .4, and. 6 have been used. In 304, also only .3,.4. and .6 have been used. However, in 305 all types of groups have been jumbled together, hence all the places available within 305 are already exhausted. Same is the case with 306, where all the main classes are already assigned except except 306.5. In the same way, 308 and 309 are also un-assigned. As it is not possible to predict the future development and growth of a new area in a subject, un-assigned classes available at random do not serve much purpose.

Use of Non-specific Headings

Some of the headings used do not give exact meaning like 305 social groups 305.3 men and women and 305.58 specific kinds of men. The term 'specific kinds of men' can be interpreted variously, and no explanatory note is provided, as to what type of men will be included here.

Conclusion

Dewey Decimal Classification has not been able to accommodate a number of the main concepts of sociology in the sociology schedule. Some of these are : Research methods, Social organization, Society, Individual/Personality, Educational sociology, Social structure, Social differentiation, Collective behavior etc. A number of other main concepts of sociology are not provided directly against the class number and only mentioned in the scope notes in the form of 'class here' and some of these are: Bureaucracy, Authority, Power, Sociology of work, Division of labor, Industrial sociology, Magic, Inequality, Social status, Values, Attitudes, Conformity, Social reform movements, Progress, Rural sociology, Urban sociology, sociology of medicine, Social policy and planning etc.

5.3 Representation of main concepts in the UDC

5.31 Arrangement of Major categories

Sociology has been allocated 301 only in UDC (1985), and following major categories or headings have been adopted by showing in bold print:

300 Sociology. Social policy. Sociography

301 Sociology

301.15 Sources and motives of social phenomena. Social significance

301.16 Social relationships

301.17 Social processes. Group formation

301.18	Social structures. Groups. Society. Social sphere
301.19	Sociological viewpoints and trends. Individual sociologists and schools
303	Methods of social sciences
308	Sociography. Description of social situation. Political and social life in various countries, peoples, races Social geography
312	Demography. Population statistics. Vital statistics

301.15 *Sources and motives of social phenomena.* Social significance This category is appropriately placed in the beginning of the schedule after 301.01 Nature and purpose, and 301.03 Scope of sociology, however, the terms used to coin the heading are not commonly used by sociologists. The category includes mostly psychological basis of human social life.

301.16 *Social Relationships.* Social relationship, social interaction and social processes are used by sociologists to denote nearly synonymous concepts. The relative significance calculated for these on the basis of their use as heading in the textbooks is as follows:

Heading	*Relative Significance*
Social interaction	1.81
Social processes	1.46
Social relations	1.14

All these can be named as sources and motives of social phenomena, as used in the UDC, and it would have been appropriate if all of these were placed under the major category' social organization' the term preferred by sociologists. The second most preferred heading is social interaction and it could have also been used.

301.17 *Social processes.* Group Formation As stated in the previous section, social processes and social relations are nearly synonymous terms. The sub-headings generally included within social processes are cooperation, compromise, accommodation, competition and conflict, but most of these are enumerated in the UDC under 301.162.1 Social relationships. The other headings enumerated under it, like rank, domination, power etc. are related to social differentiation, and some others like disintegrating processes can be accommodated under social disorganization.

301.18 *Social structures. Groups Society.* Social sphere Sociologists use the term 'social structure' and not social structures, as used in the UDC, as such, it can not accommodate differentiation, classes, stratification etc., moreover, these aspects have already been enumerated in UDC under social processes. The other main headings enumerated under this category are groups, society, social sphere. First two of these, can represent a large part of the sociological literature and the last term social sphere is not in common use. The major category 301.18 puts into one every thing which can be rightly be termedas 'heterogeneous jumble of tenuously related terms' if we use the CRG vocabulary to describe the situation. The following table would show it in a better way as to where the headings used in this section could fit under some other major categories.

Class no./ the term used in UDC		*Category where they fit better*
301.182	Crowd, mob, mass society	Social conflict, disorganization
301.183	Small groups	Social interaction, social relations
30.185.2	Racial ethnic groupings	Race, or social structure
301.185.2	Local community	Communities, Human ecology
301.186	Society Social Organization	Organized structures
301.186.2	Voluntary associations	Social relations, interaction Cooperatives
301.188.1	Economic groupings	Economic institutions Social institutions
301.188.2	Political groupings	Political institutions Social institutions

301.19 Sociological Viewpoints and Trends. Terms used in this major category suggest that history and theory of sociology canbe classed here, as it contains 301.199 Individual sociologistsand their schools. It would have been better, if this categorywas placed immediately after the heading 'subject scope, andlimits of sociology' as the category shows relation withindividual sociologists and their schools. The subject, scope andlimits of sociology is very much decided according to thesociological viewpoints and schools of sociology.

5.32 Provision for Main Concepts in the Sociology Schedule

Out of 100 main concepts of sociology identified in the present study, only 23 are available in the sociology schedule ofUDC, including demography at 312, although the terms used do nottally. Even out of these, most of the terms are used alongwith many other terms, and if we look for significant termsappearing directly against the class number as the first term,we find that only two terms - social relationships and socialprocesses. Even among the terms enumerated somewhere in betweenthe full sentence headings, the terms are hardly comparable, andin many cases only first syllable tallies. Some examples are:differentiating processes for differentiation sociallysignificant processes for social control related conceptseconomic groupings for economic institutions and biologicallyoriented trends for biological determinism (if so ?).

Table 5.8

Provision for 100 Main Concepts in the Sociology Schedule of the UDC

0. SOCIOLOGY, HISTORY, THEORIES AND METHODS

0. SOCIOLOGY, HISTORY, THEORIES AND METHODS		
1. Sociology/Scope	301	Sociology
	301.03	Subject, scope, limits of sociology
2. History	301.01	Historical development of the phenomena of human communal life
3. Theories	301.19	Sociological view points and trends Individual sociologists and schools
4. Research Methods, Techniques		
5. Scientific Method -		
I. SOCIAL ORGANIZATION, SOCIAL PROCESSES, GROUP FORMATION		
6. Social Organization	301.18	Social structures. Groups. Society. social sphere
7. Social System -		
8. Social order -		
9. Society/ Social life	301.186	Rationally determined formations. Society in the strict sense. Purposive groups. Organized structures.
10. Socio-biology	301.194	Biologically oriented trends. Organicists. Ethnological trend Instinctivists
11. Sexuality -		
12. Individual/	301.151	Socially significant characteristics of
13. Personality	—	individuals
14. Attitudes	301.151	Social psychology
15. Social Processes	301.15	Sources and motives of social phenomena Social significance

	301.17	Social processes
	301.162	Approach relationships. Compromise
16. Social relations	301.16	Social relationships
17. Social interaction	301.165	Relationship between groups and individuals
18. Groups	301.152	Group consciousness. Collective awareness. We feeling
	301.17	Group formation
	301.18	Social structures. Groups.
19. Primary groups	301.183	Numerically small groups. Set
20. Small groups	301.186.2	Voluntary associations. Cooperatives. Unions. Fraternity. Solidarity
21. Associations	301.185.4	Mental, intellectual community. Community of ideas. Friendship

II. SOCIAL INSTITUTIONS, FAMILY, POLITICAL, ECONOMIC INSTITUTIONS

22. Social Institutions	301.188.3	Social, sociable groupings
23. Kinship -		
24. Family -		
25. Marriage -		
26. Political Institutions -		
27. Government		
28. Formal Organizations -		
29. Bureaucracy -		
30. War -		
31 Economic institutions	301.188.1	Economic groupings
32. Capitalism		
33. Work -		
34. Division of labor -		
35. Industrial sociology -		
36. Leisure -		

III. CULTURE, RELIGION, SOCIAL CONTROL, EDUCATION

37. Culture -		
38. Customs -		
39. Ideology	301.152.4	Political ideology
40. Magic -		
41. Sociology of religion -		
42. Social control	301.153	Customs, convention, Public opinion
43. Values	301.153	Socially significant processes. Norms Customs
44. Norms -		
45. Morality -		
46. Socialization	301.173	Socialization
47. Conformity -		

48. Deviance -		
49. Sociology of law -		
50. Communication -		
51. Public opinion	301.153	Socially significant processes. norms. Public opinion. Fame. Ostracism
52. Sociology of education -		
53. Sociol. of knowledge -		
54. Sociology of art -		
55. Science and Technology -		
56. Industrialization -		
IV. SOCIAL STRUCTURE, STRATIFICATION, RACE		
57. Social Structure	301.172	Differentiating processes. Separation. Rank. Domination Subjection. Servitude
58. Social differentiation -		
59. Social inequality -		
60. Social stratification -		
61. Social classes -		
62. Caste -		
63. Social status -		
64. Role -		
65. Power	301.172	Differentiating processes. Separation, Rank. Domination Subjection. Servitude
66. Authority -		
67. Leadership -		
68. Social mobility -		
69. Sociology of gender -		
70. Sociol. of occupations -		
71. Racial groups	301.185.1	Organically developed communities Blood related groups. Consanguinity
72. Race relations		Racial, ethnic grouping
73. Ethnic groups	301.185.1	Racial, ethnic grouping
74. Minorities -		
V. SOCIAL CONFLICT, DISORGANIZATION		
75. Social Conflict	301.162.2	Antagonism. Confrontation.
76. Social Disorganization	301.174	Disintegrating processes.
77. Revolution -		
78. Crowd	301.182	Loose, amorphous, transitory
79. Collective behavior formations.		Crowd. Mob. Mass society
80. Social movements -		
VI. SOCIAL CHANGE -		
81. Social change -		
82. Evolution -		
83. Progress -		

VII. HUMAN ECOLOGY, COMMUNITIES		
84. Human Ecology	301.161	Socially significant milieu
85. Environment	–	environment
86. Geographic environment	-	
87. Medical Sociology	-	
88. Community	301.185.2	Local community. Spatially determined groups
89. Rural sociology	-	
90. Urbanization	-	
91. Urban Sociology	-	
VIII. POPULATION		
92. Population	312	Demography. Population statistics Vital statistics
93. Migration	-	
IX. APPLIED SOCIOLOGY, SOCIAL PROBLEMS		
94. Applied sociology	-	
95. Social planning	-	
96. Social problems	304	Reforms. Practical social problems
97. Crime	-	
98. Delinquency	-	
99. Poverty	-	
100. Sociology of aging	-	

5.321 Main Concepts enumerated in the Schedule of Other Subjects

In spite of the fact that, UDC provides detailed classification for each subject, and also that minutest details are available in the abridged edition for many a subjects, it hasbeen able to accommodate not many significant concepts of sociology , in the schedule itself. Search for these concepts/terms in the schedule of other subjects is not very convenient. See references are not adequate and the terms in the index are shown without context, e.g. the case of 'environment',where we find the sub-heading 'social 343.97' but when we go to the schedule, we find that it is in the context of criminology and criminal sociology and does not deal with social environment in general.

Out of 100 main concepts of sociology identified in the present study, 23 could be located in the sociology schedule, 54 in the schedule of other subjects that could be sued with thehelp of colon (:) device and 21 terms could not be located in thewhole schedule of UDC, these are:

Social organization	Authority	Deviance
Social system	Leadership	Social disorganization
Social order	Social stratification	Collective behavior
Social interaction	Social mobility	Human ecology
Communication	Role	Environment
Formal organizations	Social control	Urban sociology
Bureaucracy	Conformity	Applied sociology

Table 5.9

Some Main Concepts not provided in the sociology schedule of the UDC

Some Main Concepts	Provision in the UDC	
0. SOCIOLOGY, HISTORY, THEORIES AND METHODS		
1. Sociology/ Scope	-	
2. History	-	
3. Theories	-	
4. Research Methods,	-	
Techniques	-168	Scientific method
5. Scientific Method	-	
I. SOCIAL ORGANIZATION, SOCIAL PROCESSES, GROUP FORMATION		
6. Social Organization	-	
7. Social System	-	
8. Social order	-	
9. Society/ Social life	-	
10. Socio-biology	-	
11. Sexuality	-159.922.1	Sex psychology
	57.017.5	Sex and sexuality
12. Individual/	-159.923	Individual psychology
13. Personality	-159.923	Personality
14. Attitudes	-	
15. Social Processes	-	
16. Social relations	-	
17. Social interaction	-	
18. Groups	-	
19. Primary groups	-	
20. Small groups	-	
21. Associations	-	
II. SOCIAL INSTITUTIONS, FAMILY, POLITICAL, ECONOMIC INSTITUTIONS		
22. Social Institutions	-061	Organizations and other types of cooperation. Association
23. Kinship	-392.31	Kinship
24. Family	-392.3	Family life. Familial system
25. Marriage	-392.5	Marriage. Wedding. Nuptial
26. Political Institutions	-	
27. Government	-342.51	The executive. Government

28. Formal Organizations	-	
29. Bureaucracy	-342.51	The executive
30. War	-355.01	Sociology of war
31 Economic institutions	-	
32. Capitalism	-330.342.14	Capitalist economy
33. Work	-331	Work
34. Division of labor	-330.341.42	Division of labor in soci
35. Industrial sociology	-658.31	Industrial relations
36. Leisure	-379.8	Leisure
III. CULTURE, RELIGION, SOCIAL CONTROL, EDUCATION		
37. Culture	-008	Civilization. Culture. Pro
38. Customs	-	
39. Ideology	-	
40. Magic	-133.4	Magic
41. Sociology of religion	-2	Religion
42. Social control	-	
43. Values	-17.022.1	Moral values. Standards
44. Norms	-	
45. Morality	-17.022.1	Moral values. Standards
46. Socialization	-	
47. Conformity	-	
48. Deviance	-	
49. Sociology of law	-34	Law
50. Communication	-	
Symbolism	164.02	Symbolism
51. Public opinion	-	
52. Sociology of education	-37.015.4	Educational sociology
53. Sociol. of knowledge	-001	Science and knowledge in
54. Sociology of art	-7.01	Art
55. Science and Technology	-364.124	Problems of economic and technological change
56. Industrialization	-330.341.42	Industrialization
IV. SOCIAL STRUCTURE, STRATIFICATION, RACE		
57. Social Structure	-301.18	Social structures (?)
58. Social differentiation	-	
59. Social inequality	-364.14	Social inequality
60. Social stratification	-342.54	Groups within state. Social
61. Social classes	-342.54	Groups within state. Class
62. Caste	-342.54	Castes
63. Social status	-	
64. Role	-	
65. Power	-	
66. Authority	-3.076	Administrative arrangement Authorities. Departments
67. Leadership	-	
68. Social mobility	-	
69. Sociology of gender	-396	Women and society (?)

70. Sociol. of occupations	-347.232.1	Occupation
71. Racial groups	-	
72. Race relations	-	
73. Ethnic groups	-	
74. Minorities	-342.724	Ethnic minorities
V. SOCIAL CONFLICT, DISORGANIZATION		
75. Social Conflict	-	
76. Social Disorganization	-	
77. Revolution	-	
78. Crowd	-	
79. Collective behavior	-	
80. Social movements	-061.2	Movements
VI. SOCIAL CHANGE		
81. Social change	-364.122	Problems of social change
82. Evolution	-575.8	Evolution
83. Progress	-	
VII. HUMAN ECOLOGY, COMMUNITIES		
84. Human Ecology	-	
85. Environment	-	
86. Geographic environment	-308	Social geography
87. Medical Sociology	-364.444	Social medicine
88. Community	-	
89. Rural sociology	-911.373	Rural settlements
90. Urbanization	-364.122.5	Urbanization
91. Urban Sociology	-	
VIII. POPULATION -		
92. Population	-	
93. Migration	-325	Migration, colonization et
IX. APPLIED SOCIOLOGY, SOCIAL PROBLEMS		
94. Applied sociology	-	
95. Social planning	-304	Social policy
96. Social problems	-	
97. Crime	-343.9	Criminal sociology
98. Delinquency	-343.915	Juvenile delinquency
99. Poverty	-36.011.6	Poverty
100. Sociology of aging	-362.6	Welfare of the aged, elder

5.33 Terms used : Singular or Plural and Phrased Headings

A tabular presentation of some of the headings used in UDC shows that single term 'class designations' are rarely used.

Table 5.10

Use of multiple terms within a single heading in the UDC

Some Main concepts of Sociology	Form of the Term used in UDC	
Scope of sociology	301.03	Subject, scope, limits of sociology
Theoriesofsociology	301.19	Sociologicalviewpointsand trend
Society	301.186	Rationally determined formations
Social relations	301.16	Social relationships
Small groups	301.183	Numerically small groups
Government	301.188.5	Sociology of the state
Customs	301.153	Socially significant processes. Customs
Socialization	301.173	Integratingprocesses. Socialization
Social differentiation	301.172	Differentiating processes
Power	301.172	Differentiating processes. Power
Racial, ethnic groups	301.185.1	Racial,ethnic groupings
Community	301.185.2	Local community

5.34 Scattering of Related Concepts

Some of the terms are quite often used in pairs by sociologists, which helps in placing them in a filiatory sequence. The following table shows their placement in the UDC:

Table 5.11

Scattering of concept-pairs in the UDC

Some Main concepts used in pairs by sciologists	Provision in the UDC	
History and theory not provided in the UDC		
Individual and personality	159.923	Individual psychology. Personality
Family, kinship, marriage	392.3	Family
	392.31	Kinship
	392.5	Marriage
Power and authority	301.172	Power
	342.5	Power of the state
	06.041	Functions and authority of administration
Work and leisure	331	Work
	379.8	Leisure
Knowledge and ideology	001	Science and knowledge in general

	301.152.4	Political ideology
Differentiation and stratification	301.172	Differentiation process
	342.54	Social strata
Racial, ethnic groupings	305.8	Racial, ethnic, national groups
Values and norms	17.022.1	Moral values, standards
	301.152	Socially significant processes. Norms
Conformity and deviance not used in UDC		
Conflict and collective behavior	301.162.2	Estrangement relationships. Antagonism. Confrontation. Quarrel
	301.174	Disintegrating processes
Evolution and progress	575.8	Evolution
	008	Civilization, culture, progress

Table 5.12

Scattering of related concepts

Related Concepts	Class no.	Related Concepts	Class no.
Psychological basis of human communal life	301.01	Subject, scope, limits of sociology	301.03
Social psychology	301.151	Individual sociologists and their schools	301.199
Groups	301.18		
Group formation	301.17	Social processes	301.17
Group consciousness	301.152	Cooperation.	
Compromise	301.162		
Purposive groups	301.186		
Magic	133.4		
Political groupings	301.188.2	Religion	2
Sociology of the state	301.188.5		
Evolution	575.8		
Progress	008		

Use of Scope Notes or 'Notes and Instructions'

Scope notes are termed as 'notes and instructions' in UDC and these have been used at several places, but in sociology schedule such 'instructions' as 'include' 'use' 'details by common auxiliaries' 'N.B.' etc. are not used at all. However, see also', 'divide like' 'e.g. (for example)' and 'details by colon or A/Z ' have been used in sociology schedule also.

5.35 Placement of Multiple Concepts within one Class

In most of the cases, multiple concepts are jumbled together. Many times, so many concepts are placed together in such a manner that, 'class descriptions' themselves look like scope notes. An example of multiple concepts placed within a single class is like this:

301.153 Socially significant processes. Norms, Reactions. Defenses. Influence. Custom. Convention. Public opinion. Fame. Ostracism

5.36 Hospitality through Gap Device

Provision for new subjects or headings has been made at the cost of brevity of notation. On the one hand, 75 per cent main concepts of sociology are not accommodated in the sociology schedule, and on the other, a large number of un-assigned classes are available. Some of the main un-assigned classes available to accommodate new concepts are like this:

301.166 to 301.169; 301.187 to 301.189 301.197 to 301.198 .

In the present arrangement of the sociology schedule in UDC, where only 23 out of 100 main concepts of sociology are provided, the availability of un-assigned classes does not help in any way. Moreover, the provision of only 301 for sociology leaves little choice to accommodate other concepts without assigning them long notation. Thus the schedule needs to be restructured completely, so that at least 50 per cent main concepts of the subject get enumerated in the subject-specific schedule. The terminology used also needs to be amended so that it tallies with the terminology actually used by the sociologists, so that users the information retrieval systems can benefit with the exact classification of sociological literature.

Suitability of the Scheme for Classifying Micro-documents and un-specific Headings

The 'scope' of UDC as described in the 'foreword' says "UDCis a scheme for classifying information on all subjects and in all forms. The medium edition contains about a third of the material of the full edition." It may be possible to assign one or the other class number to the literature appearing as micro-documents, but it seems a tough task for the classifier, when he has to consult whole UDC for 75 per cent of the concepts used in sociology.

Some of the headings used in the UDC are not specific, as to what type of literature will be classified under them, some of which are:

301.18 Social sphere

301.15 Sources and motives of social phenomena

301.186 Rationally determined formations

5.4 Representation of main Concepts in the Colon Classification

Study based on Colon Classification Scheme (6th ed.)

For purposes of the present study CC 7th edition (1987) was not used on account of the following reasons:

1. The facet formula for sociology in the 7th edition of CC is Y, (P); (MP): (E) (2P), but the schedule for (E) (2P) is not provided;

2. Index to the 7th edition of the CC is not available;

3. Due to a large number of printing errors the class numbers and the representing them are unintelligible. On a cursory look, 30 printing mistakes are visible in a two and half page incomplete schedule of sociology.

4. It appears, sociology schedule in CC has not been revised much after the sixth edition.

5. Rules section has not been provided for sociology in the 7th ed.

On account of these difficulties, 6th edition of CC was used for the present study.

5.41 Arrangement of Major Categories in CC

Some of the major headings adopted in the Colon Classification 6th edition are as follows:

Y (P)	Y:(E) (2P)
Y1 By Age and sex	Y:1 Civilization
Y2 Family	Y:2 Physicalcharacter and feature
Y3 By residence	Y:3 Activity
Y4 Occupation	Y:4 Social pathology
Y5 By birth or status	Y:5 Demography
Y6 Abnormal or defective	Y:7 Personality
Y7 Race as social group	Y:8 Equipment

Y8 By association   Y:91 Nomenclature etc.
Y(E): (2E) (3P)
Y:1:1 Nomenclature etc.
Y:1:7 Conservation. Improvement

5.42 Provision for Main concepts of sociology in the Colon

Classification 229

Classification

Colon classification has no provision for a large number of concepts of sociology in the sociology schedule. Provision for 100 main concepts of sociology in CC is presented as followed:

Table 5.13

Provision for 100 main concepts in the Colon Classification

Related Concepts	Class no.	Related Concepts	Class no.
0. SOCIOLOGY, HISTORY, THEORIES AND METHODS			
1. Sociology/Scope	Y	Sociology	
2. History	Yv	History of sociology	
3. Theories	-		
4. Research Methods, Techniques	Y:f	Investigation	
5. Scientific Method	Y:(R17)	Scientific method	
I. SOCIAL ORGANIZATION, SOCIAL PROCESSES, GROUP FORMATION			
6. Social Organization	-		
7. Social System	-		
8. Social order	-		
9. Society/Social life	-		
10. Socio-biology	-		
11. Sexuality	-		
12. Individual/	-		
13. Personality	Y:7	Personality	
14. Attitudes	S:57	Sentiment, interest	
15. Social Processes	-		
16. Social relations	-		
17. Social interaction	-		
18. Groups	Y8	By association	
19. Primary groups	-		
20. Small groups	-		
21. Associations	**Y8**	**By association**	
II. SOCIAL INSTITUTIONS, FAMILY, POLITICAL, ECONOMIC INSTITUTIONS			
22. Social Institutions	Y,d	Social institution	

23. Kinship	-	
24. Family	Y2	Family
25. Marriage	Y217	Marriage
26. Political Institutions	-	
27. Government	-	
28. Formal Organizations	-	
29. Bureaucracy	Y9(W8)	Civil services
30. War	Y:438	War
31 Economic institutions	Y9(X)	Economic institutions
32. Capitalism	Y9(X:326)	Capitalism
33. Work	-	
34. Division of labor	-	
35. Industrial sociology	-	
36. Leisure	Y9(MY)	Leisure
III. CULTURE, RELIGION, SOCIAL CONTROL, EDUCATION		
37. Culture	Y:1	Civilization: Culture
	Y72	Primitive societies
38. Customs	Y:356	Custom
39. Ideology		
40. Magic	Y35(Δ : 87)	Magic and Witchcraft
41. Sociology of religion	Y9(Q)	Sociology of religion
42. Social control	Y:4:5	Prevention
43. Values	Y9(R43)	Social ethics
44. Norms	-	
45. Morality	-	
46. Socialization	-	
47. Conformity	-	
48. Deviance	Y:42	Degeneration
49. Sociology of law	Y9(Z)	Sociology of law
50. Communication	-	
Symbolism	Y:36	Symbolism
51. Public opinion	Y:37	Opinion
52. Sociology of education	Y9T	Sociology of education
53. Sociol. of knowledge	Y9(1)	Sociology of knowledge
54. Sociology of art	Y9(N)	Sociology of art
55. Science and Technology	-	
56. Industrialization	-	
IV. SOCIAL STRUCTURE, STRATIFICATION, RACE		
57. Social Structure	-	
58. Social differentiation	-	
59. Social inequality	-	
60. Social stratification	-	
61. Social classes	Y5	By birth or status
62. Caste	Y592	By caste
63. Social status	Y5	By birth or status

64. Role	-	
65. Power	-	
66. Authority	-	
67. Leadership	-	
68. Social mobility	-	
69. Sociology of gender	Y1	By age and sex
70. Sociol. of occupations	Y4	By occupation
71. Racial groups	Y7	Race as social group
72. Race relations	-	
73. Ethnic groups	Y73	Ethnological divisions
74. Minorities	Y58	Minority
V. SOCIAL CONFLICT, DISORGANIZATION		
75. Social Conflict	-	
76. Social Disorganization	Y:42	Degeneration
77. Revolution	Y9(W81)	Revolution
78. Crowd	-	
79. Collective behavior	-	
80. Social movements	-	
VI. SOCIAL CHANGE		
81. Social change	-	
82. Evolution	-	
83. Progress	-	
VII. HUMAN ECOLOGY, COMMUNITIES		
84. Human Ecology	Y9(U47)	Human geography
85. Environment	-	
86. Geographic environment	-	
87. Medical Sociology	-	
88. Community	-	
89. Rural sociology	Y31	Rural residence
90. Urbanization	Y33	Urban residence
91. Urban Sociology	-	
VIII. POPULATION		
92. Population	Y:5	Demography
93. Migration	-	
IX. APPLIED SOCIOLOGY, SOCIAL PROBLEMS		
94. Applied sociology	YZ	Social work
95. Social planning	-	
96. Social problems	Y:4	Social pathology
97. Crime	Y:45	Crime
98. Delinquency	-	
99. Poverty	Y:43	Poverty
100. Sociology of aging	Y13	Old person

The representation of sociological concepts in the sociology schedule of CC can be summarized as follows:

Some Main Concepts generally Adopted as main Headings	Provision in CC 6th ed.
1. History, theories, methods	Not used
2. Social organization	Not used
3. Social institutions	Not used
4. Sociology of education	Not used
5. Culture	Y:1 Culture
6. Social control	Not used
7. Social structure	Y5 By birth or status
8. Sociology of religion	Not used
9. Deviance	Not used
10. Social disorganization	(Y:4 Social pathology ?)
11. Social conflict	Not used
12. Social change	Not used
13. Human ecology	Not used
14. Population	Y:5 Demography
15. Social problems	(Y:4 Social pathology ?)

Some concepts of sociology that can be represented with the help of the concepts enumerated in other than sociology schedules are as follows:

Table 5.15

Main concepts	Provision in CC		Main Subject	
History of sociology	v	History	ACI	
Research methods	f	Investigation	PCI	
Scientific method	R17	Scientific method	R	Philosophy
Institution	d	Institution	PCI	(P)
Capitalism	X:326	Capitalism	X	Economics
Leisure	MY	Use of leisure	M	Useful arts
Sociology of art	N	Arts	N	Fine arts
Sociology of knowledge	1	Universe of knowledge	1	Universe of knowledge
Magic	Δ : 87	Magic and witchcraft	Δ	Spiritual experience
Values	R43	Social ethics	R	Philosophy
Revolution	W81	Revolution	W	Pol. Science
Human ecology	U47	Human geography	U	Geography

The instruction 'to be subdivided by (SD)' at 'Y9 others' in the sociology schedule allows to represent other concepts, not enumerated in Y (P). Under this provision, the terms or their synonyms enumerated anywhere in the whole Colon Classification scheme, can be used in sociology. Some of the concepts of sociology can be represented in the following way:

Y9(G:61)	Heredity (biological determinism?)
Y9(S5)	Sex psychology (for sexuality?)
Y9(X)	Economic institutions
Y9(T)	Sociology of education
Y9(Q)	Religious institutions
Y9(Z)	Sociology of law
Y9(L)	Medical sociology
Y9(X:75)	Planning (for social planning ?)

5.43 Terms used: Singular or Plural and Phrased Headings

Some Main Concepts of sociology	Synonymous of nearest term used in CC	
Groups	Y8	By association
Bureaucracy	W8	Civil service
Sociology of occupations	Y4	By Occupation
Leisure	MY	Use of leisure
Social classes	Y5	By birth or status
Status	Y5	By birth or status
Sociology of gender	Y1	By age and sex
Racial groups	Y7	Race as a social group
Ethnic groups	Y73	Ethnological division
Social control	Y:4:6	Treatment
Values	R43	Social ethics
Public opinion	Y:37	Opinion
Social disorganization	Y:4	Social pathology
Human ecology	U47	Human geography
Rural sociology	Y31	Rural residence
Urban sociology	Y33	Urban residence
Social problems	Y:4	Social pathology

As shown in the table 5.6, and in the table above, all termsused in CC, are in singular form. Most of the terms used to denote a class, are in the form of single or double term headings, except a few exceptions like 'race as social group' and 'physical character and feature' etc.

5.44 Scattering of Related Concepts in CC

Very few main sociological concepts are represented in CC, hence it is not possible to identify the scattering of related concepts. The provision at 'Y9 others' 'to be subdivided by (SD) will place all un-enumerated concepts of sociology together, within this category, and that will be against the idea of proper categorization and filiation of related concepts. Some of main concepts generally used by sociologists in a filiatory sequence and the provision for them in the CC is as follows:

Table 5.16

Term Generally used in pairs and provision for them in the CC

Some terms used in pairs by sociologists	Provision and placement in CC	
History and theory of sociology		No provision in the sociology schedule
Individual and personality	SN14	Individualistic psychology
	Y:7	Personality
Family, kinship and marriage	Y2	Family
		no provision for kinship
Power and authority		no provision
Work and leisure		no provision for work
Sociology of knowledge and ideology	MY	Use of leisure
	1	Knowledge, universe of
Differentiation and stratification		no provision
Status and role	Y5	Birth and status
		no provision for role
Racial and ethnic groups	Y7	Race as social group
	Y73	Ethnological division
Values and norms	R43	Social ethics
Conformity and deviance		no provision for conformity
	Y:42	Degeneration (deviance ?)
Crowd and collective behavior		no provision
Evolution and progress	G:66	Evolution
	R 4961	Progress

Provision for Scope Notes in the Schedule

Colon classification does not provide scope notes within theclassification schedules. The rules section of chapter Y explains the facets and the terms used for each facet, and some examples of the classified titles. However, instructions like 'to be divided as in . . .' , 'other divisions by (SD)', 'to be got by GD'and 'further division by (SD)' are provided at several places, so as to enable the use of isolates enumerated in the schedules of other subject schedules.

5.45 Placement of Multiple Concepts within one Class

In most of the cases, independent class numbers areprovided for each heading, except in a few cases, where alternateterms or related terms are also enumerated as seen in some of thefollowing examples:

Y:381	Material. Totem. Flag	Y:83	Light. Lamp
Y:8687	Crown. Head ornament	Y:1:5	Influence. Contact
Y:1:62	Variation. Natural selection		

5.46 Hospitality through Gap Device

Gap device has been sued to make provision for new classesthat can be added to the schedule. Some of the main un-assigned placing available are like this:

Y14, Y17 to Y19 ; Y32, Y34, Y36 and Y37 ; Y42 to Y44, Y47; Y56; Y86 to Y89 ; and Y:6.

The schedule for sociology in the Colon Classification scheme needs complete re-arrangement to accommodate a majority of the main concepts in the sociology schedule itself, and the gapdevice can hardly help in accommodating all the concepts, withoutadopting proper categorization, that is generally used in the literature of sociology.

Suitability of the Scheme for Classifying Micro-documents

Colon Classification scheme is faceted, and all the facetsof a micro-document can be represented pin-pointedly in a majority of the cases, but with the present schedule of sociology, where a majority of the main concepts are note numerated in the schedule, or in the whole scheme anywhere, the classification of micro-documents can not bring related literature in a filiatory sequence.

Un-Specific Headings

Some of the headings used in the Colon Classification scheme are non-specific. 'Y3 By residence' has sub-headings, rural and urban, but it has to be used for rural sociology and urban sociology. In 'Y4 By occupation' Sub-division is 'Y48

Leader'.In sociology, leadership is studied from the psychological point of view, from the point of view of exertion of power and authority, in connection with status and role, and also in connection with social classes, but hardly we come across any literature, where leadership is studied as an occupation. In the same way, in 'Y3 By residence' Y394 is a subdivision for 'refugee'. Refugee is studied in sociology as a social problem, in connection with displaced persons, as a kind of political migration and also in connection with adjustment of refugees in a new cultural environment, but hardly on the basis of their residential status. In this way, a majority of the concepts of sociology need reconsideration and adequate placement within the major categories to fit the literature appearing in the subject.literature.

Table 5.17

100 Main Concepts and their Representation in Some Classification Schemes

0. SOCIOLOGY,HISTORY,THEORIES AND RESEARCH METHODS

Concept	Scheme	Representation
1. Sociology	DC 301.	Sociology and anthropology class here interdisciplinary works on society
	UDC 301	Sociology
	CC Y	Sociology
		Scope of DC The terms scope, coverage, field or subject matter of Sociology sociology have not been used in DC
	UDC 301.03	Subject, scope, limits of sociology
	CC	No provision in CC for the subject, scope and limits of sociology
2. History	DC 301.09	Sociology: historical and geographical treatment
	UDC301.01	Nature and purpose of sociology...historical development of the phenomenon of human communal life
	CC Yv	History of sociology
3. Theories	DC 301.01	Sociological theory
	UDC 301.19	Sociological viewpoints and trends. Individual sociologists and schools
	CC	The term is not used in CC.
4. Research	DC 001.42	Research methods. Class here research methods not methods, not otherwise provided for. Scientific method techniques UDC 303 Methods of social sciences

		CC	The terms not used in sociology schedule. However, research methodology isenumerated in the schedule of basic subjects (CC 7th ed.)
5.	Scientific method	DC 001.42	Scientific method
		UDC 300	Methods of social sciences
		303.8	Research organization. Research procedure
		CC Y:(R17)	Scientific method

I. SOCIAL ORGANIZATION, SOCIAL PROCESSES, GROUP FORMATION

6.	Social organization	DC	no provision
		UDC	The term social organization is not used in UDC, however, the term is used in some other context at
		304	Social questions in general. critiques of social organization ' that can not be used for social organization
		CC	no provision
7.	Social System	DC	no provision
		UDC	no provision
		CC	no provision
8.	Social order	DC	no provision
		UDC	no provision
		CC	no provision
9	.Society	DC 301	Sociology and anthropology Class here inter- disciplinary works on society
		UDC 301.18	Social structures. Groups. Society. Social sphere
		CC	no provision
	Social life	DC 308	Political and social life in various countries
		UDC	no provision
		CC G:56	Social life
10	.Socio-biology	DC 304.5	Genetic factors Class here socio-biology (bio- sociology), the study of the genetic bases of human behavior. Class a specific aspect of socio-biology with the subject in sociology, e.g. the sociology of conflict 303.6
		UDC	no provision
		CC	no provision
	Heredity,	DC 304.5	Factors affecting social behavior- genetic factors Class here sociobiology (bio-sociology), the studyof the genetic bases of human social behavior
		UDC	575.5 Heredity
		CC G:61	Heredity
11.	Sexuality	DC 306.7	Institutions pertaining to relations of the sexes.

		Class here inter-disciplinary works on sex, sexual love, sexual relations
	UDC 57.017.5	Sex and sexuality
	591.551	Relation between the sexes
	612.6.06	Sexuality
	CC S5	Sex psychology
12. Individual	DC 302.5	Relation of the individual to society
	UDC 301.165	Relationship between groups and individual
	CC SN14	Individualistic psychology
13. Personality	DC	no provision in the sociology schedule
	UDC 301.151	Socially significant characteristics of individuals
	CC Y:7	Personality
14. Attitudes	DC 303.38	Public opinion Class here attitudes, attitude formation and change
	UDC 301.151	Socially significant characteristics of individuals Drives, propensities. Social psychology.
	CC S:57	Sentiment. Interest
15. Social	DC 303	Social processes processes UDC 301.17 Social processes. Group formation
	CC	no provision
16. Social	DC 302.5	Relation of the individual to society relations UDC Social relationships
	CC	no provision
17. Social	DC302	Social interaction Class here the psychological interaction principles of sociology, interpersonal relations, social psychology
	UDC301.16	Social relationships
	301.165	Relationship between groups and individuals
	CC	no provision
18. Groups	DC305	Social groups General aspects: social status, role, interactions, problems of social groups
	UDC301.18	Social structures. Groups. Society. Social sphere
	CC	no provision
19. Primary groups	DC302.34	Social interaction within small (primary) groups. Groups small enough for all members to engage in face-to face relationships at one time e.g. committees, gangs, play groups Class here friendship

	UDC	no provision
	CC	no provision
20. Small groups	DC302.34	Social interaction within small (primary) groups
	UDC301.183	Numerically small groups. Gang, circle, set
	CC	no provision
21. Associations	DC366	Association Organization formed for common purposes of a fraternal nature or for mutual assistance
	UDC 301.186.2	Voluntary associations. Cooperatives. Unions. Fraternalism. Solidarity
	CC Y8	By association

II. SOCIAL INSTITUTIONS, FAMILY, POLITICAL, AND ECONOMIC INSTITUTIONS

22. Social	DC 306	Culture and institutions Institutions: patterns of institutions of behavior in social relationships. General aspects: the roles, functions, and patterns within which the groups and members of a society conduct their lives.
	UDC	no provision
	CC	no provision
23. Kinship	DC306.83	Types of kinship systems e.g. matrilineal, patrilineal, totemic
	305.904	Persons by kinship characteristics
	UDC 17.023.32	Kinship
	301.185.1	Blood- related groups. Consanguinity. Racial, ethnic groupings
	CC	no provision
24. Family	DC 306.85	The family Including the non-consanguinal family. Class here inter-disciplinary works on family
	UDC17.023.32	Family
	17.035.3	Family
	301.185.1	Blood related groups. Consanguinity. Racial, ethnic grouping
	CCY2	Family
25. Marriage	DC 306.81	Marriage Class here inter-disciplinary works on marriage
	UDC 173.1	Marriage These places, marriage is mentioned in 340.61 various contexts, but the term is not used in the
	347.62	Sociology schedule.
	392.5	
	613.89	

	CC Y217	Marriage
26. Political	DC 306.2	Political institutions Institutions maintaining institutions internal and external peace. Class here comprehensive works on patronage, on client relationship; political sociology
	UDC	301.188.2 Political groupings
	321	Forms of political organization
	CC	no provision
27. Government	DC 306.23	Governmental institutions
	306.2	Institutions maintaining internal and external peace political sociology. Government
	UDC 342.51	Government
	CC	no provision
28. Formal	DC 302.35	Social interaction within hierarchically organized organization (complex) groups Class here bureaucracies organizational behavior
	UDC 512.741	Formal groups
	CC	no provision
29. Bureaucracy	DC302.35	Social interaction within groups- in hierarchically organized (complex) groups. Class here bureaucracies, organizational behavior.
	UDC301.188.5	Orderly, regular groupings. Groupings in a socially standardizing order. Sociology of the state.
	CCY9(w8)	Civil service
30. War	DC 303.66	War Including pacifism, sociology of war
	UDC 342.78	State of war
	CC Y:438	War
31. Economic	DC 306.3	Economic institutions Social arrangement for institutions production, distribution Class here economic anthropology; economic sociology, sociology of economic development, of consumption
	UDC 301.188.1	Economic groupings
	CC	no provision
32. Capitalism	DC 306.342	Capitalism (free enterprise)
	UDC 330.342.14	Capitalist economy
	CCX:326	Capitalist
33. Work	DC 306.36	Systems of labor Class here the sociology of work, industrial sociology
	UDC	no provision
	CC	no provision

34. Division of labor	DC306.368	Non-agricultural occupations Class here division of labor, occupations considered severally
	UDC330.341.42	Division of labour in society
	339.91	International division of labor
	CC	no provision
35. Industrial	DC 306.36	Systems of labor Class here systems of labor, sociology industrial sociology
	UDC 331.1	Industrial relations
	658.31	
	CC X:97	Industrial relations
36. Leisure	DC 306.481 2	Leisure class here free time
	UDC 331.811.8	Leisure time
	377.4	Time outside working hours, recreation and leisure
	CC MY	Physical training, sports, games, use of leisure, hobby
III. CULTURE, RELIGION, SOCIAL CONTROL, EDUCATION		
37. Culture	DC 306	Culture and institutions. Culture: the aggregate of a society's beliefs, folkways, mores, science, technology, values, arts Class here mass culture, cultural and social anthropology
	UDC17.023.36	Culture
	301.151.6	Mental, intellectual, cultural drives
	303.446.2	Cultural comparison. Cross-sectional study
	CC Y:1	Civilization. Culture
38. Customs	DC303.372	Customs and belief systems Class; here values, social ethics, social justice
	UDC 301.153	Socially significant processes, norms. Reactions. Defenses. Influence. Custom. Convention. Public opinion. Fame. Ostracism.
	CC Y:356	Custom
39. Ideology	DC 140	Ideology (philosophy)
	320.5	Ideology (Political science)
	UDC 301.152.4	Political ideology
	CC	no provision
40. Magic	DC 306.4	Cultural institutions Class here popular culture including the sociology of witch crazes, magic, symbols, eating habits, body shape
	UDC 133.4	Magic
	291.62	Magicians
	CC /\:87	Magic
41. Sociology of	DC 306.6	Religious institutions To be classed, the religion institutions must be considered from a secular, non-religious view point

		Class here sociology of religion
	UDC 291.6	Religious organization
	CC	no provision
42. Social control	DC 303.33	Social control
	UDC	no provision
	CC	no provision
	Y:4:5	Prevention
43. Values	DC 303.372	Customs and belief systems Class here values, social ethics, social justice
	UDC 364.122.8	Changes in social norms, patterns, values
	17.022.1	Standards, moral values
	CC R37	Values
44. Norms	DC 303.37	Normative methods including perception of norms
	303.372	Customs and belief systems class here values, social ethics, social justice
	UDC 301.153	Socially significant processes, norms. Reactions.
	CC R37	Value (in Metaphysics)
45. Morality	DC 303.37	Normative methods including perception of norms
	UDC 301.153	Socially significant processes, norms.
	CC Y:45R4	Moral
46. Socialization	DC 303.32	Socialization including social learning. Class here conformity
	UDC 301.173	Integrating processes. Subsidy principle. Assimilation. Stabilizing. Socialization.
	CC	no provision
47. Conformity	DC 303.32	Socialization including social learning Class here conformity
	UDC	no provision
	CC	no provision
48. Deviance	DC 302.542	Deviation Class here madness considered as a form of interaction of individual with society
	UDC	no provision
	CC	no provision
49. Sociology of	DC 306.25	Judicial institutions law UDC no provision
	CC	no provision
50. Communication	DC 302.2	Communication including semiotics Class here interdisciplinary works on communication, mass communication
	UDC 347.763	Communication
	659.3	Mass communication
	CC	no provision

Symbolism	DC306.4	Cultural institutions Class here popular culture including sociology of witch crazes, magic, symbols, eating habits, body shape
	UDC164.02	Symbolism
	291.37	Religious symbolism
	CC Y:38	Symbolism
51. Public	DC 303.38	Public opinion Class here attitudes, attitude opinion formation and change
	UDC 301.153	Socially significant processes... Public opinion
	CC Y:37	Opinion
52. Sociology of Education	DC 370.19	Educational institutions, Sociology of education
	UDC 37.015.4	Educational sociology
	CC	no provision
53. Sociol. of	DC 306.42	Sociology of knowledge Class here the sociology of Knowledge intellectual life, of information Class specific instances of the sociology of knowledge in 306.44- 306.48 (that includes language, science, technology, medicine, art and recreation)
	UDC	no provision
	CC	no provision
54. Sociology of	DC 306.489	Arts and crafts art UDC no provision
	CC	no provision
55. Science and	DC 306.45	Science Clasr here works contrasting the scientific technology and the humanistic cultures
	306.46	Technology
	303.483	Development of science and technology
	UDC	no provision
	CC	no provision
56. Industriali	DC 303.483	Development of science and technology zation UDC no provision
	CC	no provision

IV. SOCIAL STRUCTURE, STRATIFICATION, RACE

57. Social DC no provision structure	UDC 301.18	Social structures. Groups. Society. Social sphere
	CC	no provision
58. Social	DC	no provision differentiation
	UDC 301.172	Differentiating process. Individuation. Separation. Rank. Domination. Power. Subjection. Servitude.
	CC	no provision
59. Social	DC 305	Social groups General aspects: social status, role inequality interactions.... Class here ... social stratification, equality, inequality

	UDC 001.361	Equality
	177.5	Social inequality
	CC	no provision
60. Social	DC 305.512	Principles of stratification stratification
		UDC no provision
	CC	no provision
61. Social	DC305.5	Social classes Class here class structure
		classes UDC no provision
	CC	no provision
62. Caste	DC 305.512 2	Caste systems
	UDC	342.54 Castes
	177.4	Caste feeling
	CC	Y592 Caste
63. Social status	DC 305	Social groups General aspects: social status, role,..
	UDC 301.172	Rank
	CC Y5	By birth or status
		By social status (CC7)
64. Role	DC 302.15	Social role (role theory) including role conflict
	305	Social status General aspects: social status, role etc.
	UDC	no provision
	CC	no provision
65. Power	DC 303.3	Coordination and control Class here power, policy formulation
	UDC 301.172	Differentiating processes.... Power.
	CC	no provision
66. Authority	DC 303.36	Coercion e.g. authority, punishment, restraint
	UDC 17.025	Authority of the state
	CC	no provision
67. Leadership	DC 303.34	Leadership including influence cooperation
	UDC	no provision
	CC Y48	Leader (by occupation)
68. Social	DC 305.513	Social mobility mobility UDC no provision
	CC	no provision
69. Sociology of gender	DC 305.3	Men and women including trans-sexuality class here inter-disciplinary works on sex role, the sexes, gender identity, adult men and women
	UDC	no provision
	396.1	Female equality
	CC	no provision
70. Sociol. of occupations	DC 305.9	Occupational and miscellaneous groups Class here occupational mobility
	UDC	no provision

	CC Y:4:5(X)	Social pathology (occupational)
71. Racial groups	DC 305.8	Racial, ethnic and National groups Class here ethnology, cultural ethnology, ethnography, race relations
	UDC 301.185.1	Blood- related groups, consanguinity, racial ethnic groupings
	CC Y7	Race as a social group
72. Race relations	DC305.8	Racial, ethnic and National groups Class here ethnology, cultural ethnology, ethnography, race relations
	UDC 301.185.1	Blood- related groups, consanguinity, racial ethnic groupings
	342.724	Racial equality
	CC Y7	Race as a social group
73. Ethnic groups	DC 305.8	Racial, ethnic and National groups Class here ethnology, cultural ethnology, ethnography, race relations
	UDC 301.185.1	Blood- related groups, consanguinity, racial ethnic groupings
	CC Y73	Ethnological division
74. Minorities	DC 306.089	Specific indigenous racial, ethnic, national groups
	UDC 342.724	Ethnic minorities
	CC Y58	Minority
V. SOCIAL CONFLICT, DISORGANIZATION		
75. Social	DC 303.6	Conflict Class conflict in a specific area of social conflict relations with the subject in sociology, e.g. racial conflict 305.8
	UDC 301.162.2	Estrangement relationship. Antagonism. Confrontation. Quarrel
	CC	no provision
76. Social dis-organization	DC302.17	Social dysfunctions
	303.45	Social change: deterioration and decay
	UDC 301.174	Disintegrating processes. Decay. Collapse. Destructive factors
	CC Y:4	Social pathology
	Y:42	Degeneration
77. Revolution	DC 303.64	Civil war and revolution
	UDC 323.27	Revolution
	CC W81	Revolution
78. Crowd DC	302.33	Social interaction in abstract and temporary groups crowds, mobs
	UDC 301.182	Loose, amorphous, transitory, short-lived formations. Crowd, mobs
	CC	no provision
79. Collective behavior	DC	no provision

	UDC	no provision
	CC	no provision
80. Social	DC303.484	Purposefully induced change including dissent, movements radicalism Class here social innovation, social reform, social reform movements
	UDC	no provision
	CC	no provision

VI. SOCIAL CHANGE

81. Social change	DC 303.4	Social change use 303.4 for social evolution in the broadest sense, as the sum total of good and bad progressive and regressive), fast and slow changes taking place over time. Use 303.42 for detailed analysis of gradual (evolutionary) change as such. Use 303.44 for the study of social evolution considered as constant upward progress or improvement. Class social change in a specific aspect of society with the subject in sociology, e.g. changes in religious institutions 306.6
	UDC	no provision
	CC	no provision
82. Evolution	DC 303.42	Gradual (evolutionary) change
	UDC 575.8	Evolution
	CC G:8	Evolution
83. Progress	DC 303.44	Growth and development class here progress, specialization
	UDC 330.341.1	Technical progress
	CC R496	Ethics-progress, perfection

VII. HUMAN ECOLOGY, COMMUNITIES

84. Human Ecology	DC 304.2	Human ecology class here anthropo-geography, ecological anthropology, human geography
	UDC 591.5	Ecology
	CCY:81	Habitat
	U47	Human geography
85. Environment	DC 304.2	Human ecology class here ... human geography
	UDC 301.161	Socially significant milieu
	343.97	Social environment
	372.32	Environment
	343.97	Social environment
	CC Y:81	Habitat
	G:55	Environment
86. Geographic	DC 304.2	Human ecology Geographical, space, time factors environment including territoriality, time management

	UDC 301.193	Synthetic and geographical trend
	308	Social geography
	CC U47	Human geography
87. Medical	DC 306.461	Medicine Class here the sociology of medicine,of sociology health , of illness
	UDC 364.444	Social medicine
	CC	no provision
88. Community	DC 307	Communities
	UDC 301.185	Organically developed groups, communities
	301.185.2	Local community. Spatially determined groups
	301.185.3	Temporal community. Contemporaneity
	CCY:81	Habitat
89. Rural	DC 307.72	Rural communities Class here rural sociology, sociology rural villages including plantations considered as communities
	UDC 911.373	Rural settlements
	(1-22)	Village communities
	CC Y31	Rural residence
90. Urbanization	DC 307.76	Urban communities. Class here urban sociology, inter- disciplinary works on cities
	UDC 304.122.5	Urbanization
	CC Y33	Urban residence
91. Urban	DC 307.76	Urban communities. Class here urban sociology, inter-sociology disciplinary works on cities
	UDC 304.122.5	Urbanization
	CC Y33	Urban residence
VIII. POPULATION		
92. Population	DC 304.6	Population Class here demography, demographic anthropology, population geography
	UDC 312	Demography. Population statistics. Vital statistics
	CC Y:5	Demography
93. Migration	DC 304.83	Migration
	UDC325	Migration
	711.13	Population movement, distribution, densities
	CC U42	Migration
IX. APPLIED SOCIOLOGY,SOCIAL PROBLEMS		
94. Applied sociology	DC 360	Applied sociology
	UDC 304	Social questions in general. Practical social problems. Social policy

	CC YZ	Social work
95. Social	DC 303.484	Purposefully induced change including dissent, planning radicalism Class here social innovation, social reform, social reform movement
	UDC 304	Practical social problems. Social policy
	CC	no provision
96. Social problems	DC 362	Social welfare problems and services
	UDC 304	Practical social problems. Social policy
	CCY:4	Social pathology includes intemperance, degeneration, social evil and crime
97. Crime	DC 364	Crime
	UDC 301.151.56	Anti-social drives. Criminal instincts
	CC Y:45	Crime
98. Delinquency	DC 364.36	Delinquency
	UDC 343.22	Delinquents
	376.58	Juvenile delinquents
	CC	no provision
99. Poverty	DC 305.569	The impoverished Class problems of and service to the poor in 362.5
	UDC 241.53	Poverty
	CC Y:434	Poverty
100. Sociology of aging	DC 305.26	Late adulthood (gerontology-social aspects)
	UDC 362.6	Welfare of the aged, elderly, old people
	613.98	Gerontology
	CC Y13	Old person

Sociological Abstracts Classification Scheme

5.51 Arrangement of Major Categories

The classification scheme used for classifying sociological literature in the *Sociological Abstracts* has 33 main headings. Out of these, 9 headings are single-sub-heading main sections, i.e. the title of the heading and the sub-heading is the same. Some of these single sub-headings main section are'Rural sociology and agriculture', 'Urban sociology' 'sociology of education' 'sociology of religion', 'clinical sociology' etc. Out of 33 main sections only 15 have 3 or more than 3 sub-headings. First major section is 'Methodology and research technology', and the second is 'History and theory'. In any arrangement of literature on a subject, placement of 'History and theory' in the beginning appears to be a better arrangement. The their main heading is 'social psychology' and it accommodates various aspects as small groups, personality, leadership, deviance etc. In sociological literature, deviance is associated with social control, or with social disorganization, and less with social psychology, as deviance is mostly individual aspect and not collective. Next category is 'Group interactions ' and it includes only one major aspect, i.e. race relations, ethnicity, and inter-ethnic relations, implying that any user whois searching literature on racial and ethnic relations must remember that the heading used for it is 'group interactions. Fifth major section is 'Culture and social structure'. Within this section, no sub-heading related to social structure like social differentiation etc. is included. The next major section, Complex organization, includes jobs, work organization, production, employment, etc. generally included within economic institutions. The section on social change and economic development, is placed next, but it has no significant relation with complex organization,placed before it and the mass phenomena placed after it. All types of mass phenomena have been placed within one category, in the next section. Under this section social movements, public opinion, communication, collective behavior, sociology of leisure, mass culture, and sociology of sport, pertain to diverse aspects like social change, social control, and social interaction etc. and can not be fitted under one heading 'mass phenomena' as done in the Sociological Abstracts. A category by category observation of the whole arrangement makes it clear that it is not based on any thoughtful filiatory arrangement or helpful sequence. Demography and human biology also attract our attention, which is a separate section, but birth control is not placed within this section, instead, it is within family and socialization.

Table 5.18

Provision for main concepts in the Sociological Abstracts classification Scheme

1.	**Sociology/Scope**	202	**of professional interest** (teaching sociology)
2.	**History**	206	history **and present state of sociology**
		2252	history of ideas
		285	comparative and historical sociology
3.	**Theories**	207	theories, **ideas, systems**
		103	methodology (conceptual & epistemological)
		373	cognitive/ interpretive sociologies, symbolic interactionism & ethno-methodology

	2555	radical sociology
	2580	critical sociology
4. Research Methods, techniques	**100**	methodology and research technology
	104	research methods
	161	models: mathematical and other
	105	statistical methods
	188	Computer methods, media and applications
5. Scientific Method		
I. SOCIAL ORGANIZATION, SOCIAL PROCESSES, GROUP FORMATION		
6. Social Organization	267	macro-sociology: analysis of whole societies
7. Social System		
8. Social order		
9. Society/Social life		
10. Socio-biology	1844	human biology/sociobiology
	394	life cycle and biography
11. Sexuality	1940	sociology of sexual behaviour
12. Individual/		
13. Personality	312	personality and culture
14. Attitudes	**300**	social psychology
15. Social Processes		
16. Social relations		
17. Social interaction	665	social network analysis
18. Groups		
19. Primary groups		
20. Small groups	309	interaction within (small groups)
21. Associations	674	voluntary associations
II. SOCIAL INSTITUTIONS, FAMILY, POLITICAL, ECONOMIC INSTITUTIONS		
22. Social Institutions	508	social organizations
23. Kinship		
24. Family	**1941**	sociology of the family
25. Marriage		
26. Political Institutions	**900**	political sociology
	925	Voting, parties, political systems
27. Government		
28. Formal Organizations	**600**	Complex organizations
29. Bureaucracy	624	bureaucratic structure/ organizational sociology
	995	nationalism
30. War	911	interactions between societies, nations and states
	623	military sociology
31. Economic institutions	749	market structures and consumer behaviour
	3268	sociology of business
32. Capitalism	770	capitalism, socialism - world systems
	3063	marxist sociology
33. Work	621	jobs, work organization, work places and unions
34. Division of labor	686	modes of production, employment patterns, social division of labor

35. Industrial sociology		
36. Leisure	842	sociology of leisure/ tourism
	869	sociology of sport
III. CULTURE, RELIGION, SOCIAL CONTROL, EDUCATION		
37. Culture	**513**	culture
	514	Social anthropology
	850	mass culture
	1978	Sociology of death and dying
38. Customs		
39. Ideology		
40. Magic		
41. Sociology of religion	**1500**	sociology of religion
42. Social control	**1600**	social control
43. Values		
44. Norms		
45. Morality		
46. Socialization	**1976**	socialization
	1938	Sociology of the child
47. Conformity		
48. Deviance	364	deviance
49. Sociology of law	1636	sociology of law
50. Communication	828	communication
	1330	sociology of language/ socio-linguistics
51. Public opinion	827	public opinion
52. Sociology of education	**1432**	sociology of education
53. Sociol. of knowledge	2233	sociology of knowledge
	1375	sociology of literature
54. Sociology of art	**1331**	sociology of art **(creative and** performing)
	3371	visual sociology
55. Science and Technology	**1734**	sociology of science
	1772	sociology of technology
56. Industrialization		
IV. SOCIAL STRUCTURE, STRATIFICATION, RACE		
57. Culture	**0500**	culture and social structure
58. Social Structure		
59. Social differentiation	**1000**	social differentiation
60. Social inequality		
61. Social stratification	1019	Social stratification/mobility
62. Social classes		
63. Caste		
64. Social status		
65. Role		
66. Power		
67. Authority		
68. Leadership	322	leadership
69. Social mobility		

	Sociology of gender	2983	sociology of gender and gender
		2959	feminist studies
70.	Sociol. of occupations	1020	sociology of occupations and professions
71.		**0400**	group interactions
72.	Racial groups	410	interaction between (large) groups
73.	Race relations race relations,		
74.	Ethnic groups ethnicity & inter-ethnic relations		
	Minorities	2898	genocide
V. SOCIAL CONFLICT, DISORGANIZATION			
75.	Social Conflict	2858	studies in violence
		2884	terrorism
		2496	negotiation, dispute settlements
76.	Social Disorganization		
77.	Revolution		
78.	Crowd		
79.	Collective behaviour	829	collective behaviour
80.	Social movements	826	social movements
VI. SOCIAL CHANGE **0700** social change			
81.	**Social change**	**0715**	social change and economic development
82.	Evolution		
83.	Progress		
VII. HUMAN ECOLOGY, COMMUNITIES			
84.	**Human Ecology**	**1800**	demography and human ecology
85.	**Environment**	**2600**	environmental interactions
86.	Geographic environment	2682	social geography
		2681	disaster studies
87.	**Medical Sociology**	**2045**	sociology of medicine **(public health)**
		3166	clinical sociology
88.	Community	2317	sociology of communities and regions
89.	**Rural sociology**	**1116**	rural sociology **(village, agriculture)**
90.	Urbanization		
91.	**Urban Sociology**	**1218**	urban sociology
VIII. POPULATION			
92.	**Population**	**1837**	demography **(population studies)**
		1977	birth control (abortion, contraception, fertility & child bearing
93.	Migration		
IX. APPLIED SOCIOLOGY, SOCIAL PROBLEMS			
94.	Applied sociology	2148	applied sociology
		2192	sociological practice
		2046	social psychiatry (mental health)
95.	Social planning	2462	policy sciences
		989	welfare state
		2454	planning and forecasting
		2187	social service programs, delivery systems
		2460	social indicators
96.	**Social problems**	**2100**	social problems & social welfare

	2793	homeless-ness
	491	refugees
	2079	substance use/abuse & compulsive behaviors (drug abuse, addiction, alcoholism, eating disorders)
97. Crime	2147	sociology of crime and victimology
	1653	police, penology, and correctional problems
	2190	victimology
98. Delinquency	2151	juvenile delinquency
99. Poverty	**2757**	studies in poverty
	2697	famine
100. Sociology of aging	2143	social gerontology

* = headings shown in bold have been adopted as main headings in the

Table 5.19
Some main concepts used as text book heading but not used in the Sociological Abstracts

1. Scope of sociology	2. Scientific method
3. Social organization	4. Social system
5. Society	6. Social life
7. Social order	8. Social processes
9. Social relations	10. Social interaction
11. Individual	12. Attitudes
13. Primary groups	14. Associations
15. Social institutions	16. Kinship
17. Marriage	18. Government
19. War	20. Economic institutions
21. Industrial sociology	22. Ideology
23. Customs	24. Values
25. Norms	26. Morality
27. Conformity	28. Magic
29. Industrialization	30. Social structure
31. Social classes	32. Caste
33. Social inequality	34. Social mobility
35. Social status	36. Role
37. Authority	38. Power
39. Minorities	40. Social disorganization
41. Social conflict	42. Revolution
43. Crowds	44. Evolution
45. Progress	46. Human ecology
47. Urbanization	48. Migration

Table 5.20

Some main concept and the number of References on them in the Sociological Abstracts (cumulative total for 1990,1091, and 1992)

Main concept	Significance/ No. of References		Main concept	Significance/ No. of References	
0. SOCIOLOGY, HISTORY,			**43. Values**	**0.30**	**61**
THEORIES AND METHODS			44. Norms	0.55	146
5. Scientific Method	0.47	36*	45. Morality	0.11	41
I. SOCIAL ORGANIZATION,			**47. Conformity**	**0.28**	**18**
SOCIAL PROCESSES, GROUP			**56. Industrialization**	**0.32**	**121**
FORMATION			IV. SOCIAL STRUCTURE,		
6. Social Organization	**4.79**	**72**	STRATIFICATION, RACE		
7. Social System	0.42	69	57. Social Structure	2.17	254
8. Social order	0.52	70	59. Social inequality	1.49	286
9. Society	1.96	39	61. Social classes	0.91	167
Social life		30	62. Caste	0.09	38
12. Individual/	2.70	257	63. Social status	0.84	206
14. Attitudes	0.56	177	64. Role	0.35	218
15. Social Processes	1.46	38	65. Power	0.86	162
16. Social relations	1.14	128	66. Authority	0.09	37
17. Social interaction	1.81	229	74. Minorities	0.84	206
18. Groups	2.71	149			
19. Primary groups	**0.71**	**—**	V. SOCIAL CONFLICT,		
21. Associations	**0.68**	**117**	DISORGANIZATION		
II. SOCIAL INSTITUTIONS, FAMILY,			75. Social Conflict	0.74	109
POLITICAL, ECONOMIC			**76. Social Disorganization**	**0.63**	**18**
INSTITUTIONS			**77. Revolution**	**0.16**	**112**
22. Social Institutions	5.54	47	78. Crowd	0.36	11
23. Kinship	0.47	96	VI. SOCIAL CHANGE		
25. Marriage	0.58	215	82. Evolution	0.16	142
27. Government	0.45	40	83. Progress/d		
30. War	0.17	147	development	0.21	34
31. Economic **institutions**	**2.32**	**165**	VII. HUMAN ECOLOGY,		
			COMMUNITIES		
35. Industrial			84. Human Ecology	1.67	50
sociology	0.30	18	90. Urbanization	1.53	73
III. CULTURE, RELIGION, SOCIAL			VIII. POPULATION		
CONTROL, EDUCATION			**93. Migration**	**0.17**	**165**
38. Customs	0.29	25			
39. Ideology	**0.20**	**215**	IX. APPLIED SOCIOLOGY, SOCIAL		
40. Magic	**0.09**	**20**	PROBLEMS		

* 1. Sl. adopted is that of the 100 main concepts of sociology

2. Headings not adopted as class headings in the Sociological Abstracts only shown here.

Although, the number of references against each term are based on simple count of all entries appearing against that term, as such the number of entries counted, may have been duplicated in some cases, due to an article being indexed against each significant term in the title, the analysis shows that significant quantity of literature appears on most of these terms. The number of articles being published on these terms, as well the use of these terms as chapter headings in the textbooks, indicates that these terms deserve inclusion as headings in the sociological Abstracts, as most of these are 'current ' in the literature. This cross checking of the use of these concepts as heading terms also indicates that, on account of their 'currency', user demand and approach will be comparatively higher through these terms than the terms where these have been indexed. This comparative study also shows that, some concepts of sociology that used to be relatively significant earlier, as evidenced by textbook study, are now on the way to become obsolete, as indicated by quite insignificant quantity of literature appearing on them. But for such a comparative study we are dependent upon completely on Sociological Abstracts, about the concepts under which it has indexed some articles. One of the examples can be cited that of' social structure.' In the Sociological Abstracts the term is not used for hierarchical and differentiating structures of the society. According to the indexing system adopted in the Sociological Abstracts, the following terms or the concepts they represent, are loosing currency and less than expected literature is appearing on them. However, it is also possible that, the classification and indexing system adopted in the SA is responsible for showing such results.

Some Main Concepts of Sociology on which less than 50 references are included in the *Sociological Abstracts* over a period of 3 years:

Society	(39)	Social life	(30)
Social processes	(38)	Social institutions	(47)
Government	(40)	Authority	(37)
Industrial sociology	(18)	Magic	(20)
Caste system	(38)	Customs	(25)
Morality	(41)	Conformity	(18)
Crowds	(11)	Development	(34)
Progress	(7)		

Table 5.21

Some Sociological Abstracts headings covering other disciplines disciplines

Class number and the heading adopted in the SA		Related disciplines
0300	Social psychology	Social psychology
0623	Military sociology	Political institutions
0624	Bureaucratic structure	Political institutions
0700	Social change and economic development	Economic institutions
0749	Market structures and consumer behaviour	Economic institutions
0770	Capitalism/ socialism World systems	Economic institutions
1300	Sociology of language and arts	Language
1400	Sociology of education	Education
1500	Sociology of religion	Religion
1700	Sociology of science	Sciences
2000	Sociology of health and medicine	Public health and medicine
2100	Social problems and	welfare Applied sociology
2300	Community/regional development	Applied sociology
2700	Studies in poverty	Economic institutions
3200	Sociology of business	Economic institution

5.53 Terms used : Singular/Plural and Phrased Headings

Table 5.22
Some Main concepts Equivalent or near-equivalent Sociological Abstract Heading

Some main concept of Sociology	Equivalent or nera-equivalent Term of used in the SA as Heading	
Research methods technology	0100	Methodology and research
Personality	0312	Personality and culture
Biological determinism	1844	Human biology/ sociobiology
Sexuality	1940	Sociology of sexual behaviour
Associations	0674	Voluntary associations
Social institutions	0508	Social organizations
Formal organizations	0600	Complex organizations
Bureaucracy	0624	Bureaucratic structure
War	0623	Military sociology
Work	0621	Work organization
Division of labor	0686	Social division of labor
Leisure	0842	Sociology of leisure
Racial, ethnic groups	0410	Interaction between large groups
Social change	0700	Social change and economic development
Environment	2656	Environmental interactions
Communities	2317	Sociology of communities and regions
Medical sociology	2045	Sociology of medicine (public health)
Population	1837	Demography (population studies)
Crime	2147	Sociology of crime and victimology
Delinquency	2151	Juvenile delinquency
Poverty	2757	Studies in poverty

In most of the cases, the headings used in the Sociological Abstracts match with the terms being used in textbooks, and generally the terminology represents the literature of sociology better than many other bibliographical information retrieval tools. The scheme does not follow any strict rule about adoption of singular or plural headings. In case of at least 17 headings used in plural, the singular form could have conveyed the idea properly, e.g. 'environmental interaction' could have been sufficient in place of 'environmental interactions' as used in the SA.

Most of the headings used in the Sociological Abstracts are not single term headings, but some headings adopted are unnecessarily lengthy. The heading '2983 Sociology of gender and gender relations' is one case, as 'sociology of gender' is sufficient to represent the literature on the concept. In the same manner, 'sociology of occupations' could have been sufficient in place of 'sociology of occupations and professions' as used in SA.

5.54 Scattering of Related Concepts in SA

Table 5.23

Scattering of related concepts in the SA

Main concept generally mentioned together by Sociologists Abstracts	Provision in the Sociological Abstracts	
History and theories	0206	History
of sociology	0207	Theories
Individual and personality		individual not used as heading
	0312	Personality and culture
Family, kinship, marriage	1941	Family
		kinship not used as heading
		marriage not used as heading
Power and authority		both terms not used as heading
Work and leisure	0621	Job, work organization
Knowledge and ideology	2233	Sociology of knowledge
		ideology not used as heading
Differentiation and	1000	Social differentiation
stratification	1019	Social stratification
Social status and role		both terms not used as heading
Racial and ethnic groupings	0410	Interaction between (large) groups (race relations, ethnicity, and inter-ethnic relations
Values and norms		both terms not sued as headings
		Conformity and deviance
		conformity not used as heading
	0364	Deviance
Crowd and collective		crowd not used as heading
behaviour	0629	Collective behaviour
Evolution and		evolution not used as heading
progress	0700	Social change and economic development
Related concepts		Class number Related concepts
Class number		
Interaction with Social control	1600	
(small) groups	0309	

Deviance	0364	
Communication	0828	Social change and Market structures and
economic development	0715	
consumer behaviour	0749	
Sociology of science	1734	
Sociology of business	3268	
Sociology of technology	1772	
Nationalism	0995	Sociology of communities
	2317	Military sociology
	0625	Rural sociology
	1116	Sociology of education
	1432	Home-less-ness
	2793	Culture 0513
Refugees	0491	
Sociology of art	1331	
Sociology of knowledge	2233	
Culture and social Welfare state	0989	
structure	0500	
Social service programs	2187	
Social differentiation	1000	

A number of headings are explained with the help of sub-headings, that clarify the scope of the main heading adopted. Some examples are '0410 Interaction between (large) groups (race relations, ethnicity, and inter-ethnic relations' ; and "977 Birth control (abortion, contraception, fertility and child bearing)'.

5.55 Placement of Multiple Concepts within one Class

Multiple concepts are placed with one class at several places e.g. 0621 Jobs, work organization, work-places, and unions; 0715 Social change and economic development; 0624 Bureaucratic structure/ organizational sociology; and 0686 Modes of production, employment patterns, social division of labor, etc.

Hospitality through Gap Device

The classification scheme adopts a four digit class number and sub-headings can be added to a main headings, but all major headings are serially numbered, that does not allow any new major heading to be added afresh as coordinate headings without disturbing the present arrangement.

Classifying Other than Periodical literature

The scheme has been devised for the arrangement of sociological literature in the form of periodical articles. Some major headings and some minor headings within them; have been fixed and all the literature being published is somehow fitted into these headings. An user can be helped much, with the proper arrangement of literature, if some major categories are adopted and the headings and sub-headings are grouped within them. In the current arrangement, an user has to depend on the subject index, but in the index also all entries appear, wherever there is reference to that term, and the user has to select some entries relevant to his search out of all enumerated in the index against that term. Under these circumstances, the scheme can not be used for classifying other than periodical literature, unless it is supported by key term as well as concept indexing.

5.57 Un-specific Headings and Inappropriate placements

Under '0900 Political sociology/interactions' the sub-heading is '0911 Interaction between societies, nations, and states'. A question may arise as to whether the interaction between societies, nations and states, can be only political interaction. In the same manner under '0508 Social organization' not a single title could be located that has used the term 'organization' or 'social organization' in them. The heading 'famine' is under the main heading 'Environmental interactions' but sociological literature relates famine more with social problems, economic conditions, or with poverty, than with the environmental interactions as shown in the Sociological Abstracts.

Congress Subject Headings

Library of Congress Subject Headings (LCSH) is a list of heading terms, which shows, broader, related, used for, and use terms. Some terms are provided with scope note to indicate their applicability in certain situation, and also to indicate as to what type of documents these headings are applicable. The list is primarily meant for use in the U.S. Library of Congress subject catalogue. The system is in use since 1897. The present comparative study of this list with the main concepts of sociology is based on LCSH 12th edition published in 1989. The headings in the LCSH are arranged word by word in alphabetical order. The lists are also available in classified order, arranged according to the Library of Congress classification Scheme.

Table 5.24

One hundred main concepts of sociology & provision for them in the LCS Headings

0. SOCIOLOGY, HISTORY, THEORIES AND METHODS		
1.	Sociology	Sociology *
	Scope	—
2.	History	Sociology-history
3.	Theories	Social theory
4.	Research	Methods,
	Techniques	—
5.	Scientific Method	use Science-methodology
I. SOCIAL ORGANIZATION, SOCIAL PROCESSES, GROUP FORMATION		
6.	Social Organization	use Social structure
7.	Social System	Social system
8.	Social order	—
9.	Society	—
	Social life	Social life and customs
10.	Socio-biology	Socio-biology/Heredity, Human 11. Sexuality use Sex
12.	Individual	Individuality
13.	Personality	Personality
14.	Attitudes	Attitude
15.	Social Processes	Social processes
16.	Social relations	—
17.	Social interaction	Social interaction
18.	Groups	Social groups
19.	Primary groups	—
20.	Small groups	Small groups
21.	Associations	Associations, institutions etc.
II. SOCIAL INSTITUTIONS, FAMILY, POLITICAL, ECONOMIC INSTITUTIONS		
22.	Social Institutions	Social institutions
23.	Kinship	Kinship
24.	Family	Family
25.	Marriage	Marriage
26.	Political Institutions	Political sociology
27.	Government	use Political science
28.	Formal Organizations	Organizations

29. Bureaucracy	Bureaucracy
30. War	War
31 Economic institutions	Economics-sociological aspects
32. Capitalism	Capitalism
33. Work	Work
34. Division of labor	Division of labor
35. Industrial sociology	Industrial sociology
36. Leisure	Leisure
III. CULTURE, RELIGION, SOCIAL CONTROL, EDUCATION	
37. Culture	Culture/Human culture
38. Customs	Manners and customs *
39. Ideology	Ideology
40. Magic	Magic
41. Sociology of religion	Religion and sociology
42. Social control	Social control
43. Values	Social values
44. Norms	Social norms
45. Morality	Moral conditions
46. Socialization	Socialization *
47. Conformity	Conformity
48. Deviance	Deviant behaviour
49. Sociology of law use	Sociological jurisprudence
50. Communication	Communication *
Symbolism	Symbolism
51. Public opinion	Public opinion
52. Sociology of education	—
53. Sociol. of knowledge	Knowledge, Sociology of
54. Sociology of art	Art and society
55. Science and Technology	Science- social aspects
56. Industrialization	Industrialization *
IV. SOCIAL STRUCTURE, STRATIFICATION,RACE	
57. Social Structure	Social structure
58. Social differentiation	—
59. Social inequality	Equality
60. Social stratification	use Social classes
61. Social classes	Social classes
62. Caste	Caste
63. Social status	Social status
64. Role	Social role
65. Power	Power (social sciences)
66. Authority	Authority
67. Leadership	Leadership

68. Social mobility	Social mobility
69. Sociology of gender	use Sex discrimination
70. Sociol. of occupations	Occupations
71. Racial groups	Race
72. Race relations	Race relations
73. Ethnic groups	Ethnic groups *
74. Minorities	Minorities *
V. SOCIAL CONFLICT, DISORGANIZATION	
75. Social Conflict	Social conflict
76. Social Disorganization	—
77. Revolution	Revolution/s
78. Crowd Crowds	
79. Collective behaviour	Collective behaviour
80. Social movements	Social movements
VI. SOCIAL CHANGE	
81. Social change	Social change *
82. Evolution	Evolution
83. Progress	Progress
VII. HUMAN ECOLOGY, COMMUNITIES	
84. Human Ecology	Human ecology
85. Environment use	Ecology
86. Geographic environment	Anthropo-geography (?)
87. Medical Sociology	use Social medicine
88. Community	Community *
89. Rural sociology	Sociology, Rural
90. Urbanization	Urbanization
91. Urban Sociology	Sociology, Urban
VIII. POPULATION	
92. Population	Population *
93. Migration Migration *	
IX. APPLIED SOCIOLOGY, SOCIAL PROBLEMS	
94. Applied sociology	—
95. Social planning	use Social policy
96. Social problems	Social problems
97. Crime	Crime and criminals
98. Delinquency	Delinquents
99. Poverty	Poverty
100. Sociology of aging Gerontology	Aged

* Terms provided with a scope note in the LCSH have been shown with a star.

5.61 Provision for some Main Concepts of Sociology in LCSH

A comparative table showing the terms generally used in text books as headings and the form of heading suggested in the LCSH is as follows:

Table 5.25

Main concepts and the terms used for them in the LCSH

Some main concepts	Provision in the LCSH
Research methods, techniques	use science-methodology
Scientific method	not used
Society	not used
Social organization	use social structure
Social life	use manners and customs
Social order	not used
Social relations	not used
Biological determinism	Socio-biology/human heredity
Sexuality	Not used
Primary groups	Not used
Government	use political science
Organizations	use associations, institutions
Economic Institutions	Economics- sociological aspects
Sociology of education	Not used
Sociology of art	Art and society
Social differentiation	Not used
Social stratification	use social classes
Social inequality	Equality-
Sociology of gender	use sex discrimination
Morality	Moral conditions
Sociology of law	use sociological jurisprudence
Social disorganization	Not used
Science and technology	Science-social aspects
Environment	use ecology
Geographic environment	Anthropo-geography
Medical sociology	use social medicine
Social gerontology	Gerontology; Aging
Applied sociology	Not used
Social planning	use social policy

5.62 General Headings vs. Subject-specific Headings

In a general subject headings list it is possible to accommodate all headings that conform to the sub-specific demand and the form of a term used in each discipline. Some efforts arevisible to specify the terms like 'Power (social sciences)'. Many more headings need to be specified like this, to fit with the subject specific form of terms used in a subject and specific meaning attached to them. For 'social organization LCSH directs to see 'social structure'. Although there are controversies about the exact scope and applicability of the term social structure in sociology, but generally, it is taken to express the hierarchical and differentiating patterns in society, as such it is not appropriate to use social structure for social organization, i.e. they are hardly synonymous terms. Some sociologists used the term 'social life' as a synonymous term to social system, society, social order, or social organization or social interaction. LCSH makes it 'social life and customs' and directs to use the headings for it as 'manners and customs. 'Government' is used by many sociologists in place of social institutions or political sociology, and these terms go have been preferred, but directs to use 'political science for 'government', which hardly satisfies the demand of the sociologists, who may like to see some literature on government from the sociological point of view. Political science is a too broader term for searching literature on sociological aspects of government. LCSH uses 'Economics- sociological aspects' that is to be used for economic institutions, the term preferred by sociologists. It is doubtful if both these terms could be treated as synonymous. For 'delinquency' as a phenomenon, LCSH uses 'delinquents' as a group. Sociologists use the term sociology of medicine or medical sociology, but LCSH directs to use 'social medicine', a term not used by sociologists in this connection, which is evident from the fact that out of 8 dictionaries of sociology/ sciences consulted, not a single has used the word social medicine. These observations indicate that, while preparing a list of subject headings that is used by a large number of libraries, provision for some of the main concepts of each discipline needs to be kept in mind, so that the terms used by maximum number of users from that discipline are well represented and the subject-specific context is also maintained. For this purpose, a list of the main concepts of each discipline needs to be prepared, and in general headings lists some un-specific terms can be provided discipline specific context within brackets, as has been done in the case of 'power-social sciences'.

5.63 Form of the Terms and Phrased Headings used in LCSH

Provision for 100 main concepts of sociology in the LCSH is

Terms used in LCSH	55	Inverted heading used	4
Synonymous terms used in LCSH	20	Terms not represented at all	10
Instruction to use other term	11		

The LCSH is not particular about the use of singular or plural form of the heading terms, and plurals have been used liberally e.g. social groups, small groups, minorities, delinquents, crowds, and organizations etc. Most of the headings represent single concepts, but some instances can be seen where combined headings have been suggested, e.g. manners and customs, and associations, institutions etc.

Use of Phrased Headings

Headings used in LCSH fall into four categories as follows:

a. single word headings e.g. minorities, delinquents, crowds, organizations etc.;
b. a noun preceded by an adjective e.g. small groups;
c. a noun preceded by another by 'and' e.g. manners and customs;
d a noun preceded by another noun like an adjective e.g. political sociology.

Among the 100 headings to which this study is limited, the case of a noun connected with another by a preposition, or the case of phrased headings used in sociology, was not found. However, phrased headings are used in LCSH wherever required.

5.64 Treatment of Related Concepts in LCSH

Table 5.26
Treatment of terms in LCSH generally used in Pairs

Terms generally used in pairs by sociologists	Headings used in LCSH
History and theories of sociology	Sociology-history, Social theory
Social differentiation and stratification	Not used use social classes
Status and role	Social status, social role
Values and norms	Social values, Social norms
Conformity and deviance	Conformity, Deviant behaviour
Evolution and progress	Evolution, Progress

No effort is visible to have some provision for the terms that are generally used in pairs in the literature of sociology. Generally, related sub-headings are together in LCSH, by means of inversion of headings or by combination of two or more subject words. 'Sociology of knowledge' has been inverted as 'knowledge, sociology of' so as to bring all the headings related to knowledge, together. 'Rural sociology' and 'urban sociology' are also inverted as 'sociology, rural ' and 'sociology, urban' soresulting in all subdivisions of a subject falling together in the index, but for subject heading purposes this inversion can be termed as unhelpful.

5.65 Use of Scope Notes with the Headings provided in the LCSH

Scope note provides the guidelines about the subjects that need to be given a particular heading. Sometimes, the scope note also serves as a definition of the term adopted as heading, on the basis of which, the appropriateness of a heading can be judged, while assigning a heading to a particular document. Out of 100 terms relating to sociology checked in the LCSH 18 have been provided scope note. The scope note starts with the word 'Here are entered works on ' or 'Here and with local subdivisions are entered works . . .' . Scope note also prescribe the aspects of the same heading that need to be given some other heading instead of the present one.

Revision of Headings and Scope for Change

A number of headings provided in the LCSH do not tally with the terminology generally used in sociology and such headings need to be changed or specified from the subject-specific point of view. Such change is desired at least in case some main headings, that are sought by users of indexing systems, more frequently than other minor headings.

Capability of LCSH to provide specific Headings for Micro-documents

As observed in the Table 5.8 only 55 terms out of 100 terms compared are available in the same form in the LCSH. For other headings, either synonymous term is used or direction to use some other term is given. At least 10 per cent terms used in sociology have no provision at all in LCSH, as revealed by the present study of 100 terms. It appears, the requirements of a discipline like sociology, to index micro-documents, can not be met by a general headings list like.

5.7 Main Concepts suggested by Some Sociologists

Sociological specialties/ fields/areas/ aspects, suggested by 7 sociologists, one librarian and 39 fields on which International Sociological Association has formed research committees, have been classified according to the arrangement of main concepts of sociology adopted in this study. These 9 sources suggest a total of 112 areas/ concepts of sociology. On many fields/ areas/main concepts, several sources are in agreement. A comparative table showing all the concepts suggested by these sources in a classified order, with that of the main concepts of sociology identified in this study, indicates that, terms representing 83 concepts or their equivalents are among the main fields suggested by all these sources combined together. However, 30 concepts identified in this study, do not figure in any of the suggestions, and these are as follows:

Table 5.27

Main concepts not included as such by some sociologists

1.	Scope of sociology	2.	Scientific method
3.	Social processes	4.	Social interaction
5.	Attitudes	6.	Biological determinism
7.	Sexuality	8.	Primary groups
9.	Kinship	10.	Government
11.	Bureaucracy	12.	Authority
13.	Power	14.	Leadership
15.	Division of labor	16.	Capitalism
17.	Ideology	18.	Magic
19.	Social structure	20.	Castes
21.	Minorities	22.	Customs
23.	Morality	24.	Conformity
25.	Social disorganization	26.	Revolution
27.	Industrialization	28.	Environment
29.	Social problems		

Out of these, 7 terms are those, that have been identified as the comparatively more significant of sociology, but not listed by these 9 sources, and these are scope of sociology, social processes, social interaction, power, social structure, minorities, and social problems. The terms used for the main concepts of sociology by these 9 sources are presented in the table that follows in a classified order. The term suggested by each author or other sources is followed by the first three letters of the authors surname and year of suggestion.

Table 5.28

A Classified List of the Main aspects of Sociology Suggested by some Sociologists

Term	Source
0. SOCIOLOGY, HISTORY, THEORIES AND METHODS	
1. Sociology/**Cooperation**	
Sociology	Bau 1974
Scope	
Sociological perspective	Ink 1965
2. History	
History of sociology	ISA 1988
3. Theories **Social action**	**Bau 1974**
History of social thought	IES 1968
Conceptual and relationships	Ink 1965
terminological analysis	ISA 1988
General theory and	
history of sociology	Hou 1936
Sociological theory	Hor 1980
4. Research Methods, Techniques	
Logic of the social sciences	**Hou 1936**
Methods of social research	
including statistical	

methods **Hou 1936**
Research methods in sociology Some 1969
Methodology and statistics Hor 1980
Logic and methodology in
sociology **ISA 1988**
Mathematical sociology **Hor 1980**
Social surveys Bau 1974
Survey research **IES 1968**
Interviewing **Bau 1974**
5. Scientific Method Family Hou 1936
Scientific method in social
Sciences Ink 1965 Family Ser 1972
I. SOCIAL ORGANIZATION, SOCIAL
PROCESSES, GROUP FORMATION
6. Social Organization
Social Organization Bau 1974
Family research ISA 1988
Social organization Hor 1980
Sociology of organization **ISA 1988**
7. Social System **Marriage** **Les 1973**
Social systems Bau 1974
Typology (ideal type) Bau 1974
8. Social order
9. Society/Social life **Political and legal**
Society Ink 1965
institutions Ink 1965
10. Socio-biology **Political sociology** **Sme 1969**
11. Sexuality **Political sociology** **Ser 1972**
12. Individual/**Political sociology** **Bau 1974**
Individual personality Ink 1965
13. Personality **Political sociology** **ISA 1988**
Personality formation **Les 1973**
Biography and society ISA 1988
14. Attitudes
Social psychology Hou 1936
Social psychology Bau 1974
Social psychology Hor 1980
15. **Social Processes**
Social participation **Bau 1974**
Accommodation,
assimilation
16. Social relations
Interpersonal relations Bau 1974
17. Social interaction
Human behaviour Bau 1974
Social acts and social
Socio-metry Less 1968
18. Groups
Groups (including ethnic
and class) Ink 1965
Groups (sociology) **Bau 1974**
19. Primary groups
20. Small groups
Small groups research Les 1968
Sociology of small groups?
21. Associations
Associations and organizations Ink 1965
Associations institutions etc. Bau 1974
II. SOCIAL INSTITUTIONS, FAMILY
POLITICAL, ECONOMIC INSTITUTIONS
22. Social institutions etc. Bau 1974
23. Kinship
24. Family
Family and kinship Ink 1965
Family life **Les 1973**
Family **Bau 1974**
Marriage and the family **Hor 1980**
Sex customs Bau 1974
25. Marriage
Marriage and the family Hor 1980
26. Political Institutions
Political sociology Hor 1980
27. Government
National movements and
imperialism **ISA 1988**
28. Formal Organizations
Organizational sociology IES 1968
Formal and complex
organization Hor 1980
Complex organization Sme 1969
sociology Religion Les 1973
29. Bureaucracy
Sociology, of international
relations ISA 1988
Military **Les 1973**
Sociology military Bau 2974
Military sociology Hor 1980
Armed forces and conflict
resolution ISA 1988
30. War

31. **Economic Institutions**
    Economic institutions Ink 1965
    Economic sociology IES 1968
    Economy and society ISA 1988
32. Capitalism
    Communism and society Bau 1974
33. Work
    Sociology of work ISA 1988
34. Division of labour
35. Industrial sociology
    Industrial sociology Ser 1972
    Industrial sociology Bau 1974
    Industrial sociology Hor 1980
    Participation, workers
    control and self-management ISA 1988
    Labor unions Les 1973
36. Leisure
    Recreation and welfare Ink 1965
    Leisure, sports, recreation
    and the arts Hor 1980
    Sociology of leisure ISA 1988
    Sociology of sport ISA 1988

III. CULTURE, RELIGION,
SOCIAL CONTROL, EDUCATION

37. Culture
    Cultural sociology Hou 1936
    Human culture and society Ink 1965
    Cultural sociology Hor 1980
    Social anthropology Bau 1974
    Society, Primitive Bau 1974
    Comparative study of societies Sme 1969
    Comparative sociology Hor 1980
    Comparative sociology ISA 1988
38. Customs
39. Ideology
40. Magic
41. Sociology of religion
    Religious institutions Ink 1965
    Sociology of religion IES 1968
    Sociology of religion,
    beliefs, and ideologies Ser 1972
    Religion and sociology Bau 1974
    Sociology of religion Hor 1980
    Sociology of religion ISA 1988
42. Social control
    Social control Ink 1965
    Deviance and social control Sme 1969
    Social control Bau 1974
    Social control Hor 1980
    Devinance and social control ISA 1988
    Community power Bau 1974
43. Values
    Social evaluation (the
    study of values) Ink 1965
    Social values Bau 1974
    Norms
    Social norms Bau 1974
45. Morality
    Socialization
    Socialization and
    indoctrination Ink 1965
    Socialization Sme 1969
    Socialization Bau 1974
    Social perception Bau 1974
47. Conformity
48. Deviance
    Social deviance (crime,
    suicide etc.) Ink 1965
    Deviance and social control Sme 1969
    Deviant behaviour Les 1973
    Deviant behaviour Hor 1980
    Anomie Bau 1974
49. Sociology of law
    Political and legal
    institutions Ink 1965
    Sociology of law IES 1968
    Law and society Hor 1980
    Sociology of law ISA 1988
50. Communication
    Communication (including
    opinion formation,
    expression and change Ink 1965
    Communication Ser 1972
    Sociology of communication, Hor 1980
    knowledge and culture Language
    Les 1973
    Socio-linguistics Bau 1974
    Socio-linguistics ISA 1988

51. Public opinion
Collective **behaviour, crowd psychology and public opinion** — **Hou 1936**
52. Sociology of education
Educational sociology — Hou 1936
Educational and scientific institutions — Ink 1965
Sociology of education — Sme 1969
Sociology of education — **Ser 1972**
Education — Les 1973
Educational sociology — Bau 1974
Sociology of education — Hor 1980
Sociology of education — **ISA 1988**
53. Sociol. of knowledge
Sociology of knowledge — **IES 1968**
Knowledge, Sociology of — Bau 1974
Sociology of knowledge and science — Hor 1980
Sociology of communication, knowledge and culture — ISA 1988
54. Sociology of art
Aesthetic and expressive **Sociology** — **Ink 1965**
Leisure, sport, recreation and the arts — Hor 1980
sociology of arts — ISA 1988
55. Science and Technology
Sociology of science — **ISA 1988**
56. Industrialization
IV. SOCIAL STRUCTURE, STRATIFICATION, RACE
57. Social structure
58. Social differentiation
Differentiation and Student dissent stratification — Ink 1965
Social distance — Bau 1974
59. Social inequality
Equality — **Bau 1974**
60. Social stratification
Social stratification — Sme 1972
Social stratification-class and status — Ser 1972
Social stratification — Les 1973
Stratification and mobility — Hor 1980
Social stratification — ISA 1988
61. Social classes
Social classes — Bau 1974
62. Caste
63. Social status
Social stratification class and status — Ser 1972
Social status — Bau 1974
64. Role
Social role — Bau 1974
65. Power-
66. Authority-
67. Leadership-
68. Social mobility
Social mobility — **Bau 1974**
Stratification and mobility — Hor 1980
69. Sociology of gender
Women in society — ISA 1988
Sociology of youth — ISA 1988
70. Sociol. of occupations
Occupational sociology — Ser 1972
Sociology of occupations and professions — Hor 1980
71. Racial groups
Races and nationalities, — **Hou 1936**
72. Race relation
Race relations, race prejudice — Hou 1936
Race relations — Ser 1936
Race relations — Les 1973
Race and ethnic relations — Hor 1980
Ethnic, race and minority relations — ISA 1988
Black power — Les 1973
73. Ethnic groups
Ethnic relations — Les 1973
Race and ethnic relations — Hor 1980
Social integration — Ink 1965
Ethno-psychology — **Bau 1974**
74. Minorities
V. SOCIAL CONFLICT,
VI. SOCIAL STRUCTURE, DISORGANIZATION STRATIFICATION, RACE
75. Social Conflict
Social conflict (including

revolution and war)	**Ink 1965**
Alienation (social psychology)	Bau 1974
Alienaton theory and research	ISA 1988
76. Social Disorganization	
77. Revolution	
78. Crowd	
Crowds	Les 1973
Mob	Les 1973
79. Collective behaviour	
Collective behaviour-crowd psychology and public opinion	Hou 1936
Collective behavior and mass communication	**Hor 1980**
Riots	Les 1973
80. Social movements	
Social movements	Les 1973
VI. SOCIAL CHANGE-VIII. POPULATION-	
81. Social change	
Social change	Ink 1965
Social change	Sme 1969
Social change	Les 1973
Social change	Bau 1974
Social change	Hor 1980
82. Evolution	
Historical sociology (theory of evolution and progress)	Hou 1936
Social evolutions	**Bau 1974**
83. Progress	
Futures research	ISA 1988
VII.HUMAN ECOLOGY, COMMUNITIES	
84. Human Ecology	
Human ecology, regional sociology and social Sociology geography	Hou 1936
Human ecology	IES 1968
Human ecology	Hor 1980
Social ecology	ISA 1988
85. Environment	
86. Geographic environment	
Sociology of desasters	**ISA 1988**
87. Medical Sociology	
Disease and social status	Bau 1974
Sociology of health	ISA 1988
Hospitals	Les 1973
Psychiatic hospitals social aspects	Bau 1974
88. Community	
Communities: urban and rural	**Ink 1965**
Community	Bau 1974
Community	Hor 1980
Community research	ISA 1988
Community development	Bau 1974
89. Rural sociology	
Rural sociology	Hou 1936
Rural sociology	IES 1968
Rural sociology	Hor 1980
90. Urbanization welfare and social polity	ISA 1988
Urbanization	Les 1973
Urban renewal	Bau 1974
Regional and urban development	ISA 1988
91. Urban Sociology	
Urban sociology	Hou 1936
Urban sociology	IES 1968
Urban sociology	Ser 1972
Sociology, Urban	Bau 1974
Urban sociology	Hor 1980
92. Population	
Population problems and social biology	Hou 1936
Populations	Ink 1965
Demography	IES 1968
Demography	Sme 1969
Population growth	Les 1973
Demography	Hor 1980
93. Migration	
Sociology of migration	ISA 1988
94. Applied sociology and social work	Hou 1936
Social practice and social transformation	ISA 1988
Socio-technics sociological practice	ISA 1988
Applied sociology	**Hor 1980**
95. Social planning	
96. Social problems	

97. Crime		reference to problem	
Criminology	Hou 1936	children and juvenile	
Criminology	IES 1968	delinquency	Hou 1936
Criminology	Ser 1972	99. Poverty	
Crime	Les 1973	Poverty	Les 1973
Crime and criminals	Bau 1974	Poor	Bau 1974
Crime and delinquency	**Hor 1980**	Sociology of poverty, social	
98. Delinquency		100. Sociology of aging	
Child study with special		Sociology of aging	ISA 1988

* =

Hou House, Floyd Nelson	1936	Ser	Sergeant, Graham	1971
Ink Inkeles Ales	1971	Les	Les, Gerald R	1973
Sme Smelser, Neil J	1965	Bau	Baughman, James C	1974
IES Intl. Encycl. of Social Science	1968	ISA	Intl. Sociol. Assn.	1988

5.81 A Brief Description of the Dictionaries Considered

The Dictionary of Sociology by Fairchild (1940, 1955) provides maximum number of terms with brief one or two paragraph definitions, sometimes limited to even a few lines. Mitchell's dictionary (1968) has limited number of terms and short (one or half page) explanation of each term. Hoult (1969, 1977) also includes not many terms but, provides very appropriate definitions, supported with quotes from the original texts and usage in the literature of sociology. This dictionary has emphasized more on terms related to research methods and computer related terms. It also provides a detailed list of references, where usage of individual terms and treatment of concepts by sociologists can be verified. Mann (1983) includes biographical sketches of a good number of sociologists, but explanation of each term is very brief. Abercrombie (1984,1988) also has quite shorter notes on each term.

Out of the three dictionaries or encyclopedias of social sciences included, *International Encyclopedia of Social Sciences* (1968) and Kuper's *Social Science Encyclopedia* (1985) provide a separate list of the terms that they think, pertain to sociology. UNESCO sponsored Gould's Dictionary of social sciences (1964) provides definitions from various angles, i.e. sociological point of view, political point of view, psychological point of view etc. along with quotes from the original sociological texts.

A table showing the availability of main concepts of sociology, in 8 dictionaries of sociology/ social sciences and the form of the term used in them for each one of the 100 main concepts is presented in tabular form. The tabular presentation shows that:

1. The dictionaries do not adopt any fixed criteria about the use of the terms in singular or plural or about inversion of words for a term;

2. Dictionary of modern sociology by Hoult, includes maximum number of terms out of the main concepts of sociology identified in the present study; and

3. Only three main concepts history of sociology, scope of sociology, and scientific method are not included in any dictionary.

Table 5. 29

One hundred Main Concepts and the terms used for them in some Dictionaries

Main Concepts of sociology	Terms used in the dictionaries	Author FGDIHMAK	Total
0. SOCIOLOGY, HISTORY, THEORIES AND METHODS			
1. Sociology/		FGDIHMAK	8
Scope			
2. History			
3. Theories	Sociological theory	G	1
	Social theory	D	1
	Theory	DHM	3
4. Research Methods,	Sociological methods	F	1
Techniques	Methodology	GDH	3
5. Scientific Method	see Science	G	1
	see Methodology	D	1
	Scientific explanation	I	1
I. SOCIAL ORGANIZATION, SOCIAL PROCESSES, GROUP FORMATION			
6. Social Organization	Social organization	FGDH	4
	Organization	FIHM	4
7. Social System	Social system	GDHA	4
	Social systems	M	1
8. Social order	Social order	FGHA	4
	see Social cohesion	D	1
9. Society/	Society	FGDIHMAK	8
	Social life		
10. Socio-biology	Biological determinism	H	1

		Sociology, Biological	F	1
11.	Sexuality	Sexuality	G M	2
		Sexual behavior	I K	2
12.	Individual	Individual	F G H	3
		Individual psychology	I	1
13.	Personality	Personality	F D H M K	6
		Personality system	G	
14.	Attitudes	Attitude	F G D H M A	6
		Attitudes	I K	2
15.	Social Processes	Social processes	F H A	3
		Process	G	1
16.	Social relations	Social relations	F	1
		see social interaction	G	1
		Social relationships	H	1
17.	Social interaction	Social interaction	F G	2
		Interaction	F I H	3
18.	Groups	Group	F G D H A	5
		Groups	I K	2
19.	Primary groups	Primary groups	H	1
		see Group	G D A	3
		Group, Primary	F	1
20.	Small groups	Small groups		0
21.	Associations	Association	F G D H	4
II. SOCIAL INSTITUTIONS, FAMILY, POLITICAL, ECONOMIC INSTITUTIONS				
22.	Social Institutions	Social institutions	F I	2
		Institution	F G D H M A	6
23.	Kinship	Kinship	F G D I H M A K	7
		Kinship and Kinship systems	G	1
24.	Family	Family	F G D H M K	6
		Marriage- family formation	I	1
25.	Marriage	Marriage	F G D I H M A K	8
26.	Political Institutions	Political sociology	D I A	3
		Politics	F H	2
		Polity	H A	2
27.	Government	Government	F H K	3
28.	Formal	Formal organizations	A	1
		Organizations see Organization	H	1
29.	Bureaucracy	Bureaucracy	F G D I H M A K	8
30.	War	War	F G I H K	5
		see militarism	M	1
31	Economic institutions	Economic institutions		0
		Economic sociology	A	1
		Economic organization and economic system	G	1
		Economy	F H	2
		Economy and society	I	1
32.	Capitalism	Capitalism	F G D I H M A K	8

33. Work	Work	H	1
	Workers		I 1
	Work and leisure	K	1
34. Division of labor	Division of labor	G D H M A	5
Labor, Division of		F	1
35. Industrial	Industrial sociology	D D H	3
sociology	Industrial relations	I A	2
Industrial conflict	M	1	
Industry, sociology of		K	1
36. Leisure Leisure		F I H	3
Work and leisure	K	1	

III. CULTURE, RELIGION, SOCIAL CONTROL, EDUCATION

37. Culture	Culture	F G D I H M A K	8
38. Customs	Custom	F G D H A	5
39. Ideology	Ideology	F G D I H M A K	8
40. Magic	Magic	F G D H M K	
41. Sociology of	Sociology of religion	G D A	3
religion Religion:	Sociology of religion	I	1
	Religion	F G H M A	5
	Religion and ritual	K	1
42. Social control	Social control	F G D I H M A K	8
43. Values	Values	G D I A	4
	Value	F H	2
	Social values	F	1
44. Norms Norm		F G D I M A	6
	Norms	K	1
	Normative order	H	1
45. Morality	Morality	F I M	3
	Morals	F H	2
	Moral order	F G	2
46. Socialization	Socialization	G D I H A K	6
	Socialization process	F	1
47. Conformity Conformity		F G I H K	5
48. Deviance Deviance		H M	2
	Social deviance	D K	2
	Deviant behavior	G I A	3
49. Sociology of law	Sociology of law	G D A	3
	Law	I H M	3
50. Communication	Communication	F G I H M	4
	Communications	K	1
	Communication, Mass	I	1
51. Public opinion	Public opinion	F G I H A	5
52. Sociology of	Sociology of education	D A	2
education	Educational sociology	G	1
Education and society		I	1
Education		F G H M	4
53. Sociol. of knowledge	Sociology of knowledge	G D H A	4
Knowledge, Sociology of		I M K	3
54. Sociology of art	Sociology of art	F	1
Art, Sociology of		K	1

55. Science and Science Technology	Science: Sociology of science	F G H	3
		I	1
	Sociology of science	K	1
	Technology	F G I H	4
	Technological determinism see determinism	H	
	Technological society	M	1
	Technological change	A	1
56. Industrialization	Industrialization	F G I H M A	6
IV. SOCIAL STRUCTURE, STRATIFICATION, RACE			
57. Social Structure	Social structure	F G D I H M A K	8
58. Social differentiation	Social differentiation	F I M	3
	Differentiation	G H	2
59. Social inequality	Social inequality	F	1
	Inequality	F	1
	Equality	F G I H A K	6
	Equality, Social	M	1
60. Social stratification	Social stratification	F D H M	4
	Stratification	F G H A K	5
	Stratification, social	I	1
61. Social classes	Social class	F G	2
	Class	F H M A	4
	See Social stratification	D	1
	Class, Social	K	1
	Class system	H	1
62. Caste	Caste	F G I H M A K	7
	see social stratification	D	1
63. Social status	Social status	F D	2
	Status	F G I H M A	6
64. Role	Role	F G D I H M A K	8
	Social role see role	G H	2
65. Power	Power	F G H M A K	6
66. Authority	Authority	F G D H M A K	7
67. Leadership	Leadership	F G I H A K	6
68. Social mobility	Social mobility	F D I H M A K	7
	Mobility	G H	2
69. Sociology of gender	Sociology of gender	A	1
	Individual differences-sex differences	I	1
	Gender and biological sex	M	1
	Gender stratification	M	1
	Gender	A	1
	Sexual divisions	A	1
	Sexism	A	1
	Division of labor by sex	K	1
	Gender studies	K	1
70. Sociol. of occupations	Sociology of occupations	D	1
	Occupation	F G H	3
	Occupations and careers	I	1

71. Racial groups	Race	F G D I H M K	7
	Sociology of race	A	1
72. Race relations	Race relations	F I H M	4
	Racism	F G H M	4
	Race prejudice	F	1
	Race and minority group relations	G	1
	see Ethnic relations	K	1
73. Ethnic groups	Ethnic groups	G D I H A K	6
	Consciousness, ethnic	F	1
	Ethnic group relations see Race relations	H	1
	Ethnic relations see Race relations	M	1
74. Minorities	Minority	F G D I H M	6
Minority group		G H	2
V. SOCIAL CONFLICT, DISORGANIZATION			
75. Social Conflict	Social conflict	F	1
Conflict		F G D I H	5
Conflict, Social		D	1
Conflict theory		M	1
76. Social Disorganization	Social disorganization	F G H M	4
	Social disintegration	F	4
Disorganization, Community		F	1
77. Revolution	Revolution	F G I H M A	6
Revolutionary change		F H	2
Revolutions		K	1
78. Crowd	Crowd	F H	2
79. Collective behavior	Collective behavior	G D I H A	5
	Collective action	F	1
Collective behavior and crowds		K	1
80. Social movements	Social movements	I A K	3
Social movement	F G H	3	
VI. SOCIAL CHANGE			
81. Social change	Change	H	1
Social change		F G D I M A K	7
82. Evolution	Evolution	F G D I H M A K	7
83. Progress	Progress	F G H A	4
VII. HUMAN ECOLOGY, COMMUNITIES			
84. Human Ecology	Human ecology	F I H M	4
Ecology		F G D I A K	6
Cultural ecology		I	1
Ecology see Urban ecology		F	1
85. Environment	Environment	F G I H	4
Environmental studies		D M	2
86. Geographic environment	Geographic environment	F	1
	Environmentalism	H M	2

87. Medical Sociology	Medical sociology	K	1
Socialized medicine F		1	
Medical care		I	1
Medical profession		M	1
Sociology of medicine		A	1
88. Community	Community	F G D I H M A K	8
89. Rural sociology	Rural sociology	H K	2
Rural society		I	1
Sociology, Rural		F	1
Community, Village		F	1
90. Urbanization	Urbanization	F G D H A K	6
Urban revolution		I	1
91. Urban Sociology	Urban sociology	G D H	3
Sociology, rural and urban		F	1
Urban ecology: urban way of life		A	1
VIII. POPULATION			
92. Population	Population	F G I H K	5
Demography		F G D H M A	6
93. Migration Migration		F G I H M A K	7
IX. APPLIED SOCIOLOGY, SOCIAL PROBLEMS			
94. Applied sociology	Applied sociology	H A	2
Sociology, Applied		F	1
95. Social planning	Social planning	F	1
see Social policy		D	1
Social policy		F D	2
Planning, social welfare planning		I	1
Social welfare policy		K	1
96. Social problems	Social problems	I H A K	4
Social problem		F G	2
97. Crime	Crime	F G H M	4
Criminology		F G D I H M A K	8
Crime and delinquency		K	1
98. Delinquency	Delinquency	F H M A	4
Delinquency- social aspects		I	1
Delinquent		D	1
Crime and delinquency		K	1
99. Poverty	Poverty	F G D I H M A K	8
100. Sociology of aging	Social gerontology	H	1
	Gerontology	A	1
	Gerontology, social	K	1
	Aging	H A	2
	Old age assistance	F	1
Total out of 100 concepts		86 80 60 73 91 62 67	61

F	Fairchild Dictionary of sociology.	(1955)
G	Gould Dictionary of social sciences	(1964)
D	Duncan Mitchell Dictionary of sociology	(1968)
I	International Encycl. of the Social sciences	(1968)
H	Hoult Dictionary of modern sociology	(1969)
M	Michael Mann Macmillan Student Encycl. of sociology	(1983)
A	Abercrombie Dictionary of sociology	(1984)
K	Kuper Social science encyclopedia	(1985)

Table 5.30

Some Main Concepts not available in Dictionaries

Scientific method	see	Methodology	D
	see	Science	G
Social order	see	Social cohesion	D
Social relation	see	Social interaction	G
Formal organization	see	Organization	H
Class	see	Social stratification	D
Caste	see	Social stratification	D
War	see	Militarism	M
Race relations	see	Ethnic relations	K
Ethnic groups	see	Race relations	M
Ethnic group relations	see	Race relations	H
Morals	see	Normative order	H
Social change	see	Change	H
Technological determinism	see	Determinism	H

*For full name of the authors representing these first letters of their surname see at the end of the comparative table no. (5.9 ?)

5.821 Use of Singular or Plural Terms in the Dictionaries

Table 5.31

Singular or plural form of terms used in dictionaries

Terms used	First letter of Authors, or Dictionary name F G D I H M A K
Social system	G D H A
Social systems	M
Social processes	F H A
Process	G
Attitude	F G D H M A
Attitudes	I K
Communication	F G H M

Communications	K
Group	F G D H A
Groups	I K
Institution	G D H M A
Social institutions	F I
Occupation	F G H
Sociology of occupations	D
Norm	F G D I M A
Norms	K
Social movement	F G H
Social movements	I A K
Revolution	F G I H M A
Revolutions	K
Social problem	F G
Social problems	I H A K

5.83 Identification of some Main Concepts from Dictionaries

Table 5.32

No. of Dictionaries having a main Concept of Sociology

Provided in 4 Dictionariesof Sociology		Providedin 3 Dictionaries of Sociology	
0. SOCIOLOGY, HISTORY, THEORIES AND METHODS			
1. Sociology Scope	8*		
2. History			
		3. Theories	4
		4. Research Methods, Techniques	4
5. Scientific Method			
I. SOCIAL ORGANIZATION, SOCIAL PROCESSES, GROUP FORMATION			
		6. Social Organization	4
		7. Social System	4
8. Social order			
9. Society Social life	8		
10. Socio-biology			
11. Sexuality			
12. Individual/			
13. Personality	7		
14. Attitudes	8		

16. Social relations
17. Social interaction
18. Groups 7
19. Primary groups
20. Small groups
21. Associations 4

II. SOCIAL INSTITUTIONS,FAMILY, POLITICAL, ECONOMIC INSTITUTIONS

22. Social Institutions 6
23. Kinship 8
24. Family 7
25. Marriage 8
26. Political Institutions 5
27. Government
28. Formal Organizations
29. Bureaucracy 7
30. War 6
31. Economic institutions 5
32. Capitalism 8
33. Work
34. Division of labor 6
35. Industrial sociology
36. Leisure

III. CULTURE, RELIGION, SOCIAL CONTROL, EDUCATION

37. Culture 8
38. Customs 5
39. Ideology 8
40. Magic 6
41. Sociology of religion 8
42. Social control 8
43. Values 6
44. Norms 8
45. Morality
46. Socialization 7
47. Conformity
48. Deviance 7
49. Sociology of law 6
50. Communication 6
51. Public opinion 5
52. Sociology of education
53. Sociol. of knowledge 7

54. Sociology of art			
55. Science and Technology			
56. Industrialization	6		
IV. SOCIAL STRUCTURE, STRATIFICATION, RACE			
57. Social Structure	8		
		58. Social differentiation	5
59. Social inequality	7		
60. Social stratification	8		
61. Social classes	7		
62. Caste	7		
63. Social status	7		
64. Role	8		
65. Power	5		
66. Authority			
		67. Leadership	6
68. Social mobility	8		
69. Sociology of gender			
		70. Sociol. of occupations	5
71. Racial groups	8		
		72. Race relations	5
73. Ethnic groups	8		
74. Minorities	6		
V. SOCIAL CONFLICT, DISORGANIZATION			
75. Social Conflict	5		
		76. Social dis-organization	4
77. Revolution	7		
78. Crowd			
79. Collective behavior	7		
80. Social movements	6		
VI. SOCIAL CHANGE			
81. Social change	8		
		82. Evolution	7
		83. Progress	4
VII. HUMAN ECOLOGY, COMMUNITIES			
84. Human Ecology	8		
85. Environment	6		
		86. Geographic environment	3
		87. Medical Sociology	4
88. Community	8		

Concept	Dictionaries	Concept	Dictionaries
89. Rural sociology			
90. Urbanization	7		
91. Urban Sociology	5		
VIII. POPULATION			
92. Population	8		
93. Migration	7		
IX. APPLIED SOCIOLOGY, SOCIAL PROBLEMS			
		94. Applied sociology	3
95. Social planning			
		96. Social problems	6
97. Crime	7		
98. Delinquency	8		
99. Poverty	7		
		100. Sociology of aging	4

The Main concepts in this table have been divided into two categories on the basis of their availability in the number of dictionaries. The figure against each term however shows the availability of the term in total number of 8 dictionaries/ encyclopedias seen for this purpose For example the term 'war' is provided in only 3 out of 5 dictionaries of sociology consulted but if we take into consideration 3 dictionaries of social sciences also it is provided in a total of 6 out of 8 dictionaries of sociology/social sciences.

The table above, is meant to show that, at least 3 dictionaries of sociology include these concepts, as such could be treated as significant concepts of sociology.

REFERENCES

1. S R Ranganathan, *Prolegomena to library classification*. Bombay, Asia, 1967: p.72
2. *Ibid*. p. 201
3. Fred W Riggs "A new paradigm for social science terminology" *Intl. Classification* 6(3) 1979: 152
4. S R Ranganathan *op. cit*. part G
5. Classification Research Group "Need for a faceted classification as the basis of all methods of information retrieval." Proceedings of the Intl. Study Conference on Classification for Information Retrieval, Beatrice Webb House, Dorking, Eng. 13th- 17th May 1957. London, ASLIB, 1957 Appendix 2 p. 137-47
6. *Ibid*.

7. Eric de Grolier "Recent research trends in the field of information retrieval languages". Hans Wellisch ed. Subejct retrieval in the seventies: new directions. Proceedings of the Intl. Symposium, 14-15 May 1971. West Port, Greenwood, 1972: p. 29

8. F W Lancaster "Vocabulary control in information retrieval systems." in *Advances in librarianship* vol. 7. New York, Academic, 1977:p. 11

9. Susan Bury "Comparison of classification schemes for libraries" *Lib. Sci.* 17(3) 1980: 73-82

10. B S Wynar, 'Criteria for successful classification scheme' in "Classification of library materials" in *Introduction to cataloging and classification*, 4th ed. Littleton, Col., Libraries Unlimited 1972: p. 375

11. P N Kaula, "Rethinking on concepts in the study of classification". *Herald of Lib. Sci.* 23(1-2) 1984: p.40

12. Russell Langworthy "Process" in Julius Gould; William L Kolb, *A dictionary of social sciences*, London, Tavistock, 1964: p. 538-540

6
Major Findings and Conclusion

6.1 Identification of Main concepts

Identification of the main aspects, concepts or categories of a discipline is very essential for designing any bibliographic information storage and retrieval vocabulary. It is also essential that the concepts and categories so identified are able to represent other concepts within them to include the whole field of knowledge in that area. The terminology used in the bibliographic information retrieval tools, like classification schemes and indexing systems should represent the concepts of the individual disciplines in their proper perspectives. But it is not possible for any bibliographic information storage and retrieval tool, even if it represents the specific discipline, to include the terms that can represent all the aspects of a subject.

The first main objective of this study has been to develop methodology for identifying the main concepts pertaining to a discipline, specifically in social sciences. Textbook pertaining to a subject, were adjudged as the best source to identify the main concepts a discipline, as these present a cumulative and consensual view of a field of study and generally try to include most of the concepts of an area of study. Textbook also assimilate the literature appearing in a subject in the form of micro-documents. Textbook writers try to present a field of knowledge, to the best extent possible. As such, if we take a large sample of textbooks of a subject in social sciences, and classify their chapter headings, we get most of the significant concepts of that discipline, that generally forms part of the subject. The terms identified in this way, can be treated as the main concepts, and can also be used as main headings in the information retrieval tools, as these terms represent the literature of a subject and satisfy the criteria of currency and literary consensus.

The second objective of the study was to identify the main concepts of sociology with the help of the methodology stated above. A sample of 100 textbooks of sociology was taken, out of which 87 were selected, that were found to contain the chapters, generally included in a standard sociology textbook. The chapter headings were classified according to the main concept dealt in them. All the substantive terms or their synonyms used in the chapter headings by at least 3 authors out of 87 seen, were taken, and the exercise enabled to identify 100 main concepts of sociology. The classification of chapter headings also enabled to bring together, all synonymous terms generally used for a concept in the sociological literature. The terms identified in this way, out of classification of chapter headings, can be taken to represent the views of 87 sociology textbook authors, as to what they suggest as the main concepts of sociology.

Number of other sources like bibliographic classification schemes, classification schemes used in indexing/abstracting services, and some significant concepts suggested by some sociologists were also seen, and it was found that majority of the concepts identified in this study on the basis of the actual literature survey, tally in a majority of cases with the main concepts suggested by other sources.

6.1 Relative Significant of the Concepts used in Sociology

The third main objective of this study was to identify some most significant concepts out of all the main concepts used by sociologists, so that the terms representing these could be used a main headings in the information retrieval tools. The proportion of a textbook devoted by each author to a concept, in the form of chapter headings was added together, that enabled to quantify the relative significance given to that concept, by all the authors having a chapter on it. Thus, the cumulative proportion of a book devoted to a concept, made it possible to arrange all the identified concepts in descending order of significance for use as headings in the bibliographic information retrieval tools. This list in descending order of significance of concepts divides all the 100 concepts into three relative significance categories: 44 concepts that were used as chapter headings by the highest number of authors or highest proportion of these 87 textbooks was devoted to them; 26 concepts, that were dealt by lesser number of authors or lesser proportion of textbooks was devoted to them; and 30 concepts on which few authors had chapter heading in their textbooks and the proportion of books devoted to these concepts was the lowest.

The objective of this categorization is to suggest that bibliographic information retrieval tools must include the terms representing these concept in their vocabulary, and if all the terms can not be accommodated, the inclusion should be based on the relative significance of the concepts in the subject. That is to say that, highly significant concepts should be adopted as main headings in the information retrieval tools and also that, none of the significant concepts should remain un-represented in a scheme that includes sociology as a subject.

6.3 Arrangement in Filiatory and Helpful Sequence

An information retrieval tool is designed in such a manner that, all related concepts are either placed in a filiatory sequence, or if it is not possible, related concepts are connected by cross references. It is also essential that, some broad categorization of individual concepts is adopted in anarrangement, and these broad categories are termed in a manner that, all the individual concepts can be accommodated within them. Broad categorization is quite helpful for the processor of information as well as, for the users of the system, for the relative position of major categories can be easily remembered by both. Broad categorization helps a classifier, so that he can remember these main headings at the time of classifying, otherwise, it is likely that some documents are placed at the convenience of the classifier, or wherever un-assigned classes are available in a classification scheme.

Some of the main concepts of sociology, generally used as major categories in the textbooks and other literature of the subject, also appear as the headings suitable for major categories in the present study, on the basis of the highest significance given to them, by the textbook authors. The terms suggested and used as main headings are capable of including the largest number of individual concepts within them. In a relative significance range obtained for various concepts used in sociology between 8.0708 as highest and 0.0875 as lowest, the major categories adopted and their relative significance is as follows:

	Main heading terms	Significance		Main heading terms	Significance
1.	History of sociology	0.8310	11.	Social control	1.0559
2.	Theories of sociology	1.5087	12.	Deviance	2.1384
3.	Research methods	2.6350	13.	Social disorganization	0.6262
4.	Social organization	4.7906			
5.	Social institutions	5.5380	14.	Social conflict	0.7417
6.	Sociology of education	2.8657	15.	Social change	8.0708
7.	Culture	4.9952	16.	Human ecology	1.6740
8.	Sociology of religion	2.7768	17.	Population	3.0431
9.	Social structure	2.1703	18.	Social problems	0.8299
10.	Race relations	1.0559			

Majority of the literature that is generally published in sociology can be accommodated within these main headings. A filiatory arrangement of the main concepts of sociology enables to compare the arrangement done in some of the bibliographic information retrieval tools. As such the fourth main objective of the study has been, to arrange the main concepts in a filiatory and helpful sequence. Although, no arrangement of multi-dimensional concepts into a linear sequence can satisfy all the view points, and there is always scope for some improvement over the ones already in existence, still some decision has been taken, and some criteria has to be followed for any arrangement. For this purpose, following criteria were used to obtain filiatory and helpful arrangement of main concepts of sociology, in this study:

a. how a concept has been defined in the dictionaries ofsociology/ social sciences;
b. how a concept is explained with the help of other terms, thatshows relation of a concept with other concepts;
c. usage of a term in the literature of the subject;
d. how the major sections in the textbooks are further

dividedinto chapters thus showing the concepts within a majorheading;

e. related terms used by sociologists for a concept, in the formof 'see' and 'see also' references at the end of a definitionof a term;

f. terms used or shown as BT, NT,UF,RT or USE in the Library ofCongress Subject Headings; and

g. hierarchical position of a concept adopted in someclassification schemes.

The arrangement obtained on the basis of these considerations can be used/ adopted in classifying sociological literature, with some minor changes, some combination of synonymous concepts and some provision for newer and developing areas/fields of sociology.

6.4 Representation in Bibliographic Information Retrieval Tools

6.41 Representation in Dewey Decimal Classification

Adoption of major categories in the Dewey Decimal Classification is not according to their significance. Some of the main concepts of sociology have not been provided at all in the sociology schedule. Some of these are research methods, social organization, society, individual and personality, sociology of education, social structure, social differentiation, minorities, and collective behavior. A large number of headings are not mentioned directly against the class number , and only mentioned in the scope note added with the headings. Sociology of education is to be classed in education at 370, crime at 364 and social problems at 362. In most of the cases, headings in the form of phrases, instead of single or double term heading have been adopted, e.g. 306.7 'institutions pertaining to the relations of the sexes'. Even closely related concepts, generally used in pairs by sociologists have not come together in a large number of cases, e.g. conformity at 303.32 and deviance at 302.542 . The scheme has to use scope notes quite often, which could have been avoided if all the concepts were arranged within some major categories, thus placement of individual concepts itself would have explained the sub-headings to be included within them. The hospitality provided through gapdevice, can not be of much use, unless the major concepts of sociology, that are generally being dealt in the literature of the subject, are provided as main headings, against the class number directly.

6.42 Representation of Main Concepts in the UDC

Universal Decimal Classification uses only 5 major section in the sociology schedule and these are: psychological aspects, social relations, social processes, social structures, and sociological theories, and these headings are hardly capable of representing all the main concepts of sociology. UDC uses the heading 'sources and motives of social phenomena' and includes many psychological aspects within it. The heading 'social structure' does not include differentiation, stratification, social classes etc. generally included by sociologists within it. All types of possible groups have been placed together at 301.18, that accommodates racial groups, communities, and economic and political groupings.

Out of the 100 main concepts of sociology, only 23 are enumerated in sociology schedule, and a large number of them included in the schedule of psychology, political science, and social welfare etc. . Some of the main concepts not enumerated in the sociology schedule are family enumerated at 392.3, social institutions, social structure, social strata at 342.54, social status, ethnic minorities at 342.724, deviance, criminal sociology at 343.99, collective behavior, human ecology, and applied sociology. A number of related concepts are scattered e.g. groups is 301.18 but group consciousness is 301.152 . In most of the cases, even up to or 10 terms are enumerated within a single class number, e.g. at 301.18 which includes 9 terms. Gap device is available for inclusion of new concepts but not within 6 digit class numbers. In the present scheme, a classifier has to use whole schedule of UDC for 75 per cent of the main concepts of sociology. Even taking the help of index only does not provide relief, as the index does not provide full context. The scheme has provision to represent various facets of a subject through colon device, but only at the cost of the brevity of notation, as even the single facet enumerated in the sociology schedule uses 8 to 9 digits of the notation e.g. 301.185.1 racial, ethnic groupings.

6.43 Representation of main Concepts in the Colon classification

Out of 100 main concepts of sociology, only 29 are enumerated in the sociology schedule of Colon Classification, some concepts can be used through subject device, and remaining 51 are not enumerated in the whole scheme. As far as arrangement of main categories is concerned, only Y:1 culture, and Y:5 demography are used in CC out of 15 main concepts used as category headings in the present study. All other schemes provide some concepts as main headings, but CC tries to provide categoriese. by residence, by birth or status, and by association etc. ,but has been successful to devise such categories in a few cases only. The effort to categorize the concepts is he most desiredquality of a classification scheme, but if we adopt the categories suggested in the CC, such headings do not tally with the terms most often used by sociologists. This is the reason, only 9 headings used in sociology tally with the 100 main concepts of sociology. One case is of capitalism. This term is used by sociologists as heading. If we want to use a category for it, it can be placed either within economic systems or political ideologies, etc. but these headings are not much in use among the sociologists. On account of the preference of CC for category type headings, it prefers the headings in singular form only.

Abstracts Classification Scheme

To arrange sociological concepts, SA does not use any major categories and 33 main headings are all coordinate headings printed in bold. The comparative study shows that, out of 100 main concepts identified in this study, 48 are not used as headings in the Sociological Abstracts. The terms, not used as headings in it were further checked in SA index, to see if these headings have become obsolete, and as such no literature is appearing on them. It was found that except a few headings most of the terms have 50 to 256 references during a period of three years, 1990 to 1992, for which annual cumulative index was seen. This observation indicated that, literature is appearing on these concepts but they are not included as main headings in the SA, the terms are still in use and they have 3 not become obsolete. However, some concepts have less than 50 references during a period of 3 years, e.g. social processes, social institutions, and social disorganization etc. Some other concepts as social life, government, authority, industrial sociology, magic, caste system, customs, morality, conformity, crowds, and development are losing sociologists interest, if the periodical literature included and its system of indexing in the SA is adopted as criterion.

Most of the headings used in the Sociological Abstracts are necessarily lengthy, like 'sociology of sexual behavior' for sexuality, 'social division of labour' for division of labour', and 'sociology of communities and regions' for communities, etc. and in most of the cases, phrased headings have been preferred. Majority of the headings used in the Sociological Abstracts, match well with the terms being used in the textbook chapter headings and the terminology represents the literature of sociology, better than any other information retrieval tool. In SA, there is no effort to categorize the concepts, and literature on related concepts gets scattered in the arrangement, and even with the help of the subject index it is not possible to locate all the documents on the related concepts together.

LCSH being a general list of subject headings, has not beenable to provide subject headings adequately for a number of sociological concepts. In a number of cases, the term is available but there is no effort to specify the subject specific on text so that the term can be used as heading in sociology also. Some of the discipline specific terms used as headings in sociology, but not provided in the LCSH are scientific method, society, social order, social relations, primary groups, social differentiation, social disorganization and applied sociology etc. . A number of concepts are not represented in the list but the indexer is directed to use some alternative terms. Some of the terms not used in this way are, research methods, social organization, government, organizations, social stratification, sociology of gender, sociology of law, environment, and social planning. Thus, out of 100 most commonly used concepts in sociology only 55 were represented in LCSH, for 20 some synonymous term is used, in 11 cases instruction to use some other term is provided, and for 10 terms there is no provision at all.

Scope note is provided for 18 out of 100 terms, which facilitates and specifies the use of that heading to a document. The policy of inversion of headings in a number of cases, e.g. sociology, rural ; sociology, urban; heredity, human; and knowledge, sociology of, etc. are not convenient from the users point of view.

Sociology

Main concepts of sociology listed /suggested/ enumerated/guessed or identified by 7 sociologists, 1 librarian, and the areas of the 44 research committees of the International Sociological Association were classified in a filiatory sequence. The main concepts suggested by these sources, during the period 1937 to 1988 are not based on any actual literature survey. All these nine sources combined together, provide us 112 areas/fields of sociology, but these lists do not include at least 29 fields/ areas that could be identified from the textbook chapter headings as the main concepts of sociology. Among these 29 concepts, not included by any of these sources, 7 are among those that have been identified as 44 most significant concepts of sociology in this study.

6.6 PROVISION FOR MAIN CONCEPTS IN SOME DICTIONARIES

Evaluation of 5 dictionaries of sociology and 3 dictionaries/ encyclopedias of social sciences from the point of view of provision in them for the main concepts of sociology, and the form of the term used in them shows that, not dictionary includes all the main concepts or at least their synonyms, and the terms used for a concept by them are diverse. Keeping aside other aspects, a dictionary that includes maximum number of main concepts of sociology can be deemed comparatively better for analyzing sociological concepts and for their proper categorization. The analysis shows that the dictionary by Hoult that includes 90 out of the 100 main concepts of sociology, fits this criteria, and was found better than others from various other angles also. Although, it would be improper to decide the relative significance of the terms used by maximum number of dictionaries, but if we take only those terms, that have been provided at least 3 dictionaries of sociology, out of 5 consulted for the present study, a list of 76 concepts was available. On the whole, the study indicates that main concepts of sociology, that are to be represented as terms in any bibliographic information retrieval tool, can not be identified with the help of the terms sued for them, in the dictionaries of sociology.

6.7 Summary of Findings and Implications

Evaluation of the various information retrieval tools shows that neither any information retrieval tool has tried to identify the main concepts of sociology, nor the arrangement is based on proper categorization and filiatory arrangement of the main concepts. The main findings of this study as follows:

1. The study has been able to identify some concepts of sociology with the help of the terms used in the chapter headings in alarge sample of introductory textbooks of sociology. As these terms are based on their use as headings by a large number of authors, these can be treated as the main concepts of sociology. Thus, the study proves that it is possible to identify the main concepts pertaining to a discipline.

2. The identified main concepts were compared with the terms used for them some of the information retrieval tools, and the comparison proves that terminology used in these tools, does not adequately represent all the main sociological concepts.

3. The study also proves that, concepts used in a field can beranked according to their relative significance for use as main headings in the information retrieval tools, on the basis of the proportion of introductory textbooks devoted to a concept by taking a large sample of such books.

On the basis of the findings of this study a detailed classification schedule for sociology has been prepared which is shown as appendix VI.

6.71 Implications

Main concepts of sociology identified in this study, need toe provided in the information retrieval tools as class headings and subject heading terms. The study also stresses the need for proper categorization and filiatory arrangement of concepts pertaining to a discipline, while representing the terms for them in the bibliographic information retrieval tools. None of the identified concepts is new, and most of them are used in some retrieval tool or the other, and literature is appearing on them currently also, that was verified by scrutinizing the Sociological Abstracts also for a few years. Thus the terms represent the consensual view of a large number of sociologists and are in use currently in the literature, hence, if these are included as headings in the information retrieval tools, it will be fulfilling the requirement of 'educational and scientific consensus' as well as 'currency of terms', the bases which are most preferred, while selected terms for a scheme of arrangement.

The study also shows that, these are the most preferred terms among the users of the information retrieval systems pertaining to sociology. It is desirable that, a classification scheme for sociology is finalized on the basis of the findings of this study, which could be used for arrangement of macro-documents in the libraries, as well as for classifying and arranging the micro-documents for indexing and abstracting systems and services. The study also arranges the concepts and their definitions in a classified form, and the definition, explanation, and usage of a term is meant to help the organizers of the information retrieval systems in deciding the scope a concept and its related terms. If this analysis could be extended to other main concepts of sociology and classified dictionaries in the fields were available, it would great help to the organization and efficient retrieval of bibliographic information in specific disciplines.

The study is based on a survey of the textbooks of sociology, but no book could be identified that deals with all the main concepts of sociology, as such a standard textbook can be prepared by some sociologists, that includes all the main concepts of sociology. Finally it could be pointed out that, the method of identification of the main concepts of sociology used in this study, needs to be applied to other social sciences, to show how far the methodology fits for identifying their main concepts. The results can be used in designing the information retrieval tools, which will invariably include all the main concepts of the respective disciplines.

Appendices

APPENDIX I

One Hundred Textbooks of Sociology used as the main Source of Data

Year Author Title No. of Sections/Chapters

1. 1873 Spencer, Herbert Study of sociology. Ann Arbour, Univ. of Michigan, 1961: 411 p. 15*
2. 1937 Calverton, V F (ed.) *Making of society: an outline of sociology*. New York, Random House, 1937: 411 p. 8
3. 1939 Lee, Alfred McClung ed. *Principles of sociology*. 3rd ed. New York, Barnes and Noble, 1969: 420 p. 6 35
4. 1942 Barnes, Henry Elmer, *Social institutions in era of world upheaval*. 5th print. New York, Prentice Hall, 1946: 411 p. 6 19
5. 1945 Gurvitch, G; Moore, W E *Twentieth century sociology*. Jaipur, Rawat, 1980: 411 p. 136. 1947 Ogburn, W F; Nimkoff, M F *Handbook of sociology*. 5th ed. 6th print. New Delhi, Eurasia, 1979: 644 p. 7 26
7. 1949 Sprott, W J H Sociology. 3rd ed. 8th reprint. London, Hutchinson Univ. Library, 1969: 411 p. 10
8. 1950 Eldridge, Seba et al Fundamentals of sociology. New York, Thomas Y Crowell, 1950: 720 p. 7 34
9. 1950 MacIver, R M; Page, C H Society: an introductory analysis. London, Macmillan, 1974: 697 p. 3 29
10. 1951 O'Brien, Robert et al Principles of sociology: a text with adapted readings. Boston, Houghton Miffin Co., 1964: 526 p. 9
11. 1952 Freedman, Ronald et al Principles of sociology: a text with adapted readings. New York, Henry Holt, 1952: 683 p. 15
12. 1952 Levy Jr, Martin J (Structure of society). 6th reprint. Boston, NJ. Princeton Univ. Press, 1971: 584 p.

---

* No. of pages is followed by the sections/chapters in the book.

13. 1952 Merrill, Francis E; Eldridge, H W Culture and society: an introduction to sociology. 6th reprint. Englewood Cliffs, NJ., Prentice Hall, 1956: 611 p. 6 29
14. 1953 Biesanz, John; Biesanz, Mavis Introduction to social sciences: modern society. 3rd ed. Englewood Cliffs, NJ. Prentice Hall, 1978: 719 p. 3 29.
15. 1955 Broom, Leonard; Selznick, Philip Principles of sociology. 4th ed. New York, Harper and Row, 1977: 309 p. 9 -
16. 1955 Broom, Leonard; Selznick, Philip Sociology: a text with adapted readings. 7th ed. New York, Harper and Row, 1977: 411 p. bib. p.515-540 3 17
17. 1956 Frankfurt Institute for Social Research Aspects of sociology. London, Heinemann, 1973: 411 p. 12
18. 1956 Weinberg, Meyer; Shebat, Oscar E Society and men. 2nd ed. Englewood Cliffs, NJ., 1965: 694 p. 28
19. 1957 Bierstedt, Robert Social order. 3rd ed. Bombay, Tata-McGraw Hill, 1970: 411 p. 6 19
20. 1957 Gisbert, S J Fundamentals of sociology. 3rd ed. 8th reprint. Bombay, Orient Longman, 1973: 411 p. 5 17
21. 1957 Gitler, Joseph B ed. Review of sociology: analysis of a decade. New York, John Wiley, 1957: 411 p. 14
22. 1957 Mannheim, Karl Systematic sociology: an introduction to the study of society. 2nd print. London, Routledge, 1959: 167 p. 4 12
23. 1959 Merton, Robert K et al eds. Sociology today: problems and prospects. New York, Harper, 1959: 623 p. 5 25
24. 1959 Mills, C Wright (Sociological imagination). London, OUP, 1959: 234 p. - -
25. 1959 Mitchell, G Duncan Sociology: the study of social systems. 2nd ed. Delhi, Oxford, 1977: 180 p. 3 10
26. 1960 Green, Arnold W Sociology: an analysis of life in modern society. 6th ed. New York, McGraw Hill, 1972: 479 p. 4 21
27. 1960 Johnson, Harry M Sociology: a systematic introduction. New Delhi, Allied, 1960: 688 p. 7 22
28. 1961 Chinoy, Ely Society: an introduction to sociology. 2nd ed. New York, Random House, 1967: 5 21
29. 1961 Parsons, Talcott et al eds. Theories of society: foundations of modern sociological theory. New York, Free Press, 1965: 1979-5 24
30. 1961 Sutherland, Robert L et al Introductory sociology. New Delhi, Oxford and IBH, 1979: 403 p. 6 22

31. 1962 Bottomore, T B Sociology: a guide to problems and literature. 3rd ed. Bombay, Blackie, 1979: 6 20

32. 1962 Young, Kimball; Mack, Raymond Principles of sociology: a reader in theory and research. New Delhi, Affiliated East West, 1972: 373 p. 5 26

33. 1962 Young, Kimball Systematic sociology. 2nd ed. New Delhi, Affiliated East West, 1972: 376 p. 4 27

34. 1964 Douglas, Mary et al Man in society: patterns of human organization. London, Doubleday, 1964: 367 p. 16

35. 1964 Horton, Paul B; Hunt, Chester L Sociology. 6th ed. Tokyo, Mcgraw Hill, 1980: 526 p. 6 21

36. 1964 Kar, Parimal An out line of sociology. Calcutta, Bookland, 1964: 311 p. 17

37. 1965 Inkeles, Alex (What is sociology.) New Delhi, Prentice Hall, 1971:120 p. - -

38. 1965 Koller, Marvin R; Couse, Harold C Modern sociology. New York, Rinehart, 1969: 374 p. 6 22

39. 1965 Valdes, Donald M; Dean, Dwight G Sociologyin use: selected readings for introductory course. 6th reprint. New York, Macmillan, 1969: 512 p. 11

40. 1966 Goode, William J ed. Dynamics of modern society. New Delhi, Eurasia, 1975: 474 p. 7 15

41. 1966 Muzumdar, Haridas Grammar of sociology: manin society. Bombay, Asia, 1966: 728 p.3 20

42. 1967 Basu, Minendra Nath Sociology an applied limb of cultural anthropology. 2nd ed. Calcutta, World Press, 1975: 268 p. - 17

43. 1967 Bernard, Elvin L Basic sociology. 2nd ed. New York, Appleton, 1973: 533 p. glossary 495-507 6 22

44. 1967 Sachdeva, D R ; Vidyabhusan An introduction to sociology. 6th ed. Allahabad, Kitab Mahal, 1976: 684 p. 6 43

45. 1968 Goldthorpe, J E An introduction to sociology. 3rd ed. London, Cambridge Univ. Press, 1975: 221 p. 9

46. 1968 McNall, Scott G ed. Sociological perspective: introductory readings. 4th ed. Boston, Little Brown, 1977: 471 p. 5 19

47. 1968 Rocher, Guy General introduction to sociology: a theoretical perspective. Ontario, Macmillan, 1972: 580 p. 3 16

48. 1968 Sharma, Ram Nath Principles of sociology. Bombay, Asia, 1968: 460 p. 32

49. 1969 Abrahamson, Mark Sociology: an introduction to concepts

and data. New York, Van Nostrand, 1969: 340 p. 3 10

50. 1969 Smelser, Neil J; Davis, James A eds. Sociology. 3rd ed. Englewood Cliffs, Prentice Hall, 1988: 178 p. - 11
51. 1970 Coulson, Margaret A ; Riddel, Davis S (Approaching sociology: a critical introduction.) London, Routledge, 1970: 130 p. - -
52. 1970 Lenski, Gerhard; Lenski, Jean (Human societies: an introduction to macro-sociology.) New York, Mcgraw Hill, 1974 : 529 p. - -
53. 1970 Mercer, Blaine E; WAnderer, Jules J Study of society. Belmont, Calif. Wadsworth, 1970: 515 p. 16
54. 1970 Scott, W Richard Social processes and social structures: an introduction to sociology. New York, Holt, Rinehart, 1970: 637 p. 7 29
55. 1970 Wilkins, Elizabeth J Introduction to sociology. 3rd reprint London, McDonald, 1972: 416 p. 3 16
56. 1970 Worsley, Peter Introducing sociology. Hormondsworth, Penguin, 1970: 416 p. - 8
57. 1971 Gorman, Benjamin Social themes. Englewood Cliffs,NJ. Prentice Hall, 1971: 274 p. 4 11
58. 1971 Popenoe, David Sociology 7th rev. ed. Englewood Cliffs, NJ. Prentice Hall, 1988: 588 p. 16 60
59. 1971 Sergeant, Graham Textbook of sociology. London, Macmillan, 1971: 354 p. - 6
60. 1972 Berger, Peter, L ; Berger, Brigitte Sociology: a biographical approach. New York, Basic books, 1972: 372 p. - 17
61. 1972 McGee, Reece Points of departure: basic concepts of sociology). Hinsdale, Ill., Dryden Press, 1972: 208 p. - 13
62. 1973 Acuff, F Gene; Allen, Donald E From man to society: introductory sociology. Hinsdale, Ill., Dryden Press, 1973: 589 p. 423
63. 1973 Leslie, Gerald R et al Order and change: introductory sociology. 3rd ed. New York, Oxford Univ. Press, 1980: 692 p. 6 21
64. 1973 Perry, John A; Perry, Erna K Contemporary society: an introduction to social science. 4th ed. New York, Harper, 1984: 528 p. - 17
65. 1973 Perry, John A; Perry, Erna K Social web: an introduction to sociology. New York, Harper and Row,1987: 658 p. - 13

66. 1974 Potter, David; Phillip, Sarre eds. Dimensions of society. London, Univ. of London, 1974: 528 p. - 8

67. 1975 Baldridge, J Victor Sociology: a critical approach to power, conflict and change. New York, John Wiley, 1975: 497 p. 13

68. 1975 Chambliss, William J; Ryther, Thomas E Sociology: the discipline and its direction. New York, McGraw Hill, 1975: 385 p. 4 17

69. 1975 Cole, Stephen Sociological orientation: an introduction to sociology. Chicago, Rand McNally, 1975: 318 p. 9 19

70. 1975 Denisoff, R Berge; Wahrman, Ralph An invitation to sociology. 3rd ed. New York, Macmillan, 1983: 589 p. 16

71. 1975 Kenkel, William F; Voland, Ellen Society in action. New York, Harper, 1975: 534 p. 4 16

72. 1975 Stewart, Elbert W; Glynn, JAmes A Introduction to sociology. 4th ed. New Delhi, Tata-McGraw Hill, 1985: 400 p. 5 16

73. 1975 Townsend, Peter (Sociology and social policy). London, Penguin, 1975: 371 p. 24

74. 1975 Van den Verghe, Pierre L (Man in society: a bio- social view.) New York, Elsevier, 1975: 300 p. - -

75. 1976 Hebding, Daniel E ; Glick, Leonard Introduction to sociology. Reading, Mass. Addison-Wesley, 1976: 443 p. 5 13

76. 1976 Rose, Peter, I; Glazerm Myron et al Sociology: inquiring into society. 2nd ed. New York, Cranfield, 1982: 605 p. 5 16

77. 1976 Thorns, David C ed. (New directions in sociology.) London, David and Charles, 1976: 192 p. - -

78. 1976 Goode, William J Principles of sociology. 2nd ed. New York, McGraw Hill, 1988: 343p. 6 17

79. 1977 Shapiro, R Diane Foundations for sociology: a self-learning text. Chicago, Rand McNally, 1977: 407 p. 19

80. 1977 Warren, Carol A B ociology: change and conformity. Homewood, Ill. Dorsey Press,1977: 427p 6 15

81. 1978 Stewart, Elbert W Sociology: the human science. New York, McGraw- Hill, 1978: 607 p. 4 19

82. 1979 Phillips, Bernard S Sociology: from concept to practice. New York, McGraw-Hill, 1979: 524 p. glossary p. 501-10; 8 20.

83. 1979 Sherman, Howard J; Wood, James L Sociology: traditional and radical perspectives. New York, Harper and Row, 1979: 413 p. 3 23

84. 1979 Szymanski, Albert; J Goertzel; Ted George Sociology: class, consciousness, and contradictions. New York, D Van Nostrand, 1979: 344 p. - 14
85. 1980 Fletcher, Ronald (Sociology: its nature, scope and elements.) London, Batsford Academic, 1980: 255 p. - -
86. 1980 Haralambos, M; Heald, Rabin Sociology: themes and perspectives. 2nd ed. New Delhi, OUP, 1988: 594 p. p. - 13
87. 1980 Marx, Gary T ; Goodman, Norman Sociology: classic and popular approaches. New York, Random House, 1980: 436 p. - 11
88. 1981 Kubat, Daniel ed. (Paths of sociological imagination.) New York, Gordon and Breach, 1981: 584 p.- -
89. 1981 Short, James E ed. (State of sociology: problems and prospects.) Baverly Hills,Sage,1981: 303 p. - -
90. 1982 Bottomore, Tom et al eds. (Sociology: the state of the art). London, Sage, 1982: 278 p. - -
91. 1982 Larson, Richard Readings for introducing sociology. New York, OUP, 1982: 293 p. 4 -
92. 1983 Eshleman, J Ross; Cashion, Barbara G Sociology: an introduction. 3rd ed. Boston, Scott Fordman, 1988: 596 p. 6 21
93. 1983 Lee, David; Newby, Howard (Problems of sociology: an introduction to the discipline.) London, Hutchinson, 1983: 379 p. - -
94. 1983 Tischler, Henry, L et al Introduction to sociology. 3rd ed. New York, Holt Rinehart, 1986: 641 p. ref. 6 20
95. 1984 Persell, Caroline Hodges Understanding society: an introduction to sociology. 2nd ed. New York, Harper, 1987: 688 p. glossary p. 629-44 ; 6 23
96. 1985 O'Donnell, Gerard Mastering sociology. 2nd ed. London, Macmillan, 1988: p. 357 9 26.
97. 1985 Wallace, Richard C ; Wallace, W D Sociology. 2nd ed. reprint. Boston,Allen and Bacon, 1989: 611p. 6 19
98. 1986 Charon, Joel M Sociology: a conceptual approach. 2nd ed. Boston, Allyn and Bacon, 1989: 559 p. 7 18.
99. 1988 Gordon, Milton M Scope of sociology. New York, OUP, 1988: 252p. 7.
100. 1990 Shankar Rao, C N Sociology. New Delhi, S Chand, 1990: 726 p. 10 30

Note: Thirteen titles not included in the final analysis are shown within parenthesis and section and chapter column for such titles is indicated with a blank.

APPENDIX-II

Classified list of chapter headings used in 87 sociology textbooks

0. SOCIOLOGY, HISTORY, THEORIES AND METHODS

1. SOCIOLOGY

1.	1952 Study of Sociology	Merrill 1/29
2.	1956 Concept of Sociology	FISR 1/12
3.	1957 Sociology and the Social Sciences[#]	Gisbert 1/17
4.	1961 Sociology	Sutherland 1/22
5.	1962 Sociology and the Social Sciences	Young 1/26
6.	1964 Sociology and society	Horton 1/6
7.	1965 What is Sociology	Koller 1/6
8.	1966 Introduction to Sociology	Muzumdar 3/30
9.	1968 What is Sociology	Goldthorpe 1/9
10.	1968 Sociology and other Social Sciences	Sharma 3/32
11.	1970 Sociology	Worsley 1/8
12.	1973 Sociology Problems and Prospects	Bertrand 22/22
13.	1975 (What is Sociology)	Denisoff 1/16
14.	1976 Sociological point of view	Kenkel 1/16
15.	1976 Sociological perspective	Hebding 1/5
16.	1977 Sociological perspective	Rose 1/16
17.	1977 Sociological perspective	Broom 1/17
18.	1980 Introduction to Sociology	G Marx, 1/11
19.	1983 Nature and uses of Sociology	Eshleman 1/20
20.	1983 Sociological perspective	Tischler 1/20
21.	1986 Discipline of sociology	Charon 1/17
22.	1989 Sociological approach	Wallace 1/6

1.A SCOPE OF SOCIOLOGY

1.	1949 What Sociology is about	Sprott 1/10
2.	1952 Field of Sociology	Freedman 1/15
3.	1962 Scope and Methods*	Bottomore 1/6
4.	1964 Fields and Methods* of Sociology	Horton 2/21
5.	1964 Sociology: the Subject	Matter Kar 1/17
6.	1965 Extending frontiers of Sociology	Koller 21/22
7.	1967 Definition and scope	Sachdeva 1/29

8.	1970 Scope and Method*	Mercer 1/16
9.	1971 Issues and Directions	Gorman 4/4
10.	1971 Sociology: Field and its Methods*	Popenoe 1/16
11.	1973 Field	Leslie 1/21
12.	1975 Subject matter	Chambliss 1/4
13.	1977 What Sociology is about?	Shapiro 1/19
14.	1977 New direction (New Fields)	Warren 6/6
15.	1984 Contemporary areas of Sociological Inquiry	Persell 6/6

\# Headings underlined here are major sections in the textbook of respective authors and these sections have been sub- divided into multiple chapters by the authors. The infor-mation has been utilized to derive the narrower terms used in a chapter heading under a term used in the major section.

* Some headings contain multiple concepts. Such headings have been included in their respective places also, and such terms are shown here with a star(*) indicating that the headings bearing a starred term are repeated under all the significant concepts occurring in it

15.	1985 Sociological Terms and Concepts	O'Donnell 1/26
16.	1988 Nature and Methods* of Sociology	Gordon 1/7
17.	1990 Definition, scope and use	S Rao 2/39

2. HISTORY OF SOCIOLOGY

3. THEORIES OF SOCIOLOGY

1.	1957 Sociological Theory	Gitler 1/15
2.	1957 History and Theory of Sociology	Mitchell 1/3
3.	1962 Sociological Theory	Bottomore 2/20
	Social Sciences: History and Philosophy	Bottomore 4/20
4.	1959 Problems in Sociological Theory and Methodology*	Merton 1/5
5.	1964 Theories about Society	Douglas 16/16
6.	1965 Historical and Analytical foundations	Parsons 1/5
7.	1972 Models and theories	McGee 7/13
8.	1972 Historical Sociology	Rocher 10/17
9.	1973 Theories and Research	Leslie 1/5
10.	1975 Theories and Perspectives	Chambliss 1/4
11.	1975 Theories and Methods*	Cole 1/19
12.	1975 Origins of Sociology	Denisoff 2/16

13.	1976 Methods, Models, Theories	Rose 2/16
14.	1977 Theory and Method*	Warren 2/15
15.	1979 Theory and Methods*	Phillips 3/8
	Sociological Theory	Phillips 5/20
16.	1979 Theory and Method*	Szymanski 1/14
17.	1980 Methods* and Theory	Gurvitch 1/13
18.	1984 History and Theory	Persell 1/6
19.	1985 Sociological Theories	Haralambos 1/13
20.	1985 Origins, Perspectives, Techniques*	Wallace 1/19
21.	1990 Social Thought	S Rao 10/10

Other related Headings used:

1.	1971 Macro-Sociology	Gorman 3/11
2.	1977 Phenomenological and Marxist Sociologies	Warren 15/15
3.	1979 Radical Sociology	Szymanski 2/14

Concepts on which less than 3 authors have provided chapter headings are shown separately at the end of the heading bearing nearest concept.

4. RESEARCH METHODS/TECHNIQUES

1.	1949 Sociological Method	Sprott 2/10
2.	1951 Research Technique	O'Brien 1/9
3.	1957 Quantitative methods	Gitler 2/14
4.	1959 Sociological Theory* and Methodology	Merton 1/5.
5.	1962 Methods	Bottomore 1/6
6.	1964 Fields* and Methods	Horton 2/21
7.	1967 Field approach and Methods	Basu 17/17
8.	1967 Methods	Sachdeva 1/6
9.	1968 Methods and Data	McNall 2/19
10.	1968 Methods of Sociology	Sharma 2/32
11.	1969 Social Research	Abrahamson 2/10
12.	1969 Research Methods	Smelser 1/11
13.	1970 Scope* and Methods	Mercer 1/16
14	1970 Methods and Statistical Techniques	Wilkins 4/16
15.	1970 Logic and Methods	Worsley 2/8
15.	1971 Methods of Social Investigation	Sergeant 1/6
17.	1971 Field and its Methods	Popenoe 1/16

18. 1973 Methods of Social Research — Acuff 2/13
19. 1973 Methods and Techniques of Research — Bertrand 3/22
20. 1973 Method — Perry 1/13
21. 1975 Methodology — Chambliss 2/4
22. 1975 Theories and Methods — Cole 1/19
23. 1975 Research Methods — Denisoff 3/16
24. 1976 Methods, Models, Theories* — Rose 2/16
25. 1977 Collecting and Interpreting Data — Shapiro 16/19
26. 1979 Theory* and Methods — Phillips 3/8
27. 1979 Theory and Methods — Szymanski 1/14
28. 1980 Methods and Theory* — Gurvitch 1/13
29. 1982 Perspectives and Methods — Larson 1/4
30. 1983 Perspectives and Methods — Eshleman 1/5
    Methods of studying Society — Eshleman 3/20
31. 1983 Sociological Methods — O'Donnell 2/26
32. 1985 Origins, Perspectives, Techniques — Wallace 1/19
33. 1988 Nature and Methods — Gordon 2/7
34. 1990 Methods — S Rao 1/30

5. SCIENTIFIC METHOD

1. 1947 Sociology and Science — Ogburn 1/26
2. 1950 Scientific study of Social life — Eldridge 3/34
3. 1956 Empirical Social Research — FISR 8/12
4. 1975 Sociology as a Science: Myth and Method — Baldridge 2/13
5. 1975 Sociology as Science: Goals and Methods — Kenkel 2/16
6. 1976 Scientific approach — Hebding 2/13
7. 1979 Scientific Method in Sociology — Sherman 22/23
8. 1986 Sociology as a Science — Charon 2/17

I. SOCIAL ORGANIZATION, SOCIAL PROCESSES, GROUP FORMATION

6. SOCIAL ORGANIZATION

1. 1947 Social Organization — Ogburn 6/7
2. 1957 Social Organization — Bierstedt 3/5
3. 1957 Factors of Social Stability — Mannheim 11/12
4. 1961 Accommodation*and Social Organization — Sutherland 9/22
5. 1962 Social Organization — Young 3/5

6. 1964 Social Organization — Horton 3/6
7. 1965 Social Organization — Valdes 7/11
8. 1967 Social Organization — Chinoy 2/5
9. 1968 Social Organization — Sharma 15/32
10. 1969 Social Organization and Interaction* — Abrahamson 1/3
11. 1969 Social Organization — Koller 3/5
12. 1970 Social Organization: Order and Disorder — Scott 4/29
13. 1970 Social Organization — Gorman 2/4
14. 1971 Social groups* and Organizations — Popenoe 5/16
15. 1972 Organization of Society — McGee 4/8
    Social structure and Social Organization — McGee 8/13
16. 1972 Social Organization — Rocher 2/3
17. 1973 Social Organization — Leslie 4/5
18. 1975 Social Organization — Kenkel 2/4
    Social Integration and Social Organization — Kenkel 6/16
19. 1976 Social Organization — Hebding 3/5
20. 1976 Social Organization — Sachdeva 3/6
21. 1977 Social Organization — Broom 1/8
22. 1977 Social Organization — Broom (2) 2/17
23. 1977 Forms of Social Organization — Goode 3/6
24. 1977 Basic Patterns and Images of order — McNall 1/4
25. 1980 Social Organization — Gurvitch 3/4
    Social Organization and Institutions* — Gurvitch 3/13
26. 1982 Social Organization — Larson 3/4
27. 1983 Social Organization — Eshleman 4/5
28. 1986 Organization of Society — Tischler 3/6
29. 1985 Nature of Social Order — O'Donnell 18/26
30. 1985 Social Organization — Charon 2/6
    Social Order, Socialization* and Deviance* — Charon 4/6
31. 1990 Organization and Individual* — Rao 12/30

7. SOCIAL SYSTEM

9. SOCIETY/SOCIAL LIFE

1. 1947 Society — Ogburn 2/7
   Social life of man — Ogburn 2/26
2. 1950 Composition of Social Life — Eldridge 1/7

3. 1953 Society — Biesanz 7/29
4. 1956 Society — FISR 2/12
5. 1957 Roots of Social Life — Gisbert 1/5
   Nature of Society — Gisbert 3/17
6. 1960 Society — Green 3/21
7. 1961 Society and Culture* — Sutherland 1/7
   Human Society — Sutherland 2/22
8. 1964 Society — Kar 3/17
9. 1965 Personality* and Social System — Parsons 3/5
10. 1967 Society — Sachdeva 2/6
11. 1970 Social System — Wilkins 2/3
12. 1972 Society — Berger 1/17
13. 1973 Social life — Leslie 2/5
    Social Systems and Society — Leslie 6/21
14. 1973 Life in the Group: Society — Perry 3/17
15. 1975 Society — Denisoff 5/16
16. 1976 Society and its various forms — Hebding 6/13
17. 1978 Foundations of Social Life — Stewart 1/41
18. 1979 Society — Phillips 16/20
19. 1980 Becoming a Social Being: Deviance* and Social Control* — G Marx 4/11
20. 1982 Social Life — Larson 2/4
21. 1983 Society — Tischler 8/20
22. 1984 Social life: Groups* — Persell 2/6
23. 1985 Society — Wallace 3/19
24. 1986 Society — Charon 6/17

8. SOCIAL ORDER

1. 1947 Social Order — Ogburn 15/26
2. 1953 Religion * and the Social Order — Biesanz 15/29
3. 1961 Social Order, Deviance* and Change* — Chinoy 5/6
4. 1966 Socio-state* Order — Muzumdar 19/20
5. 1970 Social Order and Social Disorder* — Scott 2/4
6. 1970 Problems of Order: Social Control* — Worsley 8/8
7. 1971 Values and Norms*: Persistence* and Change* — Gorman 4/11

8. 1973 Social Control*: The maintenance of Social Order — Bertrand 16/22
9. 1968 Basic Patterns and Images of Order — McNall 1/4
10. 1985 Social Stability and Control* — O'Donnell 7/9
    Nature of Social Order — O'Donnell 18/26
11. 1986 Social Order, Institutions* and Social Control* — Charon 9/18

10. BIOLOGICAL DETERMINISM/ SOCIO-BIOLOGY/ HEREDITY

1. 1871 Preparation in Biology — Spencer 14/16
2. 1947 Contribution of Biological factor in Society — Ogburn 4/26
3. 1950 Hereditary make up — Eldridge 2/34
4. 1950 Biological factors of Social Change* — MacIver 24/29
5. 1957 Natural Conditions of Human Society: Biological — Bierstedt 2/19
6. 1957 Heredity and Environment* — Gisbert 10/17
7. 1964 Biological factors of Social Change* — Kar 15/17
8. 1967 Heredity and Environment* — Sachdeva 11/28
9. 1968 Heredity and Environment* — Sharma 8/32
10. 1971 Bio-social Development — Gorman 2/11
11. 1979 Biological and Physical* Structures — Phillips 7/8
12. 1990 Heredity and Environment* — S Rao 6/30

Other related Headings used:

1. 1957 Natural and Social Selection — Gisbert 15/17

11. SEXUALITY/ SEXUAL BEHAVIOR

1. 1964 Sexuality and Changing Sex roles* — Horton 7/21
2. 1973 Social Differentiation*: Sexuality and SexRoles* — Perry 8/17
3. 1979 Sex and Sexism — Sherman 11/23
4. 1979 Family*, Sex and Society — Szymanski 12/14
5. 1984 Sex and Sexuality — Persell 22/23

12. INDIVIDUAL

13. PERSONALITY

1. 1947 Personality — Ogburn 4/7
   Group* and Personality — Ogburn 9/26

	Culture* and Personality	Ogburn 10/26
2.	1950 Personality and Society	Eldridge 7/7
3.	1950 Individual and Society	MacIver 3/29
4.	1952 Social Structure* and Personality	Merrill 2/6
	Personality and Society	Merrill 7/29
5.	1953 Culture*, Society*, and Personality	Biesanz 1/3
	Theories of Personality Formation	Biesanz 11/29
	Personality and Social Interaction*	Biesanz 12/29
6.	1956 Personality	Weinberg 4/28
7.	1957 Society and the Individual	Bierstedt 18/19
8.	1957 Personality and Social Structure	Gitler 4/14
9.	1957 Man and his Psychic Equipment	Mannheim 1/4
	Individualization Mannheim 5/12	
10.	1959 Personality and Social Structure	Merton 11/25
11.	1960 Structure and Unity of Personality	Green 8/21
12.	1961 Personality	Sutherland 1/7
	Personality and Culture*	Sutherland 5/22
	Personality Development	Sutherland 7/22
13.	1962 Socialization* and Personality	Young 7/26
14.	1964 Personality and Socialization*	Horton 5/21
15.	1965 Individual and his Personality	Koller 6/22
16.	1965 Personality and Social System*	Parsons 3/5
17.	1967 Culture* Society and Individual*	Chinoy 4/21
18.	1967 Personality	Sachdeva 26/28
19.	1968 Individual and Society *	Sharma 16/32
20.	1970 Personality	Mercer 3/16
21.	1970 Individual and Society*	Wilkins 5/16
22.	1973 Socialization*, Personality and Culture*	Bertrand 2/6
23.	1973 Socialization* and Personality Development	McGee 3/8
24.	1973 Making of the Individual: Personality	Perry 5/17
25.	1976 Individual and Society*	Rose 4/5
26.	1979 Personality Structure	Phillips 2/8

27.	1983 Individuals within Society *	Eshleman 2/5
28.	1983 Individual in Society*	Tischler 2/6
	Socialization* and Personality	Tischler 4/20
29.	1988 Sociology and Human Nature	Gordon 4/7
30.	1990 Individual and Society*	S Rao 5/30
	Other related Headings used:	
1.	1952 Personality Disorganization	Merrill 10/29
2.	1957 Isolation	Mannheim 4/12
	Main effects of Competition and Selection on Mental Life	Mannheim 7/12
3.	1959 Sociology of Mental Illness	Merton 22/25

14. ATTITUDES

1.	1950 Interests and Attitudes	MacIver 2/29
2.	1957 Man and his Psychic Equipment	Mannheim 1/4
3.	1961 Motivational Systems	Parsons 13/24
4.	1967 Interests and Attitudes*	Sachdeva 7/2
5.	1974 Attitudes and Beliefs	Potter 6/8
6.	1980 Social Psychology	Gurvitch 6/13

15. SOCIAL PROCESSES

1.	1950 Social Interaction* and Processes	Eldridge 5/7
2.	1957 SocialProcesses	Mannheim 2/4
3.	1959 Interaction*: the Social Process	Green 4/21
4.	1961 Social Processes	Sutherland 3/7
	Accommodation and Social Organization*	Sutherland 9/22
5.	1962 Social Processes	Young 9/26
6.	1965 Social Processes	Koller 9/22
7.	1966 Social Processes	Goode 3/7
8.	1966 Processes	Muzumdar 2/3
9.	1970 Social Roles* and Social Processes	Mercer 4/16
10.	1970 Social Processes	Scott 3/6
	Social Processes in Communities*	Scott 6/7
11.	1973 Institutional* Structures and Social Processes	Bertrand 4/6
12.	1973 Social Processes	Leslie 4/21

13.	1977 Social Processes: Stability and Change*	Shapiro 11/19
14.	1990 Social Processes	S Rao 11/30
16.	**SOCIAL RELATIONS**	
1.	1947 Society and Adjustment	Ogburn 26/26
2.	1950 Social Interaction: Competition, Conflict* and Cooperation	Eldridge 20/34
	Accommodation and Assimilation	Eldridge 21/34
3.	1957 Social Contact* and Social Distance	Mannheim 3/12
4.	1961 Accommodation and Social Organization*	Sutherland 9/22
5.	1962 Social Relations	Young 2/5
6.	1966 Cooperation and Opposition	Muzumdar 10/20
7.	1968 Suggestion, Imitation, and Sympathy*	Sharma 30/32
	Social Relations, Social Control* and Social Code	Sharma 12/32
8.	1970 Integrative Processes	Scott 5/29
9.	1971 Individual Integration: Alienation and Belonging	Gorman 3/4
10.	1974 Social Relations	Potter 5/8
11.	1975 Social Relations	Chambliss 4/4
12.	1976 Roles* and Relationship	Rose 5/16
17.	**SOCIAL INTERACTION**	
1.	1947 Group Interaction	Ogburn 6/26
2.	1950 Social Interaction and Processes*	Eldridge 5/7
3.	1952 Social Interaction, Social Change,* Social Planning*	Merrill 6/6
	SocialInteraction and Social Processes*	Merrill 25/29
4.	1953 Personality* and Social Interaction	Biesanz 12/29
5.	1957 Social Contact and Social Distance*	Mannheim 3/12
6.	1961 Interaction and Social Processes*	Sutherland 8/22
7.	1961 Social Interaction	Parsons 1/24
8.	1964 Social Interaction	Horton 4/6
9.	1965 Interaction among Sub-Systems of Society	Goode 6/7

10. 1966 SocialInteraction: Communication* and Consensus — Muzumdar 7/20
11. 1967 Process of Social Interaction — Sachdeva 9/28
12. 1968 Interaction — McNall 7/19
13. 1968 Modes and Laws of Social Interactions — Sharma 11/32
14. 1969 Social Organization* and Interaction — Abrahamson 1/3
    1970 Community Organization* and Behavior — Mercer 15/16
15. 1972 Social Action — Rocher 1/3
16. 1973 Social Structure* and Interaction — Bertrand 3/6
17. 1973 Communication* and Social Interaction — Leslie 3/21
18. 1975 Social Interaction — Cole 5/19
19. 1975 Groups* influence on Behavior * — Cole 4/9
20. 1976 Socialization*, Action, Interaction — Sachdeva 2 /6
21. 1978 Group Interaction — Stewart(2) 5/19
22. 1983 Individual and Social Interaction — Eshleman 6/22
23. 1983 Social Interaction and Social Structure* — Tischler 5/20
24. 1984 Networks and Interactions — Persell 4/23
25. 1986 Social Action, Social Interaction, and Social Patterns — Charon 4/17

18. GROUP FORMATION

1. 1947 Groups and Personality* — Ogburn 9/26
2. 1950 Social Groups — MacIver 10/29
3. 1952 Group and the Individual* — Freedman 3/15
4. 1956 Group — FISR 4/12
5. 1957 Groups — Bierstedt 9/19
6. 1957 Social Groups and Social Institutions* — Gisbert 2/17
7. 1957 Sociology of Groups: Crowds*, Public — Mannheim 7/12
8. 1959 Group and the Person — Merton 3/5
9. 1961 Human Collectivities — Sutherland 4/7
   Groups and Small Group* Research — Sutherland 10/22
10. 1962 Types of Social Groups — Bottomore 6/20
11. 1962 Social Groups and Social Categories* — Young 2/26
12. 1964 Groups and Associations* — Horton 9/21
13. 1964 Social Group — Kar 4/17
14. 1966 Group — Muzumdar 1/3
    Group and Groupings — Muzumdar 2/20

15. 1968 Social Groups — Sharma 17/32
16. 1969 Group and the Individual* — Koller 3/6
17. 1970 Social Groups and Group behavior* — Mercer 6/16
18. 1971 Social Groups and Organizations* — Popenoe 5/16
19. 1973 Social Groups — Acuff 8/23
20. 1973 Groups and Large Formal Organizations* — Bertrand 9/22
21. 1973 Groups — Leslie 10/21
22. 1973 Groups — Perry 2/13
23. 1975 Groups influence on Behavior* — Cole 4/9
24. 1976 Social Groups — Hebding 5/13
25. 1976 Group basis of Society — Stewart 1/5
    Groups and Conformity* — Cole 7/19
26. 1977 Groups: Large and Small* — Goode 6/17
27. 1977 Groups: Characteristics, Kinds, and Significance — Shapiro 8/19
28. 1978 Group Interaction* — Stewart 5/19
29. 1979 Population* and Social Groupings — Bottomore 2/6
30. 1979 Groups — Phillips 6/8
31. 1980 Groups — Gurvitch 4/13
    Groups and Organizations* — Phillips 14/20
32. 1983 Social Groups and Social Organizations* — Eshleman 11/20
33. 1983 Group Structures — Tischler 6/20
34. 1984 Social life*: Groups — Persell 2/6
    Groups and Organizations* — Persell 7/23
35. 1985 Living in Groups — Wallace 3/6
    Groups and Organizations*
36. 1990 Social Groups — S Rao 1/30

19. PRIMARY GROUPS

1. 1942 Disintegration of Primary Groups and Community Disorganization* — Barnes 16/19
2. 1961 Primary Groups — Chinoy 6/21
3. 1961 Primary Groups — Parsons 4/24
4. 1967 Groups in Physical Proximity — Broom 4/8
   Primary Groups — Broom 5/9

20. SMALL GROUPS

1.	1957 Structure and Dynamics of Groups	Gitler 12/14
2.	1959 Small Group: Theory and Research	Merton 13/25
3.	1961 Groups* and Small Group Research	Sutherland 10/22
4.	1965 Small Groups	Valdes 5/11
5.	1968 Associations*: Small Groups and Bureaucracies*	McNall 8/19
6.	1970 Small Groups	Scott 4/6
7.	1973 Near Groups as Collective Behavior*	Leslie 11/21
8.	1977 Groups: Large and Small	Goode 6/17

21. ASSOCIATION

1.	1950 Associations and Interests	MacIver 17/29
2.	1957 Associations and Institutions*	Bierstedt 10/21
3.	1957 Social Institutions* and Voluntary Associations	Gitler 9/14
4.	1964 Groups* and Associations	Horton 9/21
5.	1966 Group functioning: Associations and Institutions*	Muzumdar 3/20
6.	1967 Associations	Basu 4/17
7.	1968 Association	McNall 2/4
	Associations: Small Groups* and Bureaucracies*	McNall 9/19
8.	1968 Great Associations and Institutions*	Sharma 25/32
9.	1971 Friendship and Association	Gorman 9/11
10.	1977 Associations	Broom 7/8
11.	1978 Associations	Broom 7/17

II. SOCIAL INSTITUTIONS,FAMILY, POLITICAL, ECONOMIC INSTITUTIONS

22. SOCIAL INSTITUTIONS

1.	1939 Institutions	Lee 3/6
2.	1942 Foundations and Framework of Social Institutions	Barnes 1/6
3.	1947 Interrelationship of Institutions	Ogburn 22/26
4.	1949 Society as a System of Institutions	Sprott 8/10
5.	1950 Social Institutions	Eldridge 6/7

6.	1951 Social Institutions	O'Brien 8/9
7.	1952 Community* and Social Institutions	Merrill 5/6
8.	1956 Social Institutions	Weinberg 5/28
9.	1957 Social Groups* and Social Institutions	Merrill 5/6
10.	1957 Associations* and Institutions	Bierstedt 9/21
11.	1957 Social Institutions and Voluntary Associations*	Gitler 9/14
12.	1959 Problems in the Sociology of Institutions	Merton 2/4
13.	1959 Principal Social Institutions of Simple Society	Mitchell 2/3
14.	1960 Social Institutions	Green 3/4
15.	1961 Social Institutions	Sutherland 6/7
16.	1962 Social Institutions	Bottomore 3/6
17.	1962 Social Institutions	Young 4/5
	Analysis of Institutions	Young 19/26
18.	1964 Social Institutions	Horton 10/21
19.	1965 Social Institutions	Koller 12/22
20.	1965 Social Institutions	Goode 5/7
21.	1966 Group functioning : Associations* and Institutions	Muzumdar 3/20
22.	1967 Social Institutions	Basu 6/17
23.	1969 Social Institutions	Goldthorpe 2/2
24.	1968 Institutions	McNall 4/5
25.	1968 Great Associations* and Institutions	Sharma 25/32
26.	1971 Social Groups* and Organizations	Popenoe 5/16
27.	1972 Institutions	Berger 4/17
28.	1973 Major Institutions	Broom 2/3
29.	1972 Social Institutions	McGee 7/13
30.	1973 Institutional Structures and Social Processes*	Bertrand 4/6
	Social Institutions	Bertrand 13/22
31.	1973 Social Institutions	Leslie 3/4
32.	1975 Social Institutions	Kenkel 3/4
33.	1976 Social Institutions	Rose 6/16

34. 1977 Social Institutions Goode 5/6
35. 1977 Institutions: the Fabric of Society Shapiro 9/19
36. 1977 Social Institution Warren 2/6
37. 1978 Social Institutions and Organizations Stewart 3/4
38. 1979 Institutions Phillips 5/8
39. 1980 Social Organization* and Institutions Gurvitch 5/13
40. 1982 Social Institutions Larson 4/4
41. 1983 Institutions Tischler 5/6
42. 1984 Social Institutions Persell 4/6
43. 1986 Social order*, Institutions and Social Control* Charon 9/17
44. 1989 Social Institutions Wallace 5/6
45. 1999 Social Institutions S Rao 5/10

23. KINSHIP

1. 1959 Kinship and Marriage* Mitchell 4/10
   Kinship, Family* and Neighborhood Mitchell 10/10
2. 1960 Kinship Groups and Systems Johnson 2/7
   Consanguinal Kin Groups and Class* Johnson 8/22
3. 1961 Family*, Kinship, and Marriage* Douglas 5/16
4. 1961 Kinship Parsons 4/24
5. 1962 Family* and Kinship Bottomore 10/20
6. 1964 Family*, Kinship, and Marriage* Douglas 5/16
7. 1968 Kinship, Marriage* and Family* Goldthorpe 4/9
8. 1968 Spatial Groups (Sib, Clan) Sharma 18/32
9. 1973 Social Institutions: Family* and Kinship Bertrand 13/22

24. FAMILY

1. 1942 Marriage* and the Family Barnes 15/19
2. 1947 Family Ogburn 21/26
3. 1950 Family Eldridge 25/34
4. 1950 Family MacIver 11/29
5. 1951 Family O'Brien 16/20
6. 1952 Multi-functional Institution: Family Merrill 22-23/29
7. 1953 Marriage* and Family Biesanz 13/29
8. 1956 Family FISR 9/12
9. 1956 Family Weinberg 12/28

10.	1957 Family	Bierstedt 14/19
11.	1957 Marriage* and the Family	Gitler 11/14
12.	1957 Family	Gisbert 4/17
13.	1959 Sociology of the Family	Merton 7/25
14.	1959 Kinship*, Family and Neighborhood	Mitchell 10/10
15.	1960 Family	Green 14/21
16.	1960 Marriage* and the Family	Johnson 6/22
17.	1961 Family, Kinship* and Marriage*	Chinoy 7/21
18.	1962 Family and Kinship*	Bottomore 10/20
19.	1962 Family	Young 20/26
20.	1962 Family, Kinship* and Marriage*	Douglas 5/16
21.	1964 Family	Horton 11/21
22.	1964 Family	Kar 6/17
23.	1965 Family	Koller 13/22
24.	1966 Family	Goode 11/15
25.	1966 Family	Muzumdar 15/20
26.	1967 Social units: Family	Basu 2/17
27.	1967 Family	Sachdeva 18/28
28.	1968 Kinship, Marriage and Family	Goldthorpe 4/9
29.	1968 Family	McNall 14/19
30.	1968 Family Group	Sharma 20/32
31.	1970 Family as a Social Institution	Mercer 9/16
32.	1970 Institution of Marriage* and Family	Wilkins 7/16
	Modern Family	Wilkins 12/16
33.	1970 Family	Worsley 3/8
34.	1971 Family	Popenoe 6/16
35.	1971 Family	Sergeant 3/6
	Family	Sergeant 4/13
36.	1972 Family	Berger 5/17
37.	1973 Family	Acuff 13/23
38.	1973 Social Institutions*: Family and Kinship*	Bertrand 13/22
39.	1973 Family	Leslie 17/21
40.	1973 Family	Perry 9/13
41.	1973 Marriage* and Family	Stewart 12/19
42.	1975 Family	Denisoff 8/16

43. 1975 Socialization* and the Family — Baldridge 4/13
44. 1975 Family — Kenkel 8/16
45. 1976 Family in the Modern World — Stewart 11/16
46. 1977 Family — Broom 10/17
47. 1977 Family as a Social Institution — Goode 12/17
48. 1979 Family — Warren 4/14
49. 1979 Family — Phillips 10/20
50. 1979 Origins of Family Structures — Sherman 8/23
    Marriage* and Family S — herman 10/23
51. 1979 Family, Sex, and Society — Szymanski 12/14
52. 1980 Social Institutions: Family — G Marx 8/11
53. 1983 Family Groups and Systems — Eshleman 12/20
54. 1983 Marriage*, Family and Alternative Life Styles — Tischler 13/20
55. 1984 Family — Persell 13/23
56. 1985 Family — Haralambos 8/13
57. 1985 Family — O'Donnell 2/9
    Family — O'Donnell 13-15/26
58. 1985 Marriage* and Family — Wallace 13/19
59. 1986 Family in a Changing Society* — Charon 17/17
60. 1990 Family — S Rao 16/30

25. MARRIAGE

1. 1942 Marriage and the Family* — Barnes 15/19
2. 1953 Marriage and the Family* — Biesanz 13/29
3. 1955 Courtship, Marriage and Divorce — Lee 4/35
4. 1957 Marriage and the Family* — Gitler 11/14
5. 1959 Kinship* and Marriage — Mitchell 4/10
6. 1960 Marriage and Family* in America — Green 15/21
7. 1960 Marriage and the Family* — Johnson 6/22
8. 1961 Family*, Kinship* and Marriage — Chinoy 7/21
9. 1964 Family*, Kinship*, Marriage — Douglas 5/16
10. 1967 Marriage — Sachdeva 19/28
11. 1968 Kinship*, Marriage, and Family* — Goldthorpe 4/9
12. 1968 Marriage — Sharma 22/32
13. 1969 Sexual Norms, Courtship and Marriage — Abrahamson 8/10

14.	1970 Institution of Marriage and Family*	Wilkins 7/16
15.	1973 Marriage and Family*	Stewart 12/19
16.	1979 Marriage and Family	Sherman 10/23
17.	1983 Marriage, Family* and Alternative Life-styles	Tischler 13/20
18.	1985 Marriage and Family*	Wallace 13/19

26. POLITICAL INSTITUTIONS/ POLITICAL SOCIOLOGY

1.	1871 Political bias	Spencer 11/16
2.	1942 Political and Legal* Institutions in Transition*	Barnes 3/6
3.	1947 Governing Institutions of Society	Ogburn 18/26
4.	1950 Political Institutions	Eldridge 29/34
5.	1950 Great Associations-Political	MacIver 18/29
6.	1951 Political Sociology	O'Brien 15/17
7.	1953 Governing of Man	Biesanz 3/3
	Political Systems and Philosophies	Biesanz 25-27/29
8.	1957 State	Gisbert 5/17
9.	1959 Political Sociology	Merton 3/25
10.	1059 Law* and Political Systems	Mitchell 5/10
11.	1960 American Political Order	Green 18/21
12.	1960 Polity	Johnson 4/7
	Political Institutions	Johnson 13-14/22
13.	1961 Power*, Authority*, and Political Institutions	Chinoy 13/21
14.	1961 Political Organization and Authority*	Parsons 9/24
15.	1961 Social Structure* in Economic and Political* life	Sutherland 19/22
16.	1962 Political Institutions	Bottomore 9/20
17.	1962 Political Sociology	Young 24/26
18.	1964 Politics	Douglas 8/16
19.	1964 Governmental and Economic* Institutions	Horton 14/21
20.	1964 State and Society	Kar 10/17
21.	1966 Politics and Power*	Goode 13/15
22.	1966 Socio-state Order*	Muzumdar 19/20
23.	1968 Polity	McNall 15/19

24.	1969 Political Sociology	Smelser 9/11
25.	1970 Political Organization and Behavior	Mercer 12/16
26.	1970 Political System	Wilkins 8/16
27.	1971 Politics	Gorman 7/11
28.	1971 Politics and Power*	Popenoe 15/16
29.	1971 Sociology of Politics	Sergeant 6/6
30.	1973 Social Institutions: Economic* and Political	Bertrand 15/22
31.	1973 Political Institutions	Perry 13/13
32.	1975 Political Process*: The State and Interest Groups*	Baldridge 8/13
33.	1976 Political Institutions	Stewart 15/16
34.	1977 Politics and Society	Broom 17/17
35.	1977 Political Process	Goode 13/17
36.	1978 Political Power*	Stewart 15/19
37.	1979 Political and Economic* Institutions	Phillips 12/20
38.	1979 Political Sociology	Sherman 5-6/23
39.	1980 Social Institutions: Politics	G Marx 10/11
40.	1983 Political Groups and Systems	Eshleman 15/20
41.	1983 Political Systems	Tischler 17/20
42.	1984 Power* and Politics	Persell 15/23
43.	1985 Power* and Politics	Haralambos 3/13
44.	1985 Political System	O'Donnell 9/9
45.	1985 Political Institutions	Wallace 16/19
46.	1988 Economics* and Politics	Gordon 7/7
47.	1990 Political System	S Rao 18/30
	Other related Headings used	
1.	1942 Democracy: National, State and Constitutional Government	Barnes 7/19
	Political Parties and Party Government	Barnes 8/19
2.	1953 Parties and Participation in American Democracy	Biesanz 26/29
	Communist Party: Control and Conformity	Biesanz 28/29

3.	1956 Legislative Struggle	Weinberg 21/28
	Democracy	Weinberg 7/28
	Democracy and Foreign Policy*	Weinberg 28/28

27. GOVERNMENT

1.	1947 Governing Institutions of Society	Ogburn 18/26
2.	1952 Uni-functional Institutions (Govt. etc.)	Merrill 24/29
3.	1953 Governing of man	Biesanz 3/3
	Government and its formation	Biesanz 23/29
	Variation and Change in Government	Biesanz 24/29
4.	1956 Roles of Government	Weinberg 19/28
5.	1964 Governmental and Economic* Institutions	Horton 14/21
6.	1966 Socio-state Order	Muzumdar 19/20
7.	1973 Government	Leslie 21/21
8.	1973 Government Ideology, and International Relations*	Perry 16/17
9.	1975 Government and Economy: Distributing Goods and Power*	Kenkel 11/16
10.	1985 Forms of Government	O'Donnell 24/26

28. FORMAL ORGANIZATIONS

1.	1952 Uni-functional Institutions	Merrill 24/29
2.	1957 Sociology of Groups*: Organized Groups, State*	Mannheim 9/12
3.	1959 Organizational analysis	Merton 18/25
4.	1960 Formal Organizations	Johnson 12/22
5.	1970 Formal Organizations	Scott 5/7
6.	1971 Social Groups* and Organizations	Popenoe 5/16
7.	1973 Structure of Groups* and Large Formal Organizations	Bertrand 9/22
8.	1973 Formal Organizations and Bureaucracy*	Perry 11/21
9.	1975 Formal Organizations	Cole 8/19
10.	1976 Bureaucracy* and Formal Organization	Hebding 7/13
11.	1977 Formal Organizations	Goode 7/17

12.	1980 Primary Components of Social Organization: Formal Organizations	G Marx 5/11
13.	1985 Organizations and Bureaucracy*	Haralambos 7/13

29. BUREAUCRACY

1.	1956 Bureaucracy	Weinberg 23/28
2.	1961 Bureaucracy	Chinoy 10/21
3.	1966 Bureaucracy	Goode 5/15
4.	1968 Associations*: Small groups* and Bureaucracies	McNall 8/19
5.	1971 Bureaucracy	Gorman 6/11
6.	1972 Bureaucracy	10/17
7.	1973 Bureaucracy	Acuff 17/23
8.	1973 Bureaucracy	Leslie 12/21
9.	1973 Formal Organizations* and Bureaucracy	Perry 11/17
10.	1975 Bureaucratism	Chambliss 15/17
11.	1976 Bureaucracy and Formal Organization*	Hebding 7/13
12.	1980 Organizations* and Bureaucracy	Haralambos 7/13

30. WAR

1.	1942 War as a Social institution	Barnes 10/19
2.	1947. War and International Relations	Ogburn 19/26
3.	1956 War	Weinberg 25/28
4.	1965 War	Koller 20/22
	Organizing for Peace	Weinberg 26/28
5.	1975 Military in America	Chambliss 13/17

INTERNATIONAL RELATIONS

1.	1953 International Politics and World Order	Biesanz 29/29
2.	1956 Emergence of one World	Muzumdar 13/20
3.	1956 Democracy* and Foreign Policy	Weinberg 28/28
4.	1973 Government Ideology*, and International Relations	Perry 16/17

NATIONALISM

1.	1871 Bias of Patriotism	Spencer 9/16
2.	1956 Freedom	Weinberg 8/28
	Nationalism	Weinberg 24/28
	Citizenship	Weinberg 2/28

3. 1968 Nation and National Character — Sharma 24/32

IMPERIALISM

1. 1972 Colonial System and De-colonization — Rocher 14/17
2. 1975 Imperialism and Industrialization* — Chambliss 14/17
3. 1979 Imperialism and Development* — Szymanski 10/14

31. ECONOMIC INSTITUTIONS

1. 1942 Economic Institutions — Barnes 2/6
2. 1947 Society and Economic Institutions — Ogburn 17/26
3. 1949 Economic Structure — Sprott 5/10
4. 1950 Economic Institution — Eldridge 26/34
5. 1950 Great Associations*: Economic — MacIver 19/29
6. 1953 Economy and Society — Biesanz 2/3
   Economic Decisions and Institutions* — Biesanz 16/29
   Economic Systems and Philosophies — Biesanz 18-19/29
7. 1957 Economic System — Gisbert 6/17
8. 1960 Economy — Johnson 3/7
   Economic Institutions — Johnson 9-10/22
9. 1961 Technology* and Economic Institutions — Chinoy 12/21
10. 1961 Economic Institutions — Parsons 6/24
11. 1961 Social Structure in Economic and Political life* — Sutherland 19/22
12. 1962 Economic Institutions — Bottomore 8/20
13. 1962 Economic Order — Young 23/26
14. 1964 Governmental* and Economic Institutions — Merton 14/21
15. 1964 Economic Institutions — Kar 9/17
16. 1966 Economics and Production — Goode 14/15
17. 1966 Economic Order — Muzumdar 16/20
18. 1968 Technology*, Economy, and Society — Goldthorpe 5/9
19. 1968 Economy — McNall 12/19
20. 1970 Economic Organization and Behavior — Mercer 13/16
21. 1970 Economic Systems and Social Aspects of Industry* — Wilkins 9/16
22. 1973 Economic Order — Acuff 16/23
23. 1973 Social Institutions: Economic and Political* — Bertrand 15/22
24. 1973 Economy — Leslie 20/21
25. 1973 Economy: Principles and Comparisons — Perry 14/17

26. 1973 Economy — Perry(2) 12/13
27. 1975 Technology* and Economic System — Baldridge 11/13
28. 1975 Government* and the Economy. Distributing Goods and Power* — Kenkel 11/16
29. 1976 **Economic System** — Stewart 14/16
30. 1979 **Political*** and **Economic Institutions** — Phillips 12/20
31. 1979 **Ideas***, **Institutions***, and **Economies** — Sherman 18/23
32. 1979 **Corporate Economy** — Szymanski 4/14
33. 1980 **Sociology of Economic Organization** — Gurvitch 13/13
34. 1983 **Economic Groups** and **Systems** — Eshleman 16/20
35. 1983 **Economy** — Tischler 16/20
36. 1984 **Economy** and **Work*** — Persell 14/23
37. 1988 **Economics** and **Politics*** — Gordon 5/5
38. 1985 **Work*** and **Economy** — Wallace 15/19
39. 1990 **Education*** and the **Economic System** — S Rao 17/30

Other related Headings used

1. 1953 **Consumer** — Biesanz 22/29
2. 1956 **Under-developed Countries** — Weinberg 27/28
3. 1957 **Competition** and **Monopoly** — Mannheim 6/12
4. 1961 **Economic Development** — Parsons 7/24
5. 1974 **Production** and **Allocation** — Potter 3/8

32. CAPITALISM

1. 1942 **Capitalism** and the **Economic Crisis** — Barnes 5/19
2. 1956 **Changing*** **Capitalism** — Weinberg 18/28
3. 1975 **Capitalism** — Chambliss 10/17
4. 1979 **Capitalist State** — Szymanski 8/14

Other related Heading used :

1. 1979 **Exploitation** — Sherman 3/23
   Socialist Movement: History and **Sociology** — Sherman 15/23
   Sociology of Socialism — Sherman 16/23

PROPERTY

1. 1942 Institution of **Property** — Barnes 6/19
2. 1964 **Work*** and **Wealth** — Douglas 7/16
3. 1967 **Property** and **Inheritance** — Basu 6/17
4. 1985 **Wealth** and **Income** — O'Donnell 10/26

33. WORK

1. 1964 **Work** and **Wealth*** — Douglas 7/16
2. 1970 **Work, Industry***, and **Organizations*** — Worsley 5/8

3.	1972 Work and Leisure*	Berger 12/17
4.	1974 Work	Potter 4/8
5.	1977 Work, Leisure*, and the Arts*	Warren 7/15
6.	1978 Work, and Leisure*	Stewart 16/19
7.	1984 Economy* and Work	Persell 14/23
8.	1985 Work and Leisure *	Haralambos 6/13
9.	1985 Work, and Leisure*	O'Donnell 5/9
	Meaning of Work	O'Donnell 12/26
10.	1985 Work and the Economy*	Wallace 15/19
	Other related Headings used	
1.	1968 Unemployment	Sharma 28/28
2.	1985 Changing Conditions* of Employment	O'Donnell 14/26
34.	**DIVISION OF LABOUR**	
1.	1952 Division of Labour and the Urban Community*	Freedman 11/15
2.	1957 Cooperation and the Division of Labour	Mannheim 7/12
3.	1060 Division of Labour	Green 11/21
35.	**INDUSTRIAL SOCIOLOGY**	
1.	1957 Industrial Sociology	Gitler 10/14
2.	1971 Industrial Sociology	Sergeant 5/13
3.	1979 Industrial Sociology	Sherman 4/23
4.	1979 Industrial Managers and Workers	Biesanz 20/29
5.	1956 Role of Union	Weinberg 17/28
	Industrial Worker	Weinberg 28/28
36.	**LEISURE**	
1.	1942 Leisure, Recreation and the Arts*	Barnes 19/19
2.	1960 Recreation	Green 20/21
3.	1964 People at Play	Douglas 11/16
4.	1972 Work* and Leisure*	Berger 12/17
5.	1977 Work*, Leisure, and the Arts*	Warren 7/15
8.	1978 Work*, and Leisure	Stewart 16/19
9.	1985 Work* and Leisure	Haralambos 6/13
10.	1985 Work*, and Leisure	O'Donnell 5/9
III.	**CULTURE, RELIGION, SOCIAL CONTROL, EDUCATION**	
37.	**CULTURE**	
1.	1937 Sociology and Culture	Calverton 7/8
2.	1947 Role of Culture in Society	Ogburn 3/26
	Culture and Personality*	Ogburn 10/26
3.	1950 Society and its Cultural Heritage	Eldridge 2/7

4. 1950 **Great Associations: Cultural** MacIver 20/29
5. 1951 **Culture** and **Normative Order*** O'Brien 4/9
6. 1952 **Culture** and **Society** Merrill 1/6
7. 1952 **Culture** and Society Freedman 2/15
8. 1953 **Culture,** Society and **Personality*** Biesanz 1/3
9. 1955 **Race*** and **Culture** Lee 4/6
10. 1956 **Culture** and **Civilization** FISR 6/12
11. 1956 **Culture** Weinberg 13/28
12. 1957 **Culture** and **Socialization*** Bierstedt 1/5
13. 1957 **Culture** and **Civilization** Gisbert 12/17
14. 1957 **Racial*** and **Cultural Relations** Gitler 3/14
15. 1960 Universality, Variability of **Culture** Green 5-6/21
16. 1960 **Culture** and **Socialization*** Johnson 1/7
17. 1961 **Culture** and the **Social System** Parsons 4/5
18. 1961 Society and **Culture** Sutherland 1/7
19. 1962 **Culture** and **Sub-cultures** Young 3-4/26
20. 1964 **Culture** and **Personality*** Horton 2/6
21. 1964 **Culture** Kar 2/17
22. 1965 **Culture** Koller 1/5
23. 1965 **Culture** Valdes 2/11
24. 1966 **Culture** Muzumdar 1/3
25. 1967 **Culture, Society and Individual*** Chinoy 4/21
26. 1967 **Culture** and **Civilization** Sachdeva 25/28
27. 1968 **Culture** McNall 4/19
28. 1968 **Culture** and **Civilization** Sharma 13/32
29. 1969 **Social Organization*, Culture,** and **Change*** Abrahamson 2/3
30. 1970 **Culture** and its transmission Mercer 2/16
31. 1971 **Culture** Popenoe 3/16
32. 1972 **Culture** McGee 2/8
33. 1972 **Culture, Civilization** and **Ideology*** Rocher 3/17
34. 1973 **Socialization*, Personality*,** and **Culture** Bertrand 2/6
    Social Change* and **Cultural* Growth** Bertrand 8/22
35. 1973 **Culture** and **Socialization*** Leslie 3/5
36. 1973 Product of **Social life: Culture** Perry 4/17
37. 1973 **Society*** and **Culture** Perry (2) 3/13
38. 1975 **Culture** Baldridge 3/13
39. 1975 **Social Structure*** and **Culture** Cole 6/19

40. 1975 **Culture** Denisoff 4/16
41. 1975 **Culture**: the Human Invention Kenkel 3/16
42. 1975 **Human Societies: Cultures** and **Sub-cultures** Stewart 3/16
43. 1976 **Culture** and its Acquisition* Hebding 2/5
44. 1976 **Culture** Rose 2/5
45. 1977 **Culture** Broom 2/8
46. 1977 **Culture** Broom(2) 3/17
47. 1977 **Culture**: a **design for living** Shapiro 4-5/19
48. 1978 **Culture** and **Diversity** Stewart 3/19
Educational Process*: **Transmitting the Cultural Tradition** Stewart 13/19
49. 1979 **Culture** Phillips 2/20
50. 1979 **Culture** and **Class Consciousness** Szymanski 7/14
51. 1980 **Socio-cultural Dynamics** and **Evolution*** Gurvitch 2/13
52. 1980 **Culture** and **Social Organization*** G Marx 2/11
53. 1983 **Culture** and **Society** Eshleman 4/20
54 1983 **Culture** Tischler 3/20
55. 1984 **Social life: Culture** Persell 5/23
56. 1985 **Social Patterns: Culture** Wallace 3/6
57. 1986 **Social Patterns: Social Structure,*** **Culture** Charon 3/6
58. 1990 **Individual, Culture,** and **Society** S Rao 3/10
Other related Headings used:
1. 1975 **Popular Culture** Denisoff 14/16

38. CUSTOMS

1. 1950 **Social Structures***: Sustaining Forces of **Codes** and **Custom** MacIver 1/5
2. 1957 **Custom** and **Law*** Gisbert 7/17
3. 1959 System of **Beliefs*** and **Ritual** Mitchell 6/10
4. 1960 **Religious Beliefs*** and **Rituals** Johnson 15/22
4. 1962 **Customs** and **Public Opinion*** Bottomore 13/20
5. 1964 **Law***, **Custom** and **Morality*** Douglas 9/16
6. 1967 **Folkways** Sachdeva 21/28
Custom, Law*, Fashion Sachdeva 22/28
7. 1970 **Religion** * and **Belief Systems** Wilkins 11/16
8. 1971 **Sociology of Religion*, Beliefs,** **and Ideologies*** Sergeant 12/13

39. IDEOLOGY

1.	1956 **Ideology**	FISR 12/12
2.	1960 **Ideology**	Johnson 21/22
3.	1971 **Sociology of Religion,*** **Beliefs, and Ideologies**	Sergeant 12/13
4.	1972 **Culture, Civilization** and **Ideology**	Rocher 3/17
5.	1973 **Government***, **Ideology,** and **International Relations***	Perry 16/17
6.	1979 **Ideas, Institutions***, and **Economies***	Sherman 18/23

40. MAGIC

1.	1961 **Religion*** and **Magic**	Parsons 21/24
2.	1967 **Magic, Religion*** and **Society**	Goldthorpe 9/9
3.	1990 **Religion***, **Morality***, and **Magic**	S Rao 19/30

41. SOCIOLOGY OF RELIGION

1.	1871 **Theological bias**	Spencer 12/16
2.	1942 Contemporary crisis in **Religion and Morals***	Barnes 17/19
3.	1947 **Religious Institutions**	Ogburn 20/26
4.	1950 Institution of **Religion**	Eldridge 28/34
5.	1951 **Sociology of Religion**	O'Brien 8/9
6.	1953 **Religion** and the **Social Order***	Biesanz 15/29
7.	1956 **Religion**	Weinberg 11/28
8.	1957 **Morality*** and **Religion**	Gisbert 8/17
9.	1959 **Sociology of Religion**	Merton 6/25
10.	1959 System of **Beliefs*** and **Ritual**	Mitchell 6/10
11.	1960 **Religion**	Green 17/21
12.	1960 **Religion**	Johnson 5/7
	Religious Beliefs and **Rituals**	Johnson 15/22
	Religious Groups	Johnson 16/22
13.	1961 **Religion**	Chinoy 14/21
14.	1961 **Religion** and **Social Structure***	Parsons 12/24
	Religion and **Magic***	Parsons 21/24
15.	1961 **Organized Religion**	Sutherland 21/22
16.	1962 **Religion** and **Morality***	Bottomore 14/20
17.	1962 **Religion**	Young 22/26
18.	1964 Men and their **Gods**	Douglas 6/16
19.	1964 **Religious Institution**	Horton 12/21
20.	1964 **Religion** and Society	Kar 8/17

21 1966 **Religion** Goode 10/15
22. 1966 **Religion** Muzumdar 17/20
23. 1967 **Religion** and **Morality*** Sachdeva 23/28
24. 1967 **Magic***, **Religion**, and Society Goldthorpe 9/9
25. 1968 **Religion** McNall 16/19
26. 1970 **Religious Organization** Mercer 10/16
27. 1970 **Religion** and **Belief Systems** Wilkins 11/16
28. 1971 **Religion** Popenoe 11/16
29. 1971 **Sociology of Religion, Beliefs***, **and Ideologies*** Sergeant 12/13
30. 1973 **Religion** Acuff 15/23
31. 1973 Social Institutions: **Religion and Education*** Bertrand 14/22
32. 1973 **Religion** Leslie 18/21
33. 1973 **Religion** Perry(2) 10/13
34. 1975 **Religion** and **Society** Kenkel 9/16
35. 1976 **Religion** in Society Stewart 12/16
36. 1977 **Religion** Broom(2) 12/17
37. 1977 **Religion** Warren 5/15
38. 1978 **Religion** Stewart 14/19
39. 1979 **Religion** Phillips 11/20
40. 1980 **Sociology of Religion** Gurvitch 11/13
41. 1980 Social Institutions: **Religion** G Marx 9/11
42 1983 **Religious Groups** and **Systems** Eshleman 13/20
43. 1983 **Religion** Tischler 14/20
44. 1984 **Religion** Persell 17/23
45. 1985 **Religion** Haralambos 11/13
46. 1985 **Religion** O'Donnell 23/26
47. 1985 **Religion** Wallace 14/19
48. 1990 **Religion, Morality***, **Magic*** S Rao 19/30

42. SOCIAL CONTROL

1. 1871 **Discipline** Spencer 13/16
2. 1947 **Social Control** and **Conformity*** Ogburn 8/26
3. 1949 **Public Opinion*** and **Social Control** Sprott 7/10
4. 1950 **Mores** and **Social Control** MacIver 7/29
5. 1952 **Social Control** and **Social Planning*** Merrill 27/29
6. 1961 **Deviance*** and **Social Control** Parsons 16/24
7. 1955 **Social Control** Lee 17/35

8.	1957 Forms of **Social Control**	Gisbert 3/5
9.	1960 **Social Conformity***, **Social Deviation*** and **Social Control**	Johnson 20/22
10.	1961 **Conformity*** and **Social Control**	Chinoy 18/21
11.	1962 **Regulation of Behavior**	Bottomore 4/6
12.	1962 **Social Control**	Young 5/26
13.	1964 **Social Control** and **Social Deviation***	Horton 8/21
14.	1966 **Deviance*** and **Social Control**	Goode 8/15
15.	1966 **Social Control**	Muzumdar 12/20
16.	1967 **Social Control**	Sachdeva 5/6
17.	1968 **Aggression, Conflict*** and **Social Control**	Goldthorpe 8/9
18.	1968 **Social Relations***, **Social Control** and **Social Code***	Sharma 12/32
19.	1969 **Deviance*** and **Control**	Abrahamson 10/10
20.	1969 **Deviance*** and **Social Control**	Smelser 7/11
21.	1970 **Problem of Order***: **Social Control**	Worsley 8/8
22.	1970 **Social Order*** and **Social Disorder***	Scott 4/24
23.	1971 **Deviant Behavior*** and **Social Control**	Popenoe 8/16
24.	1972 **Social Control**: the case of **Education***	Berger 9/17
25.	1973 **Social Disorganization***, **Social Deviation** and **Social Control**	Bertrand 5/6
26.	1975 **Deviant Behavior*** and **Social Control**	Chambliss 16/17
27.	1975 **Deviance*** and **Social Control**	Cole 5/9
	Social Control	Cole 11/19
28.	1977 **Prestige** as a **Control System**	Goode 4/17
29.	1977 **Social Control**: **Values***, **Norms*** and **Sanctions**	Shapiro 6/19
30.	1980 **Social Control**	Gurvitch 7/13
31.	1980 Becoming a **Social Being***: **Deviance*** and **Social Control**	G Marx 4/11
32.	1983 **Deviance*** and **Social Control**	Eshleman 7/20
33.	1983 **Social Control** and **Deviant* Behavior**	Tischler 9/20
34.	1985 **Social Stability*** and **Control**	O'Donnell 7/9
	Agencies of **Social Control**: **Family***, **Education***, **Religion***, **Law***	O'Donnell 19/26
35.	1985 **Deviance*** and **Social Control**	Wallace 6/19
36.	1986 **Social Order***, **Institutions*** and **Social Control**	Charon 9/17

37. 1988 **Social Control** and **Socialization*** Gordon 3/7
38. 1988 **Social Control** and **Socialization*** Haralambos 2/5
39. 1990 **Social Control** S Rao 6/10
    Applied Sociology:
    Problems of **Order** S Rao 28/30

43. VALUES

1. **1966** Values, Ideologies* and Symbol* System* Goode 4/7
2. 1967 **Norms*** and **Values** Sachdeva 20/28
3. 1970 **Norms*** and **Values** Scott 2/29
4. 1971 **Values** and **Norms*: Persistence*** and **Change*** Gorman 4/11
5. 1972 **Values** and alternate Meanings Sergeant 17/17
6. 1973 **Values** and **Norms*** Acuff 6/23
7. 1973 **Values, Norms*** and **Institutions*** Leslie 5/21
8. 1976 **Values** and **Norms*** Rose 4/16
9. 1977 **Social Control: Values, Norms*** and **Sanctions** Shapiro 6/19
10. 1990 **Folkways*: Mores, Values,** Norms*, **Sanctions** S Rao 20/30

44. NORMS

1. 1950 **Social Structures***: Sustaining
   Forces of **Codes** and **Custom** MacIver 1/5
   Mores and **Social Control*** MacIver 7/29
   Social Codes MacIver 8/29
   Social Codes and **Individual** life MacIver 9/29
2. 1951 **Culture*** and **Normative Order** O'Brien 4/9
3. 1952 **Normative Integration*** Freedman 5/15
4. 1957 **Norms** Bierstedt 7/19
5. 1967 **Norms** and **Values*** Sachdeva 20/22
6. 1968 **Modes** and **Laws of Social Interaction*** Sharma 11/32
7. 1970 **Norms** and **Values*** Scott 2/29
8. 1972 **Norms** McGee 3/13
9. 1973 **Values*** and **Norms** Acuff 6/23
10. 1973 **Values*, Norms** and **Institutions*** Leslie 5/21
11. 1975 **Norm** Cole 3/19
12. 1975 **Deviancy*: Going Beyond the Norm** Kenkel 16/16
13. 1976 **Values*** and **Norms** Rose 4/16

14. 1977 **Social Control***:
Values*, **Norms, Sanction** Shapiro 6/19
15. 1990 **Folkways: Mores, Values***,
Norms, **Sanctions** S Rao 20/30
Social Norms and **Social Values*** S Rao 21/30

45. MORALITY

1. 1942 Contemporary crisis in **Religion*** and **Morals** Barnes 17/19
2. 1957 **Morality** and **Religion*** Gisbert 8/17
3. 1962 **Religion*** and **Morality** Bottomore 14/20
4. 1967 **Religion*** and **Morality** Sachdeva 23/28
5. 1990 **Religion***, **Morality, Magic*** S Rao 19/30

46. SOCIALIZATION

1. 1947 **Socialization** and **Social Deviation*** Ogburn 11/26
2. 1951 **Socialization**: the **Linkage between self and Society** O'Brien 5/9
3. 1952 **Functional Integration** Freedman 4/15
Normative Integration* Freedman 5/15
4. 1955 **Socialization** Lee 1/6
5. 1957 **Socialization** and **Institutional* Structure** Gisbert 2/5
6. 1957 **Culture*** and **Socialization** Bierstedt 1/5
7. 1960 **Culture*** and **Socialization** Johnson 1/7
Socialization Johnson 5/22
8. 1961 Process of **Socialization** Parsons 14/24
9. 1962 **Socialization** and **Personality*** Young 7/26
10. 1964 **Personality*** and **Socialization** Horton 5/21
11. 1965 **Socialization** Valdes 4/11
12. 1966 **Socialization** Goode 7/15
13. 1966 Mechanism of **Socialization** Muzumdar 9/20
14. 1967 **Socialization** Basu 11/27
15. 1967 **Socialization** Sachdeva 6/28
16. 1968 **Socialization** McNall 6/19
17. 1969 **Socialization** Abrahamson 7/10
18. 1969 **Socialization** Process Smelser 3/4
Socialization Smelser 6/11
19. 1970 **Socialization** Process Scott 6/29
20. 1971 **Socialization** Popenoe 4/16
21. 1972 **Socialization** Berger 5/17

22.	1973 **Socialization** and **Personality Development***	McGee 3/8
23.	1972 **Socialization, Conformity*** and **Deviance***	Rocher 5/17
24.	1973 **Socialization**	Acuff 5/23
25.	1973 **Socialization, Personality***, and **Culture***	Bertrand 2/6
	Socialization	Bertrand 4-5/22
26.	1973 **Culture*** and **Socialization**	Leslie 3/5
	Socialization	Leslie 8/21
27.	1973 **Socialization** and **Deviance***	Perry 4/13
28.	1975 **Socialization** and the **Family***	Baldridge 4/13
29.	1975 **Socialization**	Denisoff 6/16
30.	1975 **Socialization: School without walls**	Kenkel 4/16
31.	1975 **Preservation of Societies: Socialization**	Stewart 4/16
32.	1976 **Culture** and its **Acquisition***	Hebding 2/5
	Socialization	Hebding 4/13
33.	1976 Early **Socialization**	Rose 9/16
34.	1976 **Socialization, Action, Interaction***	Sachdeva 2/6
35.	1977 **Socialization**	Broom 3/8
	Socialization	Broom 4/17
36.	1977 **Socialization**	Goode 3/17
37.	1977 **Socialization: Human Behavior as Social Behavior**	Shapiro 7/19
38.	1977 **Socialization**	Warren 11/15
39.	1978 **Socialization**	Stewart 4/19
40.	1979 **Socialization**	Johnson 5/22
41.	1979 **Socialization Process**: how they make Boys and Girls into Men and Women	Sherman **9/23**
42.	1980 **Becoming a Social being**	G Marx 3/4
43.	1983 **Socialization** as lifelong process	Eshleman 5/20
44.	1983 **Socialization** and **Personality***	Tischler 4/20
45.	1984 **Social life (Socialization**	) Persell 2/6
	Socialization	Persell 6/23
46.	1985 **Socialization**	Wallace 4/19
47.	1988 **Social Control*** and **Socialization**	Gordon 2/5
48.	1988 **Social Control*** and **Socialization**	Haralambos 2/5
49.	1986 **Socialization** and our **Social Nature**	Charon 3/17

50. 1990 **Socialization** and **Culture*** S Rao 9/30

47. CONFORMITY

1. 1947 **Social Control*** and **Conformity** Ogburn 8/26
2. 1960 **Social Conformity, Social Deviation*** and **Social Control*** Johnson 20/22
3. 1961 **Conformity** and **Social Control*** Chinoy 18/21
4. 1961 **Conformity** Parsons 17/24
5. 1971 **Roles** and **Attitudes***: **Conformity** and **Deviance*** Gorman 8/11
6. 1972 **Socialization***, **Conformity** and **Deviance*** Rocher 5/17
7. 1975 **Groups*** and **Conformity** Cole 7/19
8. 1976 **Conformity, Deviance*** and **Re-socialization*** Rose 11/16
9. 1977 **Deviance*** and **Conformity** Goode 5/17
10. 1979 **Conforming** and **Deviant Behavior*** Phillips 4/20
11. 1990 **Social Conformity** and **Deviance*** S Rao 22/36

48. DEVIANCE

1. 1947 **Socialization*** and **Social Deviation** Ogburn 11/26
   Social Control* and **Conformity** Ogburn 8/26
2. 1955 **Deviants** Lee 5/35
3. 1959 **Social Disorganization*** and **Deviant Behavior** Merton 21/25
4. 1960 **Social Deviation** and **Social Change*** Johnson 7/7
   Social Conformity, Social Deviation and **Social Control*** Johnson 20/22
5. 1961 **Social Order, Deviance,**and **Change*** Chinoy 5/5
   Conformity and **Social Control*** Chinoy 18/21
   Deviant Behavior and **Social Disorganization*** Chinoy 19/21
6. 1961 **Social Structure*** and the Motivation for **Deviant** and **Conforming Behavior*** Parsons 15/24
   Deviance and **Social Control*** Parsons 16/24
7. 1962 **Deviant Behavior** Young 26/26
8. 1964 **Social Control*** and **Social Deviation** Horton 8/21
9. 1966 **Deviance** and **Social Control*** Goode 8/15

10. 1967 **Deviant Behavior** Sachdeva 27/28
11. 1968 **Crime*** and **Deviance** McNall 18/19
12. 1969 **Deviance** and **Control*** Abrahamson 10/
10
13. 1969 **Deviance** and **Social Control*** Smelser 7/11
14. 1970 **Social Problems***, **Disorganization***
and **Deviant Behavior** Mercer 5/16
15. 1971 **Roles*** and **Attitudes:**
Conformity and **Deviance** Gorman 8/11
16. 1971 **Deviant Behavior** and **Social**
Control* Popenoe 8/16
17. 1972 **Deviance** Berger 14/17
18. 1972 **Deviant Behavior** McGee 6/8
Deviance as a failure of **Social**
Control* McGee 11/13
19. 1972 **Socialization***, **Conformity***,
and **Deviance** Rocher 2/17
20. 1973 **Social Problems*** and **Deviance** Acuff 22/23
21. 1973 **Social Disorganization***, **Social**
Deviation and **Social Control*** Bertrand 5/6
22. 1973 **Deviance** Leslie 9/21
23. 1973 **Socialization*** and **Deviance** Perry (2) 4/13
24. 1973 **Deviant Behavior** Stewart 9/19
25. 1975 **Deviant Behavior**
and **Social Control*** Chambliss 16/17
26. 1975 **Deviance** and **Social Control*** Cole 5/19
Causes of **Deviance** Cole 9/19
27. 1975 **Deviance** Denisoff 11/16
28. 1975 **Deviancy: Going Beyond the Norm*** Kenkel 16/16
29. 1976 **Deviance** and **Change*** Hebding 5/5
30. 1976 **Socialization*** and **Deviance** Perry 4/13
31. 1976 **Conformity**, **Deviance** and
Re-socialization* Rose 11/16
32. 1976 **Social Deviance** Stewart 5/16
33. 1977 **Deviance** and **Conformity** Goode 5/17
34. 1977 **Deviance** and **Stigma** Warren 13/15
35. 1978 **Diversity** and **Strain:**
Deviant Behavior Stewart 2/4

36. 1979 **Conforming** and **Deviant Behavior** — Phillips 4/20
37. 1980 Becoming a **Social Being: Deviance** and **Social Control*** — G Marx 4/11
38. 1983 **Deviance** and **Social Control*** — Eshleman 7/20
39. 1983 **Social Control*** and **Deviant Behavior** — Tischler 9/20
40. 1984 **Social life: Deviance** — Persell 2/6
41. 1985. **Deviance** Haralambos 10/13
42. 1985 **Deviance** and **Social Control*** — Wallace 6/19
43. 1986 **Social Order***, **Socialization***, **Deviance** — Charon 4/6
    Deviance and **Society** — Charon 11/17
44. 1990 **Social Conformity*** and **Deviance** — S Rao 22/36

49. SOCIOLOGY OF LAW

1. 1942 **Political*** and **Legal Institutions** — Barnes 3/6
   Law and **Justice** as a **Social Problem** — Barnes 11-12/19
2. 1956 **Judiciary** — Weinberg 22/28
3. 1959 **Sociology of Law** — Merton 4/25
4. 1959 **Law** and **Political Systems** — Mitchell 5/10
5. 1960 **Crime*** and the **Law** — Green 19/21
6. 1962 **Law** — Bottomore 15/20
7. 1964 **Law, Custom*** and **Morality*** — Douglas 9/16
8. 1977 **Law** — Broom(2) 13/17
9. 1979 **Crime*** and the **State** — Szymanski 9/14
10. 1980 **Sociology of Law** — Gurvitch 8/13

50. COMMUNICATION

1. 1942 **Communication** and the Formation of **Public Opinion*** — Barnes 4/6
2. 1950 **Herd, Crowd***, and **Mass Communication** — MacIver 16/29
3. 1951 **Communication, Interaction,** and Patterns of **Perception** — O'Brien 6/9
4. 1959 **Mass Communication** and the **Social system** — Merton 24/25
5. 1959 System of **Social Statuses*** and **Communication** — Mitchell 8/10
6. 1961 **Symbolism** and **Communication** — Parsons 18/24
7. 1961 **Collective Behavior** and **Mass Communication** — Sutherland 11/22

8. 1965 **Communication** — Koller 10/22
9. 1966 **Social Interaction, Communication** and **Consensus** — Muzumdar 7/20
10. 1968 **Symbolic Communication** — McNall 5/19
11. 1968 **Suggestion, Imitation, Sympathy** — Sharma 30/32
12. 1970 **Communication** and **Mass Media** — Wilkins 16/16
13. 1971 **Mass Media** and the **Mass Mind** — Gorman 10/11
14. 1971 **Communication** (Suggested topic) — Sergeant 1/13
15. 1973 **Communication** and **Social Interaction*** — Leslie 3/21
16. 1974 **Communication** — Potter 1/8

SYMBOLISM AND LANGUAGE

1. 1961 **Symbolism** and **Communication*** — Parsons 18/24
   Symbolism — Parsons 22/24
2. 1968 **Symbolic Communication*** — McNall 5/19
3. 1972 **Language** — McGee 5/13
4. 1976 **Symbols** and Substance — Rose 3/16

51. PUBLIC OPINION

1. 1942 **Communication*** and the Formation of **Public Opinion** — Barnes 4/6
   Molding **Public Opinion: Prejudice, Propaganda,** and **Censorship** — Barnes 14/19
2. 1949 **Public Opinion** and **Social Control*** — Sprott 7/10
3. 1950 **Public Opinion** — Eldridge 23/34
4. 1959 Study of **Consensus** — Merton 12/25
5. 1962 **Customs*** and **Public Opinion** — Bottomore 13/20
6. 1965 **Public Opinion** — Valdes 9/11

52. SOCIOLOGY OF EDUCATION

1. 1871 **Educational Bias** — Spencer 8/16
2. 1942 **Education** in Social Crisis — Barnes 18/19
3. 1950 Institution of **Education** — Eldridge 27/34
4. 1951 **Sociology of Education** — O'Brien 20/21
5. 1953 **Education** — Biesanz 14/29
6. 1957 **Educational System** — Gisbert 9/17
7. 1959 **Educational System** — Mitchell 9/10
8. 1959 **Sociology of Education** — Merton 5/25
9. 1960 **Education** — Green 16/21
10. 1961 **Education** — Chinoy 15/21

11. 1961 **Learning** Parsons 13/24
12. 1961 **Institutionalized Education** Sutherland 18/22
13. 1962 **Education** Bottomore 16/20
14. 1962 **Education** Young 21/26
15. 1964 **Education** Douglas 12/16
16. 1964 **Education, Science*** and **Technology*** Horton 13/21
17. 1964 **Education** and Society Kar 11/17
18. 1966 **Education** Goode 12/15
19. 1966 **Education** Muzumdar 18/20
20. 1968 **Education** McNall 13/19
21. 1969 **Education, Work,** and **Social Mobility** Abrahamson 9/10
22. 1969 **Sociology of Education** Smelser 10/11
23. 1970 **Education** as a Social Institution Mercer 11/16
24. 1970 **Educational System** Wilkins 10/16
25. 1970 **Education** Worsley 4/8
26. 1971 **Education** Popenoe 10/16
27. 1971 **Education** Sergeant 4/6
    Sociology of Education Sergeant 7/13
28. 1972 **Social Control***: The case of **Education** Berger 4/17
29. 1973 **Education** Acuff 14/23
30. 1973 **Education** Leslie 19/21
31. 1973 **Social Institutions***: **Religion***, and **Education** Bertrand 14/22
32. 1973 **Education** Perry (2) 11/13
33. 1975 **Education** and **Social Mobility*** Baldridge 10/13
34. 1975 **Education** and Society Kenkell 10/16
35. 1976 **Education** Stewart 13/16
36. 1977 **Education** Broom(2) 11/17
37. 1977 **Educational Sociology** Shapiro 19/19
38. 1977 **Education** Warren 6/15
39. 1978 **Educational Process: Transmitting the Cultural Traditions*** Stewart 13/16
40. 1979 **Education** Phillips 13/20
41. 1979 **Sociology of Education** Sherman 13/23
42. 1983 **Educational Groups** and **Systems** Eshleman 14/20
43. 1983 **Education** Tischler 15/20
44. 1984 **Education** Persell 16/23

45. 1985 **Education** Haralambos 5/13
46. 1985 **Sociology of Education** O'Donnell 3/9
47. 1985 **Education** Wallace 17/19
48. 1990 **Education** and the **Economic System*** S. Rao 17/30

53. SOCIOLOGY OF KNOWLEDGE

1. 1961 **Knowledge** and **Rationality** Parsons 20/24
2. 1966 **Sociology of Knowledge** Muzumdar 20/20
3. 1971 **Sociology of Religion,* Beliefs,** and **Ideologies*** Sergeant 12/13
4. 1972 **Culture, Civilization** and **Ideology*** Rocher 3/17
5. 1980 **Sociology of Knowledge** Gurvitch 10/13

54. SOCIOLOGY OF ART

1. 1942 **Leisure*, Recreation** and the **Arts** Barnes 19/19
2. 1956 **Sociology of Art** and **Music** FISR 7/12
3. 1959 **Sociology of Art** Merton 8/25
4. 1964 **Art** in Society Douglas 13/16
5. 1977 **Work*, Leisure** and the **Arts** Warren 7/15

55. SCIENCE AND TECHNOLOGY

1. 1947 Social aspects of **Innovation** Ogburn 24/26
2. 1950 **Technological factors** of **Social Change*** MacIver 25/29
3. 1953 **Great Transformation**: from **Traditional to Modern Society** Biesanz 17/29
4. 1956 **Science** and **Technology** Weinberg 10/29
5. 1957 **Industry** and **Social Change*** Gisbert 14/17
6. 1959 **Sociology of Science** Merton 9/25
7. 1961 **Science** and Society Chinoy 16/21
8. 1961 **Technology** and **Economic Institutions*** Chinoy 12/21
9. 1964 **Education*, Science** and **Technology** Horton 13/21
10. 1964 **Technology** and **Social Change*** Kar 16/17
11. 1967 **Effects of Industrialization* on Social Change*** Basu 12/17
12. 1968 **Technology, Economy*** and Society Goldthorpe 5/9
13. 1972 **Traditional Society** and **Technological Society** Rocher 7/17
    Industrialization, Development and **Modernization** Rocher 13/17
14. 1974 **Population*, Resources, Technology** Potter 1/8

15. 1975 **Technology** and **Economic System***
16. 1977 **Technology** and **Civilization*** Broom 16/17
17. 1977 Major **World Changes***: **Industrialization** Goode 16/17
18. 1977 **Industrialization***, **Urbanization*** and **Social Change*** Warren 3/15
19. 1984 **Science** and **Technology** Persell 18/23

56. INDUSTRIALIZATION

1. 1942 Evolution of **Industry** Barnes 4/19
2. 1957 **Industry** and **Social Change*** Gisbert 14/17
3. 1967 Effects of **Industrialization** on **Social Change*** Basu 12/17
4. 1970 **Economic System*** and the **Social aspects of Industry** Wilkins 9/16
5. 1970 **Work***, **Industry** and **Organizations*** Worsley 5/8
6. 1975 **Imperialism** and **Industrialization** Chambliss 14/17
7. 1973 **Industrial man** Acuff 21/23
8. 1977 Major **World Changes***: **Industrialization** Goode 16/17

IV. SOCIAL STRUCTURE, STRATIFICATION,RACE

57. SOCIAL STRUCTURE

1. 1950 **Social Structure** MacIver 2/3
2. 1951 **Groups** and **Organizations**: their **Social Structure** O'Brien 7/9
3. 1952 **Social Structure** and **Personality*** Merrill 2/5
4. 1959 **Personality*** and**SocialStructure** Merton 11/25
5. 1960 **Structure** and **Function** Johnson 3/22
6. 1961 **Religion*** and **Social Structure** Parsons 12/24
7. 1962 **Social Structure, Societies,** and **Civilization*** Bottomore 7/20
8. 1962 **Social Structures** and **Function** Young 8/26
9. 1965 **Differentiation*** and **Variation** in **Social Structures** Parsons 2/5
10. 1966 **Structural Patterns** within Society Goode 2/7
11. 1967 **Social Structure** Sachdeva 12/28
12. 1969 Basic **Social Structures** Smelser 1/4
13. 1971 **Social Structure** Popenoe 2/16
14. 1972 **Social Structure** and **Social Organization*** McGee 8/13
15. 1973 **Social Structure** and **Interaction*** Bertrand 3/6

16. 1975 **Social Structure** and **Culture*** Cole 6/19
17. 1976 **Social Structure** Rose 2/5
18. 1979 **Social Structure** Phillips 1/8
19. 1979 **Structure of Society** Sherman 17/23
20. 1983 **Social Interaction*** and **Social Structure** Tischler 5/20
21. 1984 Societies and **Social Structures** Persell 3/23
22. 1989 **Social Patterns: (Social Structure, Culture*)** Charon 3/6
Social Structure Charon 7/17
23. 1990 **Social Structure** and **Function** S Rao 4/30

58. SOCIAL DIFFERENTIATION

1. 1957 **Social Differentiation** Bierstedt 5/6
2. 1959 **Social Differentiation** and **Stratification*** Merton 19/25
3. 1961 Differentiation **and Variation** in **Social Structures*** Parsons 2/5
4. 1962 **Differentiation** and **Leadership*** Young 25/26
5. 1971 **Social Differentiation** Sergeant 2/6
6. 1976 **Social Differentiation** Hebding 4/5
7. 1976 **Differences within Societies** Stewart 2/5
8. 1983 **Social Differentiation** and **Stratification*** Eshleman 8/20
9. 1985 **Social Differentiation** O'Donnell 4/9
10. 1990 **Social Differentiation** and **Stratification*** S Rao 13/30

59. SOCIAL INEQUALITY

1. 1956 **Equality** Weinberg 9/28
2. 1971 **Inequality** Gorman 5/11
3. 1975 **Social Inequality**: Sources of **Conflict*** and **Change*** Chambliss 17/17
4. 1975 **Social Stratification** and **Inequality** Cole 8/9
Types of **Inequality** Cole 15/19
5. 1977 **Equality** and **Inequality** Goode 4/6
6. 1977 **Inequality** in **Contemporary Society** Warren 9/15
7. 1980 Structure and Process of **Inequality** G Marx 6/11
8. 1983 **Social Inequality** Eshleman 3/5
9. 1983 **Social Inequality** Tischler 4/6
10. 1984 **Social Inequality** Persell 3/6
11. 1986 **Social Inequality** Charon 5/6

12. 1989 **Social Inequality** Wallace 4/6
13. 1990 **Social Inequality** S Rao 4/10

60. SOCIAL STRATIFICATION

1. 1947 **Social Stratification** Ogburn 16/26
2. 1949 **Social Stratification** Sprott 6/10
3. 1951 **Groups*** and **Organizations***: **Social Stratification** O'Brien 16/21
4. 1952 **Rank Stratification** Freedman 6/15
5. 1952 **Social Stratification**: Caste Merrill 13/29
6. 1953 **Social Stratification** Biesanz 9/29
7. 1957 **Social Stratification** Gisbert 13/17
8. 1957 **Social Stratification** Gitler 8/14
9. 1959 **Social Differentiation*** and **Stratification** Merton 19/25
10. 1959 System of **Social Stratification** Mitchell 7/10
11. 1960 **Stratification** Johnson 6/7
12. 1961 **Social Stratification** Chinoy 8/21
13. 1961 **Stratification** and **Mobility*** Parsons 8/24
14. 1961 **Stratification** and **Mobility*** Sutherland 12/22
15. 1962 **Social Stratification** Bottomore 11/20
16. 1962 **Minorities*** in the **Stratification System** Young 12/26
17. 1964 **Social Stratification** Kar 7/17
18. 1965 **Stratification** Valdes 6/11
19. 1966 **Stratification** and **Social Mobilityy*** Goode 3/15
20. 1967 **Social Stratification** Sachdeva 20/28
21. 1968 **Social Stratification** McNall 10/19
22. 1969 **Social Stratification** Abrahamson 6/10
23. 1969 **Social Stratification** Smelser 4/11
24. 1970 **Social Stratification**: **Class***, **Status***, **Power*** Worsley 7/8
25. 1971 **Social Stratification** Popenoe 7/16
26. 1971 **Social Stratification**: **Class***, **Status*** Sergeant 10/13
27. 1972 **Class*** and **Status***: **Stratified Society** Berger 8/17
28. 1973 **Social Stratification** Acuff 9/23
29. 1973. **Social Stratification** and **Mobility*** Bertrand 10/22
30. 1973 **Social Stratification** Leslie 15/21
31. 1973 Who gets what and why: **Stratification** Perry 6/21
32. 1973 **Ranking*** and **Stratification** Perry(2) 5/13

33. 1975 **Stratification Dynamics** and the **Class System*** — Baldridge 5/13
34. 1975 **Social Stratification** and **Inequality** — Cole 8/9
35. 1975 **Social Stratification** — Denisoff 9/16
36. 1975 **Social Stratification** and **Mobility*** — Kenkel 7/16
37. 1976 **Stratification** — Hebding 8/13
38. 1977 **Social Stratification** — Broom 5/8
39. 1977 **Social Stratification** — Broom (2) 6/17
40. 1977 **Stratification System** — Goode 9/17
41. 1977 **Stratification**: Some are more **equal** than others — Shapiro 12/19
42. 1977 **Social Hierarchies** — Warren 8/15
43. 1978 **Diversity** and **Strain: Stratification** — Stewart 2/4
    Stratification: Class* and **Mobility*** — Stewart 6/19
44. 1979 **Stratification** — Phillips 4/8
45. 1979 **Class Struggle** and **Stratification** — Sherman 19/23
46. 1980 **Structures** and **Processes** of **Inequality***: **Stratification** — G Marx 6/11
47. 1983 **Social Differentiation*** and **Stratification** — Eshleman 8/20
48. 1983 **Social Stratification** — Tischler 10/20
49. 1084 **Social Stratification** — Persell 9/23
50. 1985 **Social Stratification** and **Mobility*** — Wallace 8/19
51. 1990 **Social Differentiation*** and **Stratification** — S Rao 13/30

61. SOCIAL CLASSES

62. CASTE

1. 1871 **Class bias** — Spencer 11/16
2. 1950 **Social Class** and **Caste** — MacIver 14/29
3. 1952 **Class Stratification** — Freedman 7/15
4. 1952 **Social Stratification: Caste** and **Class** — Merrill 13-14/29
5. 1956 **Social Class** — Weinberg 6/28
6. 1957 **Class** and **Caste** — Bierstedt 16/19
7. 1957 **Class Problem** — Mannheim 10/12
8. 1960 **Class** and **Mobility*** — Green 10/21
9. 1960 **Consanguinal Kin Groups** and **Class*** — Johnson 8/22
   Social, Ranking* and **Social Classes** — Johnson 18/22
10. 1962 **Social Class** and its Consequences — Young 11/26
11. 1964 **Social Class** — Horton 15/21
12. 1965 **Social Class System** — Koller 11/22

13. 1966 **Class Groupings** — Muzumdar 4/20
14. 1967 **Social Strata**: **Classes** and **Castes** — Basu 3/17
15. 1968 **Social Class** — Goldthorpe 7/9
16. 1968 **Castes** and **Social Class** — Sharma 14/32
17. 1970 **Social Status*** and **Social Classes** — Mercer 7/16
18. 1970 **Social Classes** — Wilkins 6/16
19. 1970 **Social Stratification***: **Class, Status*, Power*** — Worsley 7/8
20. 1971 **Social Stratification***: **Class, Status*** — Sergeant 10/13
21. 1972 **Stratified Community** — Berger 7/17
    Stratified Society*: **Class** and **Status*** — Berger 8/17
22. 1972 **Social Class** — McGee 10/13
23. 1975 **Stratification* Dynamics** and the **Social Class System** — Baldridge 5/13
24. 1977 **Social Hierarchies** — Warren 3/6
25. 1978 **Stratification***, **Class,** and **Mobility*** — Stewart 6/19
26. 1979 **Poverty*** and **Social Class** — Sherman 2/23
    Class Struggle and **Stratification*** — Sherman 19/23
27. 1979 **Individual** in **Class Society** — Szymanski 6/14
    Culture* and **Class Consciousness** — Szymanski 7/14
28. 1984 **Social Class** — Persell 10/23
29. 1985 **Social Class** in the United States — Wallace 9/19
30. 1985 **Social Class** — Charon 12/17
31. 1990 **Castes-Estates** and **Class** — S Rao 14/30

63. SOCIAL STATUS

64. ROLE

1. 1952 **Culture***, **Status** and **Role** — Merrill 8/29
2. 1955 **Role** — Lee 2/35
3. 1957 **Statuses** — Bierstedt 8/19
4. 1959 System of **Social Statuses** and **Communication*** — Mitchell 8/10
5. 1960 **Social Ranking** and **Social Classes*** — Johnson 18/22
6. 1961 **Social Roles** and **Culture Conflict*** — Sutherland 6/22
7. 1962 **Status** and **Roles** — Young 9/26
8. 1964 **Social Roles** — Douglas 4/16

9. 1964 **Role** and **Status** Horton 6/21
10. 1965 **Role** Valdes 3/11
11. 1967 **Role** and **Status** Sachdeva 12/28
12. 1970 **Social Roles** and **Social Processes*** Mercer 4/16
Social Status and **Social Classes*** Mercer 7/16
13. 1970 **Position** and **Roles** Scott 3/29
14. 1970 **Social Stratification***: **Class***, **Status, Power*** Worsley 7/8
15. 1971 **Social Stratification***: **Class*** and **Status*** Sergeant 10/13
16. 1971 **Role** and **Status**
17. 1971 **Role** and **Status** Popenoe 6/60
18. 1972 **Class** and **Status**: **Stratified Society** Berger 8/17
18. 1972 **Statuses** McGee 9/13
19. 1973 **Social Roles** Acuff 7/23
20. 1973 **Ranking** and **Stratification*** Perry 5/13
21. 1975 **Status** and **Role Conflict** Cole 4/19
22. 1975 **Positions** and **Roles** in Society Kenkel 5/16
23. 1976 **Roles** and **Relationship*** Rose 5/16
24. 1977 **Prestige as a Control*** **System** Goode 4/17
25. 1977 **Social Hierarchies*** Warren 3/6
26. 1990 **Role** and **Status** S Rao 2/30
Power*, **Status, Authority*** S Rao 3/30

65. POWER

66. **AUTHORITY**

1. 1949 Foci of **Power** Sprott 3/10
2. 1949 **Authority** Bierstedt 11/19
Power Bierstedt 12/19
3. 1961 **Power, Authority** and **Political Institutions*** Chinoy 13/21
4. 1961 **Political Organization*** and **Authority** Parsons 12/35
5. 1966 **Politics*** and **Power** Goode 13/15
6. 1967 **Leadership*** and **Power** Sachdeva 13/28
7. 1970 **Social Stratification***: **Class***, **Status*** and **Power** Worsley 7/8
8. 1971 **Politics*** and **Power** Popenoe 15/16

9. 1972 **Power** Berger 13/17
10. 1973 **Social Power** Bertrand 11/22
11. 1974 **Power** Potter 7/8
12. 1975 **Power** Chambliss 12/17
13. 1975 **Political Process***: The **State** and **Interest Groups*** Baldridge 8/13
14. 1975 **Government*** and **Economy***: **Distributing Goods** and **Power** Kenkel 11/16
15. 1977 **Social Power** Warren 10/15
16. 1978 **Political Power*** Stewart 15/19
17. 1984 **Power** and **Politics*** Persell 15/23
18. 1985 **Power** and **Politics*** Haralambos 3/13
19. 1985 **Pressure** and **Interest Groups** O'Donnell 25/26
20. 1986 **Social Power** Charon 13/17
21. 1990 **Power, Status***, **Authority** S Rao 3/30

67. LEADERSHIP

1. 1962 **Differentiation*** and **Leadership** Young 25/26
2. 1967 **Leadership** Basu 9/17
3. 1967 **Leadership** and **Power*** Sachdeva 13/28

68. SOCIAL MOBILITY

1. 1961 **Stratification*** and **Mobility** Parsons 8/24
2. 1961 **Stratification*** and **Mobility** Sutherland 12/22
3. 1964 **Social Mobility** Horton 14/21
4. 1966 **Social Stratification*** and **Mobility** Goode 3/15
5. 1967 **Population***, **Social Mobility** and the **Refugees*** Basu 13/17
6. 1969 **Education***, **Work** and **Social Mobility** Abrahamson 9/10
7. 1971 **Social Mobility** Sergeant 5/6
8. 1973 **Social Stratification** and **Mobility** Bertrand 10/22
9. 1975 **Social Mobility: Racial***, **Sexual*** and **Legal Barriers*** Baldridge 6/13
10. 1975 **Social Stratification*** and **Mobility** Kenkel 7/16
11. 1978 **Stratification***, **Class*** and **Mobility** Stewart 6/19
12. 1985 **Social Mobility** O'Donnell 11/26
13. 1985 **Social Stratification*** and **Mobility** Wallace 8/19

69. SOCIOLOGY OF GENDER

1. 1957 **Stratification: Women and Men** Bierstedt 13/19
2. 1964 **Sexuality*** and **Changing Sex Roles** Horton 7/21
3. 1973 **Social Differentiation***: **Sexuality*** and **Sex Roles** Perry 8/21
4. 1975 **Social Mobility***: **Racial***, **Sexual**, and **Legal Barriers** Baldridge 6/13
5. 1975 **Discrimination against Blacks*** and **Women** Cole 17/19
6. 1977 **Inequality***: **Women and Men** Goode 11/17
7. 1977 **Women's Studies** Shapiro 19/19
8. 1978 **Stratification***: **Sex** and **Age** Stewart 8/19
9. 1979 **Sex** and **Age Roles** Phillips 9/20
10. 1979 **Sex*** and **Sexism** Sherman 11/23
11. 1980 Structures and Process of **Inequality***: **Sex Stratification** G Marx 7/11
12. 1983 **Gender** and **Age Differentiation*** Eshleman 10/20
13. 1983 **Gender Roles** Tischler 12/20
14. 1984 **Gender Roles** and **Inequality*** Persell 12/23
15. 1985 **Women** and Society Haralambos 9/13
16. 1985 **Gender Role Inequalities*** Wallace 11/19

70. SOCIOLOGY OF OCCUPATIONS

1. 1959 **Study of Occupations** Merton 20/25
2. 1966 **Occupation** Goode 4/15
3. 1971 **Occupational Sociology** Sergeant 8/13
4. 1977 **Occupations** and **Professions** Goode 14/17

71. RACIAL GROUPS

73. ETHNIC GROUPS

1. 1950 **Ethnic** and **Racial Groups** MacIver 15/29
2. 1952 **Race** and **Social Structure*** Merrill 12/29
3. 1955 **Race** and **Culture*** Lee 4/6
4. 1957 **Color** and **Creed** Bierstedt 17/19
5. 1961 **Racial** and **Ethnic Groups** Chinoy 9/21
6. 1961 **Ethnic Solidarity** Parsons 3/24
7. 1961 **Race** and **Race Conscious Groups*** Sutherland 13/22
8. 1964 **Physical Differences** Douglas 2/16
9. 1964 **Race** Kar 13/17

10. 1966 **Race Groups** Muzumdar 6/20
11. 1968 **Race** and **Racism*** Sharma 23/32
12. 1971 **Racial** and **Ethnic Minorities*** Popenoe 9/16
13. 1976 **Race** and **Ethnicity** Rose 8/16
14. 1977 **Race** and **Ethnicity** Broom 14/17
15. 1978 Diversity and Strain:
    Race and **Ethnic Groups** Stewart 2/4
16. 1979 **Biological*** and **Physical Structures** Phillips 7/8
    Ethnic Groups Phillips 8/20
17. 1979 **Race, Ethnicity**, and **Racism*** Sherman 7/23
18. 1979 **Racism** and **Capitalism*** Szymanski 11/14
19. 1988 **Race** and **Ethnicity** Gordon 5/5

72. RACE RELATIONS

1. 1953 **Inter-group Tensions** in a
   Multi-Group Society Biesanz 20/29
2. 1956 **Prejudice** FISR 11/12
3. 1956 **Racial Discrimination** Weinberg 11/28
4. 1957 **Race Problem** Gisbert 11/17
5. 1957 **Racial** and **Cultural*** **Relations*** Gitler 13/14
6. 1959 **Sociology of Race** and
   Ethnic Relations Merton 17/25
7. 1961 **Ethnic Solidarity** Parsons 3/24
8. 1961 **Race*** and **Race Conscious Groups** Sutherland 13/22
9. 1964 **Race** and **Ethnic Relations** Horton 17/21
10. 1966 **Ethnic Relations** Goode 2/15
11. 1968 **Minority Relations** McNall 9/19
12. 1968 **Race*** and **Racism** Sharma 23/32
13. 1970 **Minority*** **Group Relations** Mercer 8/16
14. 1971 **Race Relations** Sergeant 11/13
15. 1973 **Inter-group Relations** and
    Minority* **Problems** Bertrand 21/22
16. 1975 **Discrimination against**
    Blacks*, and **Women*** Cole 17/19
17. 1975 **Inter-group Relations** Denisoff 10/16
18. 1975 **Minority*** **Group Relations** Kenkel 15/16
19. 1976 **Minority*** **Groups**: Relations
    and **Reactions** Hebding 9/13
20. 1977 **Race** and **Ethnic Relations** Goode 10/17
21. 1977 **Minority*** **Relations**: **Prejudice** and
    Discrimination Shapiro 13/19

22. 1979 **Race***, **Ethnicity** and **Racism** — Sherman 7/23
23. 1979 **Racism** and **Capitalism*** — Szymanski 11/14
24. 1983 **Racial** and **Ethnic Differentiation*** — Eshleman 9/20
25. 1985 **Race** and **Ethnic Relations** — Wallace 10/19

74. MINORITIES

1. 1955 **Minorities**: **Racial, Ethnic***, **Class*** — Lee 35/35
2. 1960 Americas **Minorities** — Green 12/21
3. 1962 **Minorities** in the **Stratification*** **System** — Young 12/26
4. 1965 **Minority Groups** — Koller 18/22
5. 1968 **Minority Relations*** — McNall 19/19
6. 1970 **Minority Group Relations*** — Mercer 8/16
7. 1970 **Minority Groups** and **Social Organization*** — Wilkins 14/16
8. 1971 **Racial*** and **Ethnic Minorities*** — Popenoe 9/16
9. 1973 **Social Adjustment** of **Minorities** — Acuff 20/23
10. 1973 **Inter-group Relations*** and **Minority Problems** — Bertrand 21/22
11. 1973 **Minorities** — Leslie 16/21
12. 1973 **Majority** and **Minorities** — Perry 6/13
13. 1973 We and They: **Majority** and **Minorities** — Perry(2) 7/21
14. 1975 **Discrimination against Blacks***, and **Women*** — Cole 17/19
15. 1975 **Minority Group Relation*** — Kenkel 15/16
16. 1976 **Minority Groups**: **Relations*** and Reactions — Hebding 9/13
17. 1976 **Racial** and **Ethnic Minorities** — Stewart 7/16
18. 1977 **Minority Relations***; **Prejudice** and **Discrimination** — Shapiro 13/19
19. 1978 **Minorities**: **Racial** and **Ethnic** — Stewart 7/19
20. 1983 **Racial** and **Ethnic Minorities** — Tischler 11/20
21. 1984 **Minority Groups** and **Age Inequality*** — Persell 11/23
22. 1986 **Minorities** and **Social Structure*** — Charon 14/17

V. SOCIAL CONFLICT, DISORGANIZATION

75. SOCIAL CONFLICT

1. 1937 Sociology and **Social Conflict** — Calverton 6/8
2. 1966 **Management of Stress** in Social Systems — Goode 6/15

3.	1967 **Conflict** and **Tension** in **Human Society**	Basu 10/17
4.	1968 **Aggression, Conflict** and **Social Control***	Goldthorpe 8/9
5.	1968 **Social Change*** and **Social Conflict**	McNall 4/4
	Social Conflict and **Social Movements***	McNall 17/19
6.	1973 **Social Conflict**	Acuff 11/23
7.	1975 **Contradictions** and **Conflicts**	Chambliss 11/17
8.	1975 **Conflict** and **Change***	Kenkel 4/4
9.	1986 **Social Conflict** and **Social Movements**	Charon 15/17

76. SOCIAL DISORGANIZATION

1.	1942 **Family** and **Community Disorganization**	Barnes 5/6
2.	1947 **Social Disorganization**	Ogburn 25/26
3.	1959 **Social Disorganization** and **Deviant Behavior***	Merton 21/25
4.	1961 **Deviant Behavior*** and **Social Disorganization**	Chinoy 17/21
5.	1967 **Social Disorganization**	Sachdeva 28/28
6.	1968 **Social Disorganization**	Sharma 25/32
7.	1970 **Social Problems*, Disorganization,** and **Deviant Behavior***	Mercer 5/16
8.	1970 **Social Order *** and **Social Disorder**	Scott 4/29
9.	1973 **Social Disorganization, Social Deviation*** and **Social Control***	Bertrand 5/6
	Social Disorganization and **Social Problems**	Bertrand 17/22
10.	1977 **Social Disorganization**	Warren 5/6
11.	1990 **Social Disorganization** and **Social Problems***	S Rao 8/10

77. REVOLUTION

1.	1965 **Social Change*** and **Revolution**	Goode 7/7
2.	1972 **Revolutionary Process**	Rocher 15/16
3.	1975 **Social Movements*** and **Revolution**	Baldridge 9/13
4.	1979 **Social Movements*** and **Revolution**	Szymanski 14/14

78. CROWD

1.	1947 **Group Behavior***	Ogburn 3/7

2. 1950 **Herd, Crowd** and **Mass Communication*** MacIver 16/29
3. 1952 **Crowd** as **Collective Behavior*** Merrill 16/29
4. 1956 **Masses** FISR 5/12
5. 1968 **Crowd Behavior*** and **Group Mind** Sharma 31/32
6. 1957 **Sociology of Groups***: **Crowd, Public** Mannheim 8/12

79. COLLECTIVE BEHAVIOR

1. 1947 **Group* Behavior** Ogburn 3/7
2. 1950 **Collective Behavior** Eldridge 22/34
3. 1952 **Collective Behavior** Merrill 4/6
   Crowd* as **Collective Behavior** Merrill 16/29
   Public* as **Collective Behavior** Merrill 17/29
4. 1955 **Collective Behavior** Lee 2/6
   Collective Behavior including **Social Movements*** Lee 7-11/35
5. 1957 **Collective Behavior** Gitler 5/14
6. 1961 **Collective Behavior** and **Mass Communication*** Sutherland 11/22
7. 1964 **Collective Behavior** in **Mass Society** Horton 18/21
8. 1964 **Collective Behavior** Kar 5/17
9. 1965 **Collective Behavior** Koller 8/22
10. 1967 **Collective Behavior** Sachdeva 15/28
11. 1968 **Crowd Behavior** and **Group Mind** Sharma 21/32
    Human Nature and **Collective Behavior** Sharma 32/32
12. 1970 **Social Groups*** and **Group Behavior** Mercer 6/16
13. 1971 **Collective Behavior** and **Social Movements*** Popenoe 12/16
14. 1973 **Collective Behavior** Acuff 10/23
15. 1973 **Near Group*** and **Collective Behavior** Leslie 11/21
16. 1973 **MassSociety** and **Collective Behavior** Perry 12/17
17. 1973 **Collective Behavior** Perry(2) 8/13
18. 1975 **Collective Behavior** Denisoff 13/16
19. 1976 **Collective Behavior** Hebding 11/13
20. 1976 **Trends in Societies: Collective Behavior** Stewart 3/5

21. 1977 **Collective Behavior** Broom 7/8
Collective Behavior Broom(2) 8/17
22. 1977 Diversity and Strain:
Collective Behavior Stewart 2/4
Collective Behavior Stewart 11/19
23. 1979 **Collective Behavior (as Social Change)** Phillips 19/20
24. 1983 **Collective Behavior** and **Social Movements*** Wallace 7/19
25. 1983 **Social Movements*** and **Collective Behavior** Tischler 18/20
26. 1984 **Social Change***, **Collective Behavior** and **Social Movements*** Persell 19/23

80. SOCIAL MOVEMENTS

1. 1952 **Social Movements** as **Collective Behavior*** Merrill 18/29
2. 1955 **Collective Behavior** including **Social Movements** Lee 7-11/35
3. 1967 **Social Movements** Sachdeva 16/28
4. 1968 **Social Conflict*** and **Social Movements** Mcnall 17/19
5. 1971 **Collective Behavior*** and **Social Movements** Popenoe 12/16
6. 1972 **Social Movements** and **Pressure Groups*** Rocher 12/17
7. 1975 **Social Movements** and **Revolution*** Baldridge 9/13
8. 1975 **Social Movements** Denisoff 15/16
9. 1976 **Social Movements** Hebding 12/13
10. 1976 **Social Movements** Rose 15/16
11. 1979 Sociology of **Protest Movements** Sherman 14/23
12. 1979 **Social Movements** and **Revolution*** Szymanski 14/14
13. 1983 **Social Movements** and **Collective Behavior*** Tischler 18/20
14. 1983 **Collective Behavior*** and **Social Movements** Wallace 7/19
15. 1984 **Social Change***, **Collective Behavior*** and **Social Movements** Persell 19/23

16.	1986 **Social Conflict*** and **Social Movements**	Charon 15/17
VI.	**SOCIAL CHANGE**	
81.	**SOCIAL CHANGE**	
1.	1942 **Political** and **Legal*** **Institutions** in Transition *	Barnes 3/6
	Contemporary **crisis** in **Religion** and **Morals***	Barnes 17/19
2.	1947 **Socio-Cultural Change**	Ogburn 7/7
	Socio-Cultural Change	Ogburn 23/26
3.	1949 **Social Change**	Sprott 9/10
4.	1950 **Social Change**	MacIver 3/3
	Cultural factors* of **Social Change**	MacIver 26/29
5.	1951 **Social Change** and **Social Planning***	O'Brien 1/9
6.	1952 **Social Interaction***, **Social Change** and **Social Planning**	Merrill 6/6
	Social Change and **Social Problems***	Merrill 26/29
7.	1956 **Changing Capitalism** *	Weinberg 18/28
8.	1957 **Social Change**	Bierstedt 5/5
	Problems of **Social Change**	Bierstedt 19/19
9.	1957 Agencies of **Social Change**	Gisbert 4/5
	Industry and **Social Change**	Gisbert 14/17
10.	1957 **Social Stability** and **Social Change**	Mannheim 4/4
	Causes of **Social Change**	Mannheim 12/12
11.	1960 **Social Change**	Green 4/4
12.	1960 **Social Deviation*** and **Social Change**	Johnson 7/7
	Social Change	Johnson 22/22
13.	1961 **Social Change**	Chinoy 20/21
14.	1961 **Social Change**	Parsons 5/5
	Change and **Development***	Parsons 24/24
15.	1961 **Social Change**	Sutherland 7/7
	Changing Social World	Sutherland 22/22
16.	1962 **Social Change**	Bottomore 5/6
	Change, Development, Progress*	Bottomore 17/20
	Factors of **Social Change**	Bottomore 18/20
17.	1962 **Social Dynamics**	Young 5/5
	Social and **Cultural*** **Change**	Young 6/26

18.	1964 **Social Change** and **Progress***	Douglas 15/16
19.	1964 **Social Change** and **Social Policy***	Horton 6/6
	Social and **Cultural Change**	Horton 21/21
20.	1964 **Social Change**	Kar 14/17
	Technology and **Social Change**	Kar 16/17
21.	1965 **Social Change** and **Revolution**	Goode 7/7
22.	1965 **Social** and **Cultural Change**	Valdes 8/11
23.	1966 **Social Change**	Muzumdar 11/20
24.	1967 **Effects of Industrialization*** on **Social Change**	Basu 12/17
25.	1967 **Social Order, Deviance*** and **Change**	Chinoy 5/6
26.	1967 **Social Change**	Sachdeva 6/6
27.	1968 **Social Change** and **Social Conflict***	McNall 4/4
28.	1968 **Social Change**	Sharma 10/32
29.	1969 **Social** and **Cultural Change**	Abrahamson 4/10
30.	1969 **Social Change**	Smelser 8/11
31.	1970 **Social Change** and **Social Planning***	Mercer 16/16
32.	1970 **Changing Society**	Wilkins 3/9
33.	1971 **Values*** and **Norms***: **Persistence***, and **Change**	Gorman 4/11
33.	1971 **Urban*** **Development** and **Community*** **Change**	Popenoe 14/16
	Social change	Popenoe 16/16
34.	1972 **Change**	Berger 15/17
35.	1972 **Social Change**	Rocher 3/3
	Revolutionary Process	Rocher 15/17
	Social Change	Rocher 11-12/17
36.	1973 **Socio-cultural Change**	Acuff 12/23
37.	1973 **Socio-cultural Change**	Perry 9/17
	Institutions* in **Transition**	Perry 13/17
38.	1973 **Social** and **Cultural*** **Change**	Perry(2) 7/13
39.	1973 **Social Change** and **Cultural*** **Growth**	Bertrand 8/22
40.	1974 **Social Change**	Potter 8/8
41.	1975 Historical Process:**Social Change**	Chambliss 3/4
42.	1975 **Social Change**	Cole 7/9
	Change from Simple to Complex Societies	Cole 13/19
	Marxist Theory of Social Change	Cole 14/19

43.	1975 **Social Change**	Denisoff 16/16
44.	1975 **Conflict*** and **Change**	Kenkel 4/4
	Social and **Cultural Change**	Kenkel 12/16
45.	1976 **Social Change**	Hebding 13/13
46.	1976 **Continuity** and **Change**	Rose 5/5
	Social Change	Rose 14/16
47.	1976 **Changing Institutions***	Stewart 4/5
	Sociology and **Social Change**	Stewart 5/5
48.	1977 **Social Change**	Goode 6/6
49.	1977 **Social Processes***: **Stability and Change**	Shapiro 11/19
50.	1977 **Industrialization***, **Urbanization*** and **Social Change**	Warren 3/15
51.	1978 Sources of **Change**	Stewart 4/4
52.	1979 **Social Change**	Phillips 8/8
53.	1979 **Social Change**	Sherman 0/23
	Sociological Analysis of History	Sherman 21/23
54.	1980 **Socio-cultural Dynamics** and **Evolution**	Gurvitch 2/13
	Social Causation and **Change**	Gurvitch 3/13
55.	1983 **Human Ecology*** and **Change**	Eshleman 5/5
	1983 **Changing Community***	Eshleman 19/20
	Nature of **Social Change**	Eshleman 20/20
56.	1983 **Social Change**	Tischler 6/6
57.	1984 **Social Changes** and Issues	Persell 5/6
	Social Change, Collective Behavior* and **Social Movements***	Persell 19/23
58.	1985 **Social Change**	O'Donnell 8/9
	Reasons and Process of **Social Change**	O'Donnell 21-22/26
	1985 Changing Conditions of **Employment***	O'Donnell 14/26
59.	1986 **Dynamic nature of Society**	Charon 6/6
	Social Change	Charon 16/17
	Family* in a **Changing Society***	Charon 17/17
60.	1989 **Social Change**	Wallace 6/6
61.	1990 **Social Change**	S Rao 7/10

82. EVOLUTION

83. PROGRESS

1.	1950 **Social Evolution**	MacIver 27/29
	Social Evolution and **Social Progress**	MacIver 28/29
2.	1957 **Social Evolution** and **Progress**	Gisbert 17/17
3.	1961 **Change*** and **Development**	Parsons 24/24
4.	1962 **Change*, Development, Progress**	Bottomore 17/20
5.	1964 **Social Change*** and **Progress**	Douglas 15/16
6.	1964 **Social Evolution** and **Progress**	Kar 17/17
7.	1968 **Social Evolution, Social Progress**	Sharma 9,14/32
8.	1980 **Socio-cultural Dynamics*** and **Evolution**	Gurvitch 2/13

VII. HUMAN ECOLOGY, COMMUNITIES

84. HUMAN ECOLOGY

85. ENVIRONMENT

1.	1947 **Human Ecology** and **Population***	Ogburn 5/7
2.	1950 **Geography*, Ecology*** and the **Community***	Eldridge 3/7
	Community and **Human Ecology**	Eldridge 11/34
3.	1950 **Society** and **Environment**	MacIver 2/5
	Environment and Life	MacIver 4/29
	Total **Environment** and **Accommodation**	MacIver 6/29
4.	1952 **Ecological aspects** of **Community***	Merrill 21/29
5.	1955 **Human Ecology**	Lee 5/6
	Eco-System and **Ecology**	Lee 22/35
6.	1957 **Heredity*** and **Environment**	Gisbert 10/17
7.	1959 Organism and its **Physical Environment**	Green 2/21
8.	1961 **Communities**: **Ecology** and **Urbanization**	Chinoy 11/21
9.	1961 **Ecology** and **Communities***	Sutherland 14/22
10.	1962 **Human Ecology**	Young 17/26
11.	1964 **Human Ecology**	Horton 5/6
12.	1965 **Population** and **Ecology**	Valdes 10/11
13.	1967 **Human Ecology**	Sachdeva 4/6
	Heredity* and **Environment**	Sachdeva 11/28
14.	1968 Society and **Environment**	Sharma 5/32
	Heredity* and **Environment**	Sharma 8/32

15. 1971 **Population*** and **Ecology** Popenoe 13/16
16. 1973 Man and **Ecology** Acuff 23/23
17. 1973 **Human Ecology** and **Environmental Problems** Bertrand 20/22
18. 1973. **Population***, **Urbanization***, and **Ecology** Perry 10/17
20. 1977 **Population*** and **Ecology** Broom 8/8
21. 1977 **Demography*** and **Human Ecology** Shapiro 17/19
22. 1979 **Human Ecology** Phillips 18/20
23. 1979 **Ecology** and **Population*** Szymanski 13/14
24. 1980 **Human Ecology** Gurvitch 13/13
25. 1983 **Human Ecology** and **Change*** Eshleman 5/5
26. 1983 **Demography*** and **Ecology** Tischler 19/20
27. 1985 **Population*** and **Environment** Wallace 18/19
28. 1990 **Heredity*** and **Environment** S Rao 6/30

86. GEOGRAPHIC ENVIRONMENT

1. 1947. **Geographical factor** in Society Ogburn 5/26
2. 1950 **Geography, Ecology*** and **Community*** Eldridge 3/7
   Geographical factor and **Culture*** Eldridge 9/34
3. 1950 **Geography** and People MacIver 5/29
4. 1957 **Natural Condition of Human Society: Geographic** Bierstedt 1/19
5. 1977 **Geography** and **Social life** Goode 8/17

87. MEDICAL SOCIOLOGY

1. 1959 **Sociology of Medicine** Merton 10/25
2. 1961 **Health** and **Welfare Organization*** Sutherland 20/22
3. 1969 **Medical Sociology** Smelser 11/11
4. 1971 **Medical Sociology** Sergeant 11/11
5. 1977 **Medical Sociology** Shapiro 19/19
6. 1983 **Population*** and **Health** Eshleman 18/20
7. 1984 **Population** and **Health** Persell 20/23

88. COMMUNITY

1. 1947 **Communities** Ogburn 12/26
2. 1950 **Geography***, **Ecology*** and **Community** Eldridge 3/7
   Community and **Human Ecology*** Eldridge 11/34
3. 1950 **Community** MacIver 12/29
4. 1951 **Human Communities** O'Brien 2/9
5. 1952 **Community** and **Social Institutions*** Merrill 5/6

Entry	Source
Ecological* aspects of Community	Merrill 11/29
Community and Social Institutions*	Merrill 20/29
6. 1956 Community Studies	FISR 10/12
7. 1956 Community Power	Weinberg 20/28
8. 1957 Rural* Community	Gitler 7/14
9. 1959 Modern Community Trend	Green 13/21
10. 1961 Communities: Ecology* and Urbanization*	Chinoy 11/21
11. 1961 Population* and Communities	Sutherland 7/7
Ecology* and Communities	Sutherland 14/22
12. 1962 Folk* and Urban* Communities	Young 16/26
13. 1964 Changing Community	Horton 20/21
14. 1968 Communities	McNall 9/19
15. 1969 Comparative Study of Societies	Smelser 2/11
16. 1970 Community Organization and Behavior*	Mercer 15/16
17. 1970 Social Processes* in Communities	Scott 6/7
18. 1970 Community	Worsley 6/8
19. 1971 Urban* Development and Community Change*	Popenoe 14/16
20. 1972 Community	Berger 6/17
21. 1973 Community	Acuff 18/23
22. 1976 Nature of Community	Rose 12/16
23. 1979 Community	Phillips 15/20
24. 1983 Changing Community	Eshleman 19/20
25. 1983 Communities	Tischler 7/20
26. 1990 Individual* and Community	S Rao 7/30

89. RURAL SOCIOLOGY

Entry	Source
1. 1950 Rural Trade area and the Metropolitan* Region	Eldridge 13/34
2. 1953 Farmer in an Industrializing World	Biesanz 2/29
3. 1956 Modern Farmer	Weinberg 15/28
4. 1957 Rural Community*	Gitler 7/14
5. 1959 Trends in Rural Sociology	Merton 16/25
6. 1962 Folk* and Urban* Communities*	Young 16/26
7. 1967 Rural Community*	Sachdeva 17/28
8. 1968 Village Community*	Sharma 6/32

90. URBANIZATION

91. URBAN SOCIOLOGY

1.	1950 **Spatial Patterning of City**	Eldridge 12/34
	Rural* **Trade area** and the **Metropolitan Region**	Eldridge 13/34
2.	1950 **City, Country** and **Region**	MacIver 13/29
3.	1952 **Urban Community**	Freedman 10/15
	Stratification* in **Urban Society**	Freedman 12/15
	Social Change* in **Urban Society**	Freedman 14/15
4.	1952 **City Planning**	Merrill 28/29
5.	1957 **City, Country, Suburb**	Bierstedt 15/19
6.	1957 **Urban Community**	Gitler 6/14
7.	1959 Comparative **Urban Sociology**	Merton 15/25
8.	1961 Contemporary **Urban Community**	Sutherland 16/22
9.	1962 **Folk*** and **Urban Communities***	Young 16/26
	Metropolitan areas and **Suburbs**	Young 18/26
10.	1961 **Communities: Ecology** and **Urbanization**	Chinoy 11/21
11.	1967 **Urban Community**	Sachdeva 18/28
12.	1968 **Rural-Urban contrast**	Sharma 7/32
13.	1970 **Urbanization**	Wilkins 13/16
14.	1971 **Urban Development** and **Community*** **Change**	Popenoe 14/16
15.	1971 **Urban Sociology**	Sergeant 13/13
16.	1973 **Cities**	Leslie 14/21
17.	1973 **Population***, **Urbanization** and **Ecology***	Perry 10/17
18.	1975 **Population*** and **Urbanization**	Baldridge 12/13
19.	1975 **City**	Kenkel 14/16
20.	1976 **Urban Living**	Rose 13/16
21.	1976 **Trends in Societies:Urban Trend**	Stewart 3/5
22.	1977 **Urbanization**	Broom 15/19
23.	1977 Major World Changes: **Urbanization**	Goode 16/17
24.	1977 **Industrialization***, **Urbanization** and **Social Change***	Warren 3/15
25.	1978 **Urbanization**	Stewart 18/19
26.	1980 **Demography*** and **Urbanization: Urban Community**	G Marx 11/11

27. 1984 **Urbanization** and **Sub-urbanization** Persell 21/23
28. 1985 **Social Change***: **Urbanization** and **Modernization*** Wallace 19/19

VIII. POPULATION

92. POPULATION

1. 1947 **Human Ecology*** and **Population** Ogburn 5/7
   Distribution of Population Ogburn 13/26
   Growth of Population Ogburn 14/26
2. 1950 **Population traits** and **Trends** Eldridge 14/34
   How many People Eldridge 14/34
   Population: Problem of Quality-policy Eldridge 17-18/34
3. 1951 **Human Population** O'Brien 3/9
4. 1952 **Population** and **Social Structure*** Merrill 11/29
5. 1953 **Population**: its **Growth** and **Distribution** Biesanz 8/29
6. 1955 **Population** Lee 23/35
7. 1957 **Natural Condition of Human Society: Demographic** Bierstedt 3/19
8. 1957 **Population** Gisbert 16/17
9. 1957 **Population Research** Gitler 3/14
10. 1959 Problem of **Demographic Social Structure*** Merton 3/4
    Sociology of Demographic Behavior Merton 14/25
11. 1960 **Population** Green 9/21
12. 1961 **Population** and Society Chinoy 4/5
13. 1961 **Population** and **Communities*** Sutherland 5/7
14. 1962 **Population** and **Social Groupings*** Bottomore 2/6
15. 1962 **Population** and **Resources** Young 14/26
    Population Differentials Young 15/26
16. 1964 **Demography** and **Population Problems** Bertrand 19/22
17. 1964 **Population** Horton 19/21
18. 1965 **Demography** Koller 15/22
19. 1965 **Population** and **Ecology*** Valdes 10/11
20. 1967 **Population** Sachdeva 19/28
21. 1968 **Population** McNall 11/19
22. 1970 **Population Characteristics** and **Trends** Mercer 14/16
23. 1971 **Population** and **Ecology*** Popenoe 13/16

24. 1971 **Demography**	Sergeant 3/13
25. 1973 **Population**	Acuff 19/23
26. 1973 **Population**	Leslie 13/21
27. 1973 **Population, Urbanization*, Ecology***	Perry 10/17
28. 1974 **Population, Resources, Technology***	Potter 1/8
29. 1975 **Population** and **Urbanization***	Baldridge 12/13
30. 1975 **Demography**	Denisoff 12/16
31. 1975 **Social Demography**	Kenkel 13/16
32. 1976 Trends in Societies: **Population**	Stewart 3/5
Growth of Human Population	Stewart 8/16
33. 1977 **Population** and **Ecology***	Broom 8/8
34. 1977 **Population**	Broom(2) 9/17
35. 1977 Major World Changes:	
Population Growth	Goode 16/17
36. 1977 **Demography** and **Human Ecology***	Shapiro 17/19
37. 1978 **Population**: Trends and Consequences	Stewart 17/19
38. 1979 **Population**	Phillips 17/20
39. 1979 **Ecology*** and **Population**	Szymanski 13/14
40. 1980 **Demography** and **Urbanization***:	
Urban Community	G Marx 11/12
41. 1983 **Population** and **Health***	Eshleman 18/20
42. 1983 **Demography** and **Ecology***	Tischler 19/20
43. 1984 **Population** and **Health***	Persell 20/23
44. 1985 **Population** and **Environment***	Wailace 18/19
45. 1985 **Demographic** and **Social**	
aspects of **Population**	O'Donnell 6/9
Effects of **Population Change**	O'Donnell 16/26
46. 1990 **Population Problem** and **Beggary**	S Rao 26/30

93. MIGRATION

1. 1950 Man as a **Migrant**	Eldridge 16/34
2. 1955 **Migration** and **Mobility**	Lee 26/35
3. 1967 **Population*, Social Mobility***	
and the **Refugees***	Basu 13/17
4. 1972 **Migration**	McGee 13/13
5. 1985 **Migration**	O'Donnell 17/26

94. APPLIED SOCIOLOGY

1. 1959 **Applications of Sociology**	Merton 5/5
2. 1965 **Applied Sociology**	Valdes 11/11

3. 1967 **Uses of Sociology** Chinoy 6/6
4. 1975 **Role of Sociologists** and the **Uses of Sociology** Cole 9/9
5. 1979 **Applied Sociology**: **Policy, Planning, Problems** Bottomore 6/6
6. 1979 **Applications of Sociology** Sherman 2/3
7. 1990 **Applied Sociology** S Rao 9/10

IX. APPLIED SOCIOLOGY, SOCIAL PROBLEMS

95. SOCIAL PLANNING

1. 1951 **Social Change*** and **Social Planning** O'Brien 9/9
2. 1952 **Societal Planning** Freedman 15/15
3. 1952 **Social Interaction, Social Change*** and **Social Planning** Merrill 6/6
   Social Control* and **Social Planning** Merrill 27/29
4. 1961 **Health** and **Welfare Organization*** Sutherland 20/22
5. 1962 **Sociology, Social Policy**, and **Social Planning** Bottomore 19/20
6. 1970 **Social Change*** and **Social Planning** Mercer 16/16
7. 1975 **Social Reformism**: **Race*** and **Education*** Baldridge 13/13
8. 1964 **Social Change*** and **Social Policy** Horton 6/6

96. SOCIAL PROBLEMS

1. 1949 **Social Problems** Sprott 10/10
2. 1952 **Social Change*** and **Social Problems** Merrill 26/29
3. 1955 **Social Problems** Lee 6/6
   Social Problems Lee 28-34/35
4. 1962 **Social Problems** Bottomore 20/20
5. 1967 **Social Problems** Basu 15/17
   Social Pathology Basu 14/17
6. 1967 **Social Problems** Sachdeva 29/29
7. 1969 **Problem areas in Society** Koller 5/6
8. 1970 **Social Problems, Disorganization***, and **Deviant Behavior*** Mercer 5/16
9. 1972 **Youth** Berger 11/17
10. 1973 **Social Problems** and **Deviance*** Acuff 22/23
11. 1973 **Social Problems** Bertrand 6/6

12. 1990 **Social Disorganization*** and
Social Problems S Rao 8/10
Juvenile Delinquency*, **Youth unrest** and the
Problems of the Aged S Rao 25/30
Applied Sociology*:
Problems of the aged S Rao 28/30

FUTURE STUDIES

1. 1952 **Society of the Future** Merrill 29/29
2. 1966 **Emergence of one World** Muzumdar 13/20
3. 1971 **Possible Near Futures** Gorman 11/11
4. 1975 **Change*** **from Simple to Complex Societies** Cole 13/19
5. 1977 **Emerging World System: Socio-political Changes*** Goode 17/17

97. CRIME

98. DELINQUENCY

1. 1956 **Delinquency** Weinberg 13/28
2. 1957 **Sociology of Delinquency** and **Crime** Gitler 14/14
3. 1959 **Criminology Research** Merton 23/25
4. 1960 **Crime** and **Law*** Green 19/21
5. 1960 **Crime** and **Punishment** Kar 19/21
6. 1965 **Crime** Koller 19/22
7. 1968 **Crime** and **Deviance*** MCNall 18/19
8. 1968 **Crime** Sharma 27/32
9. 1970 **Delinquency** and **Anti-social Behavior** Wilkins 15/16
10. 1971 **Criminology** Sergeant 2/13
11. 1973 **Crime** and **Delinquency** Bertrand 18/22
12. 1977 **Criminal Behavior** Shapiro 14/19
13. 1977 **Crime** and **Delinquency** Warren 14/15
14. 1979 **Crime** and the **State*** Szymanski 9/14
15. 1980 **Criminology** Gurvitch 9/13
16. 1985 **Crime** and **Delinquency** O'Donnell 20/26
17. 1990 **Juvenile Delinquency, Youth** Unrest and **Problems of the Aged*** S Rao 25/30

Other related Headings used:

1.	1973 **Total Institutions (Punishment, Prison, Mental care)**	Stewart 10/19
2.	1975 **Labeling Theory**	Cole 10/19

99. POVERTY

1.	1968 **Poverty**	Sharma 29/32
2.	1975 **Poverty** in America	Baldridge 7/13
3.	1979 **Poverty** and **Social Class***	Sherman 2/23
4.	1985 **Poverty**	Haralambos 4/13

100. SOCIAL GERONTOLOGY/AGING

1.	1965 **Gerontology**	Koller 17/22
2.	1972 **Old Age, Illness,** and **Death**	Berger 16/17
3.	1979 **Age** and **Ageism**	Sherman 12/23
4.	1985 **Aging in Industrial Society**	Wallace 12/19
5.	1990 **Juvenile Delinquency*, Youth Unrest,** and the **Problems of the Aged**	S Rao 25/30

APPENDIX III

Definition of some terms used or related to the study

1. Classification "Classification as process, consists of distinguishing each entity in the universe concerned from all other entities by recognizing its relationships with its coordinates, superordinates and collaterals. For convenience of reference, these relationships can be called `COSCO relationships'" G Bhattacharyya "General theory of subject headings" Lib. Sci. 11, 1974: p.24

"An ordering whose objects are assigned to mutually exclusive and jointly exhaustive classes. At each step of a classificatory analysis (division) its objects are treated dichotomously: they either fall or do not fall into a class. A classification ;thus requires a single criterion called fundamentum divisionis, the basis of division. When multiple criteria or dimensions are involved, we have a typology and/or a taxonomy." Giovanni Sartori "Guidelines for concept analysis: glossary" Social science concepts: a systematic analysis. London, Sage, 1984:p.73

"A documentary language which groups concepts into classes, uses mostly hierarchical relations for arrangement of classes, and reflects the structure; of arrangement by notation." Gernot Wersig; Noveling Ulrich comp. Terminology of documentation Paris, UNESCO Press, 1976: p. 132

2. Classifying and Classification "The verb classify has two meanings: primarily to relate individuals by their likeness, by a perpetual and conceptual process, that is, to regard them as being in classes, in classifications... distinct again is the verb class, which means to relate, to refer, to assign, a thing to a relevant class, regarding some characteristics." H E Bliss "A bibliographic classification: principles; and definition." in Lois Mai Chan et al eds. Theory of subject analysis. Colorado, Libraries Unlimited, 1986: p. 78

3. Classificatory Language "A classificatory language differs from a natural language in that it does not predicate any thing, but simply states subjects. Its parts of speech will therefore not perform; the same function in an analet as do words in a sentence." B C Vickery "Systematic subject indexing" Jl. of Documentation 9, 1953: 48-57 (reprinted in L M Chan Ibid p. 125-135)

4. Category "A category denotes either the name given to any class of things, actions, or relationships which recur with sufficient (relative) uniformity and frequency as to render the class a useful subject of predication; or the class the class itself. When rigorously defined and placed in a system of classes, it becomes a scientific category. ... All technical terms and concepts in social sciences are categories in the sense that they denote name, a class of observable things, actions, or relations. Nothing can be observed as a datum for science that can not be named or categorized." Read Bain in Gould; Kolb eds. Dictionary of social sciences. London, Tavistock, 1964: p.77

" 1. A `class' of high generality; 2. A general facet applying to a lot of subject fields." in Wersig op. cit. p. 124

5. **Compatibility** "Compatibility is the ability of one information system to accept the original indexing and abstracting data to another information system for any given subject coverage that is common to both systems." W Hammond "Dimensions of compatibility" in S M Newman ed. Information systems compatibility. Washington, Spartan Books, 1965: (quoted by Alan Gilchrist " Intermediate languages for switching and control" ASLIB Proceed. 24(7) July 1972: p. 390

"Implies the use of some kind of manipulation to make the results and products of processing in one system usable in another." Alan GilChrist ibid. p. 390

6. **Concept** "Any unit of thought; a mental image formed by generalization" Wersig op. cit. p. 56

"The basic unit of thinking. It can be said that we have a concept of A (or of A-ness) when we are able to distinguish A from whatever is not A" Sartori op. cit. p. 74

7. **Subordinate Concept** A concept is subordinated to another concept if it has been established by one step of division, i.e. it has

one 'specific characteristic' the super-ordinate concept does not possess." Wersig op. cit. p. 58

8. **Superordinate Concept** A 'concept' is a superordinate concept if it has several subordinate concepts which are established by one step of division, i.e. it possesses one 'generic characteristic' which the 'subordinate concept does not possess." Wersig op. cit. p. 58

9. **Context** "Any setting in which a; word is used, to be specified as follows: 1.author context; 2. disciplinary context; 3. field or subfield context; or 4. theoretical context" Sartori op. cit. p. 74

10. **Controlled Vocabulary** "May be defined as a limited set of terms that must be used to index documents, and to search for these documents, in a particular system." F W Lancaster "Vocabulary control in information retrieval systems. Advances in Librarianship vol.7. New York, Academic Press, 1977: p. 2

11. **Definition** "Concepts are constructed from definitions. a definition is a system of terms, such as the sentences of a language, the symbols of logic, or the notation of mathematics, that informs the investigators as to t he phenomenon denoted by a concept. For example, the concept `conflict' only has meaning when it is defined. One possible definition might be: `conflict equals interactions among social units in which one unit seeks to prevent the other from realizing its goals.' Such a definition allows scientists to visualize the phenomena that is denoted by a concept." Jonathan Turner Structure of sociological theory Homewood, Ill. Dorsey Press, 1978: p. 3

"Verbal determination of a `concept' by distinguishing it from other concepts." Wersig op. cit. p.56

12. **Descriptor** "The meaning to be associated with each descriptor is carefully drawn or assigned in such a fashion as to best serve the purposes of the user population- even it this privately-assigned meaning may change or distort the usual meaning publicly attached to the term. In this sense, a descriptor `is not a word in ordinary language'. It is a private term for retrieval purposes only. It is an arbitrary word-symbol for a particularly chosen scope of meaning or application for use by a particular group of people with a particular collection." Calvin M Mooers "Descriptors" in Encycl. of Lib. and Inf. Sci. vol. 7 New York, Marcel Dekker, 1972: p. 34

"A descriptor is any authorized entity identifier that can be used for retrieving other entities. If the retrieving entities are concepts, we speak of `subject descriptors'." Dagobert Soergel Organizing information: principles of database and retrieval systems. Orlando, Academic Press, 1985: p. 62

13. **Discipline** "The word is used here in the sense of a field of

related studies in which there develops a community of scholars with common interest, who stimulate one another in their investigations, a set of related techniques, a cumulative body of knowledge and certain generally accepted principle of practice. Such a discipline also tends to acquire an apparatus- associations, periodicals, publications, and research and training centers." Frank Lorimer "Development of demography" in P M Hauser; O D Duncan eds. The study of population. Chicago, Univ. of Chicago, 1959: p. 158

"When ever we consider any branch of learning as an intellectual discipline, we have in mind the premises on which the men in the field rest their work, the ideas and currents of thought, which unite or separate them, the characteristic style of reasoning or argument which they use, the types of data considered, the manner in which they are collected, and the manner in which they are ;treated." Alex Inkeles What is sociology: an introduction to the discipline and the profession. New Delhi, Prentice Hall, 1971: p. 106

"Sociology is an academic discipline. The word discipline is important, for it implies an order, a systematic study of a topic. A discipline has a history, a group of scholars who together investigate a portion of reality and are viewed by themselves and others as a branch of knowledge. All disciplines have rules that scholars must follow to prove their ideas and to check each other's work." Joel M Charon Sociology: a conceptual approach. 2nd ed. Boston, Allyn and Bacon, (1986) 1989: p. 4

"An organized field of study or branch of learning dealing with specific kinds of subjects and for subjects considered from specific points of view." L M Harod Librarian's glossary". London, Clarion Books, 1977: p. 278

14. **Document Analysis** "The analysis of the subject contents of documents with the aim to select all the characteristics according to which the documents should be able to be found in retrieval." Wersig op. cit. p. 98

15. **Documentary Language** "An `artificial language' used by documentation systems for purposes of indexing, storage, and retrieval." Wersig op. cit. p. 67

16. **Facet** "The total subclasses resulting from the application of a single characteristic is called a facet." J Mills A modern outline of library classification. London, Chapman and Hall, (1960), 1968: p. 8

17. **Hierarchy** "The network between concepts constituted by hierarchical relations." Wersing op. cit. p. 127

18. **Indexing** "Assignment of index terms to documents or objects with the aim to be able later on to retrieve the documents or

objects according to the selected concepts designated by the index terms." Wersig op. cit. p. 98

19. **Indexing Language** "The task of an indexing language is to represent concepts and statements with a sufficient degree of predictability and fidelity. Any kind of language that serves this purpose is (or can be used as) an indexing language". Robert Fugman "Towards a theory of information supply and indexing: treatise IV- on retrieval system theory" Intl. Class. 6(1), 1979: p. 14

20. **Information Retrieval** "The action of or methods and procedures for recovering specific information from a collection of stored data." Wersig op. cit. p. 140

"It consists of four stages:

1. identifying the exact subject of the search;

2. locating this subject in a guide which refers the searcher to one or more documents;

3. locating the document; and

4. locating the required information in the documents."

D J Foskett Classification and indexing in the social sciences. London, Buttorworths, (1963) 1974: p. 6

21. **Information Retrieval Language** "If we take the loose definitions of `information' to mean knowledge in transit; `retrieval' to mean recovery by investigation; and `language' to mean a vocabulary and way of using it, then we can, perhaps, accept the suggestion that an IRL is a vocabulary and way of using it to recover by investigation, knowledge, which is in transit. Furthermore, by loosely defining: `vocabulary' to mean the works in a language (in an alphabetical list) and `index' to mean a list of names, subjects etc, with references, we can see that `IRL' is approximately synonymous with `index vocabulary'. A G A Pickford "Some problems of using an unstructured information retreival olanguage in a co-ordinate indexing system." ASLIB Proceed. 23(3) March 1971: p. 133

22. **Isolate** "An isoolate is an object or class of obejcts, a process or class of processes, or an abstract term or class or such terms." J E L Farradane "A scientific theory of classification and indexing" Jl. of Documentation 6, 1950: 83-99; 8, 1952: 73-92 (reprinted by Vickery in L M Chan op. cit. p. 131)

"A single concept of any degree of complexity which can be considered in isolation for purposes of definition, or for placing in a classification ." Wersig op. cit. p. 127

23. **Lead in Term** "is any term or other symbol for which a relationship to a descriptor is established so that a user looking under

the term is directed to the descriptor." Dagobert Soergel Organizing information. op. cit. p. 62

24. **Subject** "Any concept or concept combination looked as an entity" Wersig op. cit. p. 58

25. **Subject Heading** "A word, term or a phrase chosen to express a concept or a concept combination in indexing and to constitute an entry." Wersig op. cit. p. 58

26. **Term** "Although a word may have several senses, only one of them is intended when it is used as a term. Hence, a word is a term only when it designates one of tis possible meanings." Fred W Riggs "A new paradigm for social science termino-logy". Intl. Class. 6(3), 1979: p. 152

27. **Terminology** "Terminology is the system of terms to denote - that is to name- the classes or ranked isolates in a scheme for classification." S R Ranganathan Prolegomena to library classification. 3rd ed. Bombay, Asia Pub. House, 1967: p. 201

"Terminology of a scheme for classification is the system of terms in a language, denoting or naaming ;the clases of the scheme, the language being the natural one ore the jargon of a profession or trade." S R Ranganathan ibid p. 72

"The discipline concepred with the formation and naming of a concept, either in a special sub-field or in the aggregate of all subject fields..... An organized set of technical terms whose meaning has been explained or defined." Wersig op. cit. p. 55

" 'Important words' that are carriers of concepts, that can be said to constitute, in some meaningful sense, units of thinking." Sartori op. cit. p. 17.

Bibliography

Adam, R. "Language and information retrieval in the social sciences", *ASLIB Proceed,* 34(9) 1982; 394-405.

Austin, Derek "Vocabulary control and information retrieval" *ASLIB Proceedings* 38(1) 1986: 1-15.

Beteille, Andre "Language of the social sciences" *Intl. Social Sci. Jl.* 9(3) 1977: 531-32.

Brown, Julie S; Gilmartin, Brian G. "Sociology today: lacunae, emphases and surfeits" *American Sociologist* 4 Nov. 1969: 283-91.

Bury, Susan "Comparison of classification schemes for libraries" *Lib. Sci.* 17(3) 1980: 73-82.

Carroll, J M; Roeoff, R "Computer selection of key words using word frequency analysis" *American Documentation* 20, 1969: 227-33.

Christ, J M *Concepts and subject headings; their relation in information retrieval and library science.* Scarecrow Press, 1972:

Coates, E J "Significance and term relationship in compound headings" in L M Chan *Theory of subject analysis* colorado, Libraries Unlimited, 1986: p. 181-95

Dahlberg, I *Guidelines for the establishment of compatibility between information languages in the social sciences.* (Prepared for UNESCO Division for the Development of Social Sciences) Frankfurt, Index Verlag, 1980:

———— ; "Towards establishment of compatibility between indexing languages" *Intl. Classification* 9(2) 1981: 86-91; 10 (1) 1983: 5-8

Davis, C H "Integrating vocabularies with a classification scheme" *American Documentation* 19, 1968: 101.

Dewey, Harry "Relationship between the headings in the subject catalogue and the classification number of books" in Jean M. Perrault ed. *Conf. on Reclassification: Rationale and Problems.* University of Maryland, April 4-6, 1968: p. 57-78

Farradane, J E L "Concept organisation for information retrieval" *Information Storage and Retrieval* 3, 1967: 297-314.

————— ; "Analysis and organisation of knowledge for retrieval" *ASLIB Proceed.* 22 (12) 1970: 607-16.

Foskett, D J "Problems of indexing and classification in the social sciences" *Intl. Social Sci. Jl* 23(2), 1971: 244-55.

————— ; "Social sciences in the general classification schemes," *Classification and Indexing in the Social Sciences* 2nd ed. London, Butterworths, 1974: p. 64-83.

————— ; "Classification for community development" in *ibid.* p. 190-193.

————— ; Foskett, Joy "London Education Classification" *Education Libraries Supplement* 6, 2nd ed. 1974.

————— ; Bury, Susan "Concept organisation and universal classification systems" in *Universal Classification, Subject Analysis and ordering Systems.* 4th Intl Study Conference on Classification Research, Augsberg, 1982. Frankfurt, Index Verlag, 1982: p. 35-44.

Fugman, R "Complementarity of natural and indexing languages" *Intl. Classification* 9(3) 1982: 140-4.

Gollner, Ernest "Concepts and society" in *Concept of kinship and other essays on anthropological method and explanation* Oxford, Basil Blackwell, (1973) 1987: 18-46.

Gilchrist, Alan "Intermediate languages for switching and control" *ASLIB Proceed.* 24(7) July 1972: 387-411.

Gopinath, M A "Symbiosis between classification and thesaurus" *Lib. Sci.* 24(2) Dec 1987: 211-225.

————— ; "Subject analysis and classification." *DRTC Annual Seminar* 7(2) 1969: 699-712.

————— ; Mahapatra, V K "Geographical schedule in CC, UDC, and DC" *Lib. Sci.* 3, 1966: 168-211.

————— ; Prasad, K N "Compatibility of the principles for design of thesaurus and classification schemes" *Lib. Sci.* 13(2) June 1976: 56-66.

Haykin, D J "Subject headings: fundamental concepts" in Lois Mai Chan et al. *op. cit.* p. 105-112.

Kyle, Barbara "Towards a classification for social science literature" *Amer. Documentation.* 9, 1958: 168-183.

————— ; "Merits and demerits of various classification schemes for the social sciences." *UNESCO Bul.* 14(2) 1960: 54-60.

Larsen, Otto N ; Catton, William R Jr *Conceptual sociology: a manual for exercises relation concepts to specimens, principles and definition*. New York, Harper and Row, 1962: p. 275.

Lee, M E "Word-word associations in document retrieval systems" *American Documentation* 20, 1969: 27-38.

Tilakovic, Ljerka "Criteria for testing and evaluating a library bibliographic classification" *Informatica* 19(6) Nov.-Dec. 1985: 379-385.

Meillet, Antone "How worrds change their meanings" in Talcott Parsons et. al. eds. *Theories of society*. New York, Free Press, (1961) 1965: 1013-1017.

Meyriat Jean "Social science information languages: A comparative analysis" *Intl. Classif.* 7(2) July 1980: 60-65.

Milestead, J L "Term Source: internal or external" in *Subject Access Systems* New York, Academic, 1984: p. 103-119.

Neelameghan, A; Venkataraman, S "Formulation of kernel terms for a subject and isolate terms for a classification schedule for use in the synthesis of class number by computer" *Lib. Sci.* 6, 1969: 71-93.

Piaget, Jean "Classification of disciplines and inter-disciplinary connections" *Intl. Social Sci. Jl.* 16, 1964: 553-70.

Rada, Roy et. al. "Creating and evaluating entry terms" *Jl. of Documentation* 44(1) 1988: 19-41.

Rajan, T N Handling compound terms in indexing systems" *Jl. of Lib. and Inf. Sci.* 1(2) Dec. 1976: 169-90.

Ranganathan, S R "Design of depth classification: methodology" *Lib. Sci.* 1, 1964: 1-41.

————— ; "Recall value and entry word in heading" *Lib. Sci.* 6, 1969: 289-306.

————— ; Neelameghan, A "Basis for study of compatibility and capability of the Colon Classification Scheme with the Universal Decimal Classification Scheme" *Lib. Sci.* 7, 1970: 97-109.

Riggs, Fred W "A paradigm for social science terminology" *Intl. Classification* 6 (3) 1979: 150-58.

————— ; "Importance of concepts: Some considerations on how they could be designated less ambiguously" *Amer. Sociologist* 14(4) 1979: 172-185.

————— ; "A conceptual encyclopaedia for the social sciences" *Intl. Social Sci. Jl.* 111, Feb. 1987: 109-125.

Robertson, S E; Sparck Jones, K "Relevance weighting of search terms" *JASIS* 27(3) May 1976: 129-46.

Rodrigues, Robert D "Hulme's concept of literary warrant" *Classification and Cataloguing Qly*. 5(1) 1984: 17-26.

Rolling, L "Role of graphic display in concept relationships in indexing and retrieval vocabularies" in Lois Mai Chan et al. eds. *op. cit*. p. 273-86.

Sartori, Giovanni et al. eds. *Tower of Babel: on the definition and analysis of concepts in social sciences*. Intl. Studies Association, Occasional Paper no. 6. Pittsberg, University of Pittsberg, 1975: p. 452.

Seetharama, S. "Term concept relationships in information retrieval thesaurus" *Lib. Sci*. 13(2) June 1976: 67-73.

Small, Barbara *Term bank for tomorrow's world*. London, ASLIB, 1983: 212.

Soergel, Dagobert "A general model for indexing languages: the basis for compatibility and integration: in Hans Wellisch ed. *Subject retrieval in the seventies*. West Port, Greenwood, 1972: 36-61.

Stinchcombe, Arthur L "Origin of sociology as a discipline" *Acta Sociologica* 27(1) 1984: 51-61.

"Subject headings and canon of currency" *Lib. Sci*. 6, 1969: 191-92.

Svenonius, Elaine "Unanswered questions in the design of controlled vocabularies" *JASIS* 37(5) 1986: 331-340.

Swift, D F et al. *A case study in indexing and classification in the sociology of education*. Open University, 1973.

Thesaurus of sociological indexing terms. 2nd ed. San Diego, CA. Sociological Abstracts Inc. April, 1989.

Timasheff, N S "Basic concepts of sociology" *American Jl. of Sociology* 58(2) Sept. 1952: 176-86.

Trivedi, B I "Classification of demography" *Annals of Lib. Sci*. 6(2) 1959: 44-49.

Urrwin, Anthony G "Revision of classification schemes: policies and practices" *Jl. of Librarianship* 10(1) 1978: 19-38.

Varma, S R "Treatment of statistics in UDC, LC and CC: a comparison" *Indian Lib. Movement* 5(3) 1978: 90-93.

Vickery, B C "Classificatory principles in natural language indexing systems" in A Maltby ed. *Classification in the 1970's*. London, Bingley, 1972: p. 167-91.

Wepsiec, Jan "Library of Congress subject headings pertaining to society" *Cataloguing and Classification Qly*. 2(3-4) 1982: 1-29.

Wersig, G. "Experiences in compatibility research in documentary languages" in A. Neelameghan ed. *Ordering systems for global information networks*. Proceedings of the 3rd Intl. Study Conference on Classification Reserch, Bombay, 1975. Bangalore, DRTC, 1979: 204-211.

Whitelock, P. J. "A descriptor bank for social science terms", *Intl. Classification* 9(3) 1982: 142-151.